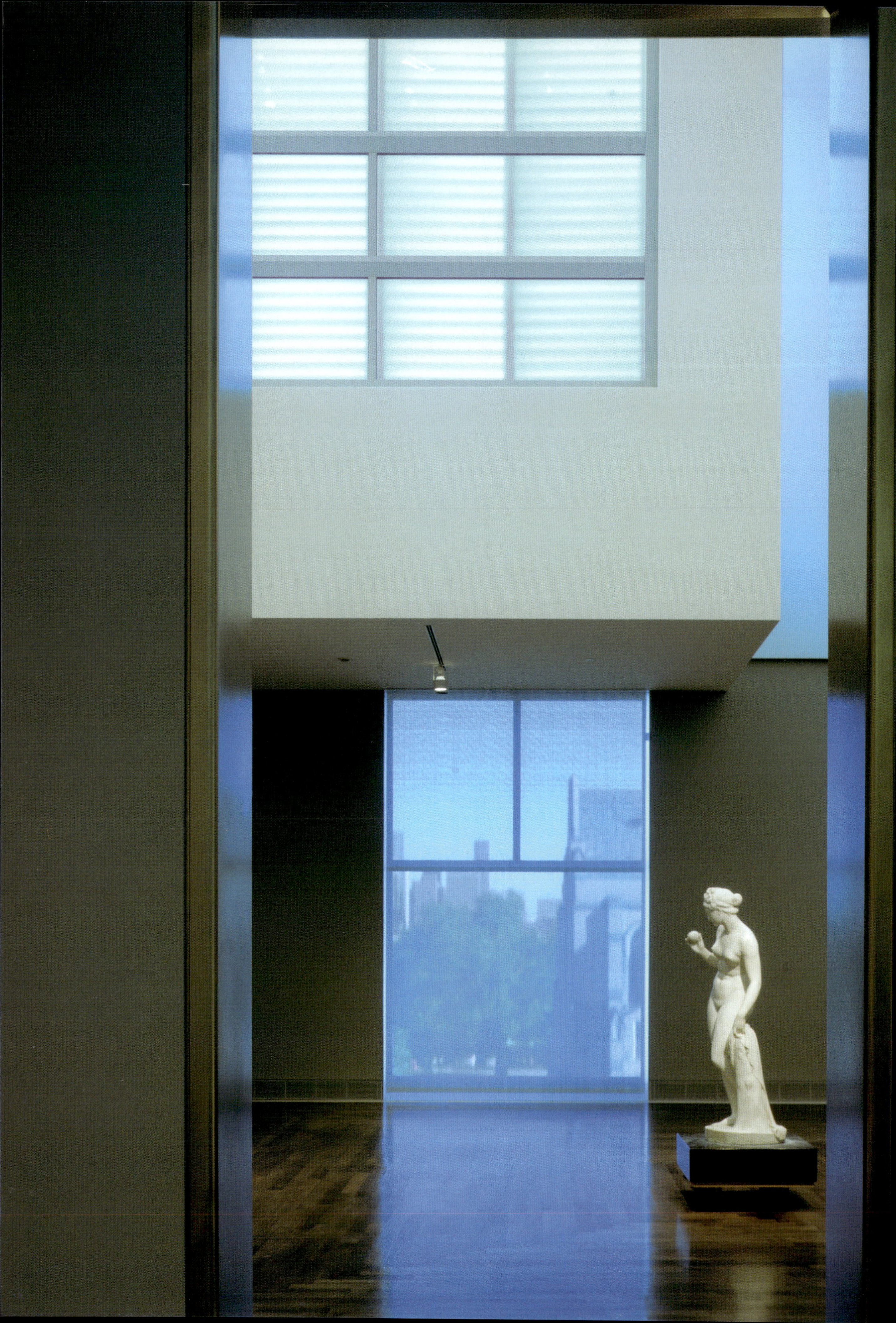

DESIGNING THE NEW MUSEUM

ROCKPORT

Acknowledgments

AUTHOR
James Grayson Trulove

Nora Greer has my profound gratitude for her tireless and indispensable contributions to the success of this book, including writing, editing, and project management. I would also like to thank Il Kim for his advice and keen eye in helping to select many of the projects featured and to Steel Colony for his assistance in coordinating the many tasks associated with assembling a book of this magnitude and complexity.

I am grateful to David C. Levy for offering a valuable perspective of a museum director faced with building a new addition by a renowned architect.

Thanks to Rockport Publishers and particularly to Jay Donahue and Winnie Prentiss for their support and encouragement as this book was being created.

And the many architects and their design teams for creating these destination museums and to the photographers who captured them so vividly.

FIRST PUBLISHED IN THE UNITED STATES OF AMERICA BY ROCKPORT PUBLISHERS INC.

33 COMMERCIAL STREET | GLOUCESTER |
MASSACHUSETTS | 01930.5089
TELEPHONE > (978) 282.9590 |
FACSIMILE > (978) 283.2742 | WWW.ROCKPUB.COM
ISBN 1-56496-689-5
10 9 8 7 6

CREDITS

DESIGN > JENNIFER STERLING DESIGN / SAN FRANCISCO
PRINTED >
PRINTED > PRINTED IN CHINA.

DESIGNING THE NEW MUSEUM:

BUILDING A DESTINATION

JAMES GRAYSON TRULOVE

with a foreword by David C. Levy

ROCKPORT PUBLISHERS

GLOUCESTER MASSACHUSETTS

Table of Contents

1 DESIGNING THE NEW MUSEUM

2 *BY*
David C. Levy

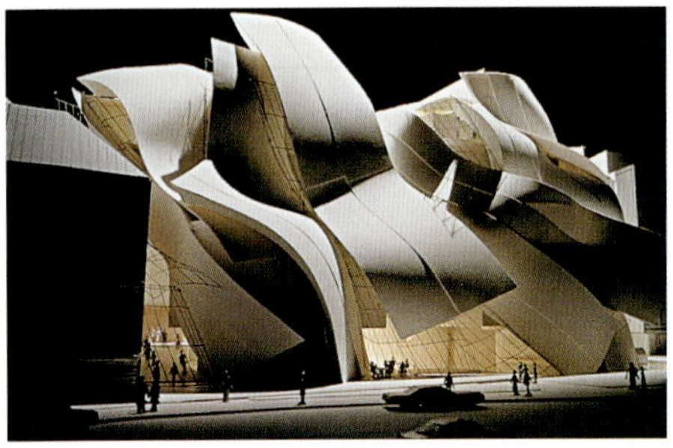

In the late 1950s New York City's Guggenheim Museum commissioned the most important object in its collection—Frank Lloyd Wright's great inverted cone of concrete and glass on 89th Street and Fifth Avenue. This was a public acknowledgment that the aesthetic of an era is as strongly embodied in its architecture as in its painting and sculpture. It was perhaps the first, and certainly the most daring, declaration by a major museum that, in this regard, its obligation to art and culture requires it to put its money where its mouth is. In retrospect it is odd that this idea, though widely accepted in principle, had not found tangible expression in more than a century of museum design.

The building of the Guggenheim did not, however, start a groundswell of innovative museum architecture. With the possible exception of The National Gallery's 1975 East Wing by I. M. Pei, good architects of the 1960s and '70s built good museums that were, for the most part, merely modern adaptations of 19th century ideas—museums as cultural temples. To be sure, they had modern amenities, but little or no attempt was made to integrate these buildings conceptually into the contemporary artistic experience. At best, they were regarded as elegant receptacles for their museums' collections; almost never as part of those collections.

In the 1980s, almost three decades after Wright paved the way, Renzo Piano and Richard Rogers again rocked the museum world with the design of the Centre Pompideau. Though far less innovative than Wright's Guggenheim, this museum set an extraordinary new record by becoming the most visited destination in Europe—not for its content, but for the building itself. This time there was a discernible effect and, as this book documents, subsequent museum design became progressively more responsive to the issues and sensibilities of contemporary architecture as a valid goal in itself. Nowhere has this idea been given fuller expression than by Frank Gehry (and again by the Guggenheim) in Bilbao, Spain.

There is some irony in the fact that the Guggenheim's Director, Tom Krens, initially believed that he could take advantage of his museum's great holdings, which were larger than he could show at any one time in New York, while performing an innovative and important service to the international cultural community. Making masterpieces from the Guggenheim available to cities that lacked great art works of their own, Krens reasoned, would provide a cultural resource for their citizens, attract tourists, and make a valid, income-generating use of a collection that would otherwise languish in storage.

No. 1 Frank Gehry's design for the addition to the Corcoran Gallery of Art in Washington, D.C.

Krens's strategy was also calculated to address the debatable practice through which museums habitually accumulate important works of art with full knowledge that their limited exhibition space virtually precluded their being placed on public view for more than a minimal time. As the collection continues to grow, this situation becomes even more acute. Although Krens certainly, and successfully, set out to continue the Guggenheim's great architectural tradition by commissioning one of the most daring architects of our time, it is nevertheless a somewhat unanticipated, funny and, from an architectural point of view, rather wonderful outcome of Krens's ingenuous, creative, and public spirited plan that Gehry's building has completely upstaged the art exhibited inside.

The grimy industrial city of Bilbao, hitherto uncharted by the tourist industry, now has one-and-half million annual visitors (twice its most optimistic initial projections) who come from every corner of the globe solely to experience its amazing new work of architecture. Most of them do not even bother to check the exhibition schedule in advance!

Yet it would be a profound disservice to suggest that the object of museum design is merely the creation of a destination building, or worse, some kind of architectural billboard. The museum-as-Disneyland would be cynical response to the evolving new needs of the cultural and architectural communities. Nevertheless, the role of museums changed substantially in the last half of the twentieth century and it is now an imperative that the nineteenth-century paradigm, which continues to be anachronistically reflected in much museum architecture, be radically reexamined.

The unfolding of the twenty-first century is likely to witness a radical architectural shift, and museums must accept a mandate to be in its vanguard. This, after all, is intrinsic to their mission. In addition architecture, always driven by advances in technology (wood to stone, stone to concrete, concrete to steel, etc.) is just beginning to respond to the latest technological revolution. Frank Gehry's buildings are among the first to exploit the full aesthetic implications of computer-aided design/computer-aided manufacture (CAD/CAM). CAD/CAM makes possible a whole new vocabulary of complex curves and related shapes that would have been unthinkable—and unbuildable—in the past.

This vocabulary, however, goes far beyond any evolutionary notion of architectural economics or aesthetics. It is a quantum break and, consequently, unlikely to find its fullest expression in commercial building. If, like medieval cathedrals, museums understand and accept their full responsibility to the art of their time, including their

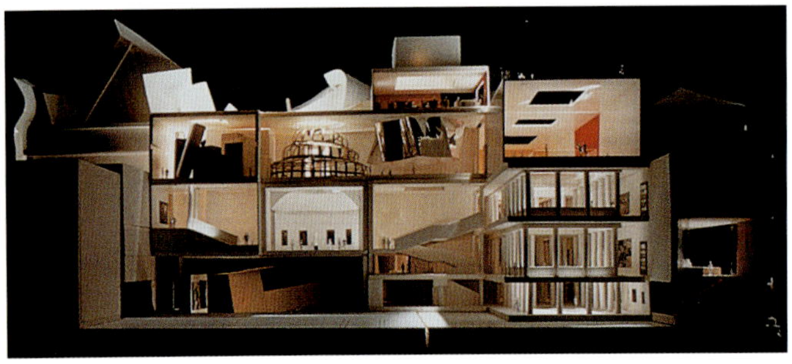

responsibility to the urban environment as a whole, then they are best positioned to lead the way and to explore the new and radically different architectural forms made possible by the digital revolution.

My own experience has underscored both the nature and the complexity of this obligation. Just two years ago the Trustees of the Corcoran Gallery of Art, Washington D.C.'s oldest museum and only college of art, decided to complete its nineteenth-century master plan with a final addition to its great neo-classical building. This was a daunting assignment, as the original building, across from The White House and designed in the 1890s by the distinguished Beaux Arts architect, Earnest Flagg, is generally considered to be one of the finest in the city. The Corcoran chose Frank O. Gehry as the architect for this project, not only making a sharp stylistic break with the architecture of the original building, but taking a radical and potentially controversial step in what may be America's most architectural conservative city.

Working with a committee of lay trustees, none of whose backgrounds included professional experience in either architecture or design, we began an extended year-long dialogue, lead by the distinguished critic Paul Goldberger whom the committee had invited as advisor and alter ego. The committee also had extended conversations with ten of the world's leading architects.

The purpose of this exercise was to establish a level of discourse that would do justice to the responsibility we were assuming—the creation of a major work or architecture, in White House Park and at the center of our national capital. The goal was to engage in a full exploration of the intellectual and civic principles at stake. Not surprisingly, we learned a great deal.

We learned that architectural selection is difficult and inherently flawed. We might summarize our view of the process as follows:

- Architectural competitions are probably the best (and most politically viable) means available to an institution selecting an architect. However, they are, by definition and time limitations, unable to be responsive and interactive with the profoundly subtle needs of a complex client. This is because competitions are unable to duplicate the architect/client interaction that should be at the heart of the design experience.

  To minimize this difficulty, we gave our competing architects six months to complete their submissions (rather than the more usual charette-type approach), and we requested that they use this relatively extended time to work as closely as possible with us. In a limited way, this helped, but it certainly did not solve the problem.

No. 2 The interior of the model of the addition to the Corcoran Gallery of Art in Washington, C.C., designed by Frank Gehry.

- Architectural competitions tend to select competing finalists representing a smorgasbord of design philosophies; e.g., a historical contextualist, a modernist, a post-modernist, etc. This approach almost inevitably focuses the selection debate on the competing architectural styles represented, not on the actual quality of the final presentation or its underlying creative process.

  We addressed this issue by reviewing the qualifications of sixty architects, reducing this number to ten, and engaging in extended interviews with that semi-final group. But we resolved most of our differences about design direction prior to commissioning the design competition itself. Therefore, the three architects selected to submit full design presentations—Frank O. Gehry, Santiago Calatrava, and Daniel Libeskind—were each viewed as progressive modernists. There was no question of choosing "one from column A or one from column B" at this point in the process.

- The hardest thing to remember in the competition process (and the most important to know) is that its goal is not the choice of a design—it is the choice of an architect. Whatever the desired result of a competition design presentation may be it should not, in the end, be the creation of a piece of sculpture. A building is a living, working environment and its initial design will undergo enormous transformation before ground is broken for its construction. So it is the thought process, the design attitude, and the design sensibility of the architect that will determine the success or failure of a building.

As this is written, the Corcoran has completed some ten months of the design process itself, working with Frank Gehry and his staff to resolve the extraordinarily subtle complexities of a building program that should stand the test of time for the next two centuries. Completing such a task in our national capital is about many things; it is about aesthetics, money, politics, and turf. But most of all, it is about a balance between civic and aesthetic responsibility. Because, in the end, a museum bears the burden to explore the new with respect for the past; to respond to the aura of its urban environment while leading it forward, and to set an example for architects, artists, and the public in the decades and centuries to come.

As the new Corcoran rises from the ground over the next few years, we hope we will have met the challenge of this daunting task. The works of architecture in this book represent different approaches to this obligation, by architects, trustees and government. Some fail; many succeed. Yet the study of this work is critical to the future of art and architecture in the century to come.

1 *ART OR ARCHITECTURE?*

2 *BY*
Il Kim

In today's worldwide museum-building rush, architects, supported by the notion of "museum as a large work of art that houses smaller works of art," proudly materialize their pure architectural ideology in their designs. These progressive museum buildings have become the manifestation of contemporary architectural discourse. At the same time, new museum buildings are mega-income sources within the economic structure of cities. Such is the case of the Guggenheim Museum Bilbao, conceived as an urban, economic catalyst, wherein a world-renowned architect, Frank O. Gehry, created an innovative design which in turn has attracted a large number of visitors/tourists and stimulated economic growth throughout the city. Thus we see new museum buildings that are architecturally radical yet enticing.

Because of this intense architectural/cultural trend, one can experience and appreciate many diverse and attractive exhibition spaces. (It is said that today in the United States alone at least 50 new museums or large-scale additions are under construction.) Critics of these new buildings, however, are concerned that although innovative and eye-catching, the architecture, unlike traditional museum buildings, overwhelms the works of art they present and detracts from the concentration of the viewer. The critics further complain that new museums are more and more becoming places for entertainment, and what is more significant for the museums is not the art inside but very often the building itself. Thus among today's polemical issues are the role of new museums as places of entertainment, and their ability to draw people back to buildings that are often more alluring than their contents.

Today, it is difficult to judge which museum designs are appropriate, because we have lost the strict norms for the social role of museums that were defined through political and educational discourse in the nineteenth and twentieth centuries. In the early nineteenth century, many museums were built for the purpose of public education. And unlike spare contemporary displays, almost every square inch of their walls was covered by works of art. By the end of the century, visiting museums had become a major part of the leisure of the European middle class. And magnificent buildings that manifested architectural innovations, an example of which is Karl Friedrich Schinkel's Altes Museum in Berlin, completed in 1828, were part of the attraction.

Most of us visit a museum to see a particular exhibition, for educational purposes or just for fun, and it may be true that if a museum is an interesting building, we will go back there every now and then. However, we often find ourselves judging a museum favorably only when we experience a coherence between good exhibits placed in a space that enhances their allure, and architectural spaces, the characteristics of which are emphasized and even defined by the very existence of the objects on display. When discussing a new museum we should not simply praise or criticize its innovative architectural design, but we should carefully examine the exhibition spaces that it provides. In another words, is it simply a magnificent building or is it also a magnificent museum?

Of course, museums can be entertaining. With successfully designed museums, however, the entertainment does not end just as simple fun. The experiences of many layers of fine interlace between exhibit and space can stimulate the visitor's thinking and occasionally lead to a spark of enlightenment. It is this process that deeply satisfies the visitor.

Each of twenty-four new museum projects depicted in *Designing the New Museum: Building a Destination* offers unique solution to the question of how to create those thoughtful interlaces under a variety of circumstances. Through a subtle combination of spatial arrangements, control of movement, careful use of different materials, and the creation of narrative, the architects who designed these new museums provide intellectual stimulation even for those who come to museums just for fun. And in so doing, those architects successfully combine art and architecture to make their museum buildings crucial, irreplaceable parts of the learning experience.

GENERAL INTEREST ART MUSEUMS

Gerard L. Cafesjian Pavilion

1 *PROJECT*
Gerard L. Cafesjian Pavilion | *Scottsdale Museum of Contemporary Art / Arizona*

2 *ARCHITECT*
William P. Bruder Architecture, Ltd. | *New River, Arizona*

When the city of Scottsdale, Arizona, wanted to expand its arts facilities, it turned to an unusual source—the re-use of a cinema complex located next to its existing Center for the Arts. The complex of theaters was chosen for the raw space offered—some 18,500 square feet (1,665 square meters) of exhibition space. The challenge for architect William P. Bruder was to replace Hollywood glitz with urbane sophistication.

A rectangular building, the old cinema complex was a dusty-buff stucco. Bruder first painted this surface a dark purplish gray. Then to enliven it, he ran a new façade down the entire length of the building. Now, at the south end, patrons arrive to find a huge glass wall designed by sculptor James Fraser Carpenter. Made of sheets of dichoric glass, it encloses a small sculpture court and announces the museum's artistic orientation. The remaining front façade is clad in panels of silver galvanized steel, which shimmer in the desert sun. To create what Bruder calls the look of a "handmade quilt," these steel panels range randomly in width from 1 foot (300 mm) to 4 feet (1,143 mm). At the north end, the façade bulges in homage to the curving Center for the Arts building across the street.

Visitors enter through the opening in the front façade, which is brightly lit at night, and are drawn along curving walls to the galleries beyond. On a sunny day, a side trip into the iridescent court created by Carpenter's glass wall is a necessity. Otherwise the visitor passes the circular metal reception desk and bookstall to one side and a café to the other. In the galleries—once the heart of the cinemas—Bruder stripped the interiors, revealing the industrial timber trusses of old ceilings. Here, he delicately threaded new mechanical and electrical services and created flexible gallery spaces. The Green Eye of the Pyramid by Stanislav Libensky and Jaroslava Brychtova—the centerpiece permanent exhibition—beckons the visitor deep into the galleries.

No. 1-4
Description

Caption
Photo

No. 1 View through James Fraser Carpenter's glass sculpture to the courtyard and the original cinema facade.

No. 2 Reflected in the curve at the south end of the building is the neighboring Scottsdale Center for the Arts, from which the new museum's curving shape is borrowed.

No. 3 Inside the court made by Carpentre's sculptured wall, the light constantly changes in direction and color. The old building is to the left.

No. 4 The dichroic glass bends around the building's south corner to form a sculpture court.

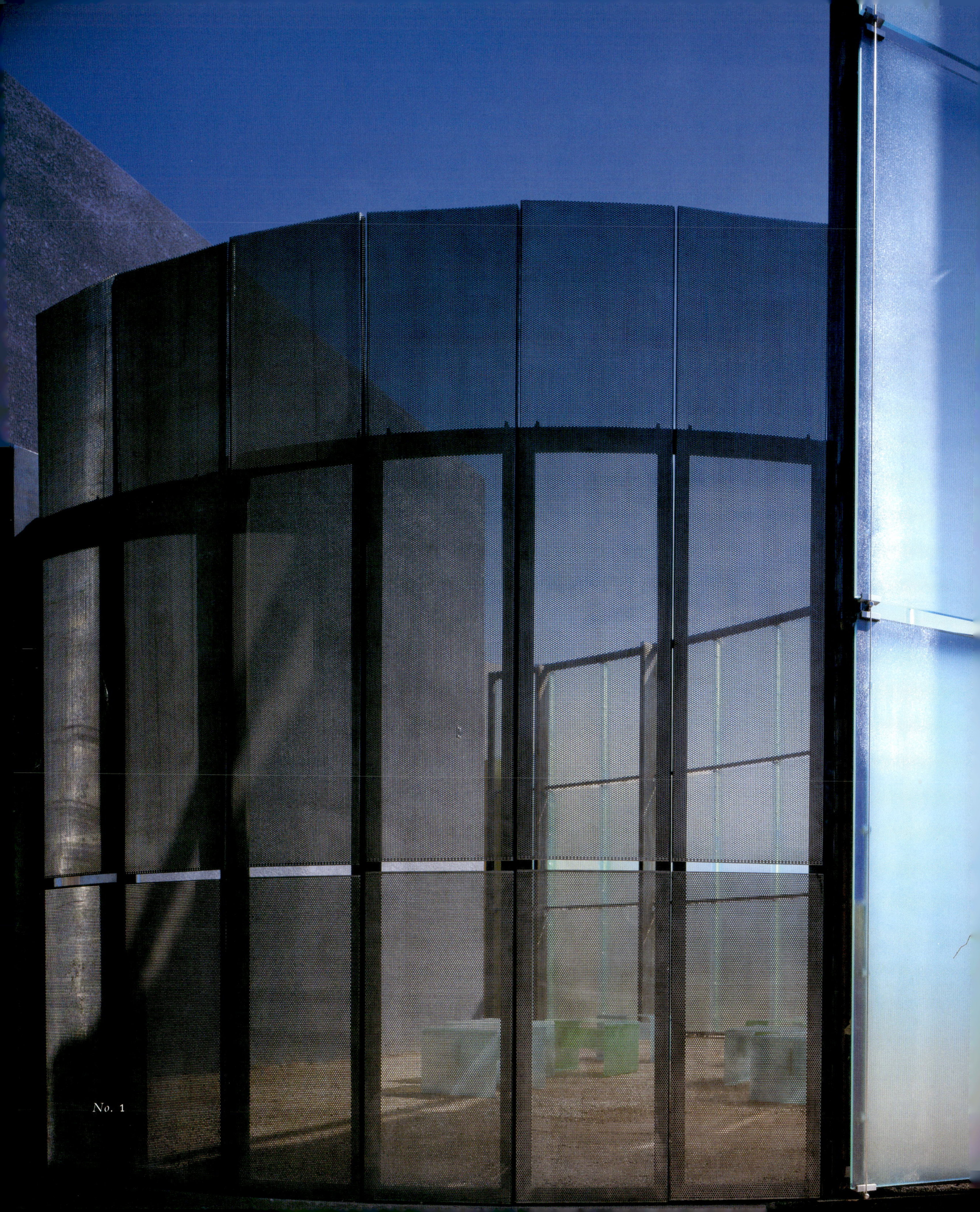

No. 1

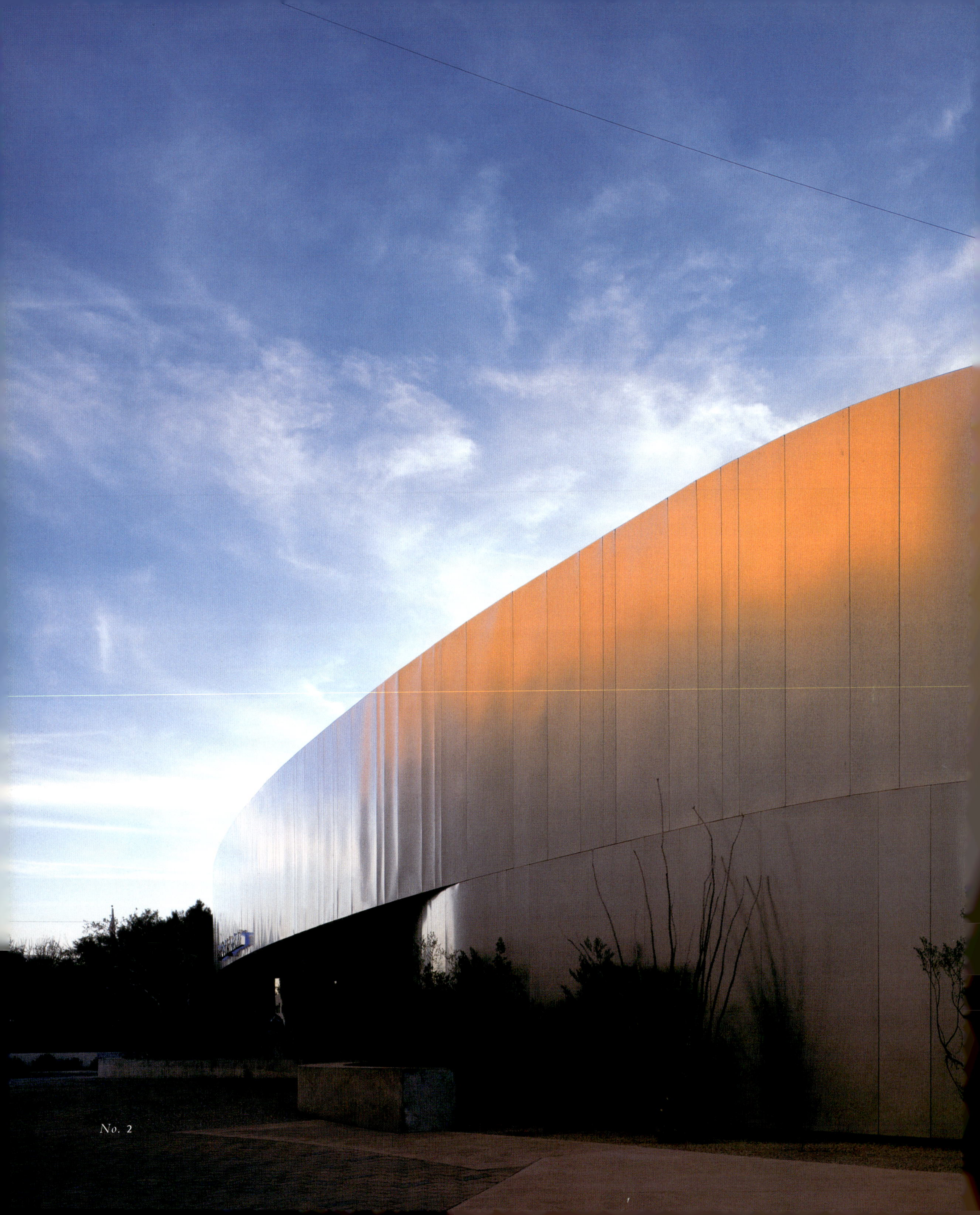

No. 2

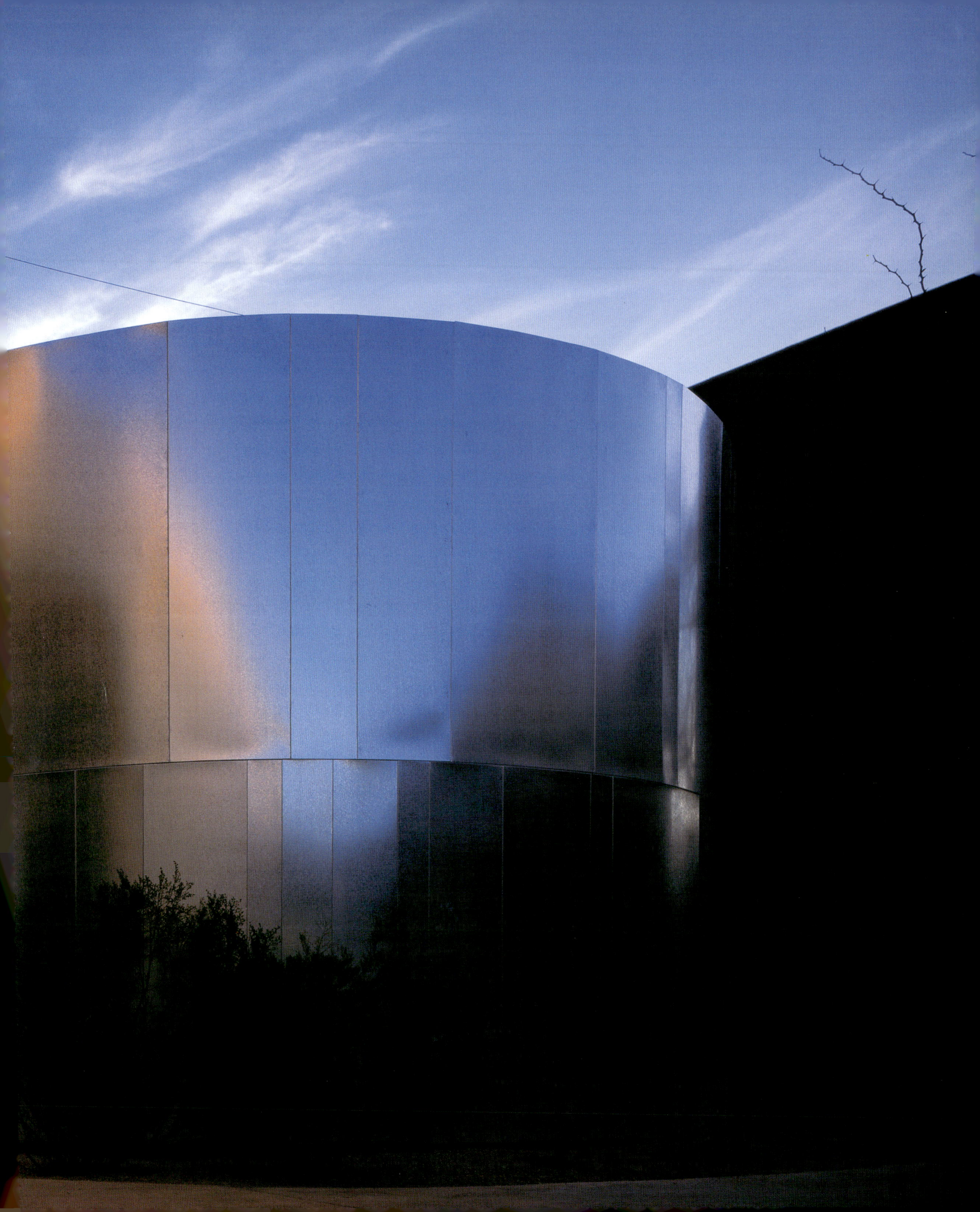

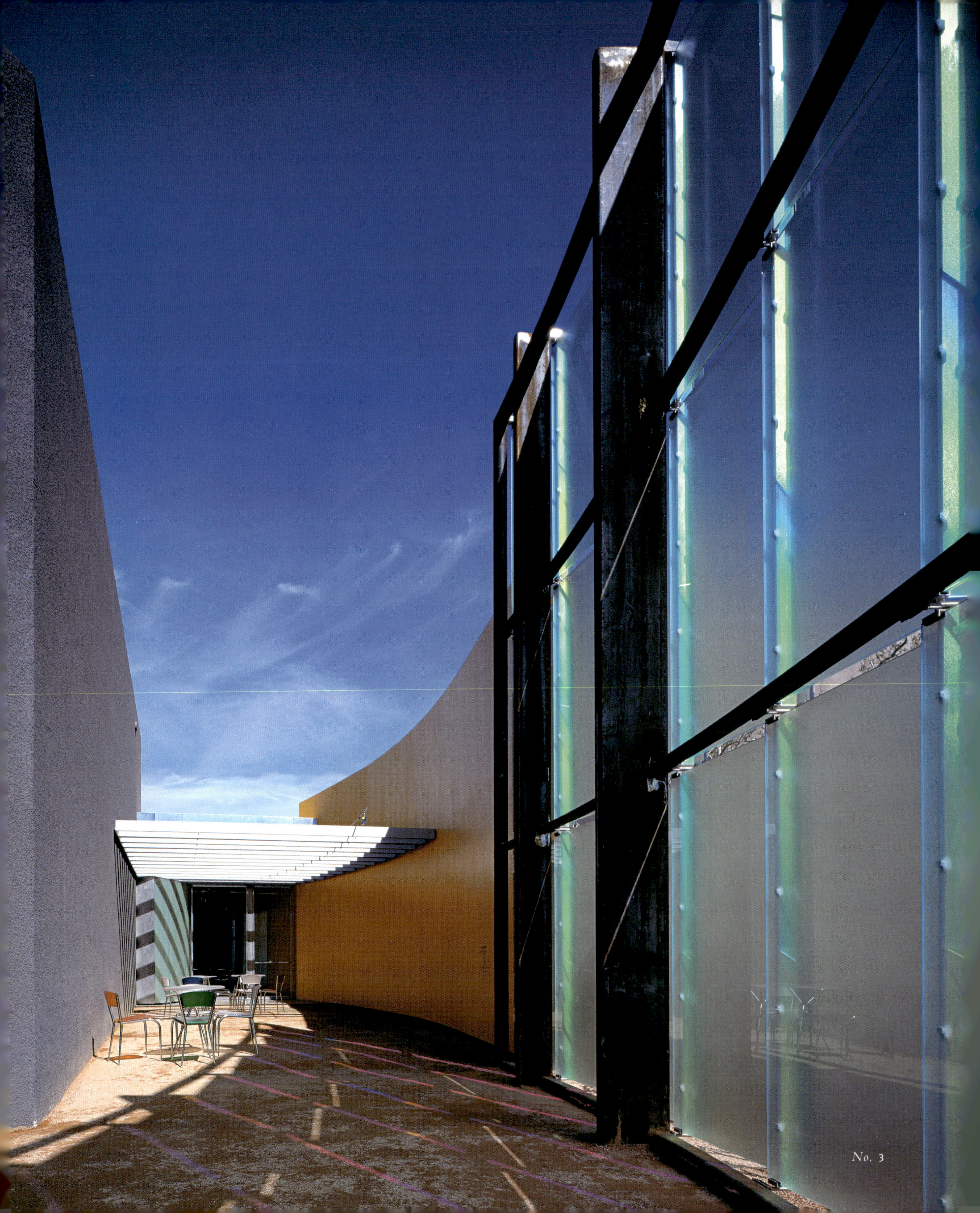

No. 3

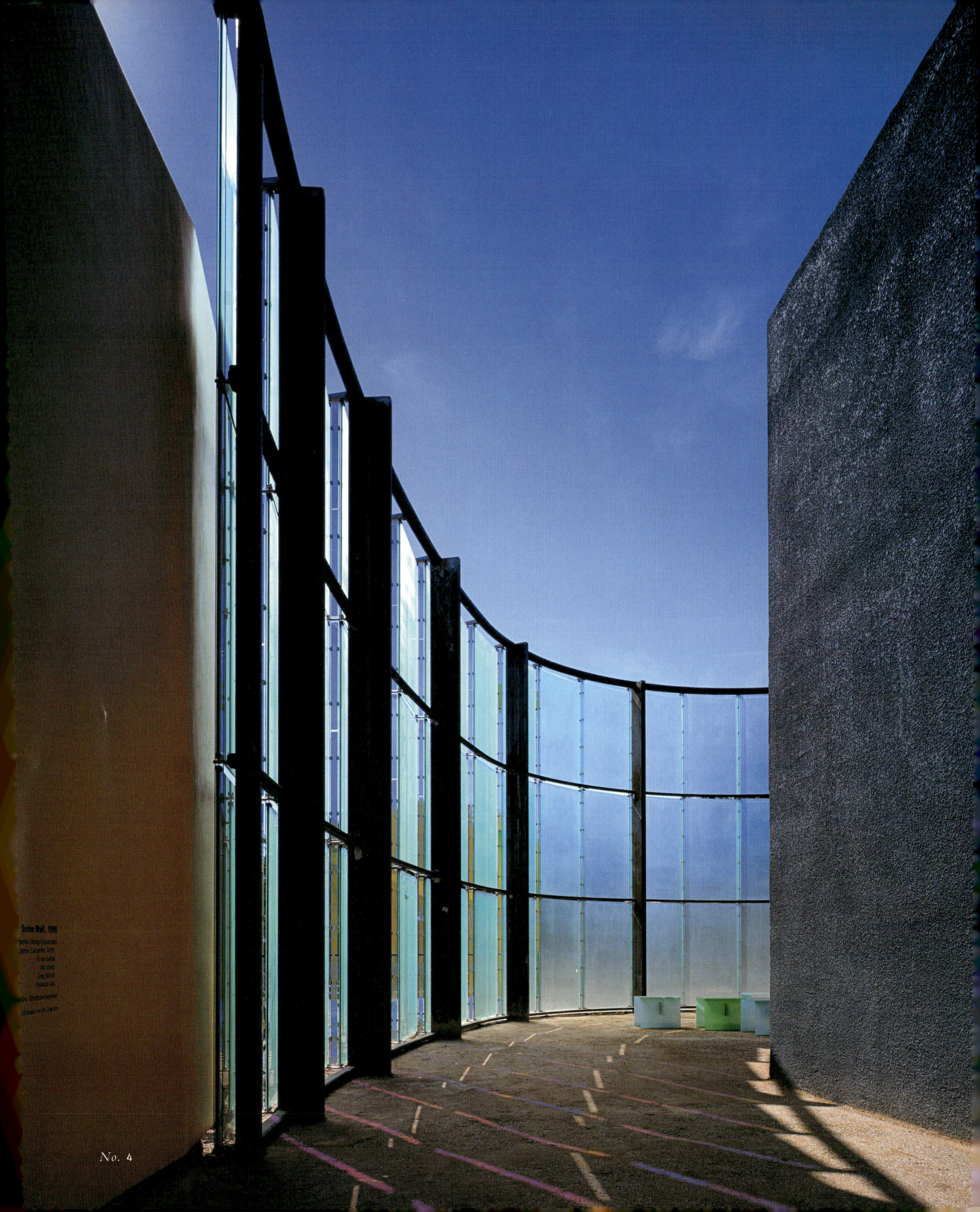

No. 4

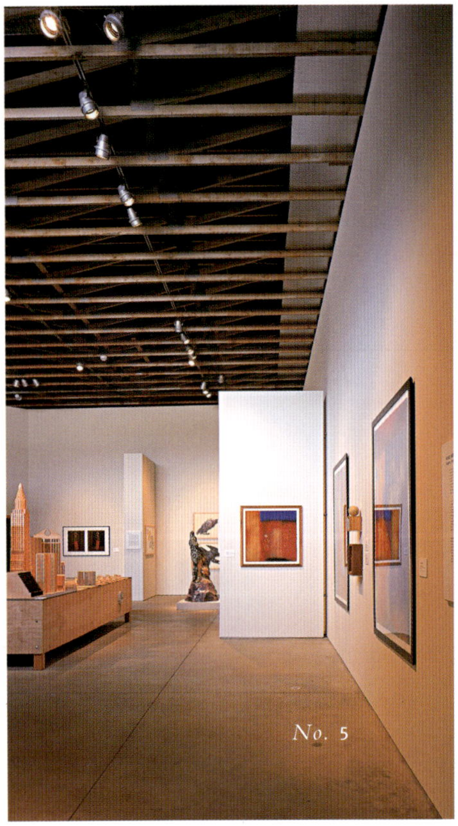

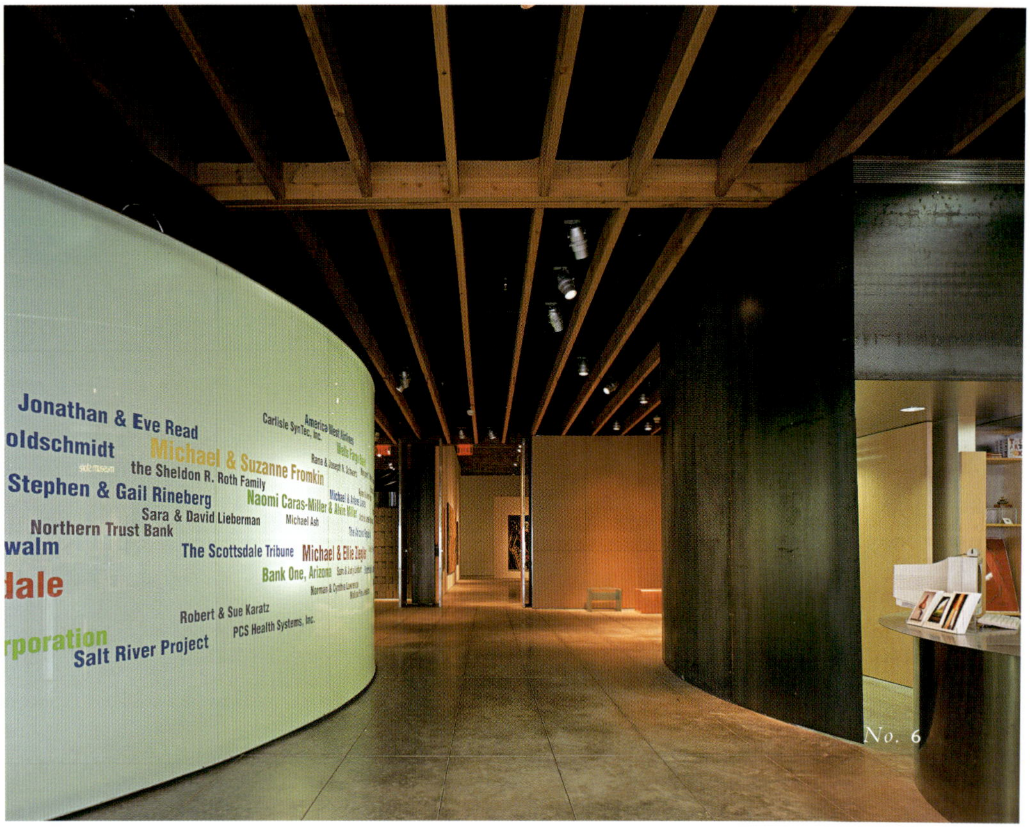

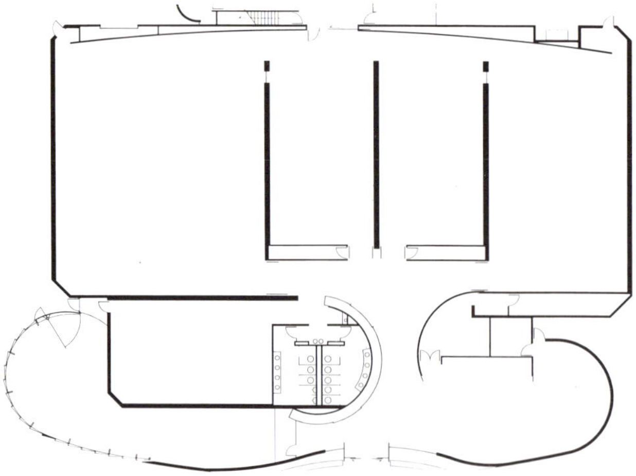

No. 5-7

DESCRIPTION

CAPTION

PHOTO

No. 5 Track lighting is integrated into the exposed timber trussed ceiling.

No. 6 Visitors are drawn forward into the galleries by two curving walls, one of which lists donors and sponsors.

No. 7 The flexible interior provides adaptable space for changing exhibitions.

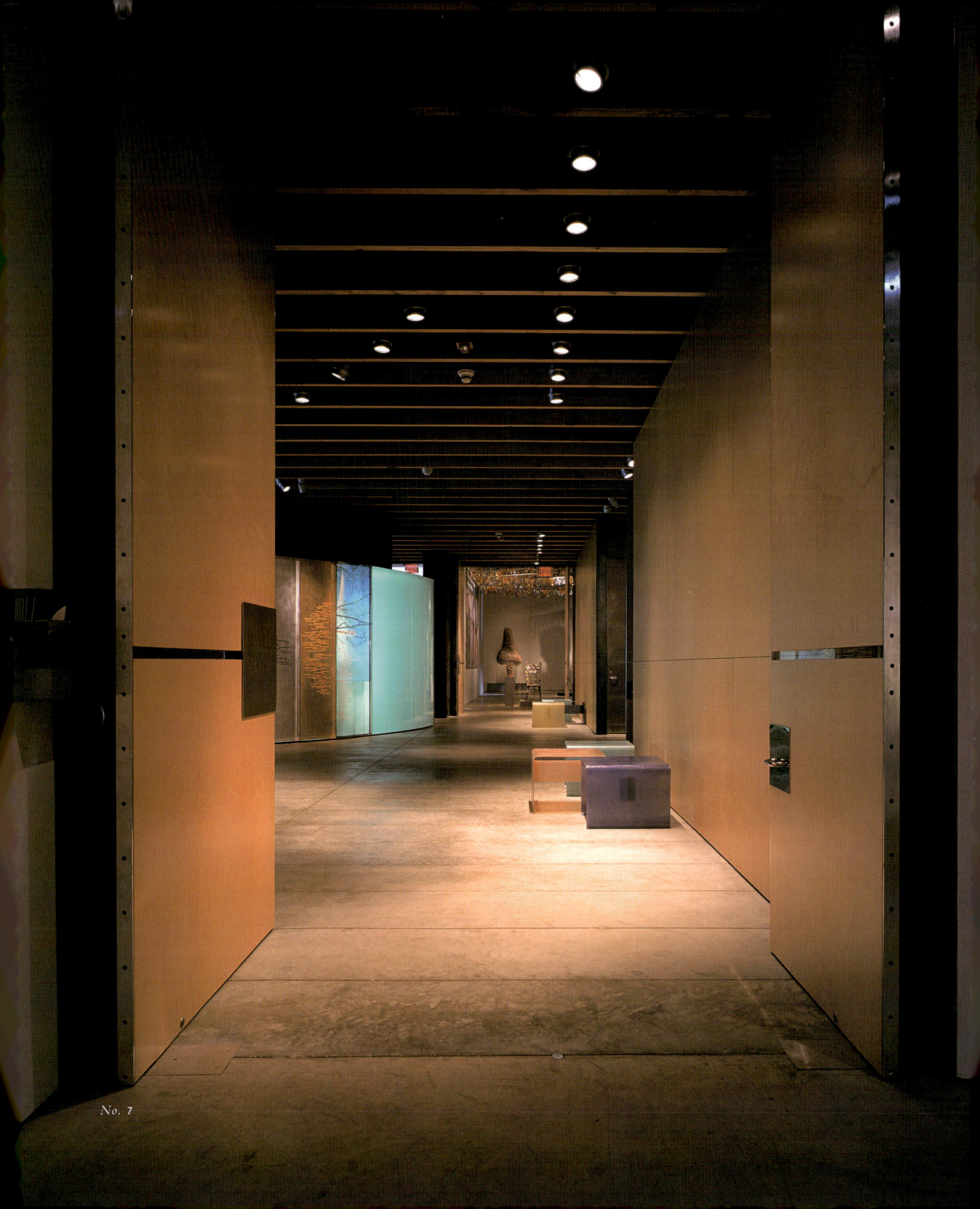
No. 7

Mass MoCA

1 *PROJECT NAME*
Mass MoCA | *North Adams, Massachusetts*

2 *ARCHITECT*
Bruner / Cott | *Cambridge, Massachusetts*

Vacant for ten years, a nineteenth-century industrial complex in northwestern Massachusetts has been given new life as an art museum/vacation center. The focal point of the 13-acre site is Bruner/Cott's design for Mass MoCA, a scheme that seamlessly blends old architecture with new to create a museum that enlivens the contemporary art it showcases.

Originally built in 1872 for Arnold Printworks, a cotton fabrics company, the complex was used from 1940 to 1985 by the Sprague Electric Company. As it was the primary source of employment in North Adams, the town fell into hard times after the plant closed. Its close proximity to Williams College and Tanglewood helped spark interest in the birth of Mass MoCa, which eventually was founded by a public/private partnership. The 160,000-square-foot (14,400 square meter) museum opened in 1999, although it was considered economically viable only by leasing 40,000 square feet (3,600 square meters) for office and retail space.

A sign announces Mass MoCA using the same typeface and standing where the Sprague sign stood for four-and-a-half decades. As visitors enter the main courtyard, they first encounter Building 3, which was cut down to its foundation walls to become an outdoor gallery. Building 3 also symbolically serves as the "cemetery of the Abbey," a grass "reflecting pool" for the clock tower, the centerpiece of the complex.

The lobby of Mass MoCA is the entire first floor of Building 10. Visitors enter through a vestibule richly textured with industrial materials—doors are randomly paned in gridded or ribbed glass and flooring changes from rustproof red metal grates over raw earth to rubber matting and finally to cast steel. The Performing Arts Theater (Building 11) is a multi-functional, state-of-the-art, "black" box, which can be organized as a 650-seat conventional stage or for performance-in-the-round or for video-cinema screening.

The architect's intention was to retain the historic, add new elements where needed, and, in the end, create a single piece that is both old and new, with the intervention almost invisible. Therefore, patinae of the past were retained and merged with the new. Great care was taken to create galleries of disparate scale and finish. The largest galleries, which appear most straightforward, were, in fact, changed the least. There, forests of columns were removed and trusses fabricated to create open spans. The spaces that appear most finished were generally found in the worst condition. Gallery heights range from one to three stories; one gallery runs the length of a football field.

No. 1
Description

CAPTION PHOTO

No. 1 The bridge to the museum entrance.

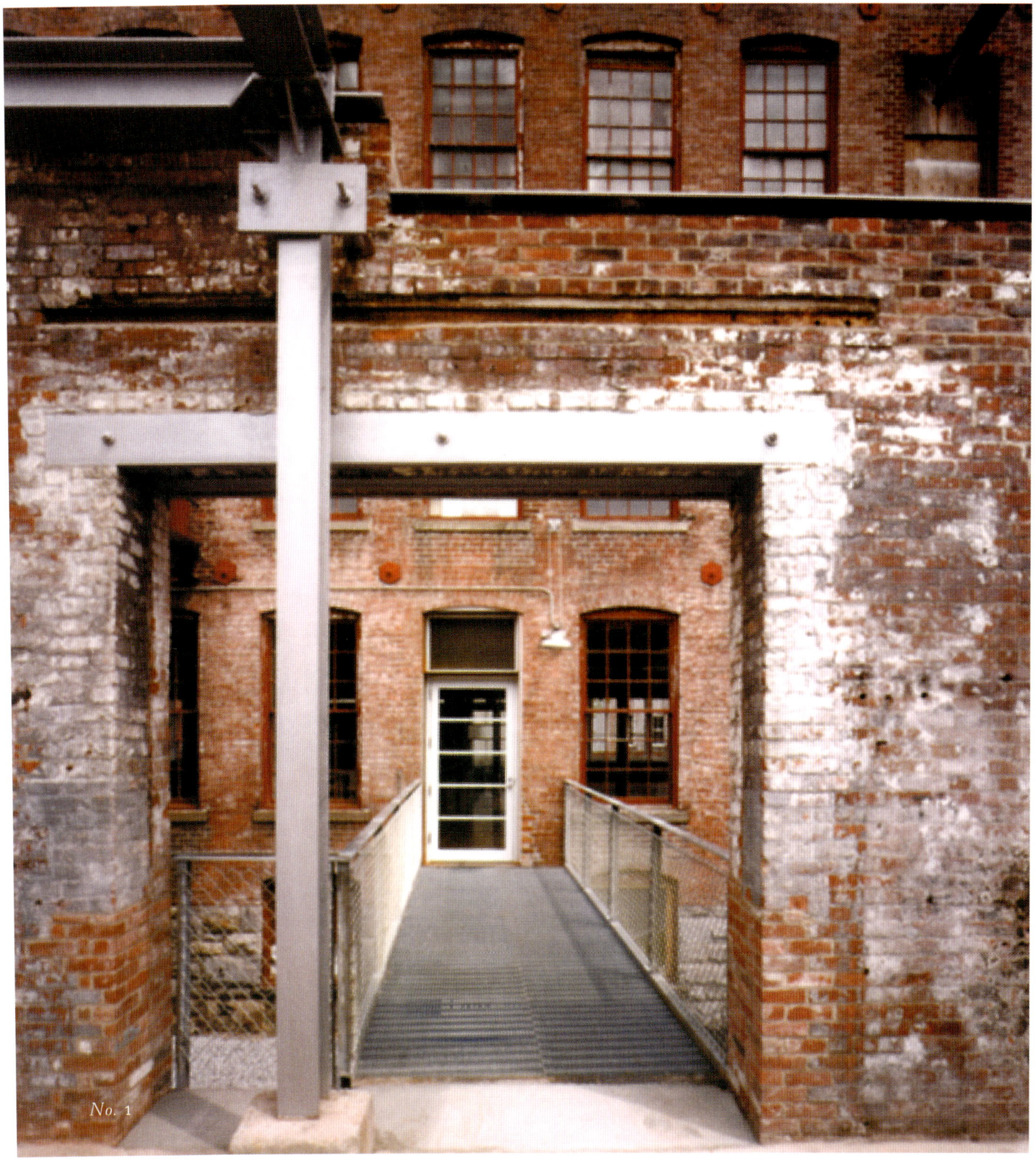
No. 1

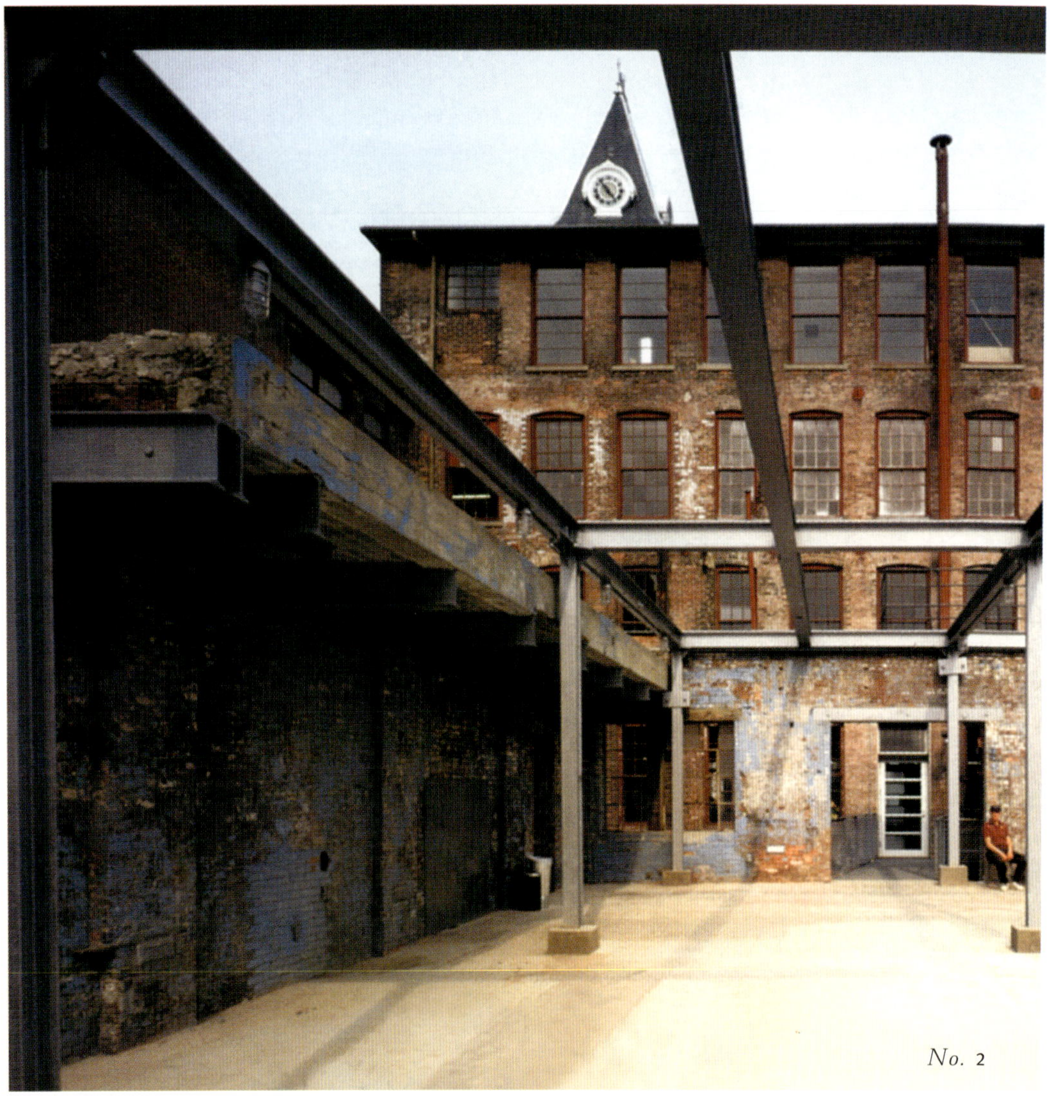

No. 2

Photo: Robert Polidori

No. 2-3 Description

CAPTION PHOTO

No. 2 A performance courtyard as seen through the entryway.

No. 3 The entrance court and a sculpture "Tree Logic." The old foundation is visible in the foreground.

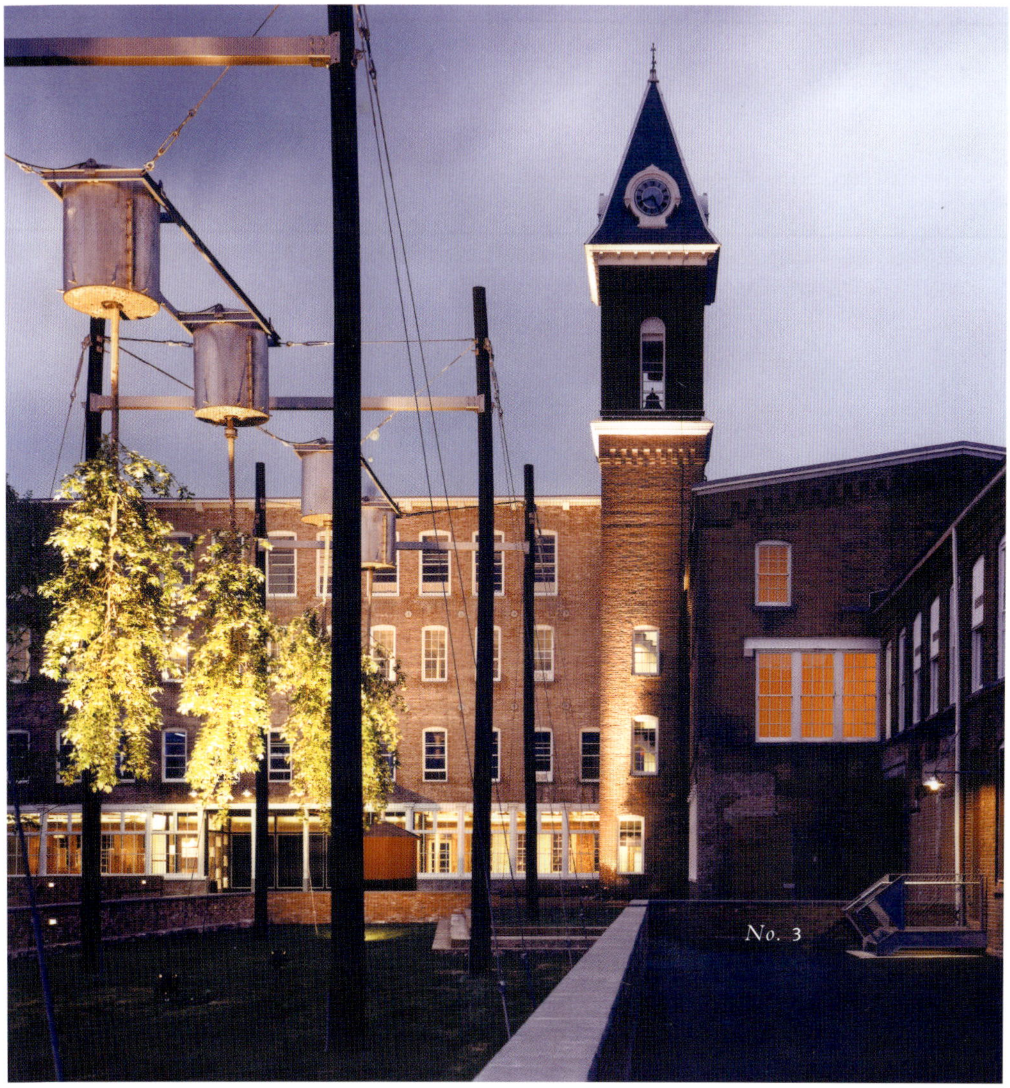

Photo: Peter Vanderwarker

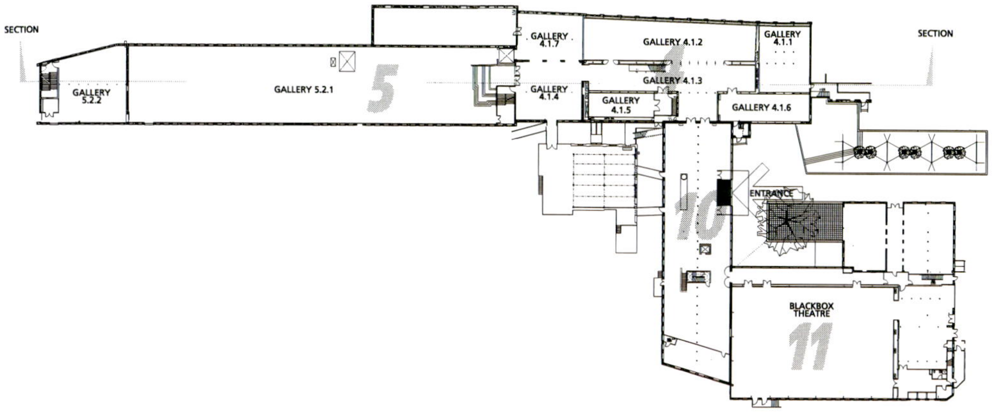

No.

GENERAL INTEREST

No. 4

DESCRIPTION

CAPTION

PHOTO

No. 4 GALLERY 4.1.2, ROSENQUIST INSTALLATION, WITH COMPLETED TRUSSES, OVERLOOK AND BALCONY.

Photo: ROBERT POLIDORI

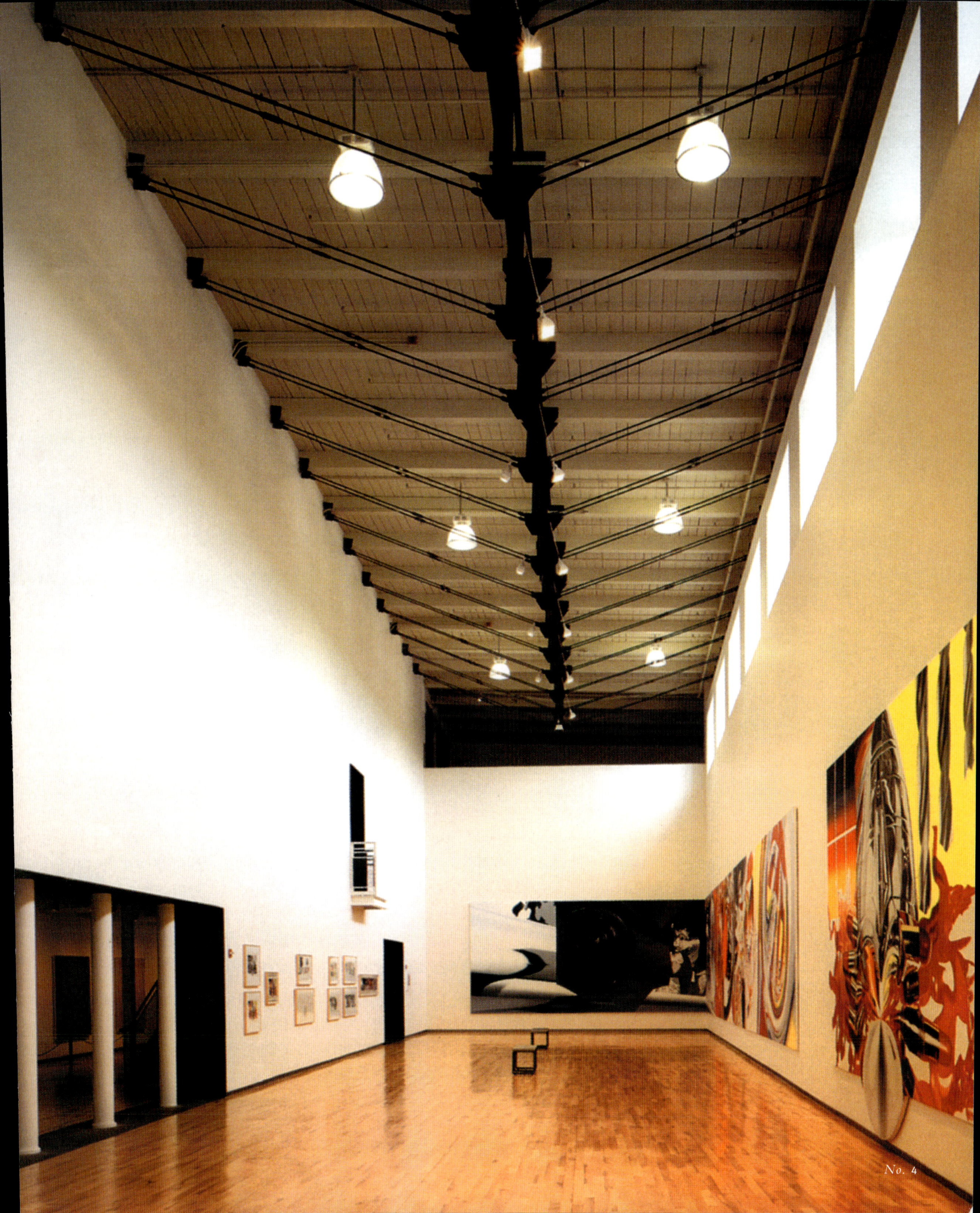

No. 4

Photo: Peter Vanderwarker

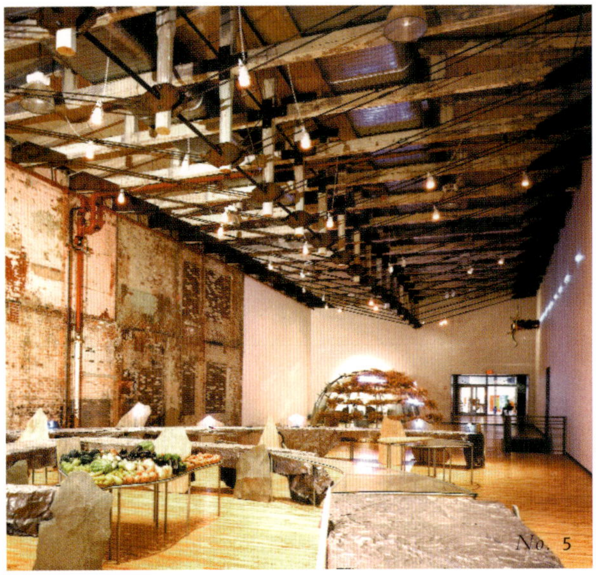

Photo: Robert Polidori

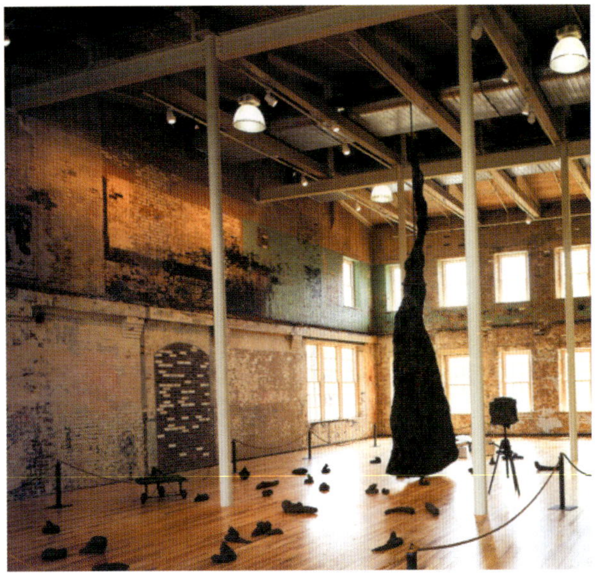

No. 5-8

DESCRIPTION

CAPTION

PHOTO

No. 5 Gallery 4.2.2, Merz installation, with fabricated trusses

No. 6 A Joseph Beuys installation in a gallery where the floors and columns have been removed to create a two-story space.

No. 7 Detail of gallery 4.1.1

No. 8 Gallery 5.1 with concret floor in new two-story space

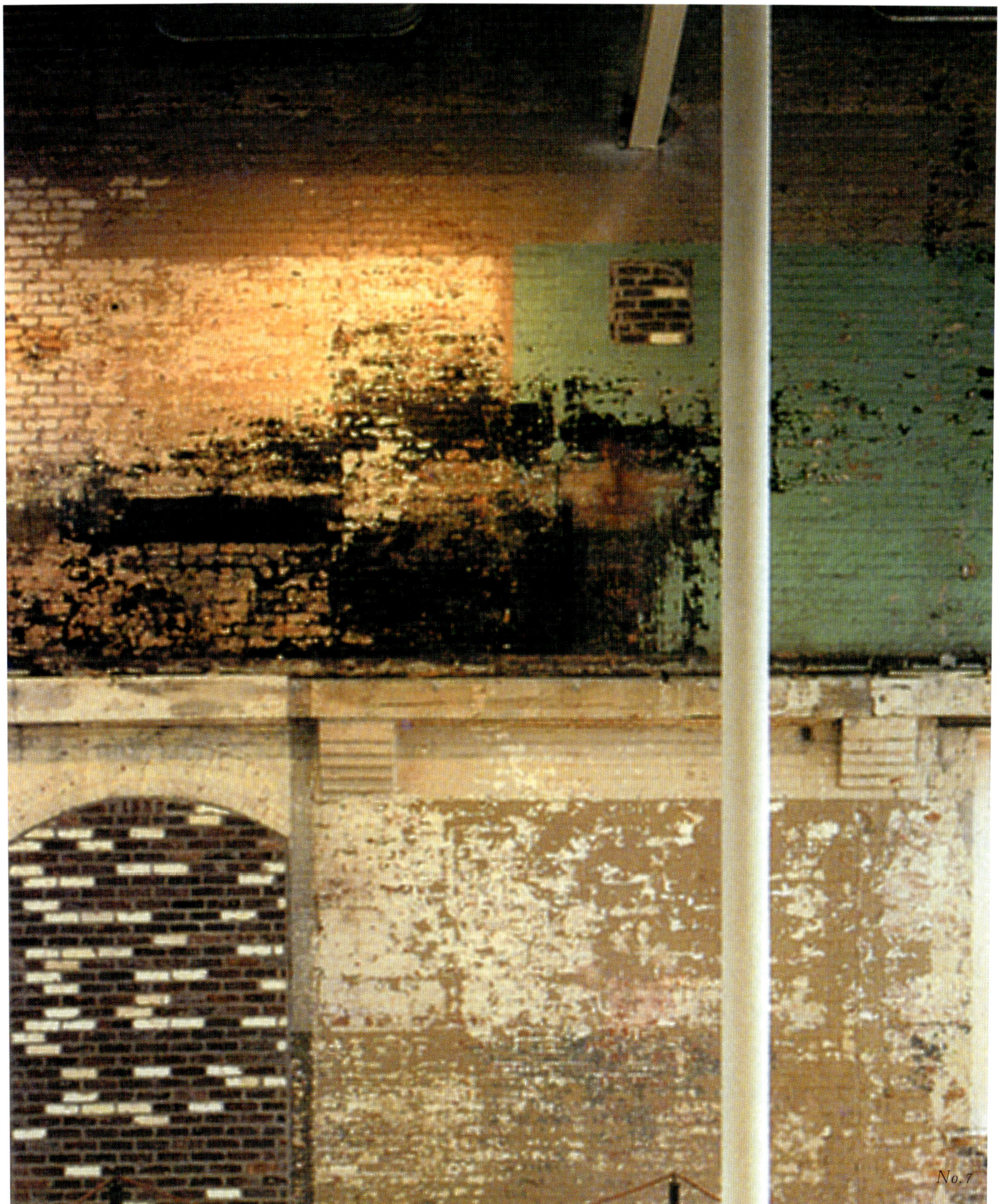
No.7

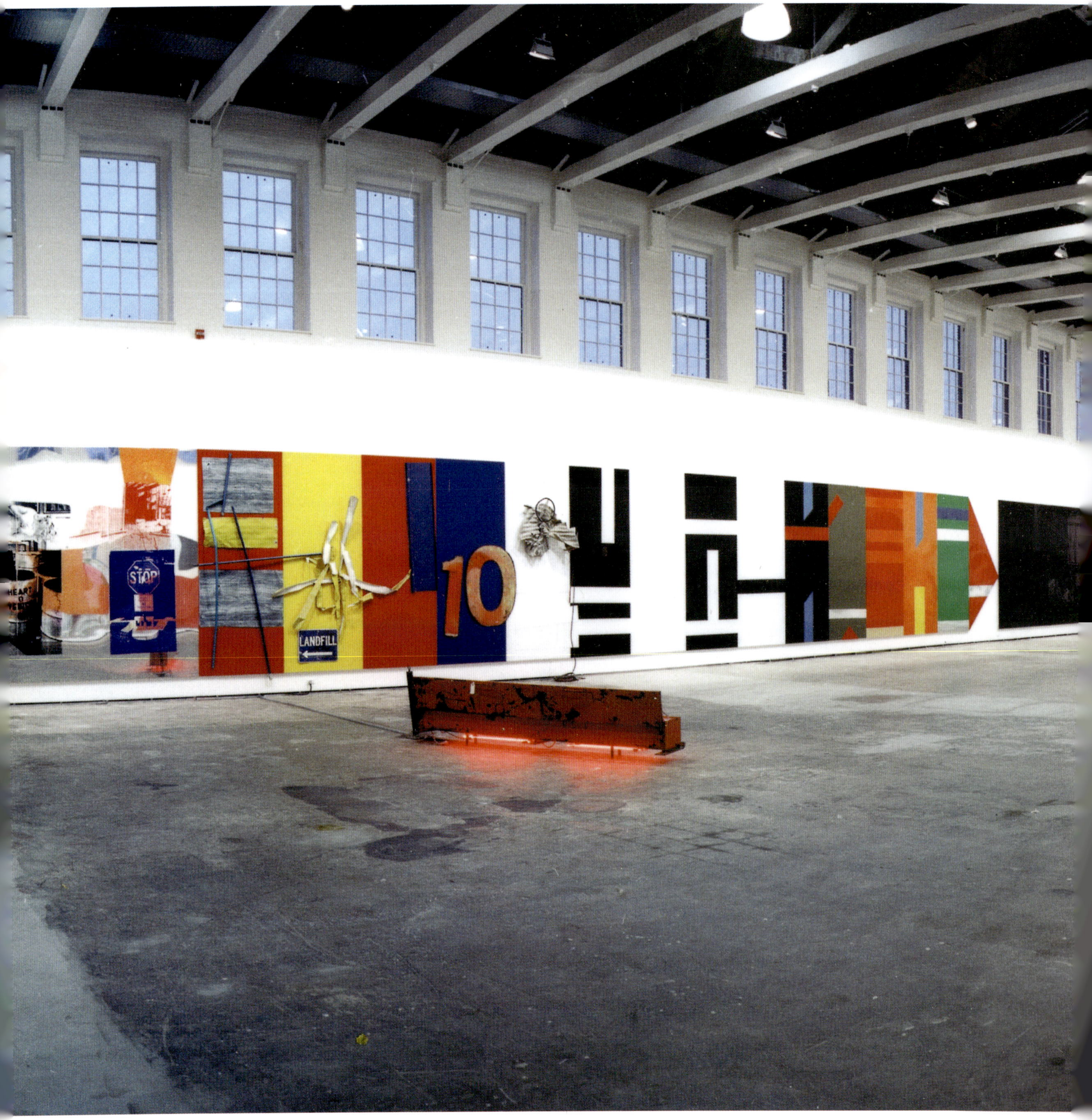

Photo: Nick Whitman

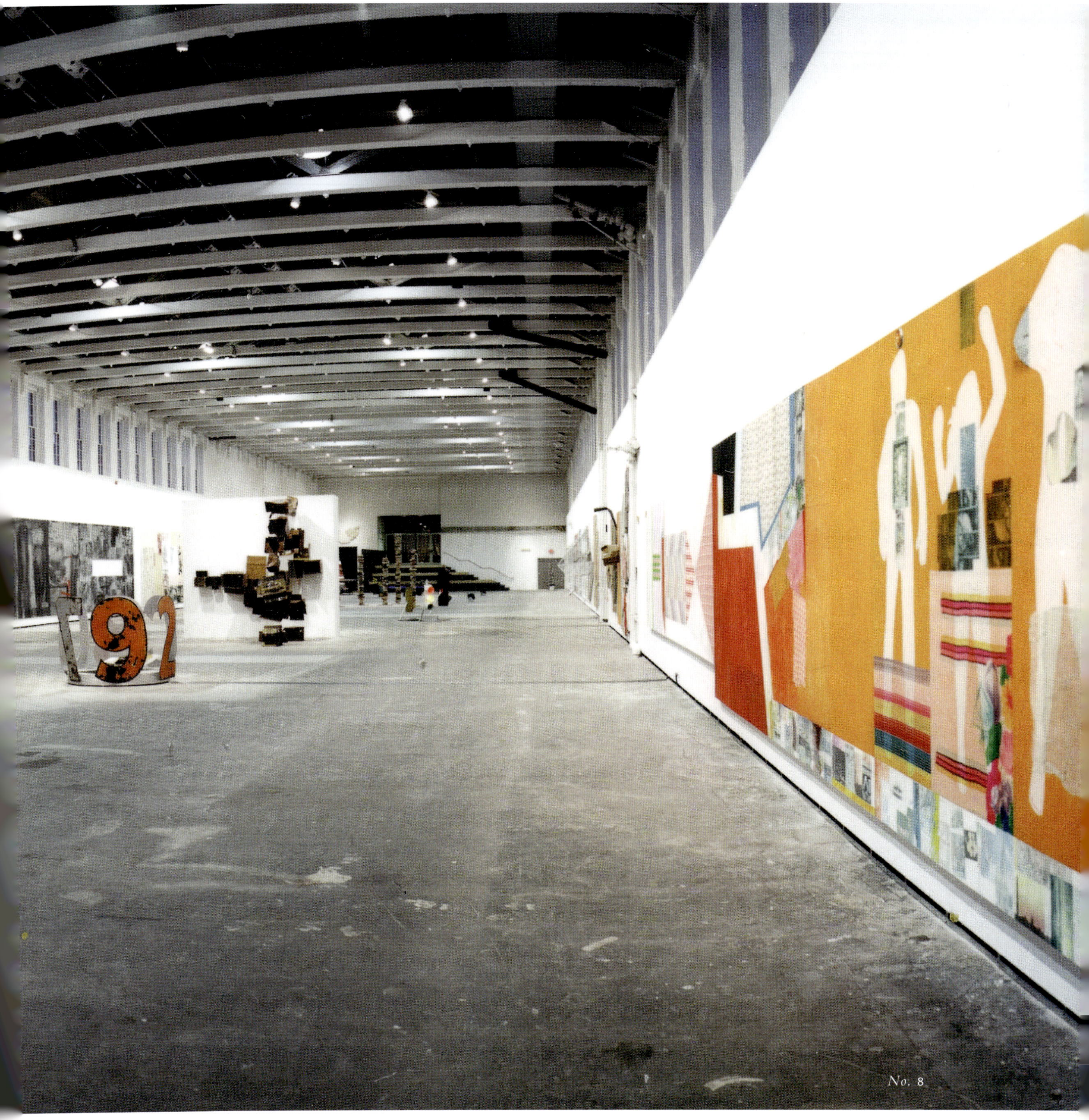

No. 8

Museum of Contemporary Art

1 *PROJECT*
Museum of Contemporary Art | *North Miami, Florida*

2 *ARCHITECT*
Gwathmey Siegel & Associates Architects | *New York, New York*

It's an unusual civics lesson today when a city trades parking for culture, but that's what North Miami did. As part of an urban revitalization project, the Museum of Contemporary Art was inserted between City Hall and the Police Headquarters. An assemblage of brightly colored, cubist objects, the museum forms an animated destination point that beckons art enthusiasts inside. Its presence creates a new cultural center downtown.

Designed by Gwathmey Siegel, the 24,000-square-foot (2,160-square-meter) building consists of four interconnected buildings of earth-hued stucco, concrete and glass block, galvanized corrugated metal panels and steel. These objects are carefully organized in the architect's language of arrival, procession, circulation, scale, and proportion. Together they form a unique horizontal and vertical grid. They serve as a "gate-bridge" between the civic buildings on both sides. The building components are colored in the painterly tradition of Braque and Picasso. Their materiality reflects the tradition of South Florida and that of Mexican architect Luis Barrigan.

In front of the museum, the public plaza is outlined by a 28-foot (23.1-meter) grid of palm trees, a reflecting pool, a flexible pavilion, and a museum arcade. The overall design is meant to "provide a continuous and enriched dialogue between architecture and art, providing and challenging while enthusing a sense of reflection and calm."

The open interior allows space for recognition of local artists, such as Teresita Fernandez and Jose Bedia, as well as established artists like Dan Flavin and Louise Nevelson.

No. 1 Description

Caption Photo

No. 1 The museum consists of cubist forms placed between City Hall and Police Headquarters.

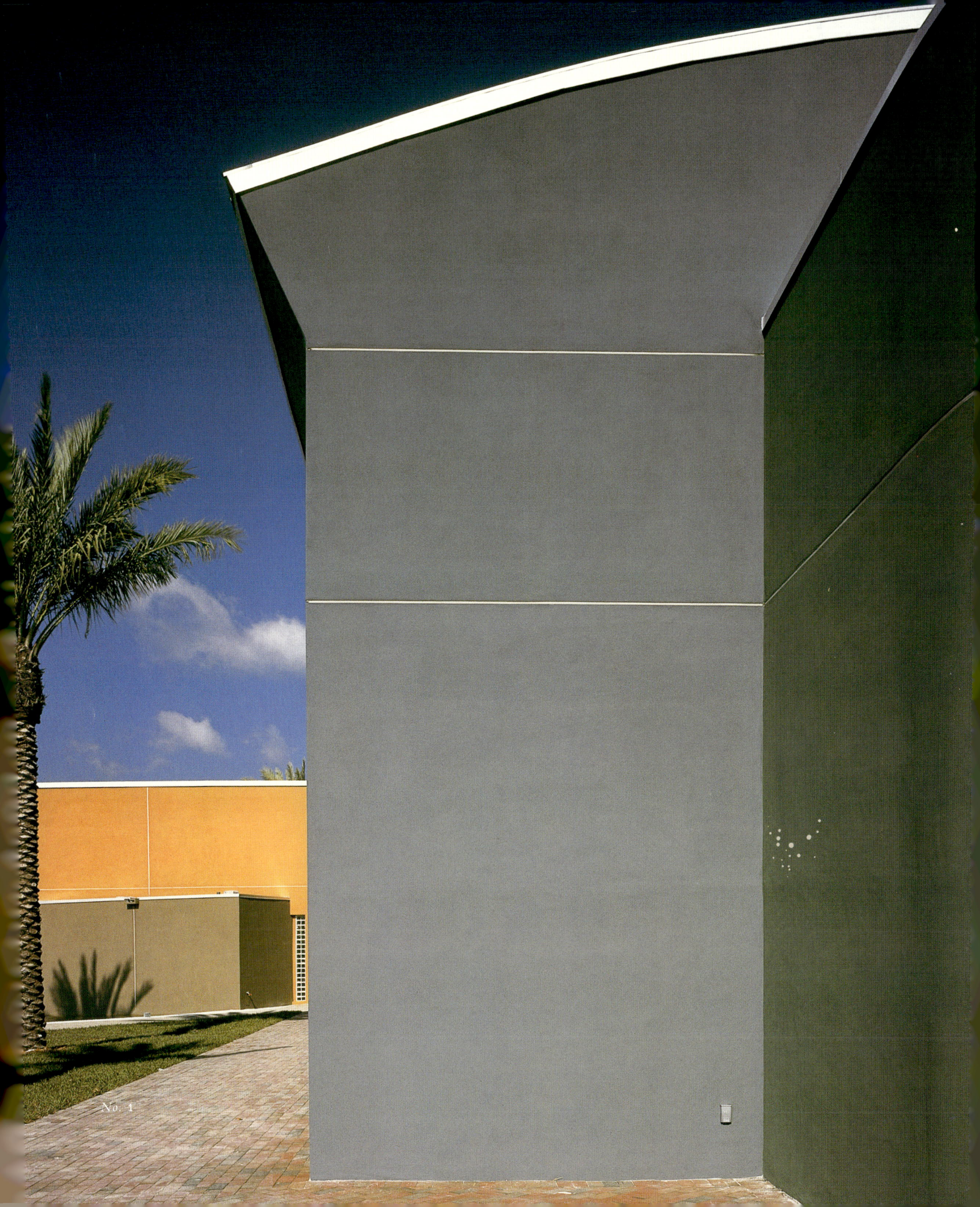
No. 1

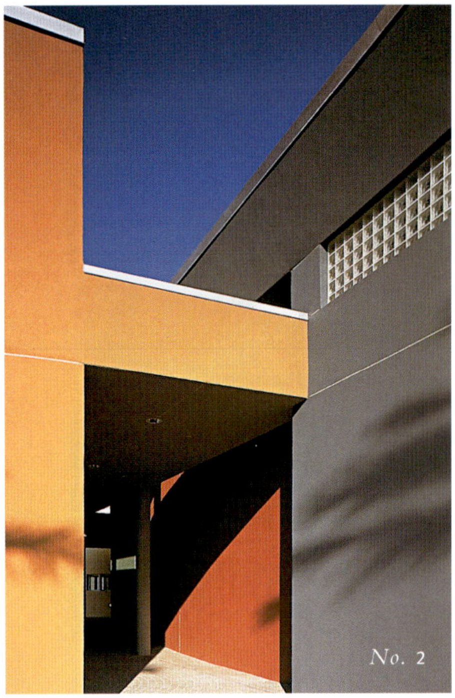
No. 2

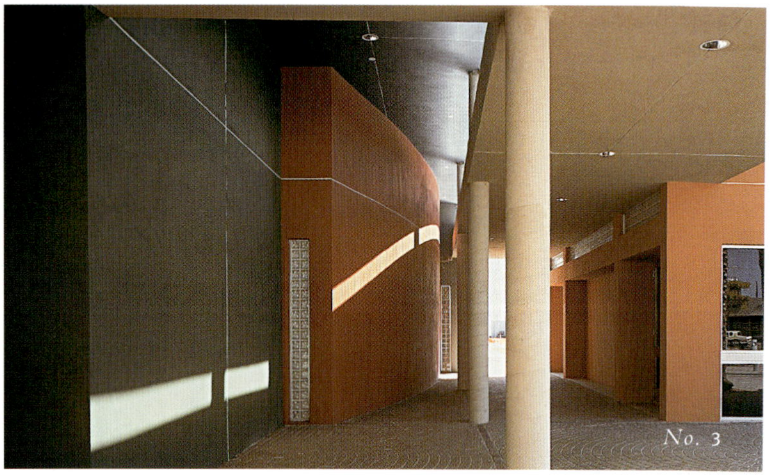
No. 3

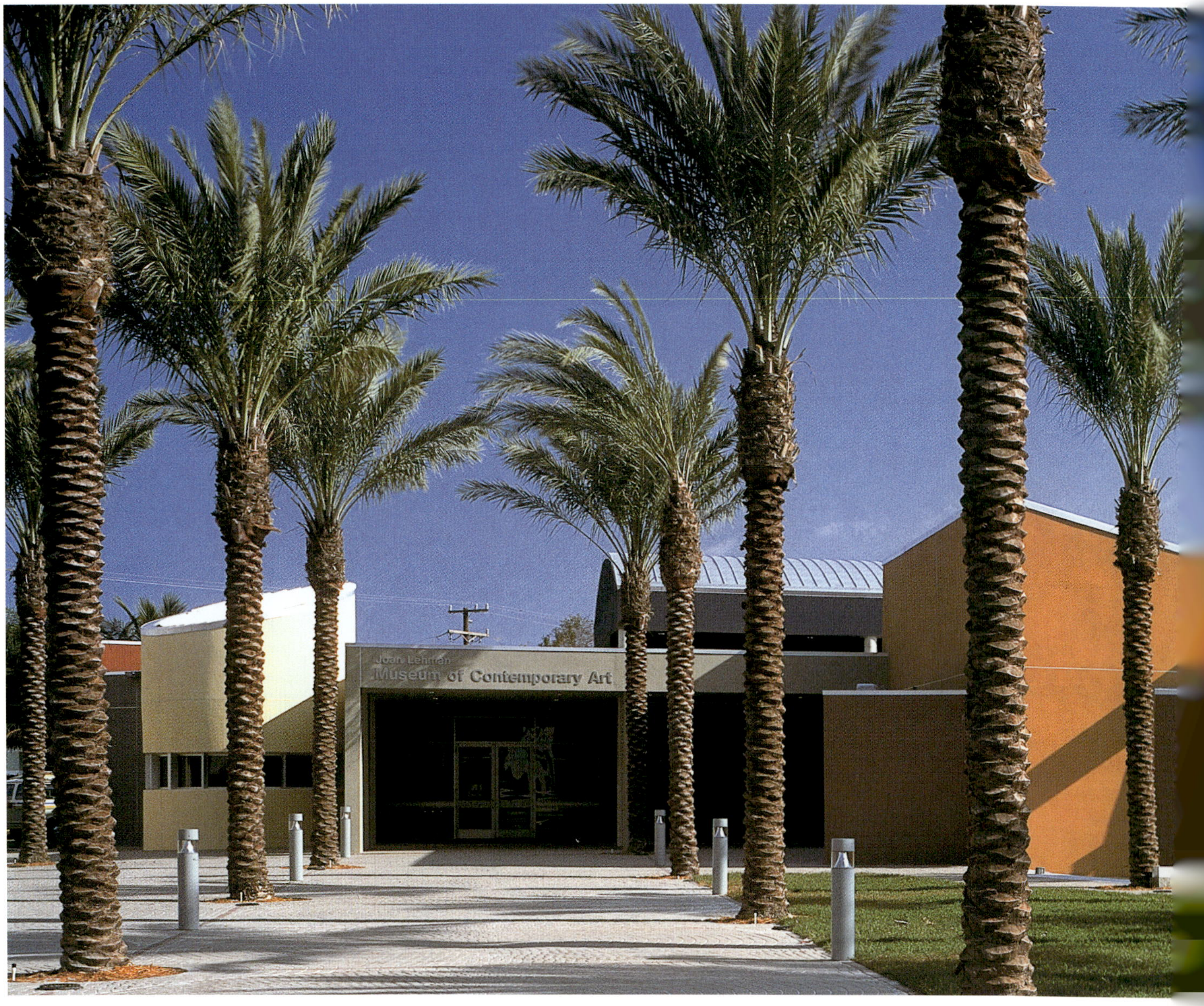

No. 2-4

DESCRIPTION

CAPTION

PHOTO

No. 2 East façade with the museum store and entry arcade. The exterior is painted stucco.

No. 3 The entry arcade carries the bold color scheme of the exterior into the museum's interior.

No. 4 As viewed from across the pubic plaza, the 24,000 square-foot (2,160-square-meter) building is defined by four interconnected elements that frame an existing sculpture courtyard and form a visual collage.

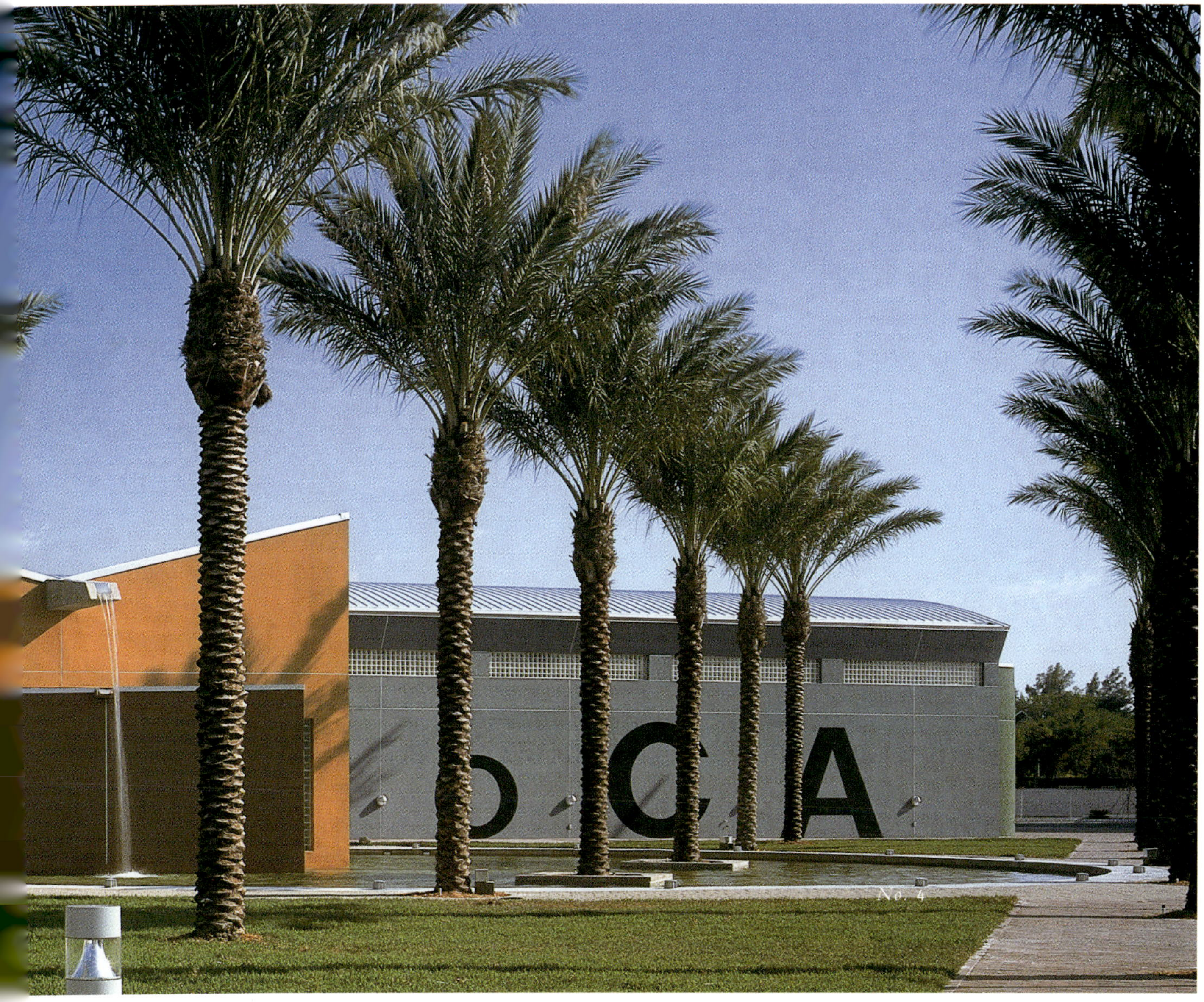

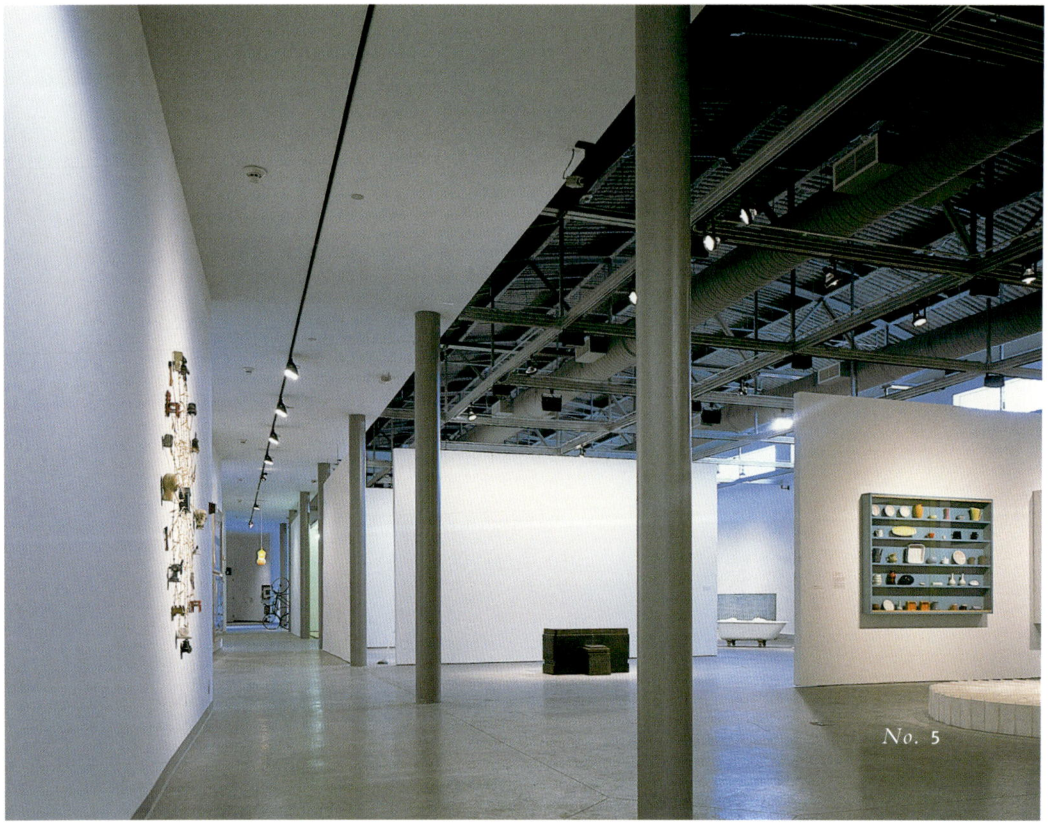

No. 8

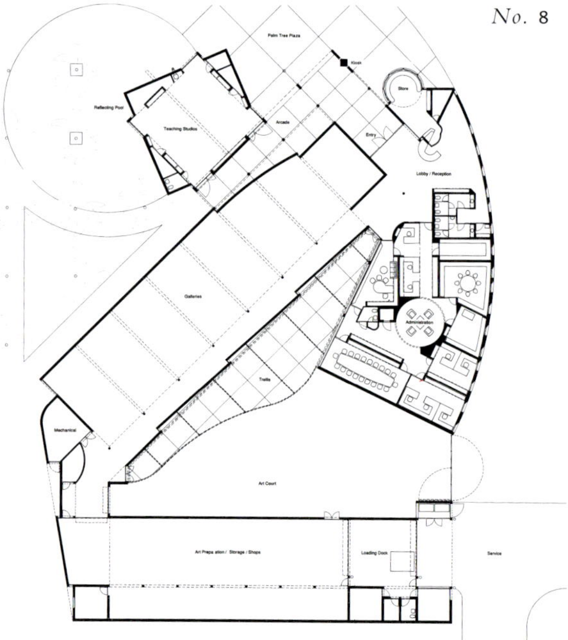

CAPTION

PHOTO

No. 5, 6 & 7 The dynamic interiors create a continuous dialogue between architecture and art, provoking and challenging an atmosphere that is both reflective and calming.

No. 8 The floor plan shows the relationship of the four-interconnected building elements and the courtyard.

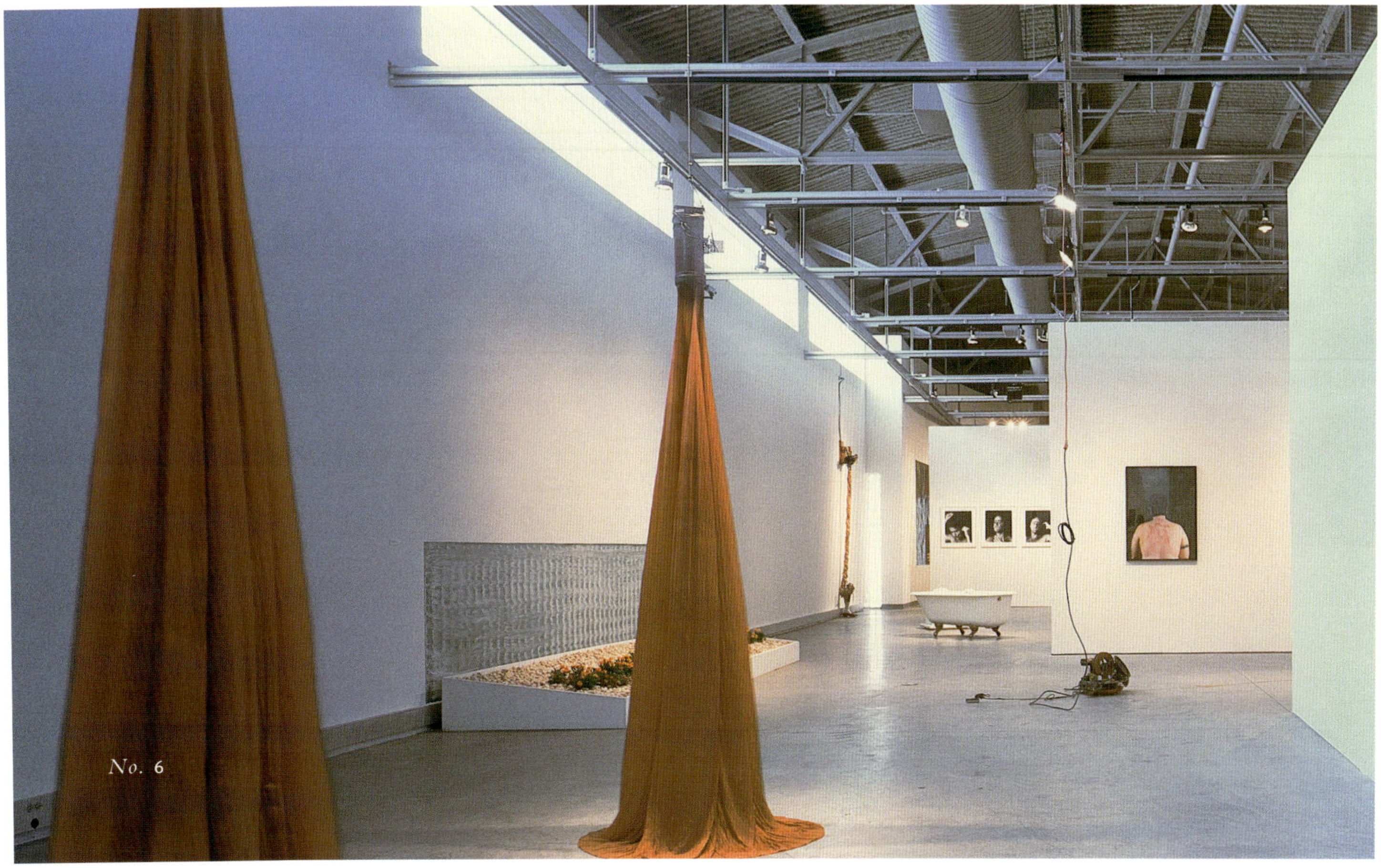

No. 6

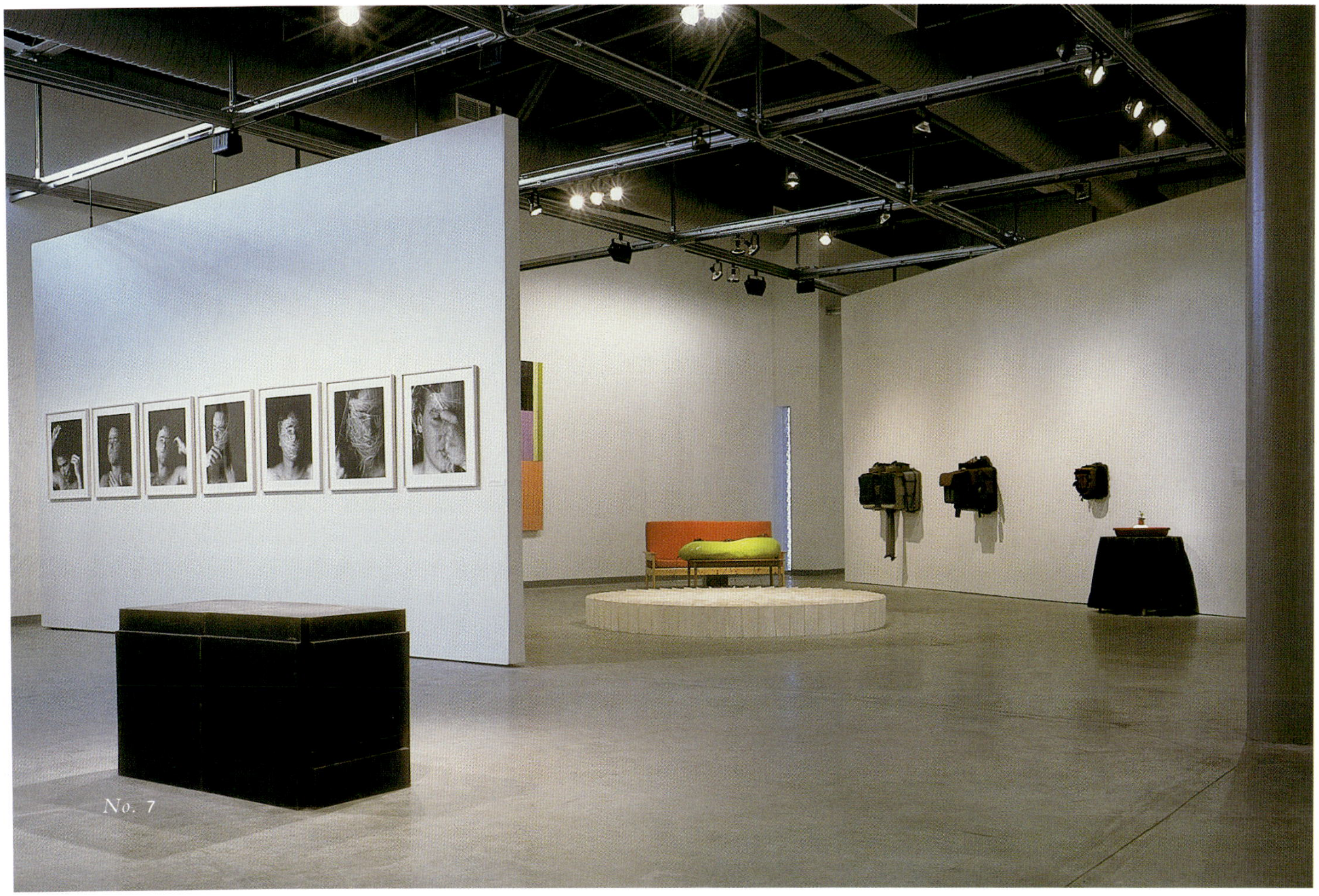

No. 7

Kiasma

1 *PROJECT*
Kiasma, Museum of Contemporary Art | *Helsinki, Finland*

2 *ARCHITECT*
Steven Holl Architects | *New York City*

For the design of Kiasma, Steven Holl Architects faced an intimidating task: Insert a new building of prominence among other major civic monuments in the heart of a vibrant capital city. Not only would the new museum face the Parliament building to the west, but also Eliel Saarinen's Helsinki Station lay to the east and Alvar Aalto's Finlandia Hall to the north. The solution is a signature building that geometrically relates to these city sites, as well as to the Töölo Bay and beyond.

Symbolically shaped in the gesture of two hands clasping, the Museum of Contemporary Art is a bold building of unadorned clarity. Complexity comes through a skillful manipulation of materials—aluminum, glass, and zinc. The 130,000-square-foot (11,700-square-meter) building is carefully sited to visually link with Finlandia Hall and also to engage in a "natural line" with the adjacent landscaped park and Toolo Bay. Eliminating the intermediate scale in the building's architecture creates a "language of silence".

This design, however, brings to the interior two special characteristics—it provides a variety of spatial experiences and permits an abundance of natural light to enter the galleries. The galleries are typically semi-rectangular in shape with one wall curved; however, slight variations in room shapes and sizes exist due to the gentle curves in the building. These rooms are meant to be silent, but not static; they are differentiated through their irregularity. Asymmetry defines the movement through these spaces, so that the overall design becomes a slightly warped "gallery of rooms." The visitor, therefore, is confronted with continuous unfolding or changing perspectives that connect the internal experience to the overall concept of intertwining or "Kiasma."

The building is shaped to take advantage of the horizontal natural light found in this northern city. The slight variation in room shape and the gently curving exterior façade allows natural light to enter several ways at once. The curved "Wall of Ice" lets light penetrate though glass planks with translucent insulation while horizontal light is deflected down through upper and lower levels. The curved roof section with its "bowtie" skylights introduces another means for distributing light to galleries below the top level. All twenty-five galleries are naturally lit.

No. 1
Description

Caption
Photo

No. 1 Exterior materials include aluminum, glass, and zinc—all carefully manipulated by Holl.

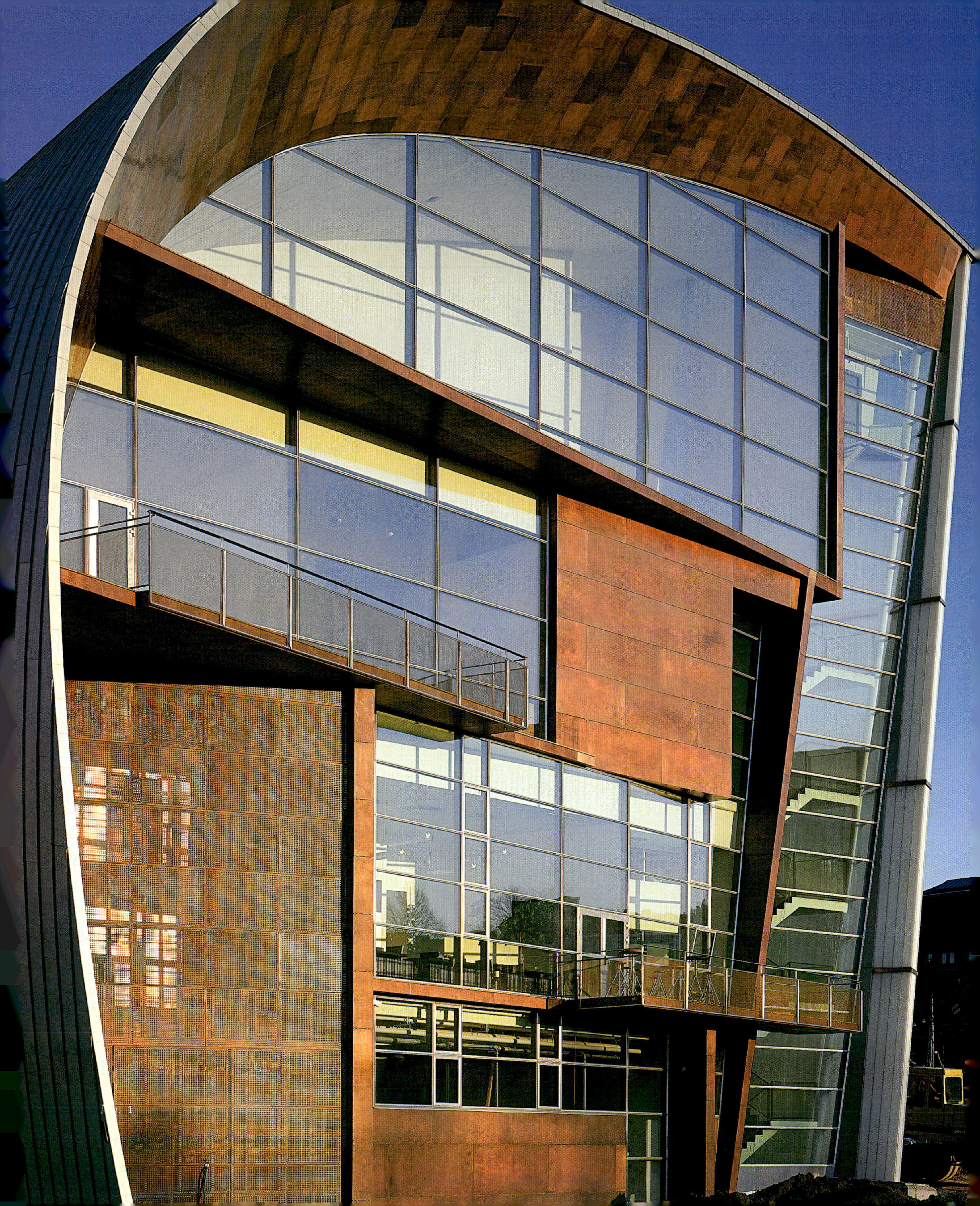

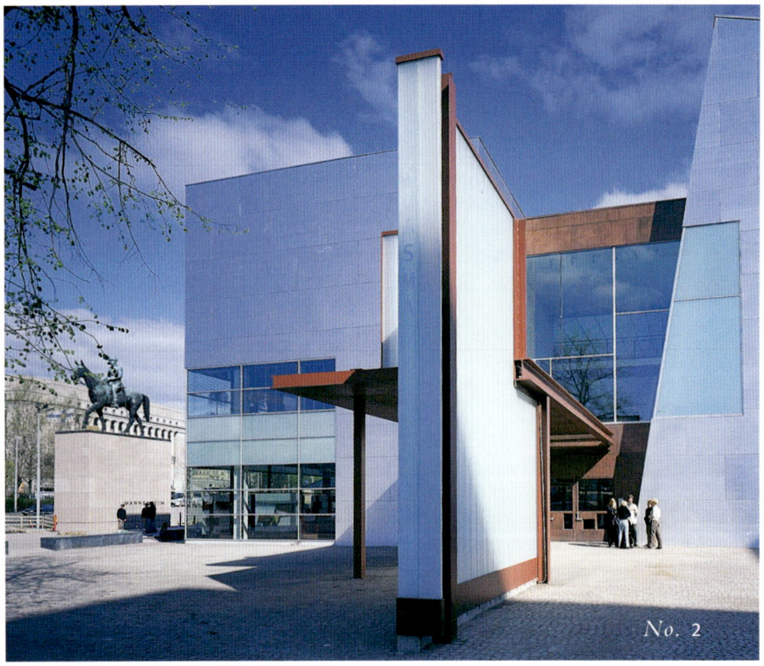

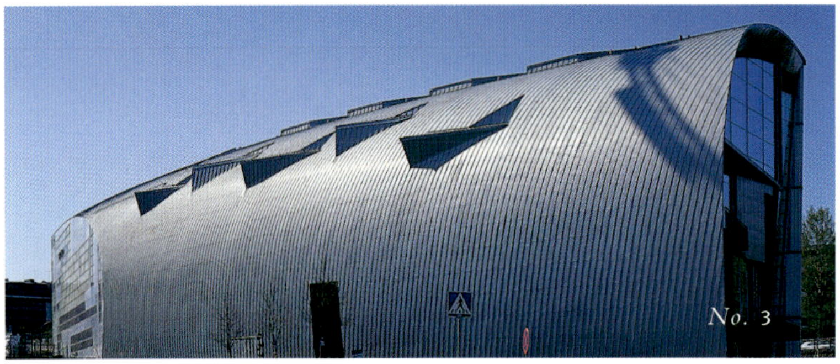

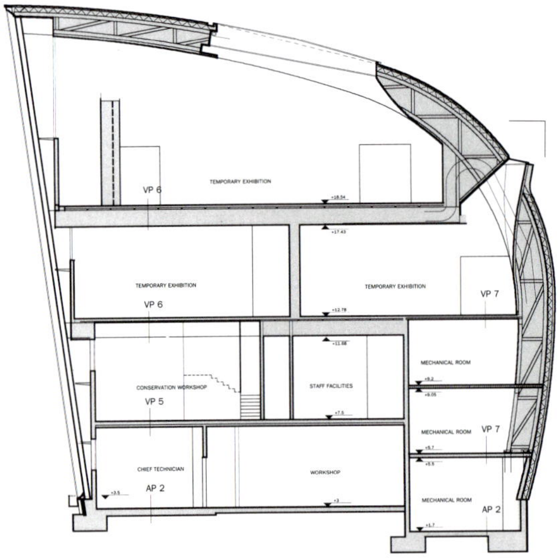

No. 2-4

DESCRIPTION

CAPTION

PHOTO

No. 2 Entrance facade

No. 3 View of the curved section of the roof with "bowtie" skylights.

No. 4 The concept of Kiasma involves the intertwining of the building's mass with the geometry of the city and the landscape. Each are reflected in the shape of the building, an implicit cultural line curves to link Finlandia Hall designed by Alvar Aalto while engages a natural line with the landscape and Töölo Bay at Helsinki's heart.

No. 4

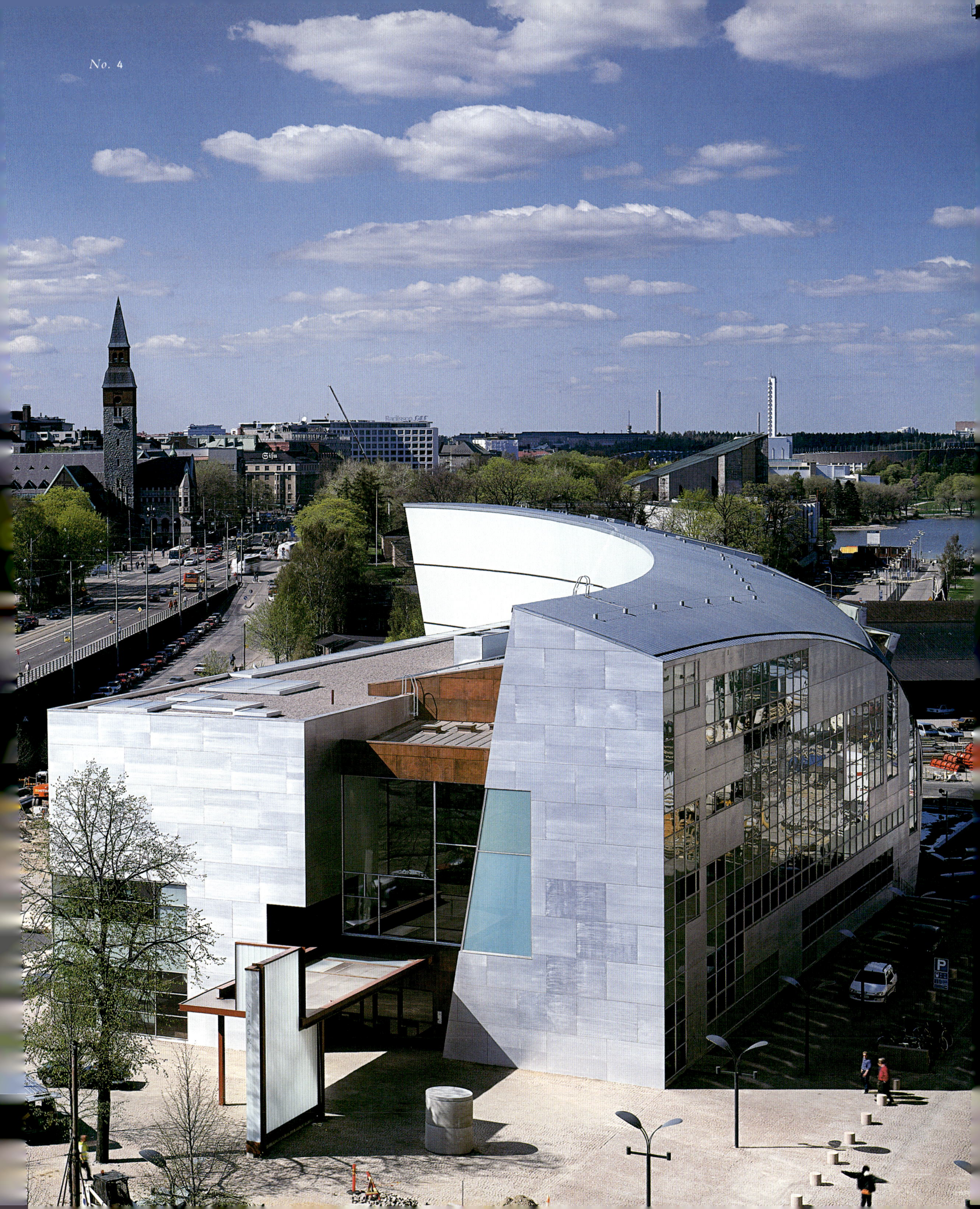

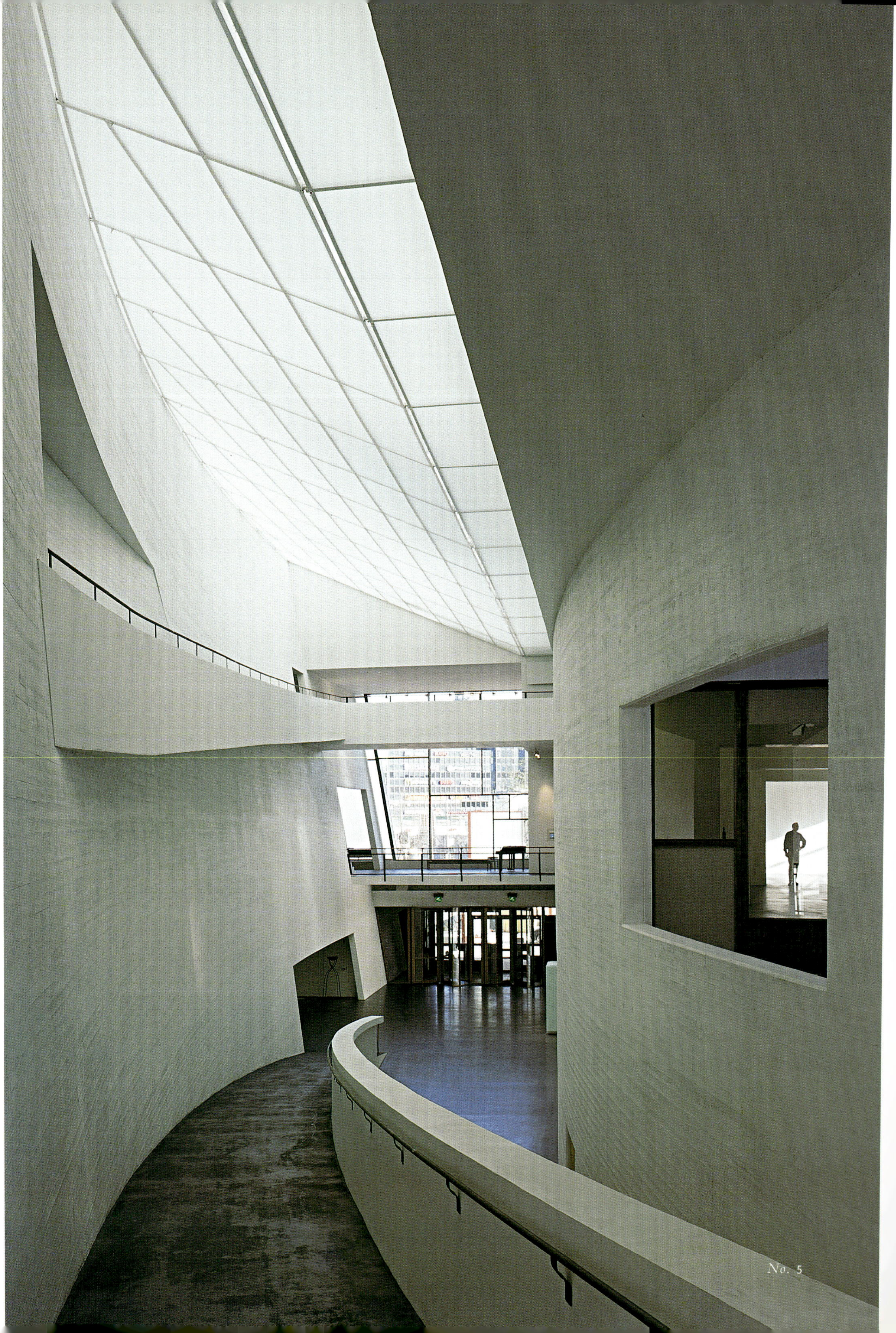

No. 5

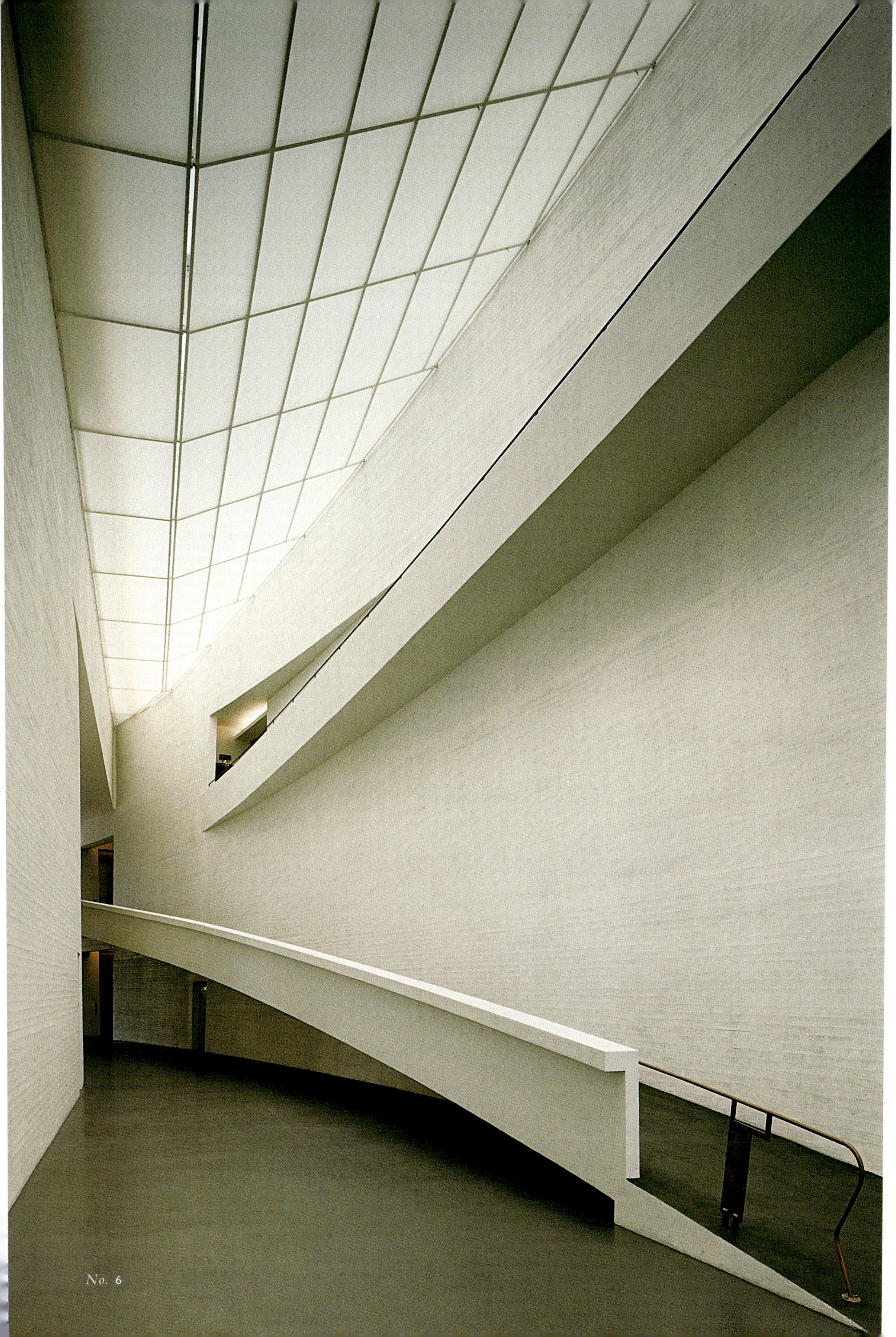

No. 6

No.

GENERAL INTEREST

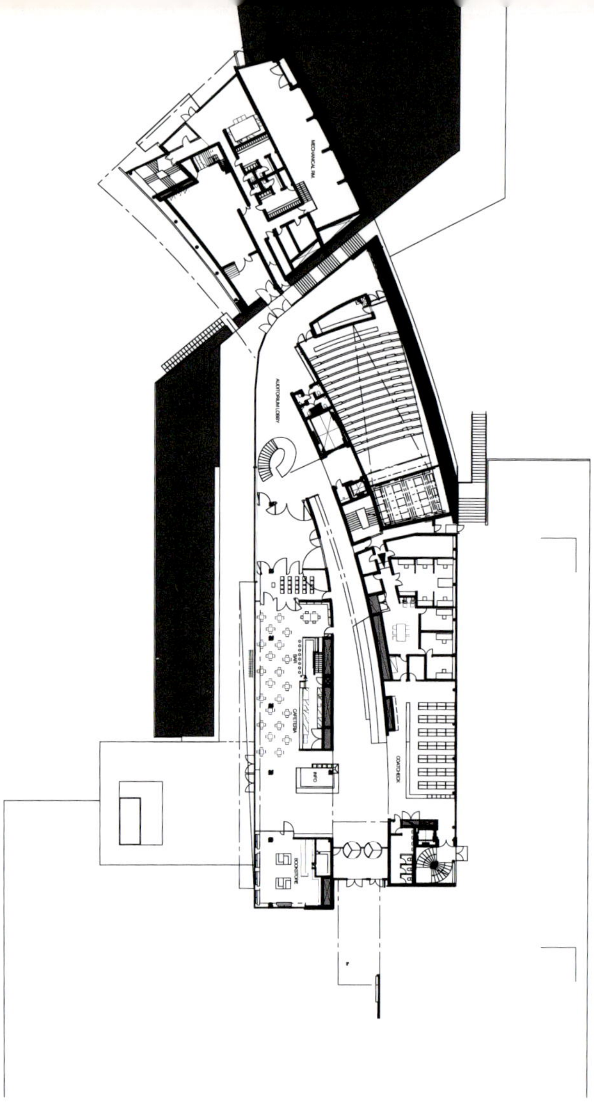

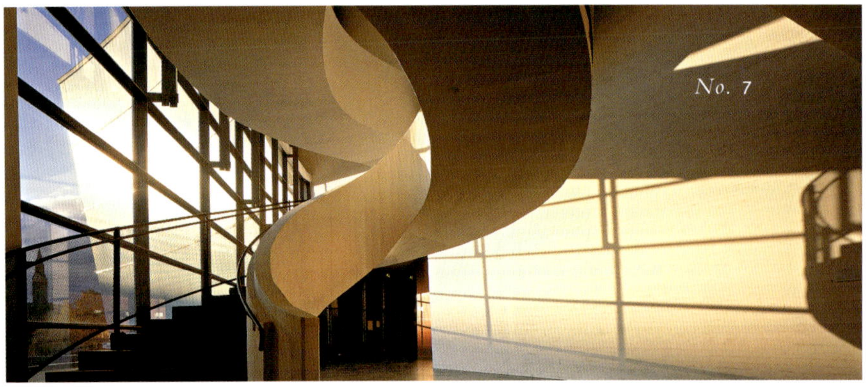

No. 5-12

DESCRIPTION

CAPTION

PHOTO

No. 5-12 Asymmetry defines movement through a series of spatial sequences such that the overall design becomes a slightly warped 'gallery of ruins.' The visitor is confronted with a continuous unfolding of changing perspectives that connect the internal experiences with the overall concept of intertwining or Kiasma. The general character of the galleries, which are typically semi-rectangular with one wall curved, allows for a silent yet dramatic backdrop for the exhibit of contemporary art. Slight variations in room shapes and sizes are due to the gently curving section of the building, which allows the horizontal natural light to enter in several different ways.

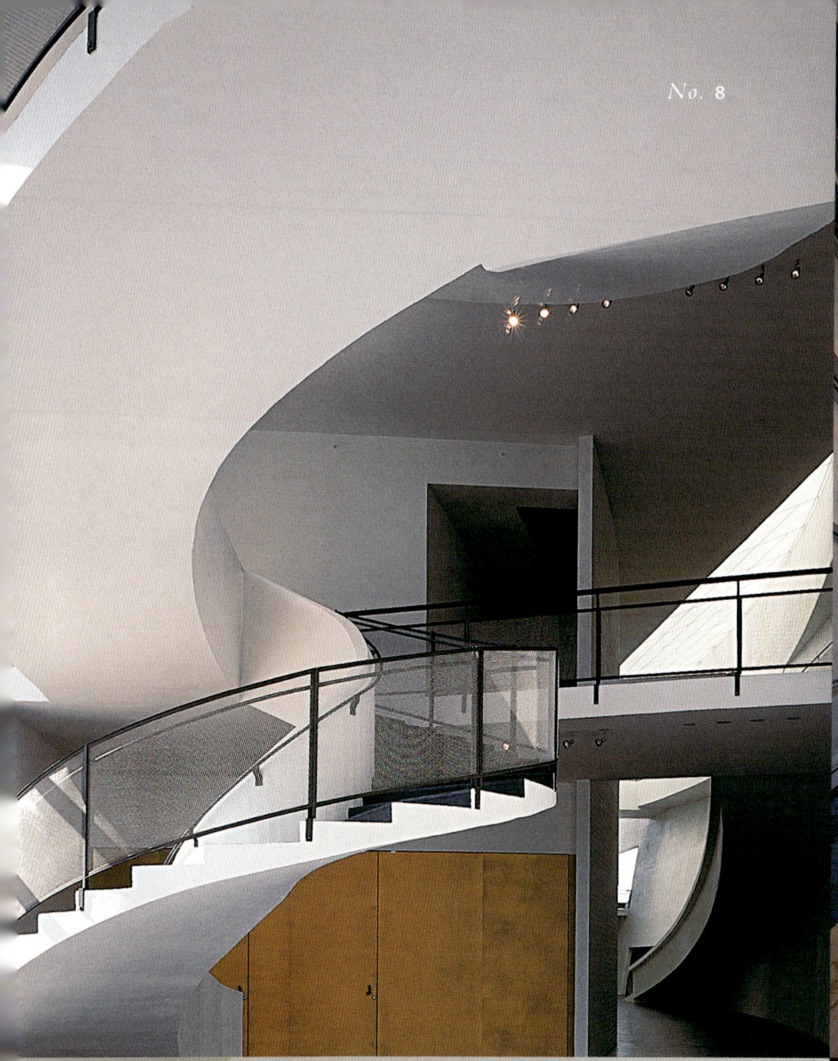
No. 8

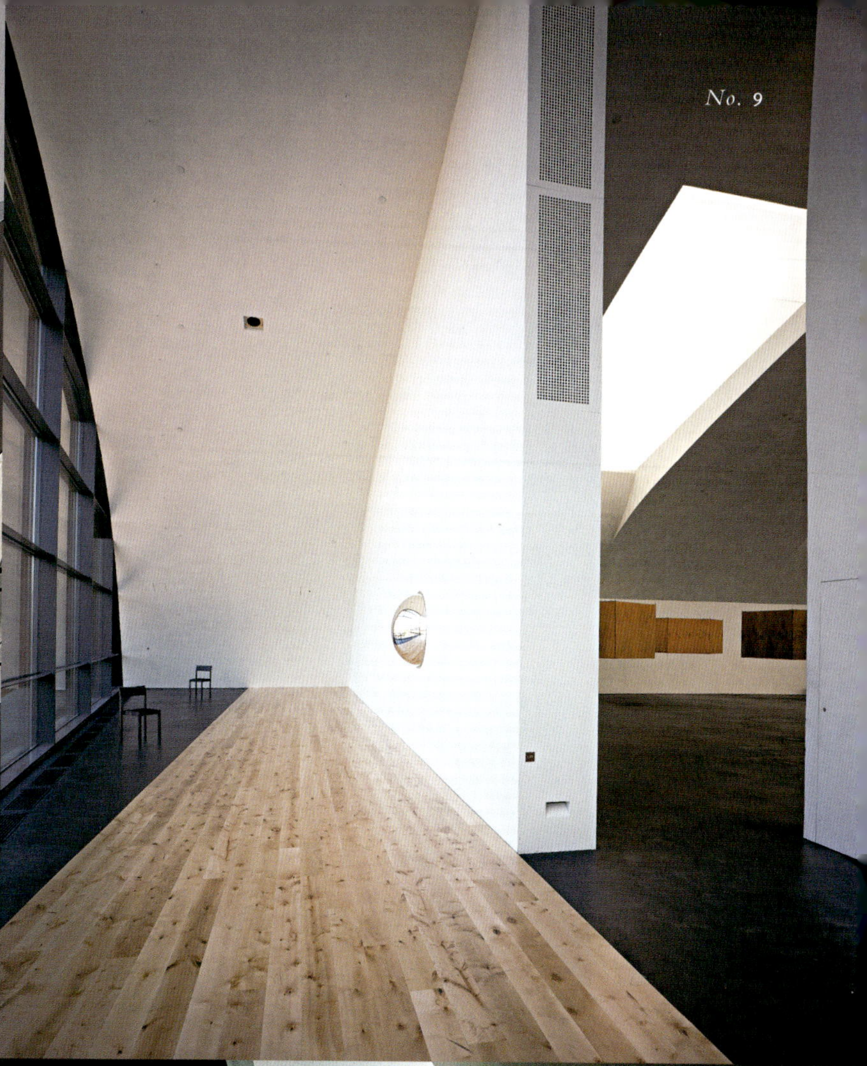
No. 9

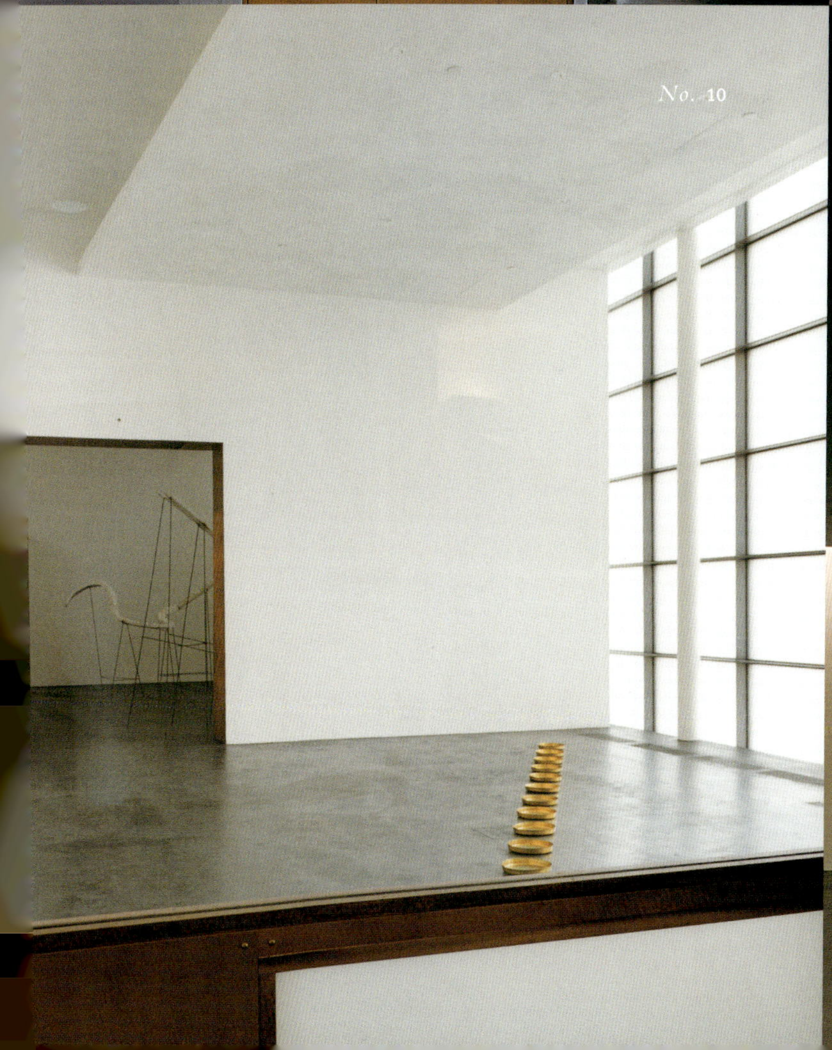
No. 10

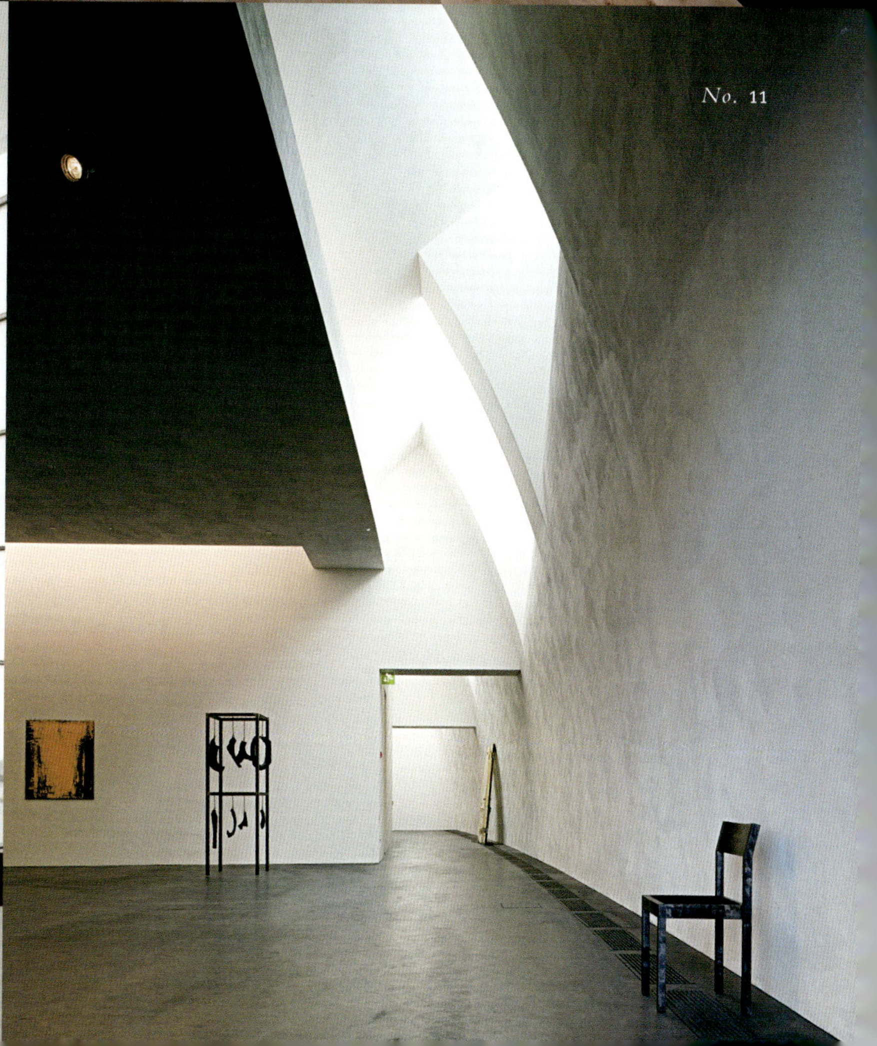
No. 11

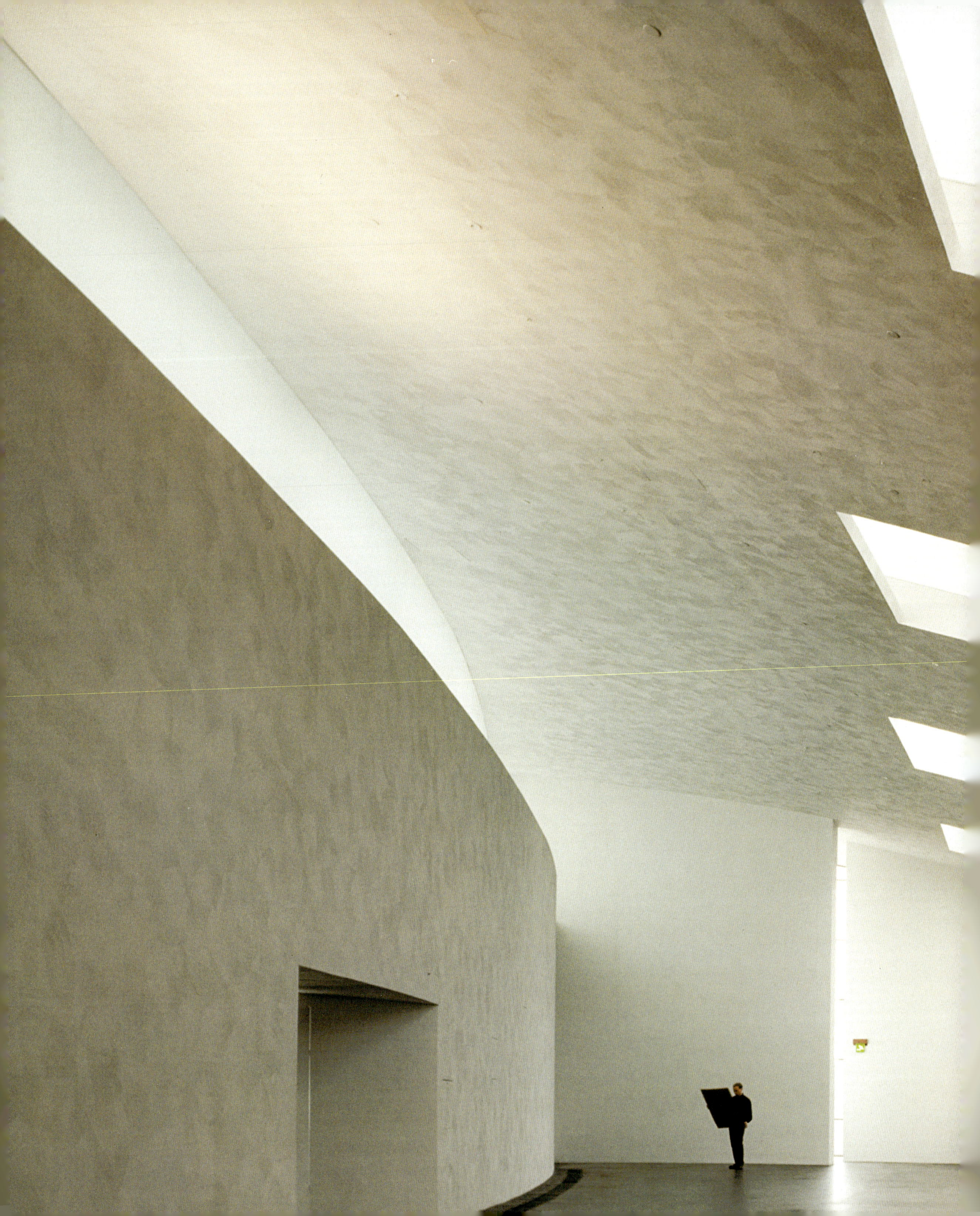

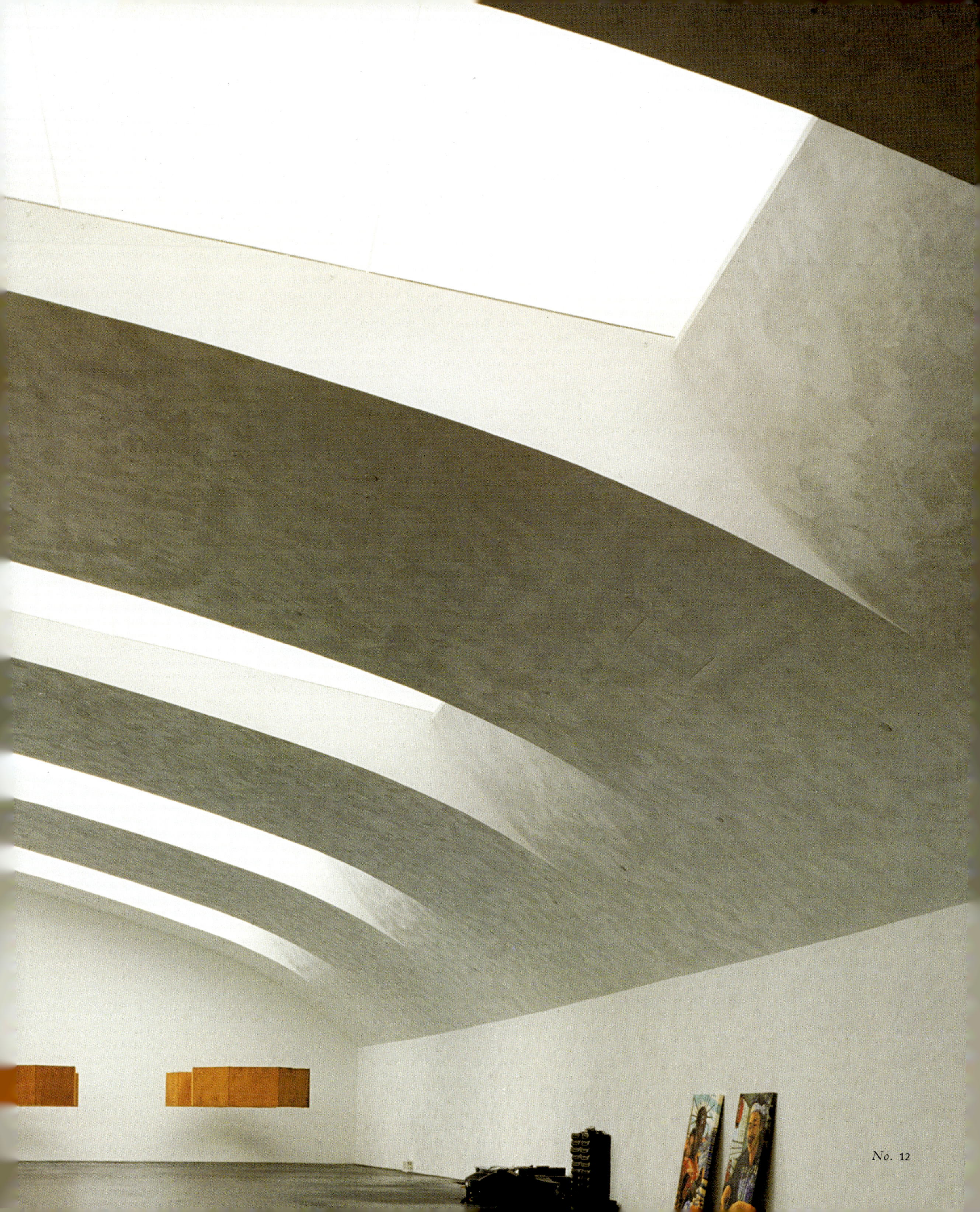

No. 12

Audrey Jones Beck Building

1 *PROJECT*
Museum of Fine Arts | *Houston, Texas*

2 *ARCHITECT*
José Rafael Moneo | *Madrid, Spain*

For the addition to the Museum of Fine Arts, Houston, (MFAH), José Rafael Moneo faced an urban design challenge as well as an architectural one: Insert a huge addition directly across from the existing landmark museum in a city that relies more on automobile than pedestrian traffic. His solution is a full-city block limestone box—an extremely understated exterior solution, which turns inward to reveal a wondrous light-filled exhibition space.

MFAH's original building is a 1924 Beaux Arts structure overlayed by two glass and steel Mies van der Rohe additions. The Beck Building, designed to house European art from antiquity to 1920, connects to the main building by tunnel. Moneo brought the Indiana limestone façade up to the edge of the site's surrounding sidewalks, breaking the heavy massing only at the entrance. The porte-cochere and elegant bronze doorframes at the entrance, in essence, bow to the original building. Pass by this limestone box and wonder at the monolithic architecture.

Walk inside, though, and feel exhilarated. You emerge from the low-ceilinged entrance foyer into the light-filled central three-story atrium. Straight ahead, a staircase of Portuguese limestone ascends to the third floor in a single run. On the other side of the atrium, an escalator moves upward in the opposite direction but with the same final destination. Upstairs, three galleries housing Impressionist and Old Master paintings, line the atrium's perimeter. A large Tiffany window announces the American galleries in the lower level.

Moneo devised a unique system of overhead lanterns to provide a consistent amount of daylight to the galleries while filtering out damaging ultraviolet rays. From the exterior the lanterns resemble old-fashioned air-conditioning units.

No. 1
Description

Caption Photo

No. 1 Clad in Indiana limestone, the massive three-story, block-long building occupies the entire block to the sidewalk's edge. The entrance features a porte-cochere for valet parking. The entrance doorframes are constructed of bronze Dakota mahogany granite details.

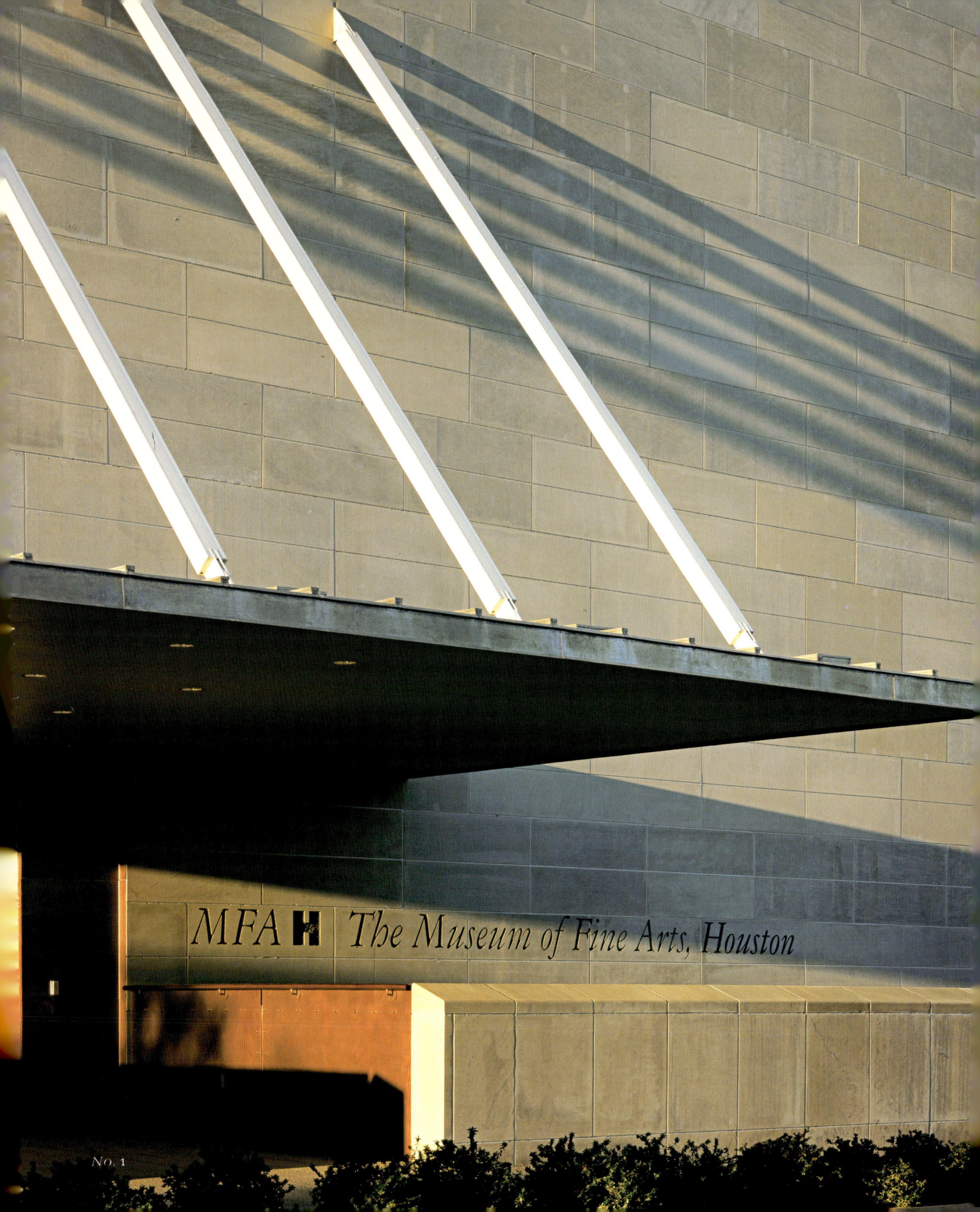

No. 1

No. 2-3

DESCRIPTION

CAPTION

PHOTO

No. 2 THE MOST DISTINCTIVE EXTERIOR FEATURE OF THE MUSEUM IS THE SKYLIGHT-STUDDED ROOF. THESE SKYLIGHT LANTERNS ARE CENTRAL TO THE INNOVATIVE NATURAL LIGHTING SYSTEM, WHICH IS DESIGNED TO PROVIDE IDEAL CONDITIONS FOR LOOKING AT ART. EACH SKYLIT GALLERY CONTAINS COMPUTER-CONTROLLED ELECTRIC LIGHTS THAT SUPPLEMENT NATURAL LIGHT AS NEEDED. THE DESIGN OF THE LANTERNS WAS SUBJECTED TO EXTENSIVE TESTING, RESULTING IN ILLUMINATION THROUGHOUT THE DAY THAT IS REMARKABLY CONSISTENT.

No. 3 RAFAEL MONEO'S DESIGN FOR THE BECK BUILDING REFLECTS HIS INGENIOUS ATTENTION TO LIGHT AND DETAIL FROM THE INNOVATION NATURAL LIGHTING SYSTEM TO HIS CAREFUL SELECTION OF ELEGANT BUILDING MATERIALS. THE MUSEUM'S ENTRANCE IS OPPOSITE THE EXISTING LAW BUILDING. TOGETHER THE LAW AND BECK BUILDING YIELD OVER 150,000 SQUARE FEET METER DEDICATED TO THE MUSEUM'S ENCYCLOPEDIC COLLECTION OF ART AND TEMPORARY EXHIBITIONS. THE BECK BUILDING CONSISTS OF OVER HALF OF THE 84,000 SQUARE FEET METER OF GALLEY SPACE.

No.

GENERAL INTEREST

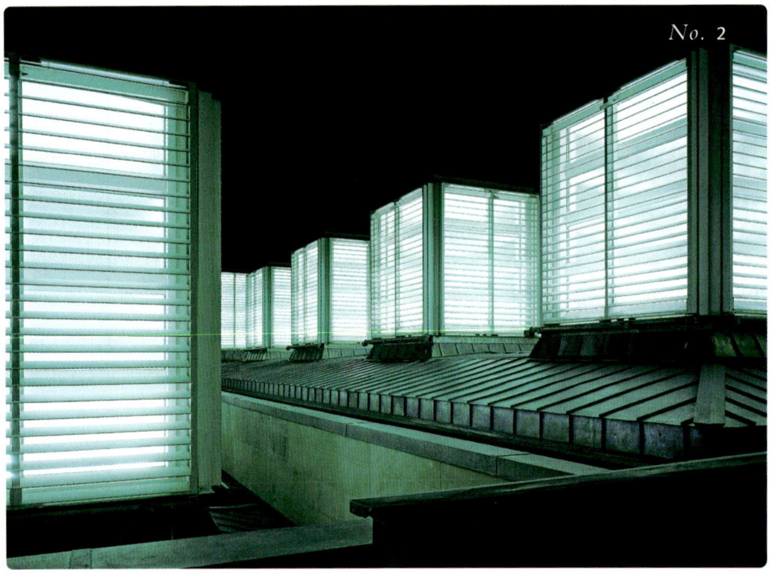

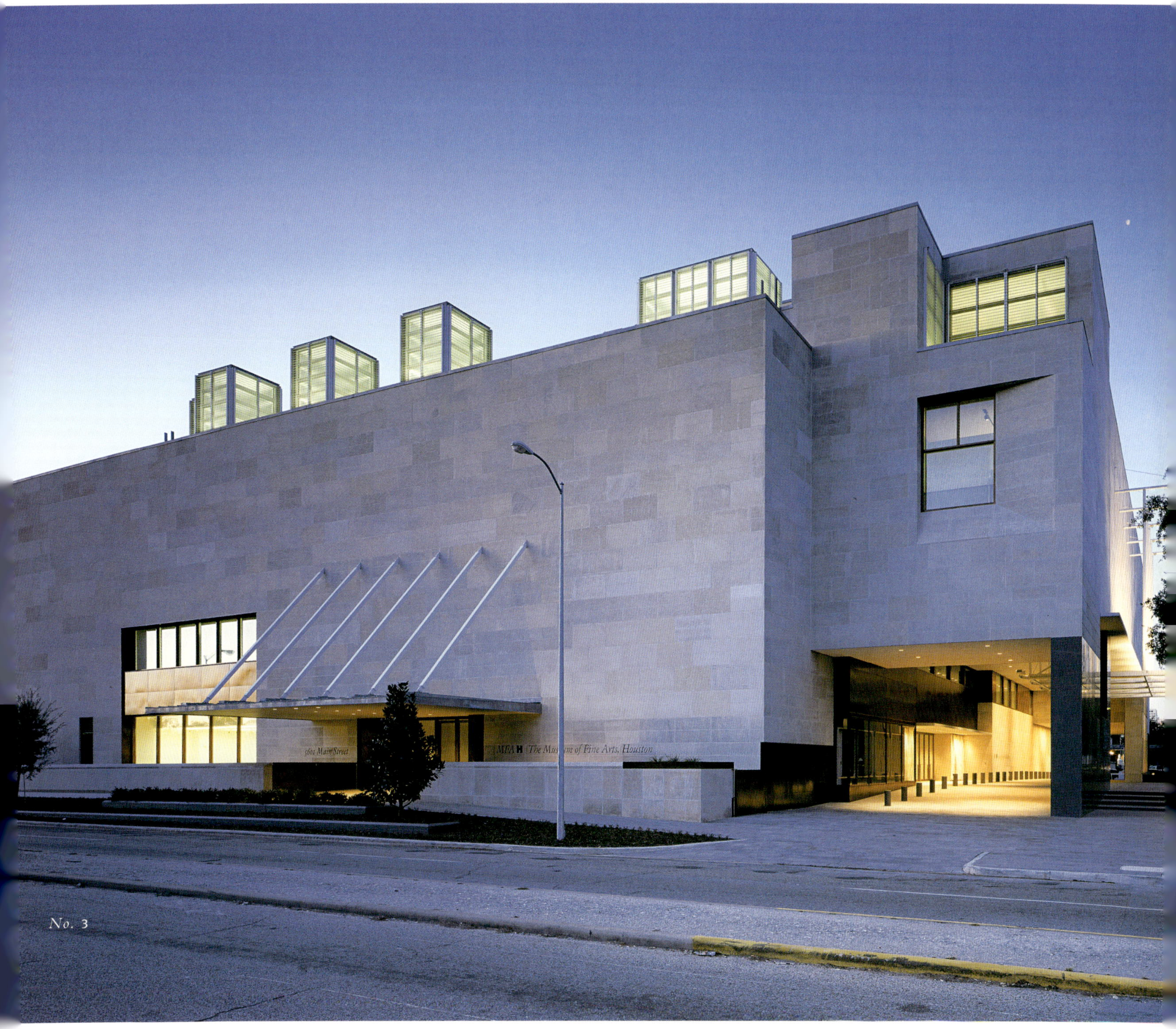

No. 3

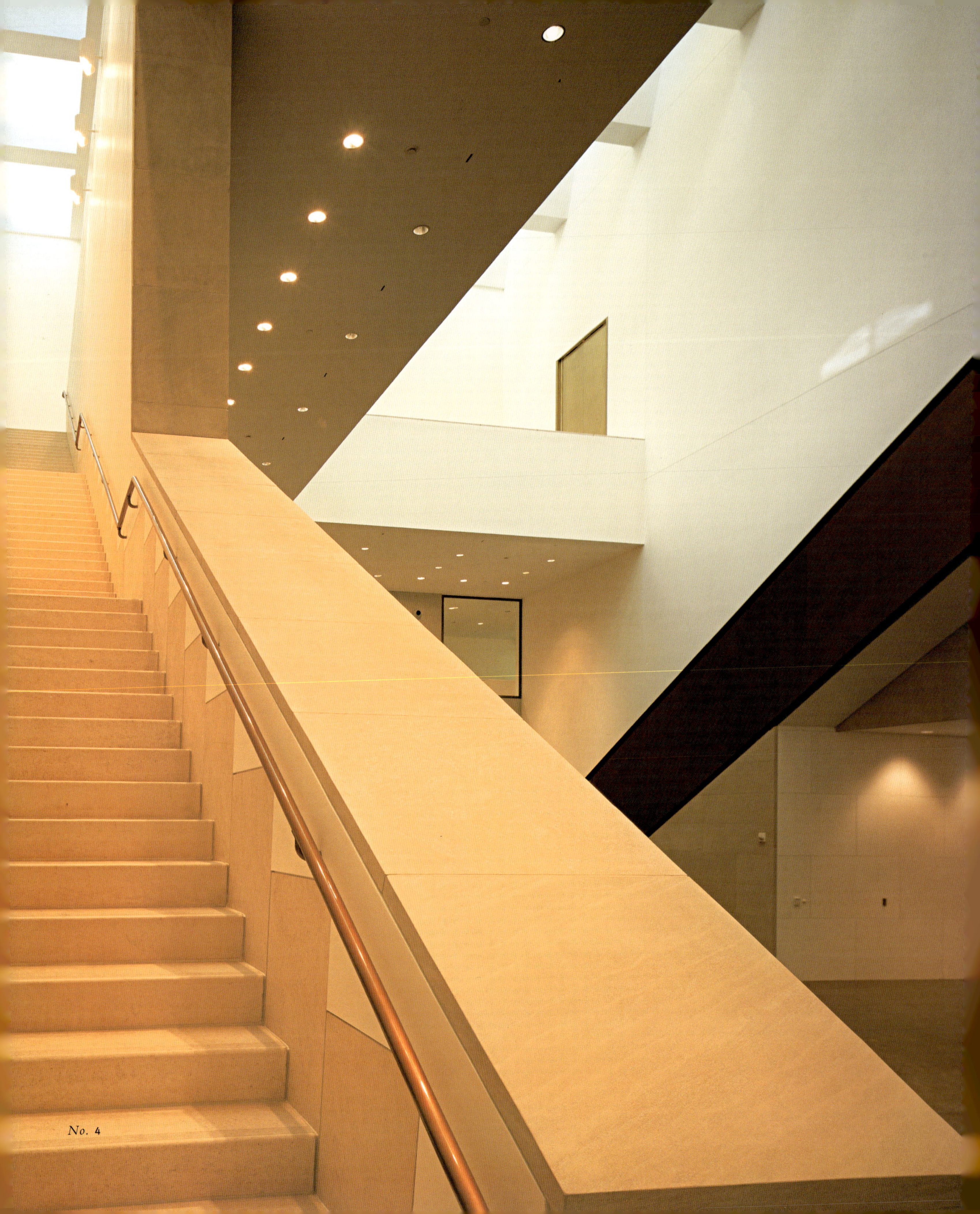

No. 4

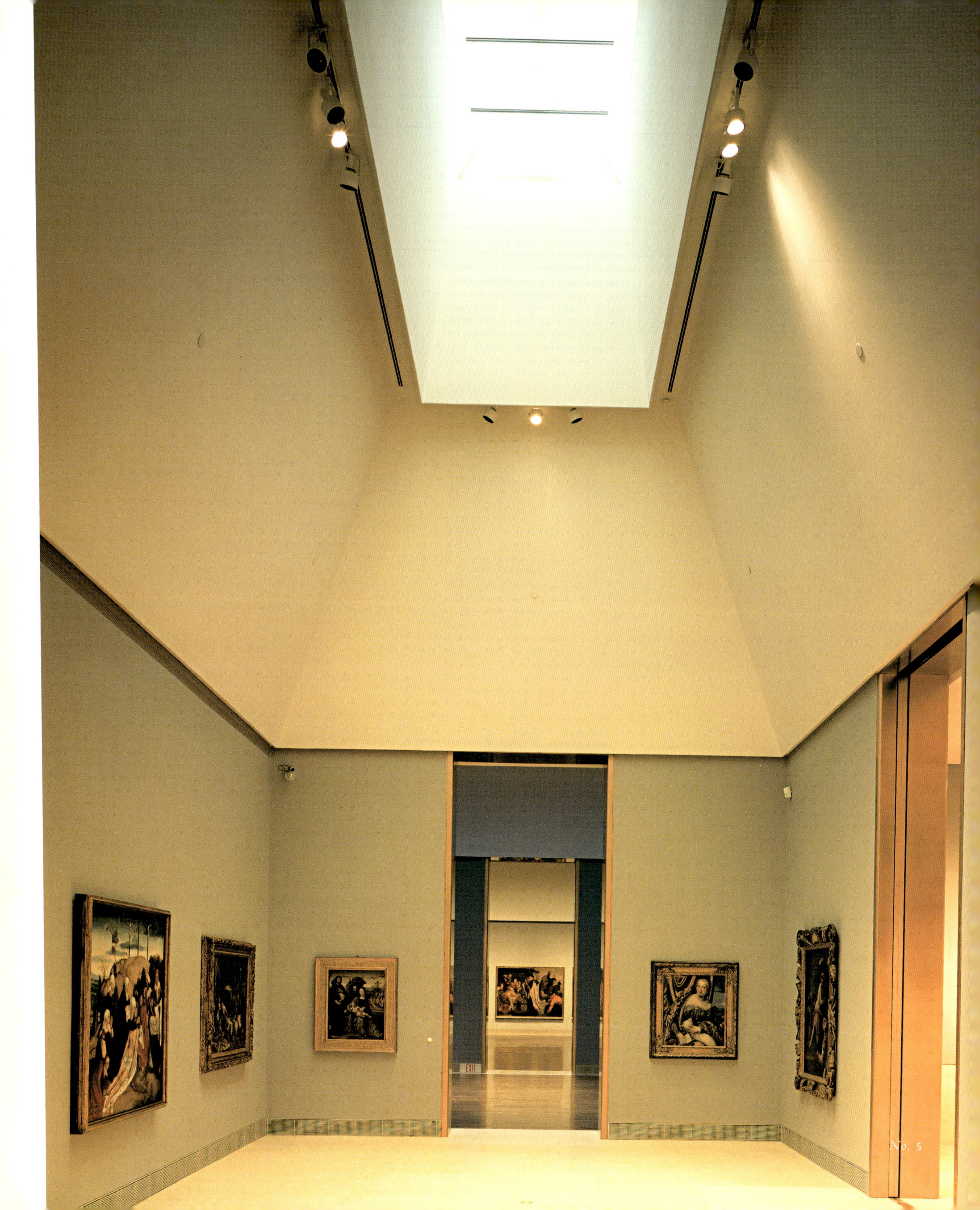

No. 5

Audrey Jones Beck Building
First Floor

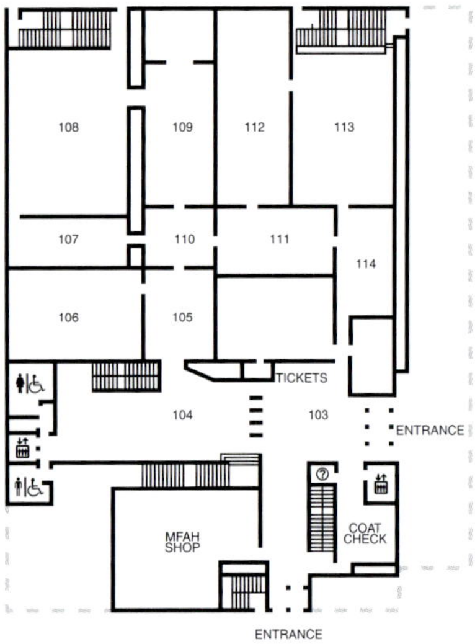

Audrey Jones Beck Building
Lower Level

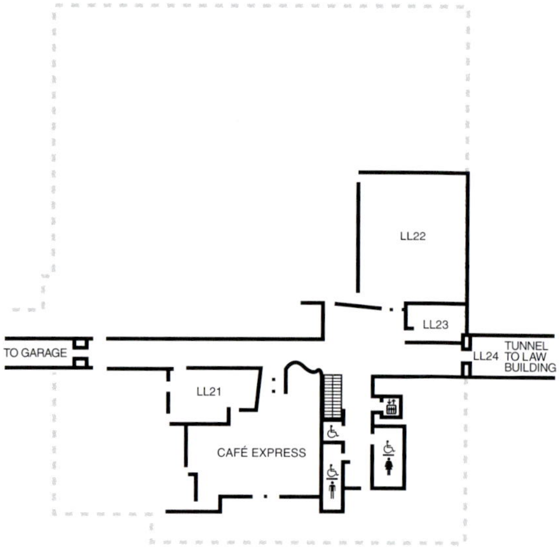

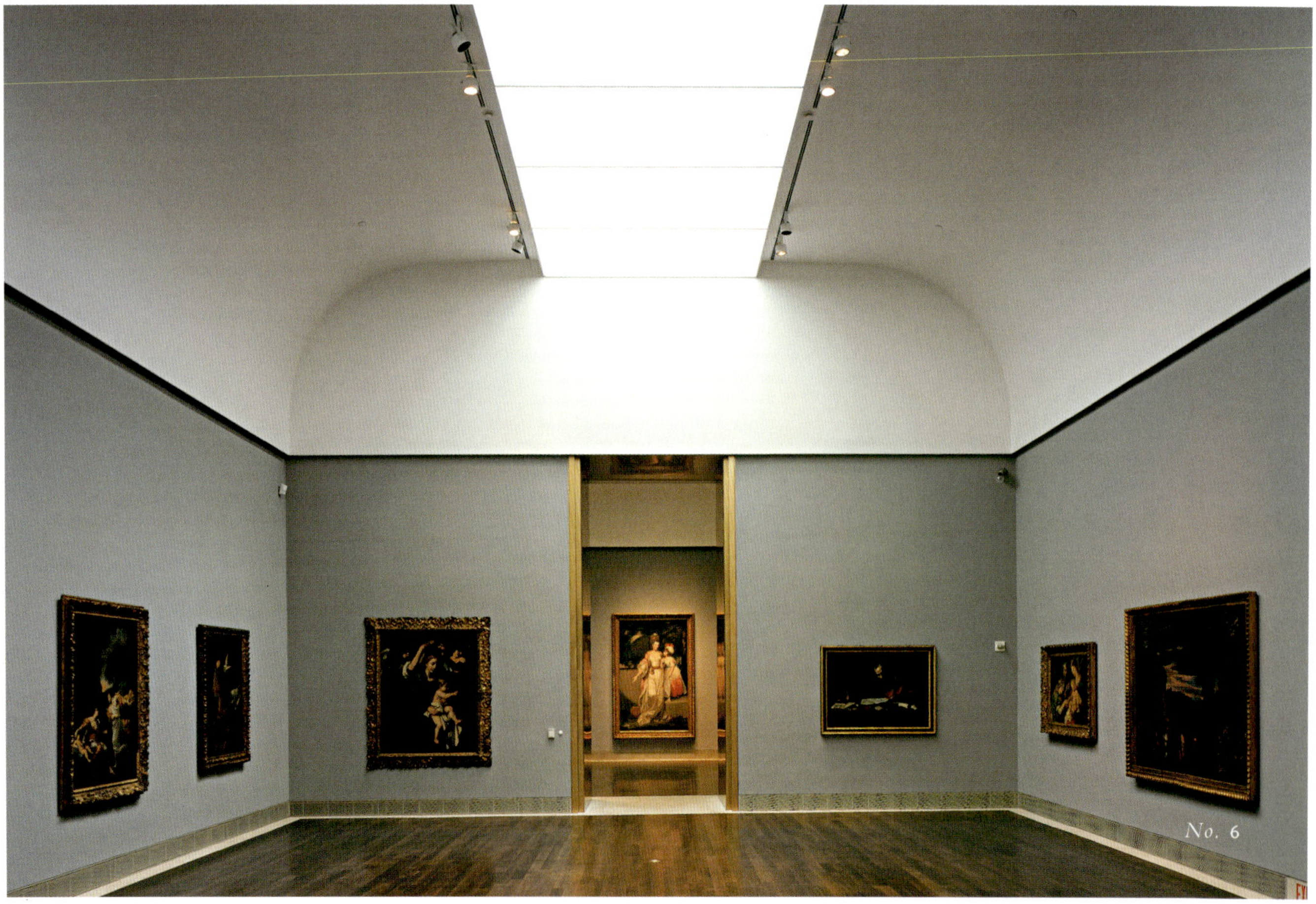
No. 6

No. 4-7

DESCRIPTION

CAPTION

PHOTO

No. 5 A STAIRCASE OF PORTUGUESE LIMESTONE ASCENDS THREE STORIES.

No. 6, 7 & 8 THE NATURAL LIGHT STREAMING THROUGH THE GALLERIES ALLOWS VISITORS TO VIEW PAINTINGS AS ORIGINALLY INTENDED, SINCE MOST, IF NOT ALL, OF THESE WORKS WERE CREATED BEFORE THE ADVENT OF ELECTRIC LIGHT.

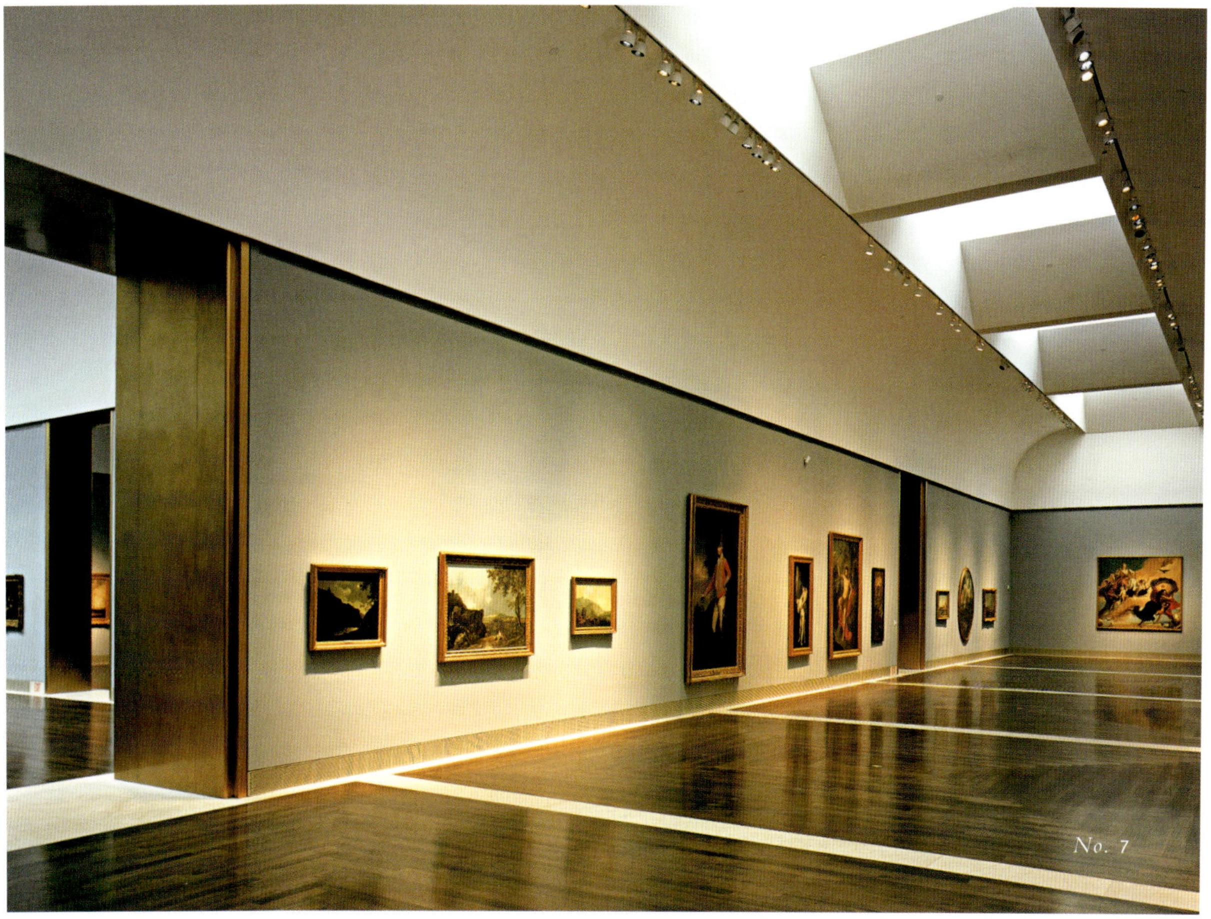

No. 7

Miho Museum

1 *PROJECT*
Miho Museum | *Shiga, Japan*

2 *ARCHITECT*
Pei Cobb Freed & Partners | *New York, New York*

At first sight, the Miho Museum appears as an optical illusion—glass temples rising out of the haze that settles over the mountains outside of Kyoto, Japan. Unless you enter the building, that's all you'll experience, since 80 percent of the structure is underground, sculpted gently to meet the contours of the land beneath. The museum's design is architect I.M. Pei's homage to nature—and a breathtaking one at that.

Pei was limited by environmental regulations. He could only expose the limestone-and-glass façade 13 meters (42.9 feet) above ground. Drawing on angular geometries of earlier work (such as the National Gallery of Art in Washington, D.C., and the addition to the Louvre in Paris), Pei created a series of skylights and custom-designed space frames of tubular steel and glass. For the Miho Museum, the skylights are fitted with imitation wood, so the dark profiles become abstractions of the thatched roofs of the Japanese *irimoya* tradition. These triangulated shapes seem to embrace the landscape as they reach toward the heavens. At the same time, tempered by louvers, an abundance of the sun's brilliance pours through the skylights into the underground spaces.

The museum lies across a valley from Misono, the headquarters and religious retreat of the Shinji Shumeikai, whose collection of Japanese, Asian and Near Eastern art fills the museum. Guests enter the museum via a winding path that leads through a curved, stainless steel-paneled tunnel bored through a mountainside. From the tunnel, visitors cross a spectacular cable-stayed bridge that suspends 120 meters (396 feet)over a deep ravine. Their destination is a plaza, the stairs of which rise to the museum's moon-gated entry.

Devoted to Japanese art, the museum's north wing museum is organized around a Japanese garden . A small tea house is tucked into a gallery corner. The south wing is dedicated to antiquities from China to the Roman Empire. The area has two levels, with each gallery focusing on one object. Throughout courtyards, gardens, and windows demonstrate the Skakkei technique of framing close and distant views.

No. 1
Description

Caption Photo

No. 1 View as visitors emerge from the tunnel that connects the visitor's entrance to the museum.

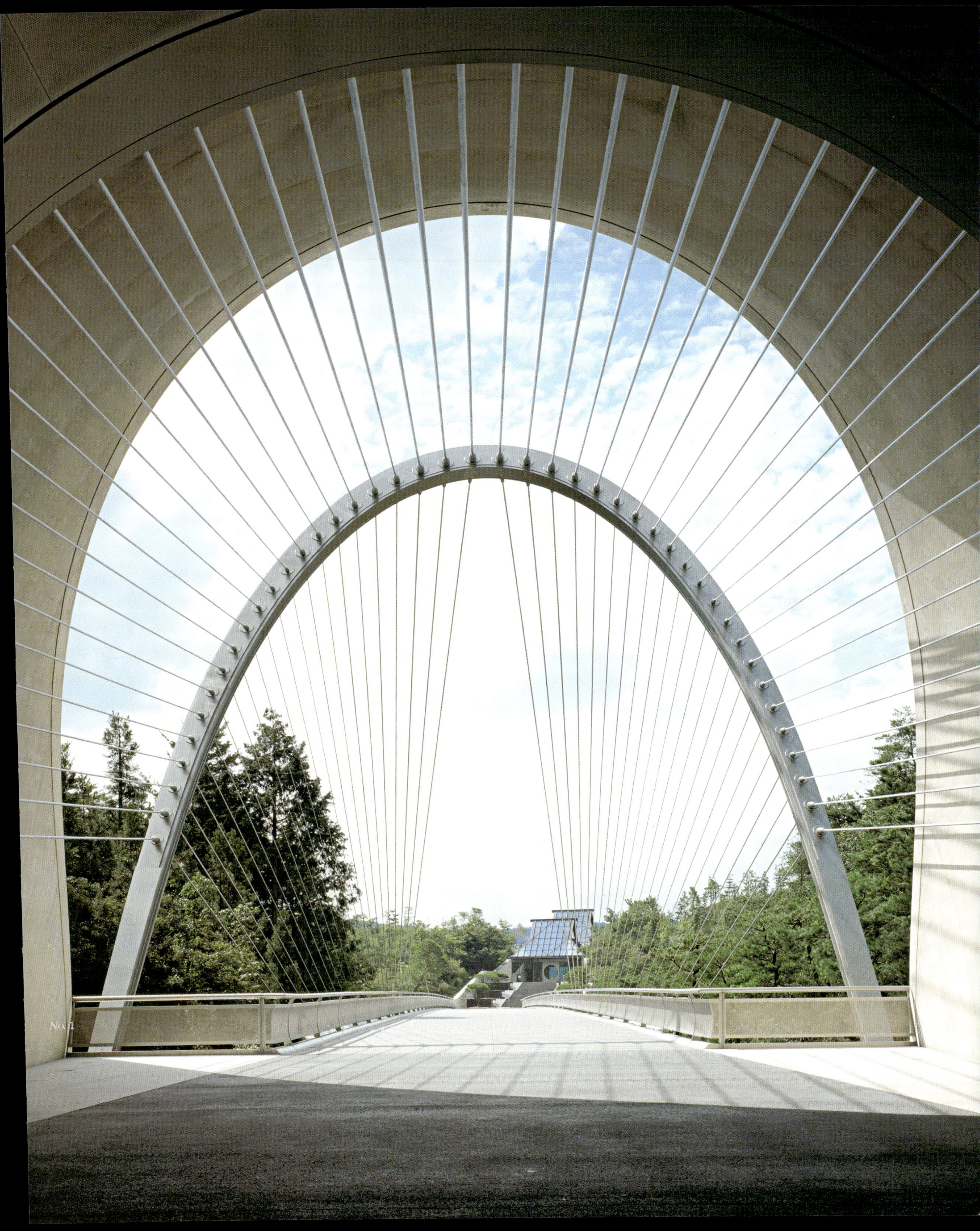

No. 1

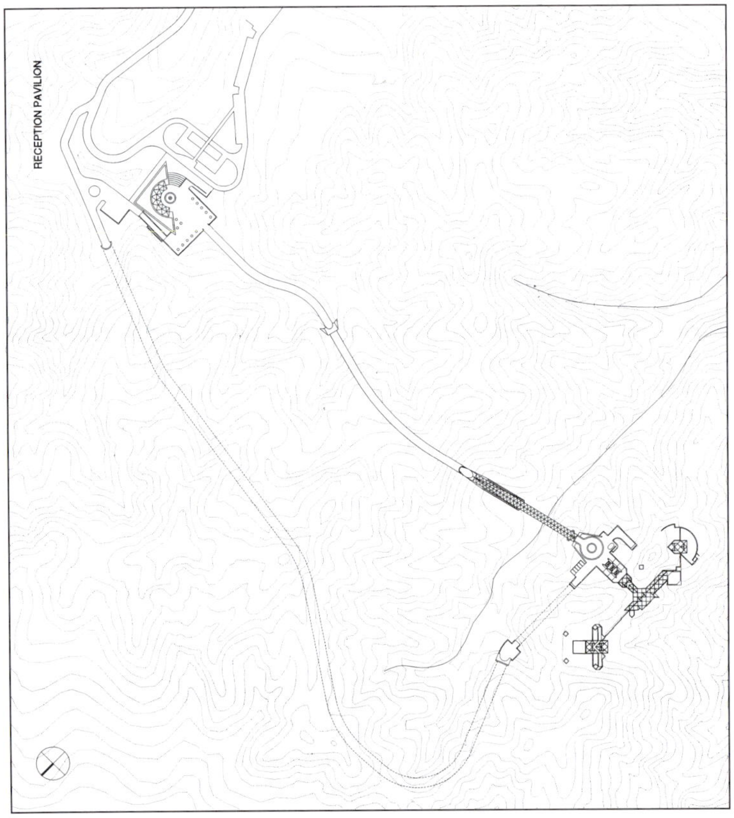

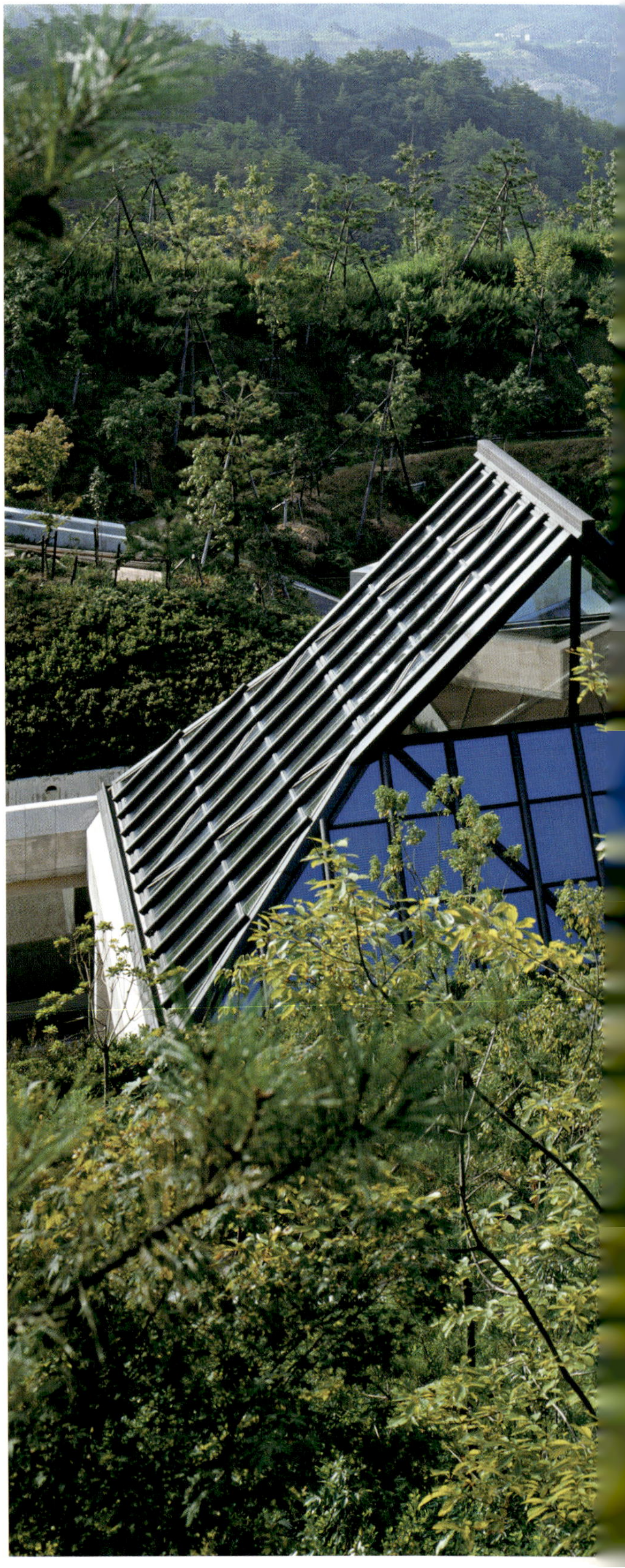

CAPTION PHOTO

No. 2 The museum is situated on 240 acres in the mountains outside Kyoto, Japan.

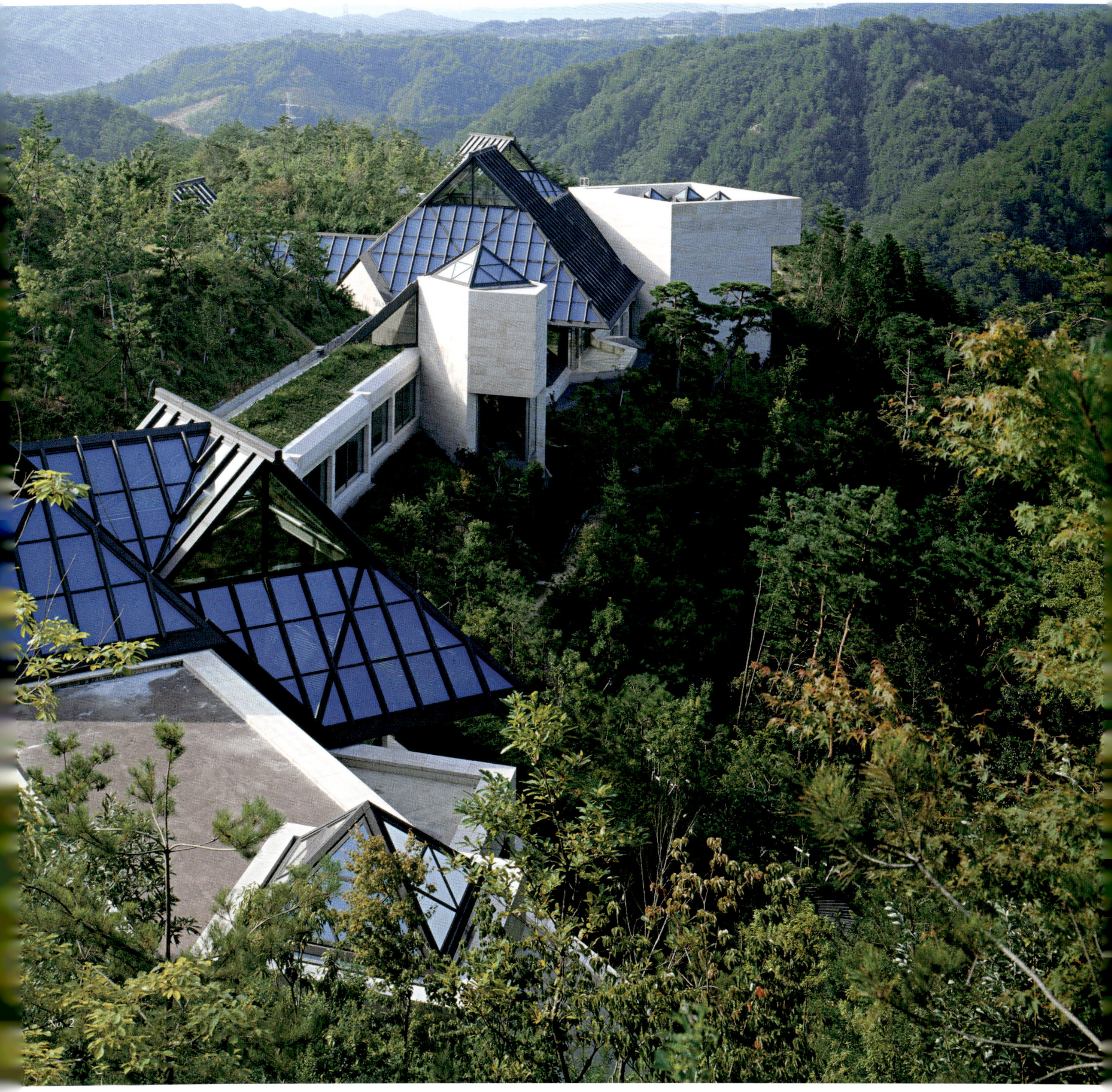

No. 2

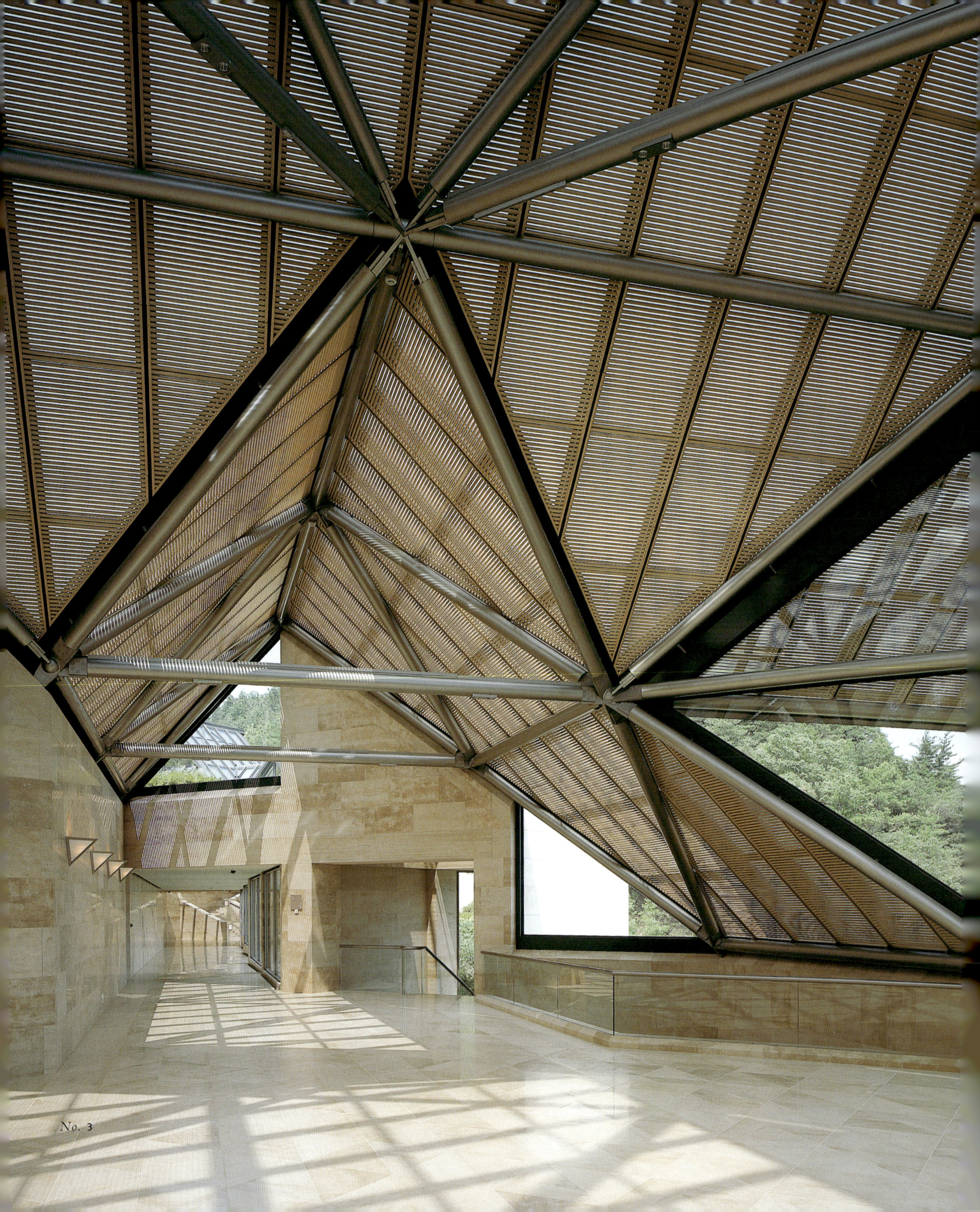

No. 3

No. 3-7

DESCRIPTION

CAPTION

PHOTO

No. 3 & 6 Throughout the interior, light filters in through aluminum sunscreens. The surface of the sunscreens have been digitized to evoke the grain, texture and warmth of local woods.

No. 4 & 5 Gallery spaces focus predominantly on one object.

No. 7 Where possible, the interior galleries are visually connected with the outside landscape.

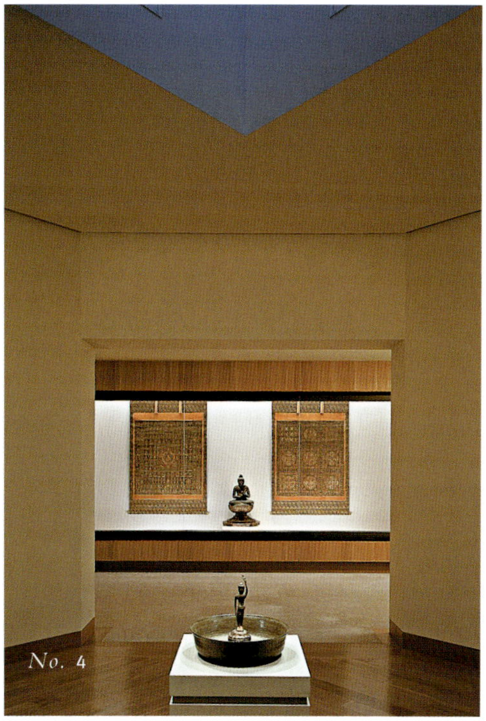

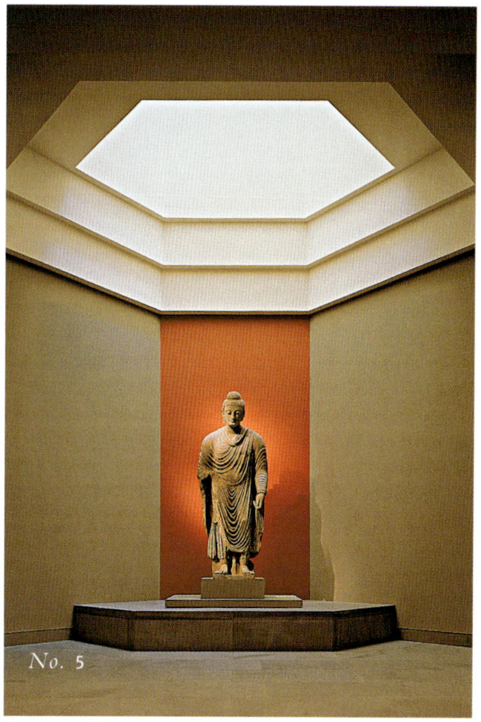

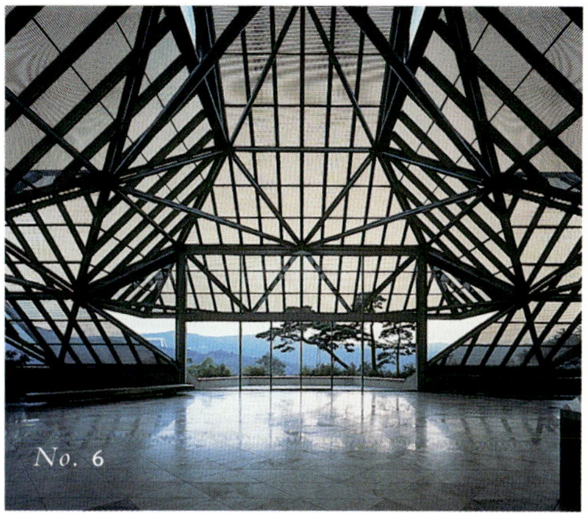

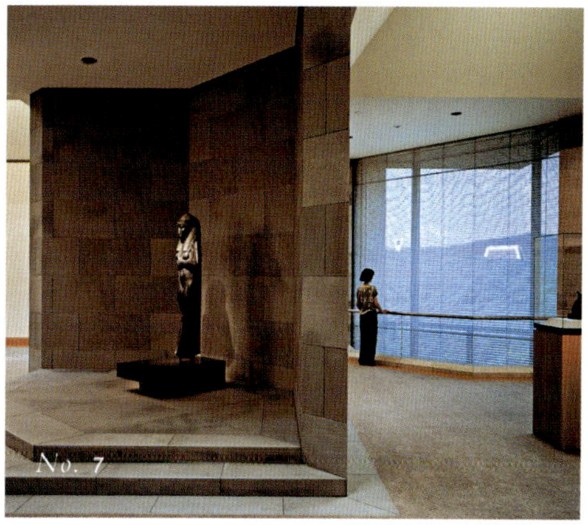

Iris and B. Gerald Cantor Center for the Visual Arts

1 *PROJECT*
Iris and B. Gerald Cantor Center for the Visual Arts at Stanford University | *Palo Alto, California*

2 *ARCHITECT*
Polshek Partnership Architects | *New York, New York*

In 1989 the Loma Prieta earthquake brought great devastation to Northern California and to several historical buildings on the campus of Stanford University, including the Stanford Art Museum. Rather than just rebuilding the old, new elements were juxtaposed against the existing to create an exciting new composition—and a new arts center for the campus.

The original building consisted of a late nineteenth-century fragment and a late twentieth-century intervention. Polshek's goal is to blur the distinctions between the new and old, so the visitor moves freely from one to the other, never cognizant of the seams. By adding 37,000 square feet (6,570-square-meters) to the existing 73,000-square-foot (3,330-square-meter) building, in effect, a whole new precinct of the campus would be created. The new building houses flexible galleries, classrooms, art storage space, a café, bookstore and special events room, and a series of outdoor sculpture courts and gardens. Unlike the older building, which is rigidly symmetrical, the new design responds to asymmetrical site conditions, resulting in the creation of important outdoor spaces, as well as indoor ones.

The addition borrows scale and proportion from the old, yet casts the new in a modern idiom. A rotunda placed on the main axis becomes the new ceremonial heart of the building and functions as a modern twin of the original entrance hall. A two-level spine mediates between the old and new portions and affords views and access into the sculpture court that sites between them. Designed to be flexible, one of the two new 6,000-square-foot (540-square-meter) galleries is naturally lit. The other is artificially lit and can be used for different exhibition purposes. At night, the transparency of the new addition against the solid walls of the former museum draws visitors inside.

No. 1
DESCRIPTION

CAPTION PHOTO

No. 1 A screen wall surrounds the new addition's rotunda.

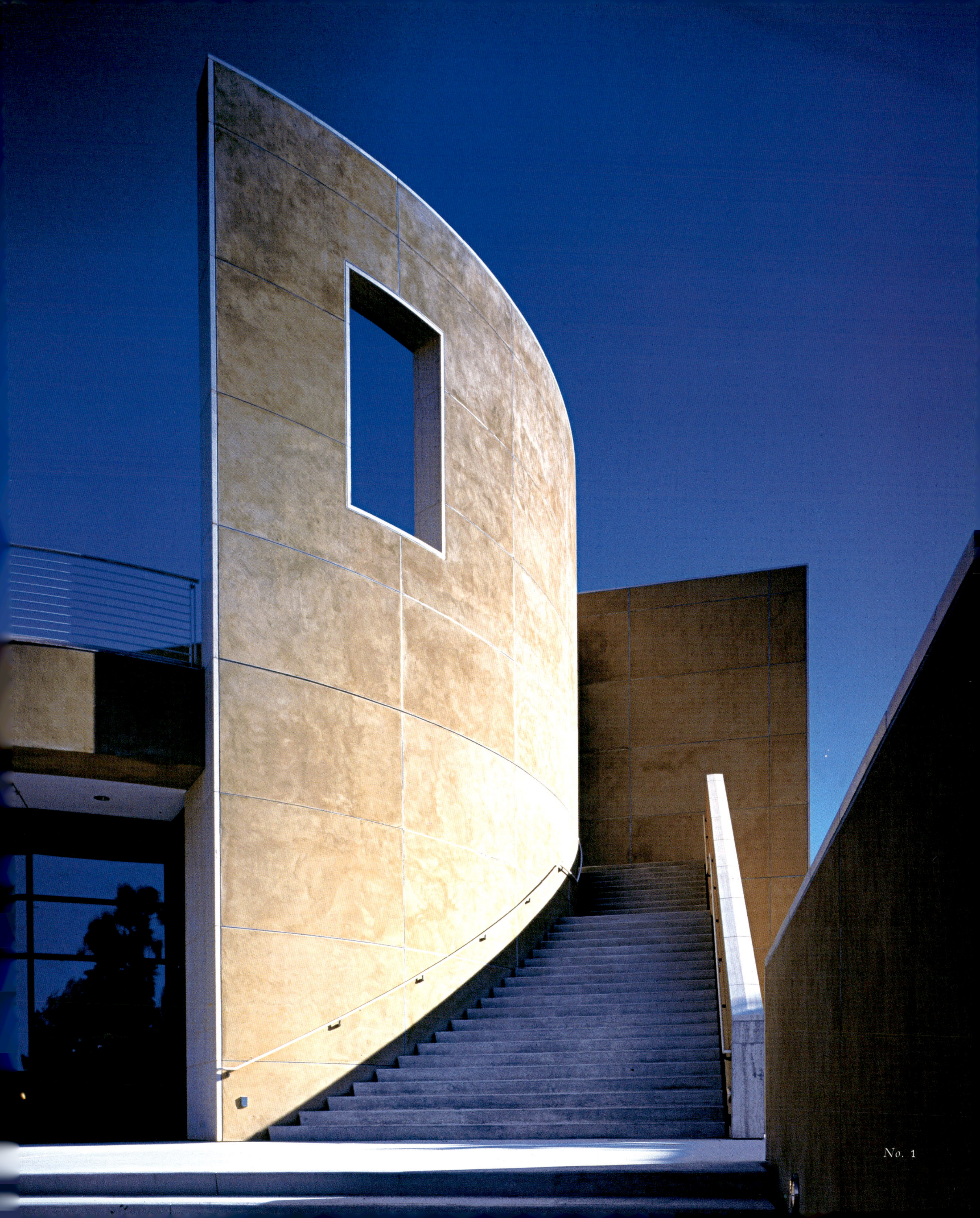

No. 1

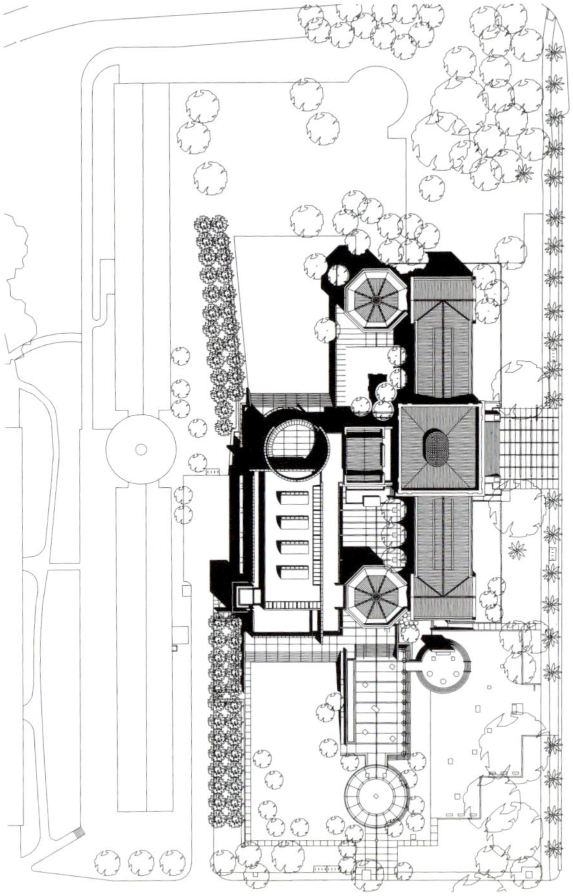

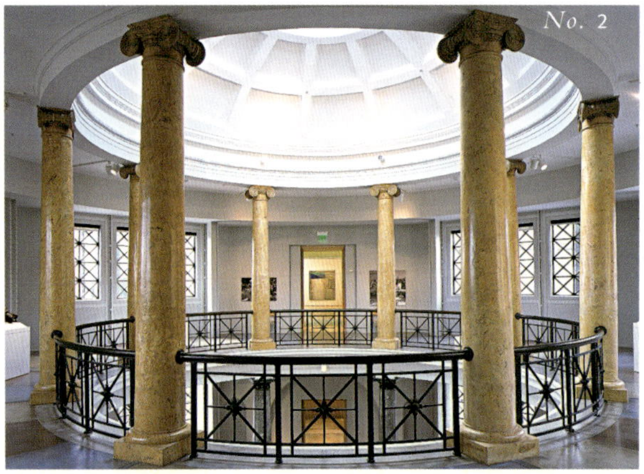

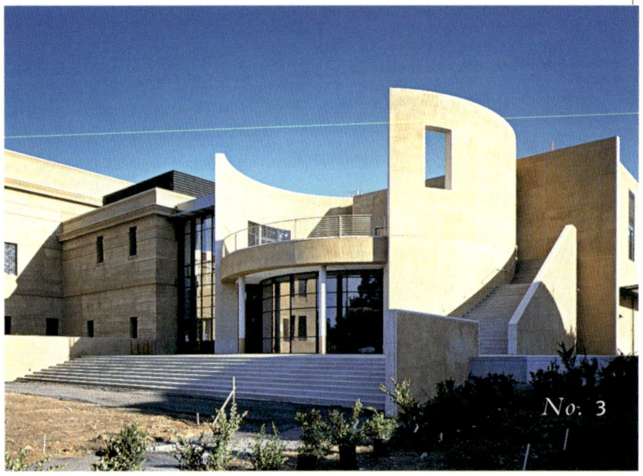

No. 2-4
DESCRIPTION

CAPTION PHOTO

No. 2 The rotunda of the existing structure regained its splendor.

No. 3 The screen wall and canopy comprise the south wall of the addition as serve to reduce its scale.

No. 4 The architect's effort to connect the inside and outside of the museum is profoundly illustrated in this view from the sculpture court back from the new addition (on the left) and the old (on the right). Also evident is the functional role that the spine plays as the mediator between the old and new buildings.

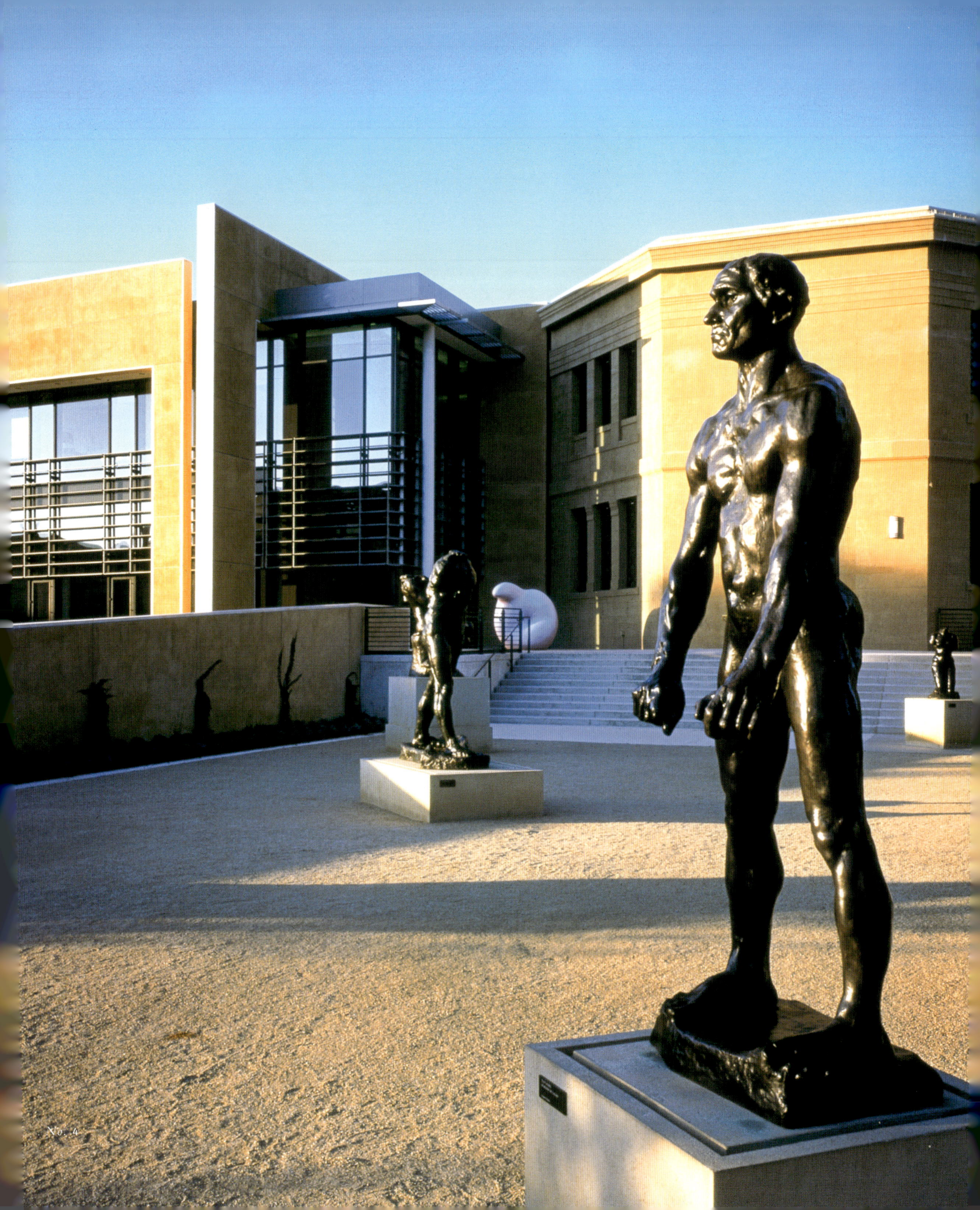

No. 4

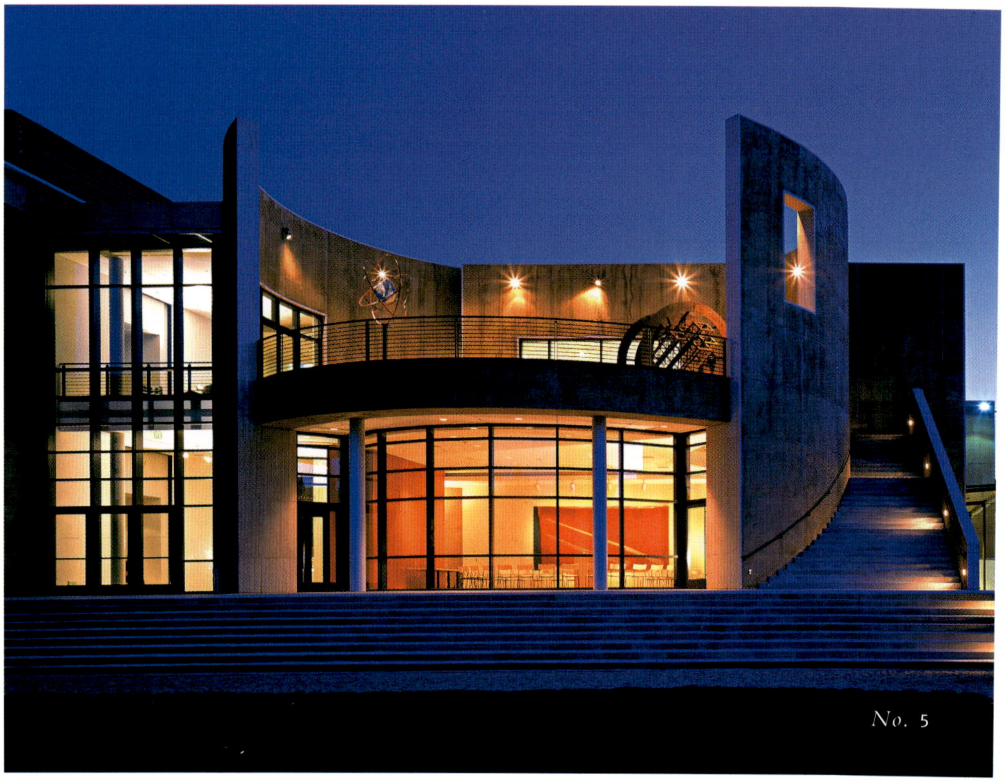

No. 5

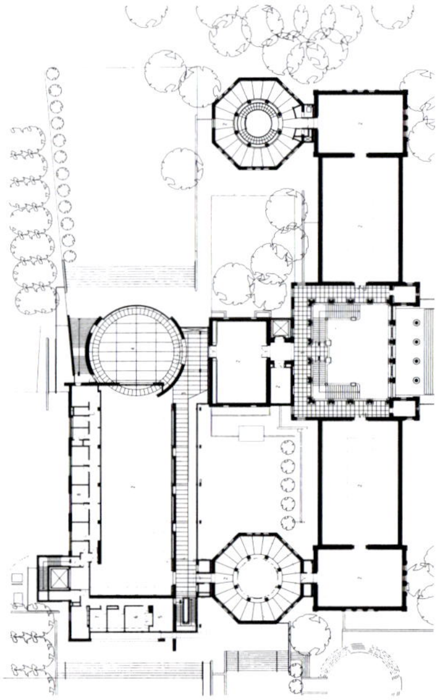

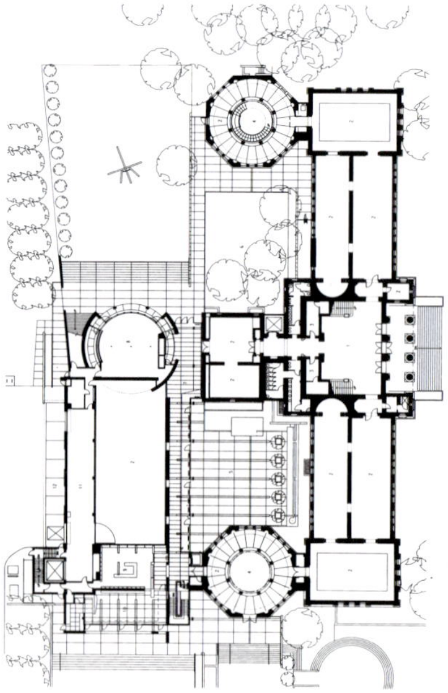

No. 5-6

DESCRIPTION

CAPTION

PHOTO

No. 5 The Arts Center seen at night.

No. 6 The museum contains two new galleries, both of which can be subdivided for exhibitions.

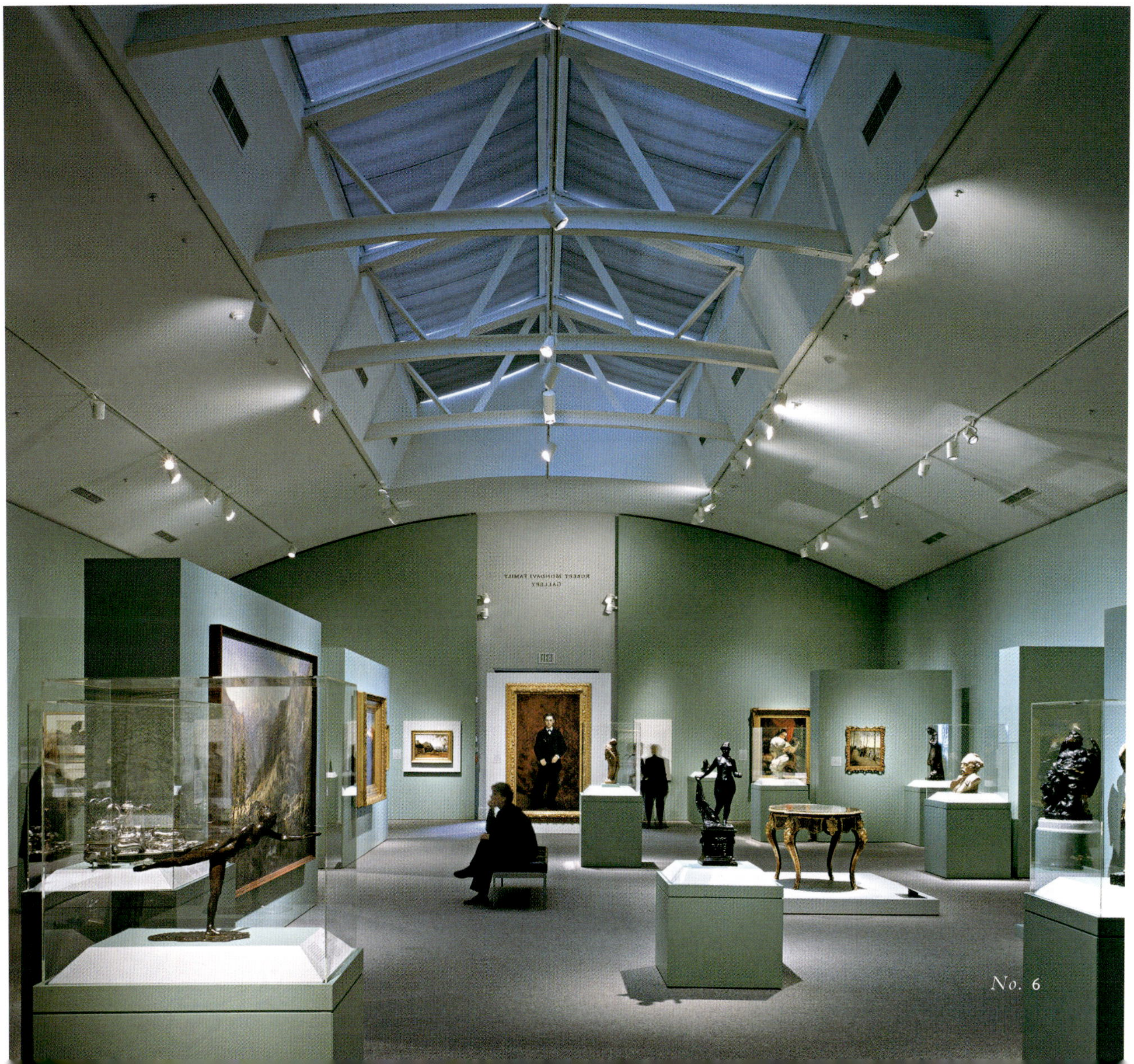

Museu de Serralves

1 *PROJECT*
Museu de Serralves | *Oporto, Portugal*

2 *ARCHITECT*
Álvaro Siza | *Oporto, Portugal*

When the Museu de Serralves opened its doors in June 1999, it not only presented to the world a stunning collection of fine arts but also an exquisite sun-dappled museum designed by Portugal's most brilliant contemporary architect Álvaro Siza.

The 140,000-square-foot (12,600-square-meter) museum houses the extensive collection of contemporary art gathered by the Serralves Foundation, a public/private consortium of more than 50 partners—in all some 1,650 pieces of post-1960s art, with emphasis on Spanish artists. The foundation is located in a pink Art Deco house at Parque de Serralves in Oporto, Portugal, a 44.5-acre (18-hectare) park of formal gardens, pastures, woods, and agricultural fields located in the heart of the city. Siza takes advantage of the site, for the museum is to be understood in a gradual, unfolding, ambulatory manner.

The approach is a lengthy series of entries. The visitor first enters a breach in the original stone wall, confronts a small pavilion, passes down a long, covered walkway, skirts a garden, and then arrives at the main entrance to the museum. The exterior surfaces are unadorned white stucco, the only decoration being manipulations of form and space. Inside, Siza organized the circulation vaguely in an H-shape—a double corridor of galleries, 14 in all, with occasional, lateral links, all united by a large U-shaped gallery. His goal was to blur the lines between corridor and room to create a sense of ambiguity and threshold, to set up a rhythm between areas of circulation and display.

What is most remarkable is Siza's manipulation of light. In a number of galleries, he suspended from the ceilings what appear to be very large, thick inverted Parson tables, their legs cut off, creating the impression of monoliths hovering overhead. In fact, these objects front skylights and also air-conditioning equipment and artificial light. Almost magically, natural light pours over the sides, washing the surrounding walls and supplemented by artificial light only when necessary.

No. 1-2
Description

Caption Photo

No. 1 The exterior of the building is constructed of granite and stucco.

No. 2 The bright Portuguese light reflects off the granite and white stucco walls of the museum, giving it form and substance.

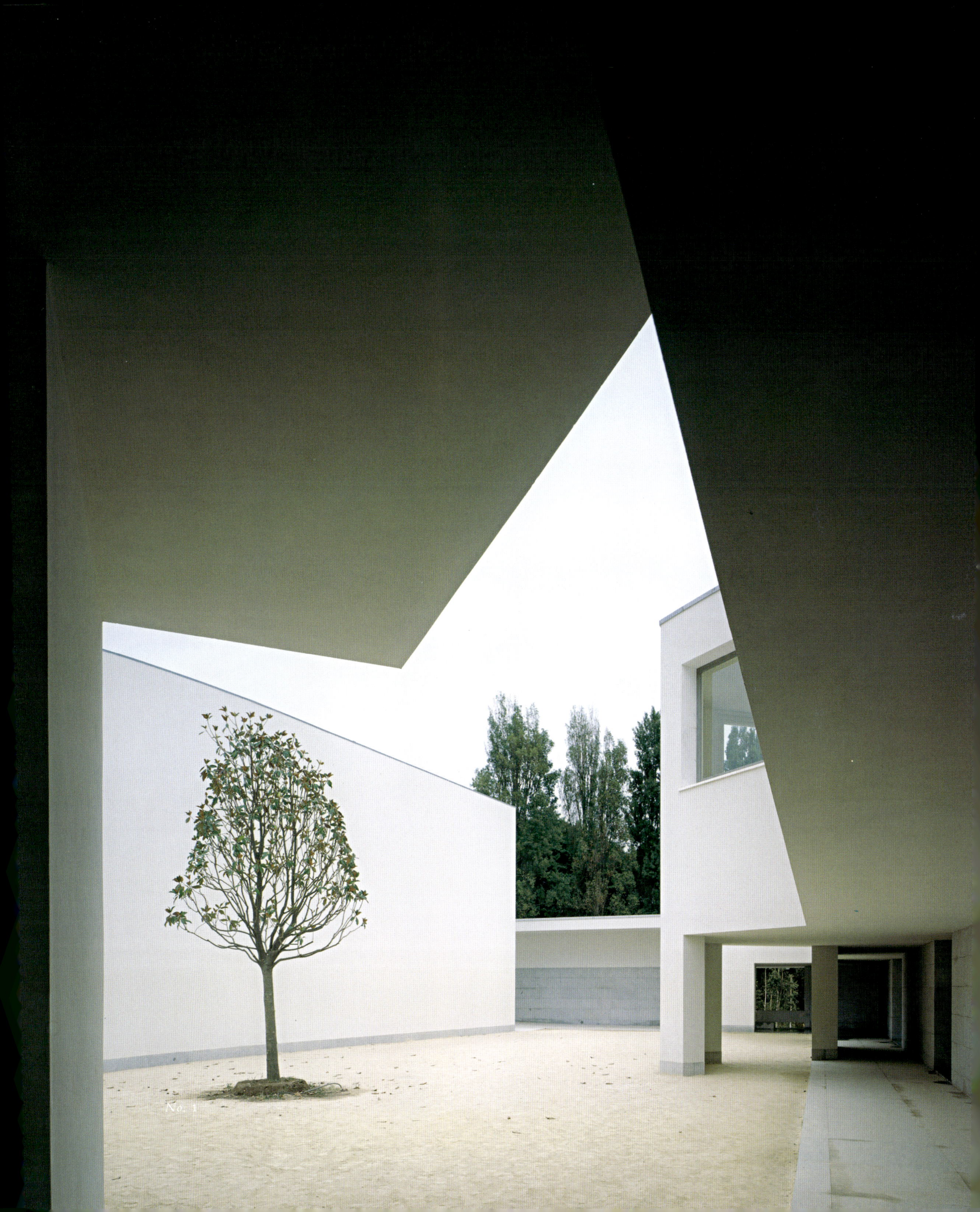

No. 1

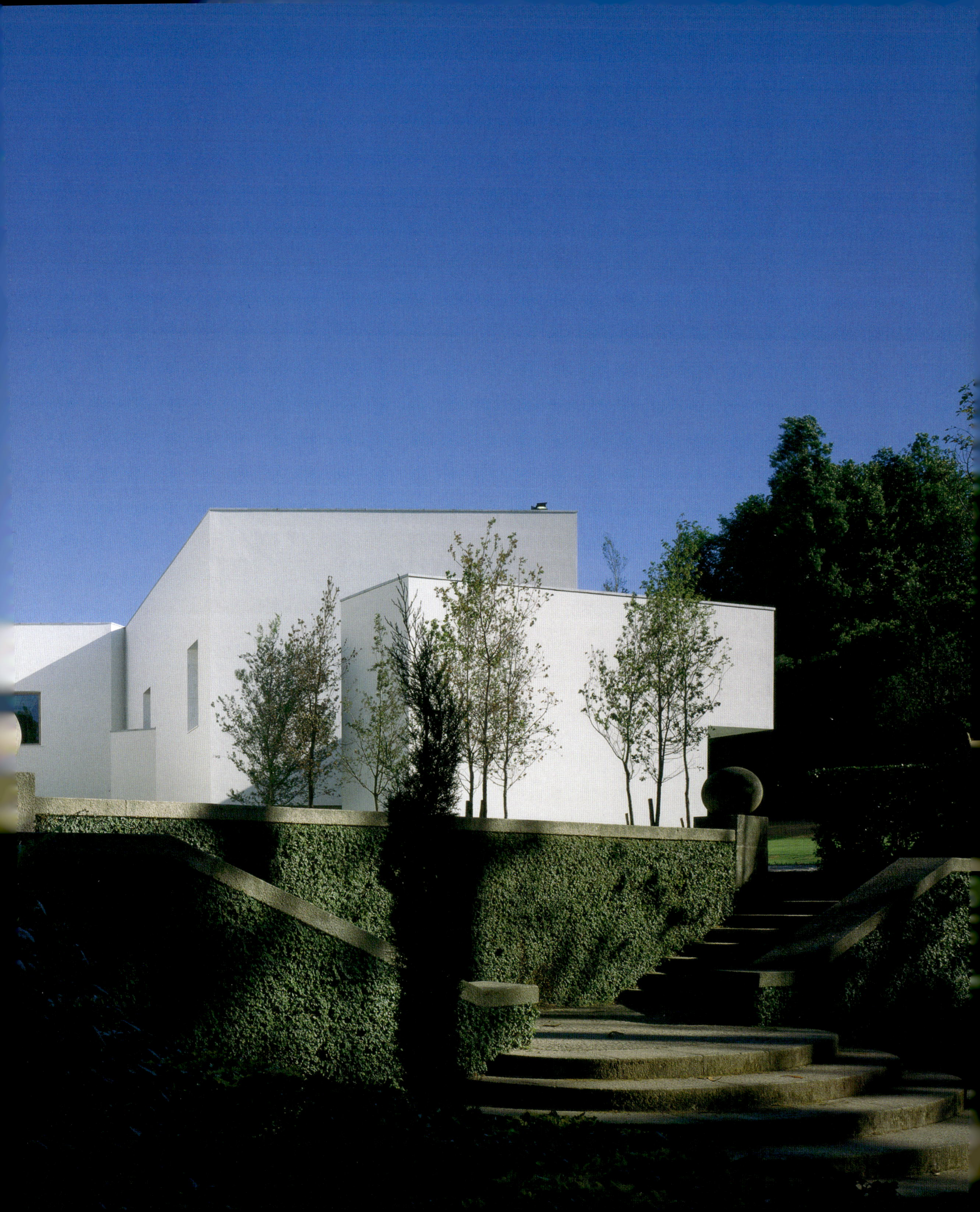

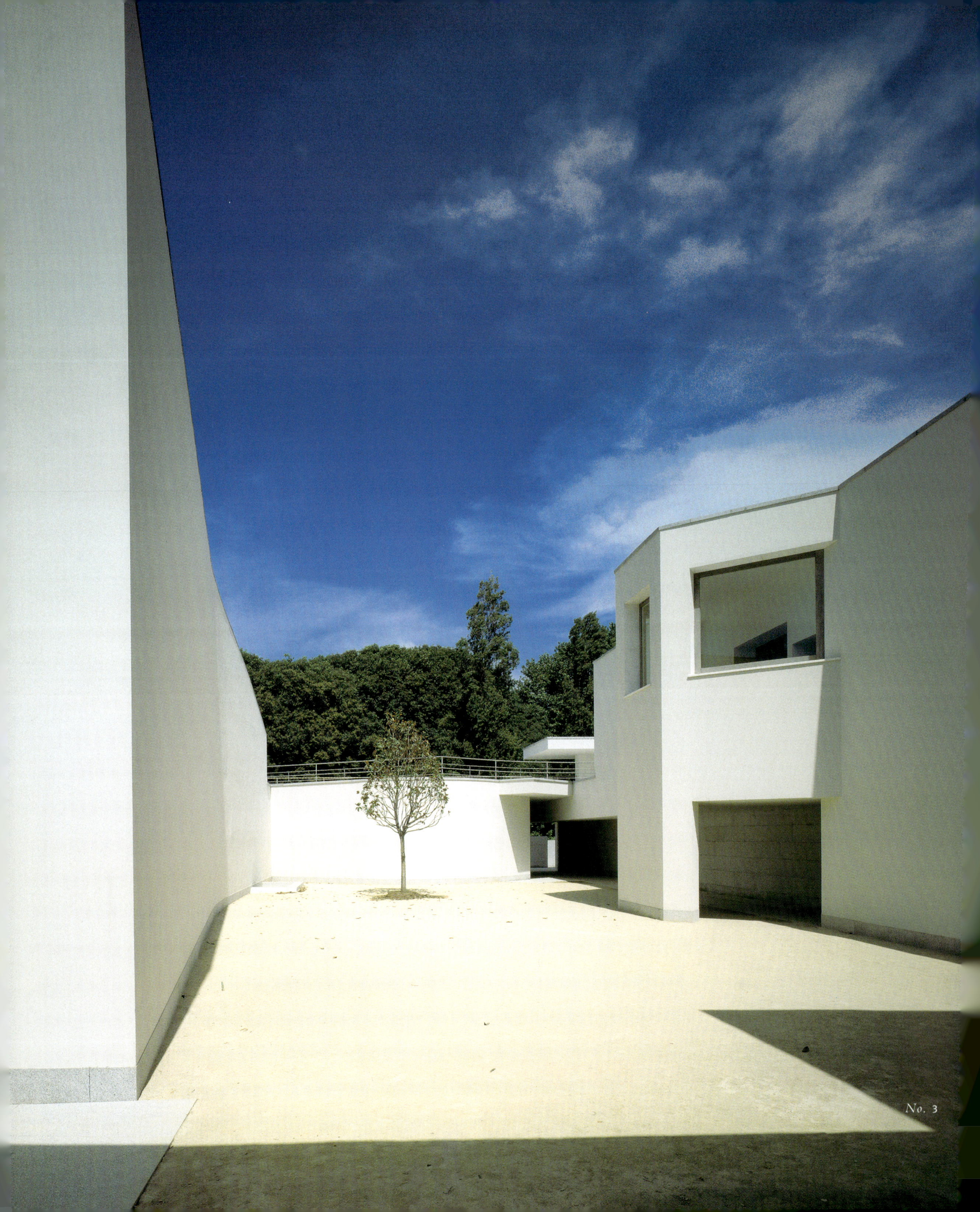

No. 3

No. 3-9

DESCRIPTION

CAPTION

PHOTO

No. 3-9 The architect carefully orchestrated the entry sequence to th museum and the exterior views around the building.

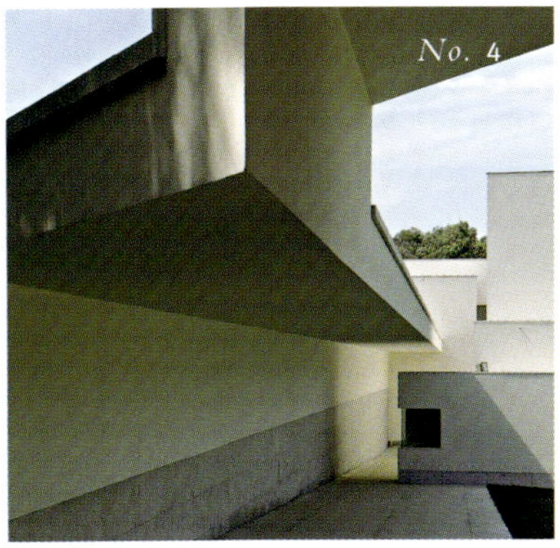

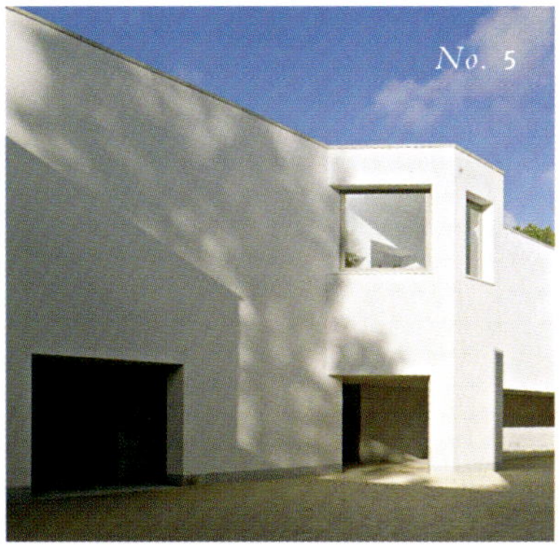

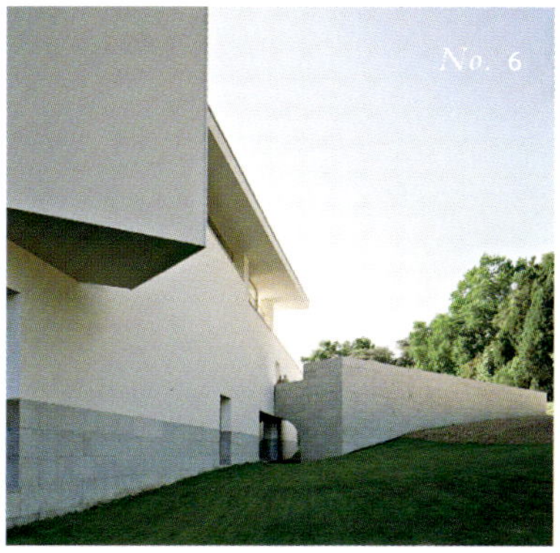

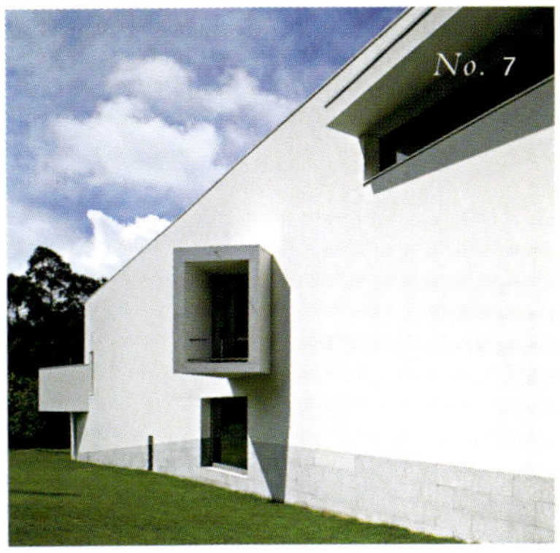

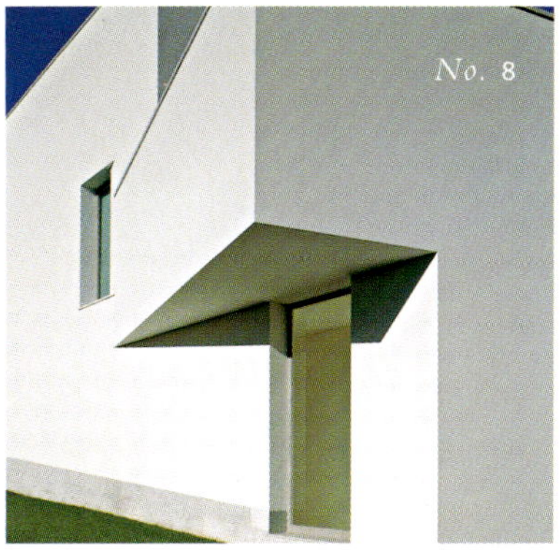

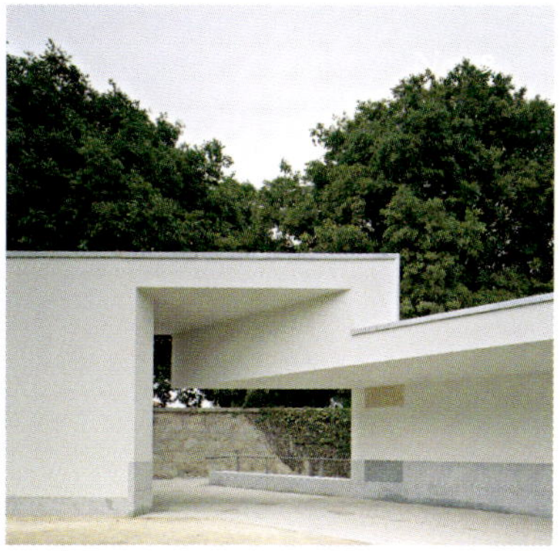

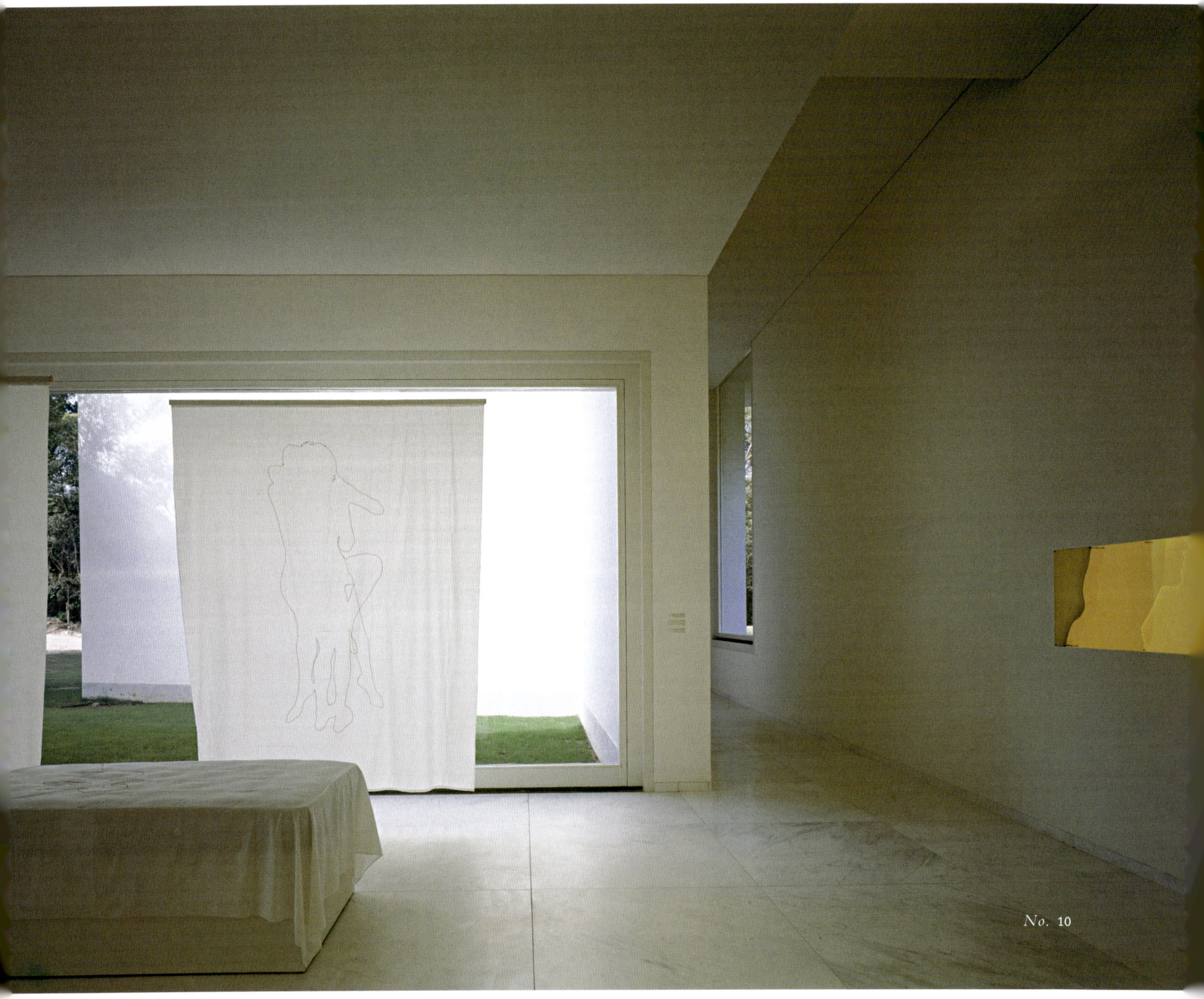
No. 10

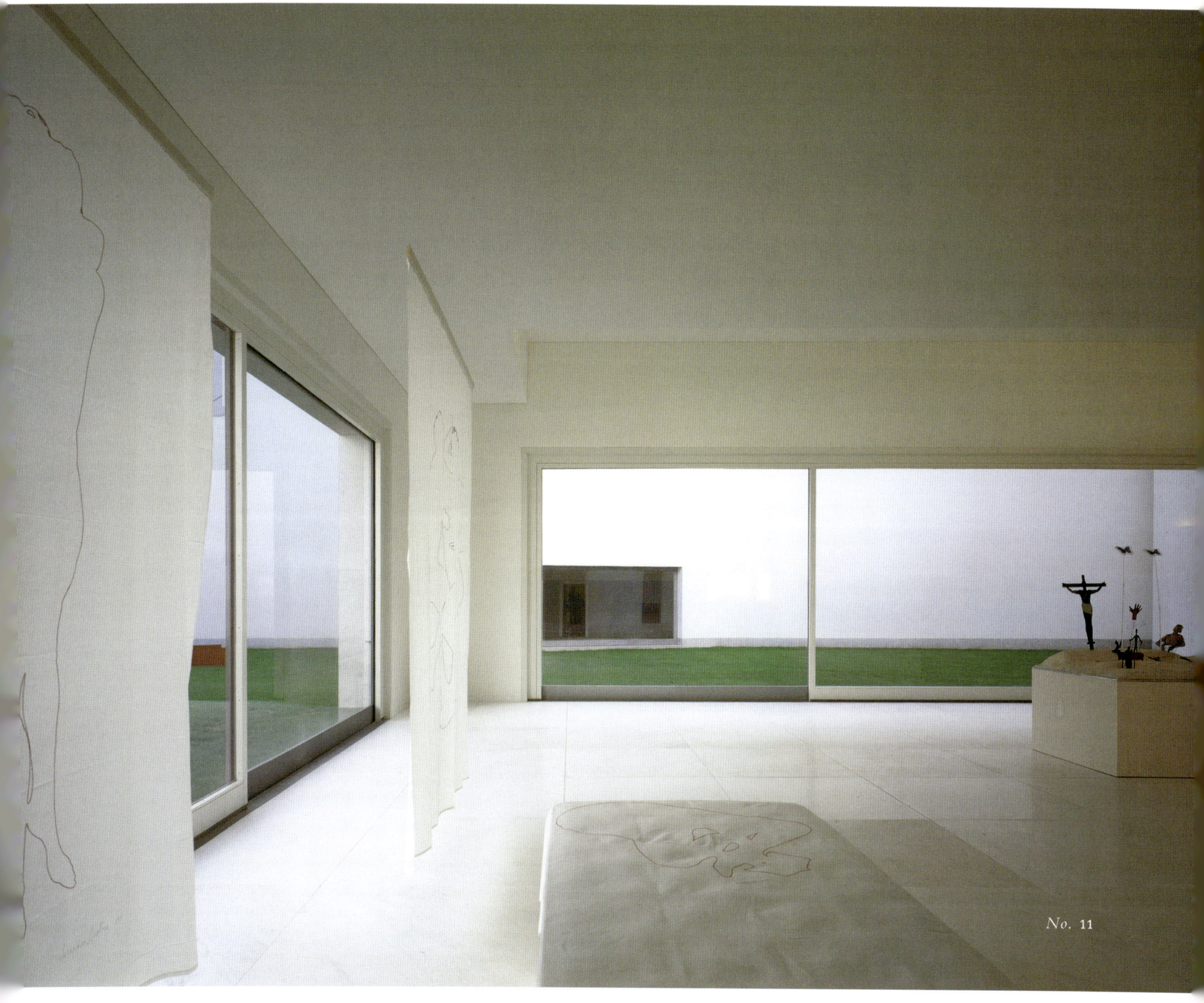

No. 11

CAPTION

PHOTO

No. 10 & 11 Galleries are united around and make use of the light from one of two U-shaped courtyards.

No. 12-15 The museum's galleries are softly lit by diffused nature light, In some instances, to create this quality of light, the architect suspends large platforms over large skylights.

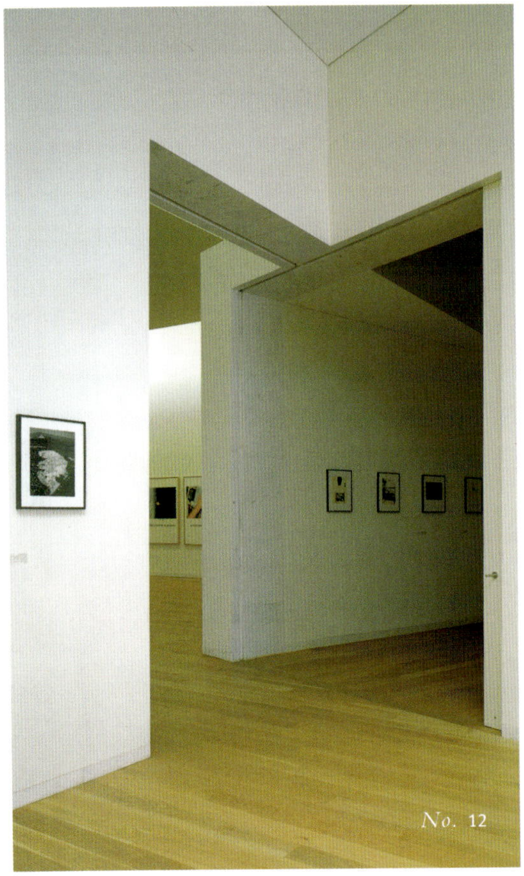
No. 12

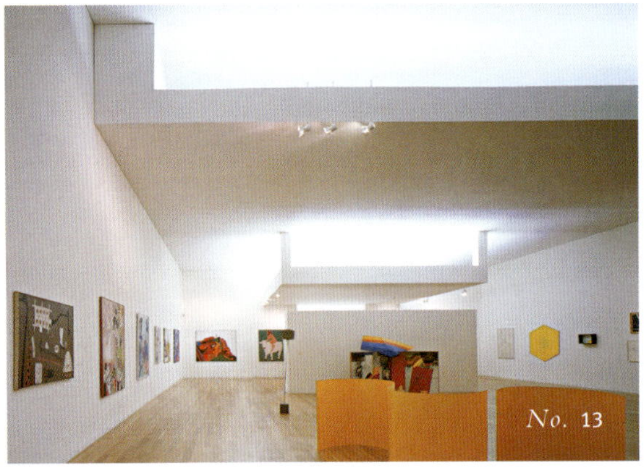
No. 13

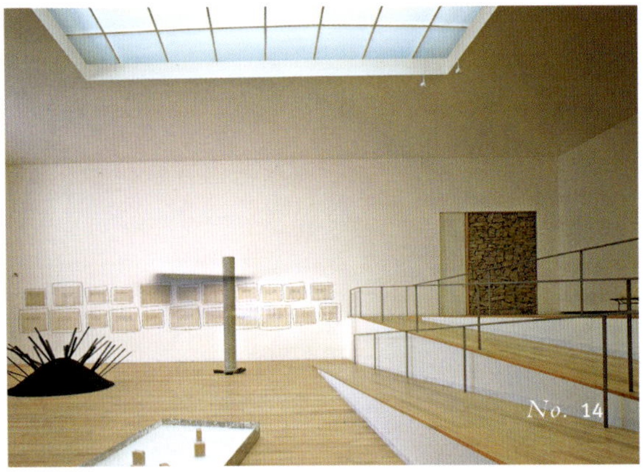
No. 14

No. 15

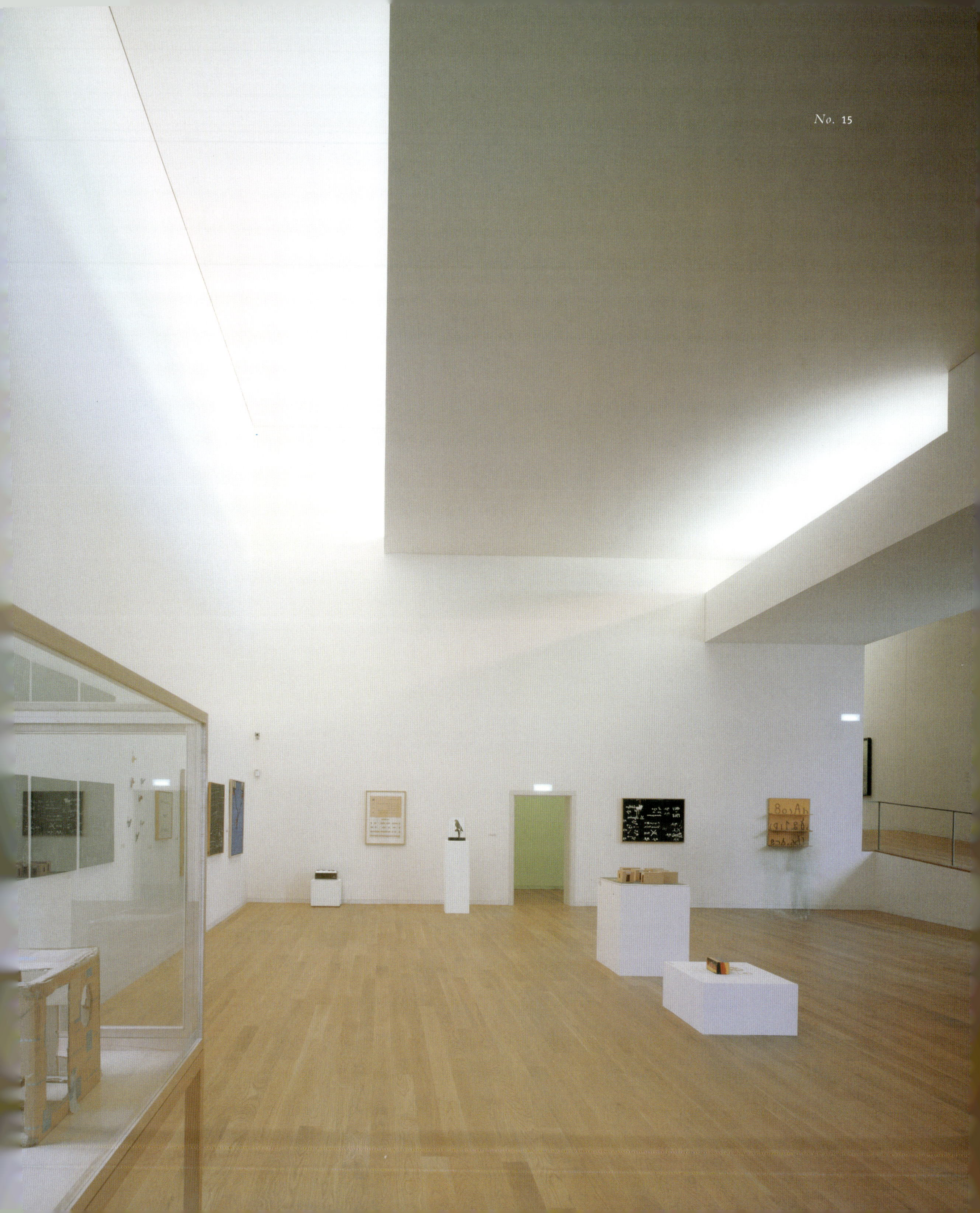

Gulf Coast Museum of Art

PROJECT

1 Florida Gulf Coast Arts Center | *Pinellas County Botanical Gardens*
Clearwater, Florida

ARCHITECT

2 Thompson and Rose | *Cambridge, Massachusetts*

The local climate and quality of light as well as the local flora and fauna influenced the design of the Florida Gulf Coast Arts Center—its simple volumes, light-weight structures, and the admittance of an abundance of natural light. Such is the work of Thompson and Rose, a firm that strives to successfully weave together architecture and the landscape.

The new 50,000-square-foot meter arts center spreads out on land between the 60-acre botanical gardens and the Pinellas waterway. There, galleries house the center's permanent modern art collection. Studios hold classes for instruction in painting, photography, metalsmithing, sculpture, ceramics, printmaking, fiber arts, woodworking, and glass blowing.

In developing the design, Thompson and Rose analyzed the specific site conditions—the movement of the sun, the topography, the geological conditions, the water and wind movement, the flora and fauna and species. The goal was to create an architecture that "sees" it sites, an architecture that stands in relationship to its surroundings and heightens the experience and effect of the natural environment.

For the arts center, the structures are simple volumes of concrete block with light-weight steel joists supporting membrane roofs. Metal clad light monitors punctuate the simple volumes and provide ambient north light to the studios and galleries. Overhanging awnings provide shade to the south, west, and east. These components—sculpted roof lights and projecting sunshades—reveal the unique influence of the Florida sun to determine a building's shape.

A curved colonnade runs along the studio and shop buildings and becomes an outdoor classroom. A path for pedestrians, the colonnade is defined by a lightweight steel structure.

No. 1

Description

Caption

Photo

No. 1 The museum acts as a backdrop to the sculpture garden.

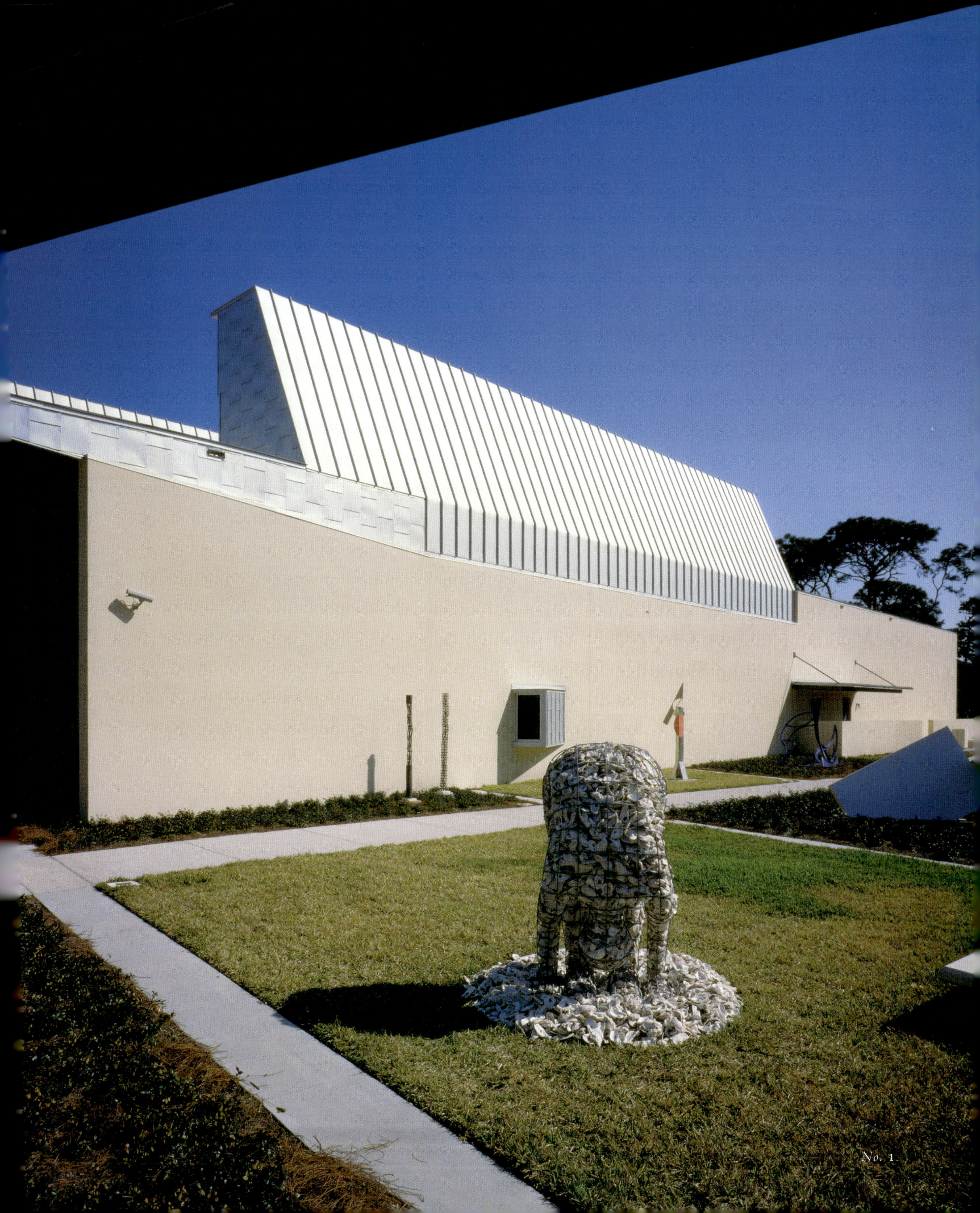

No. 1

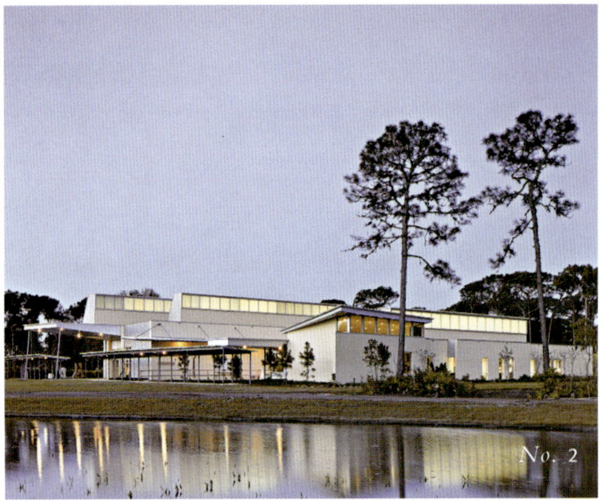
No. 2

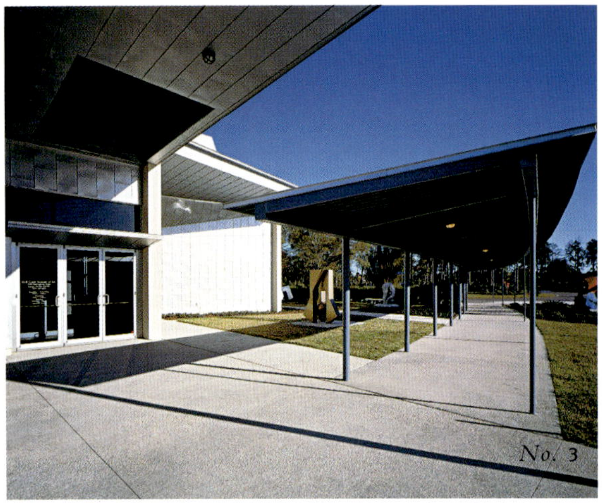
No. 3

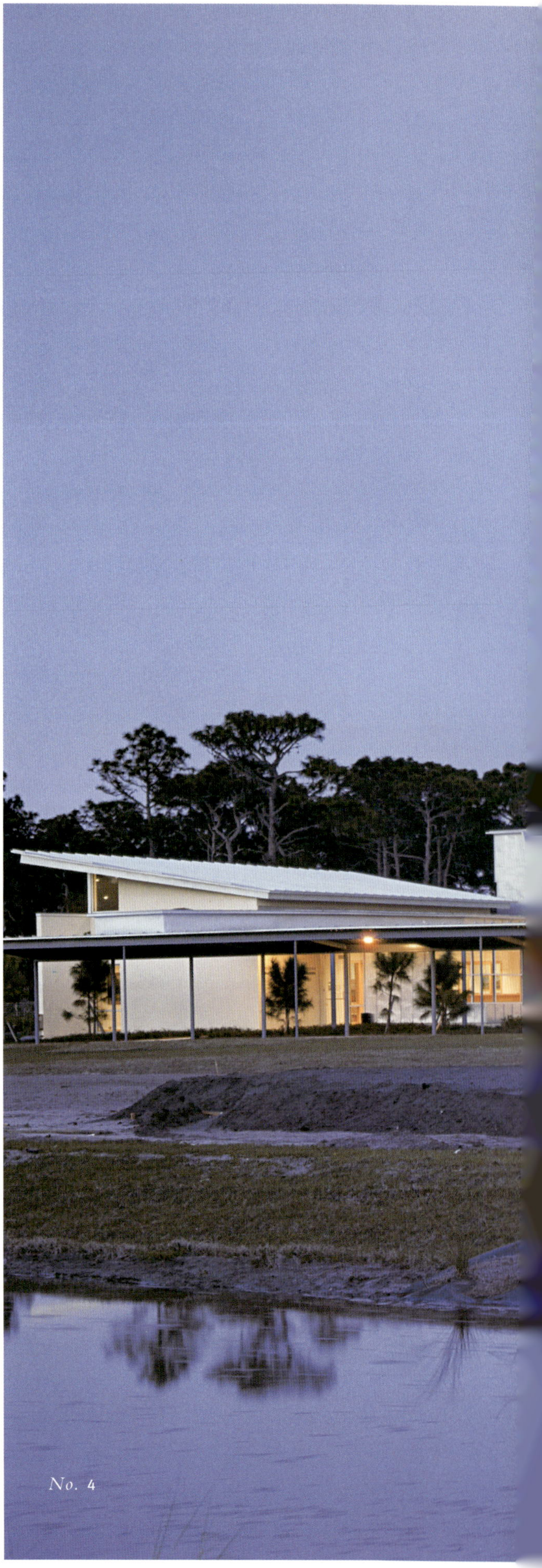
No. 4

CAPTION PHOTO

No. 2 At dusk, interior lights glow through the sun awnings.

No. 3 A covered walkway leads to the nearby botanical gardens.

No. 4 The lightweight steel structure responds to the Florida climate.

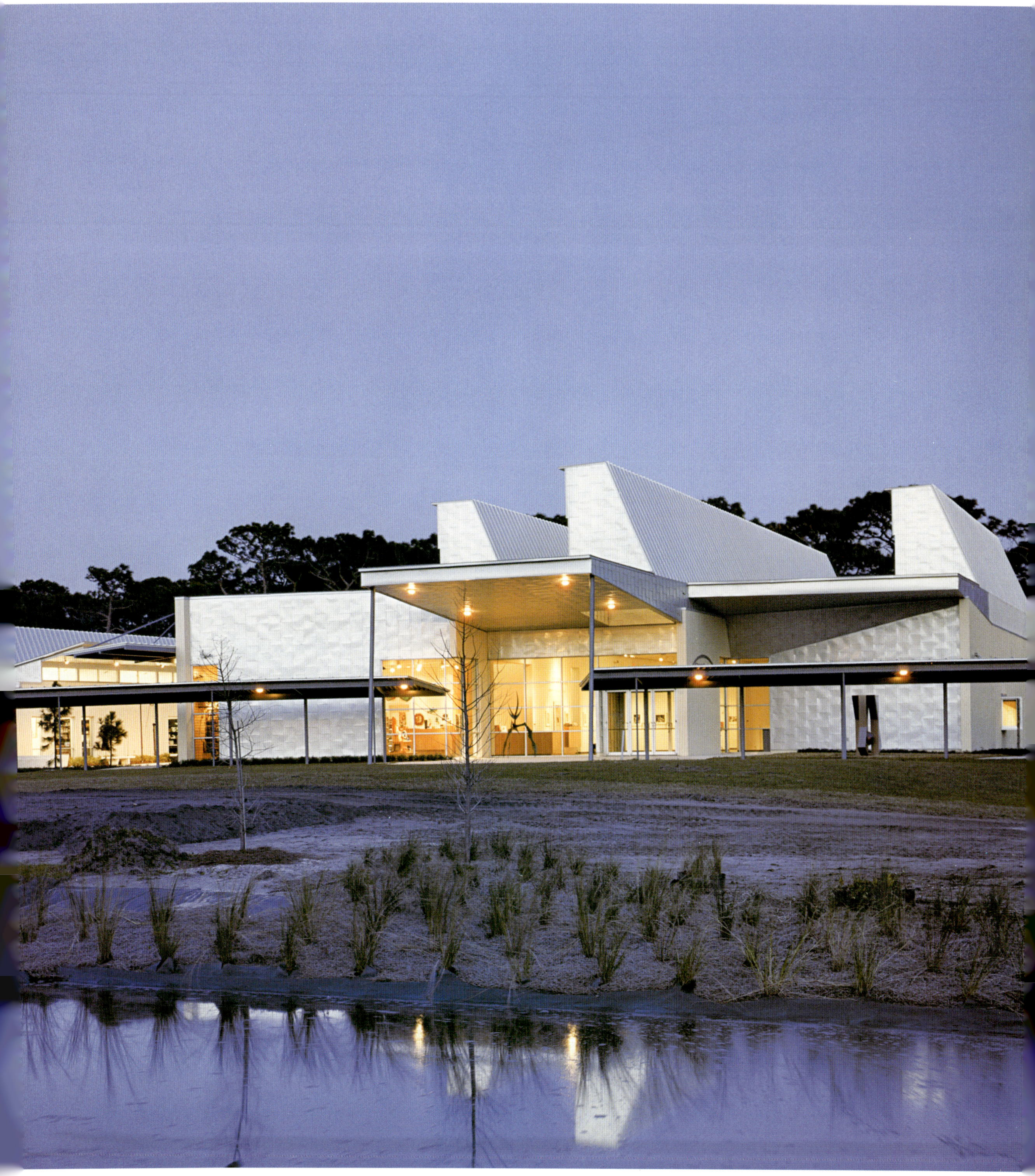

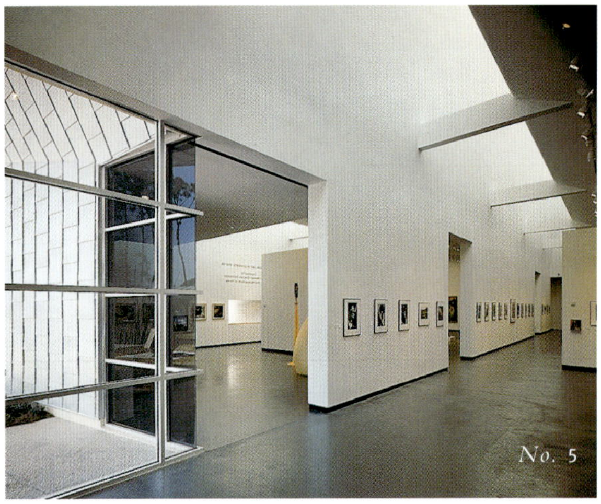
No. 5

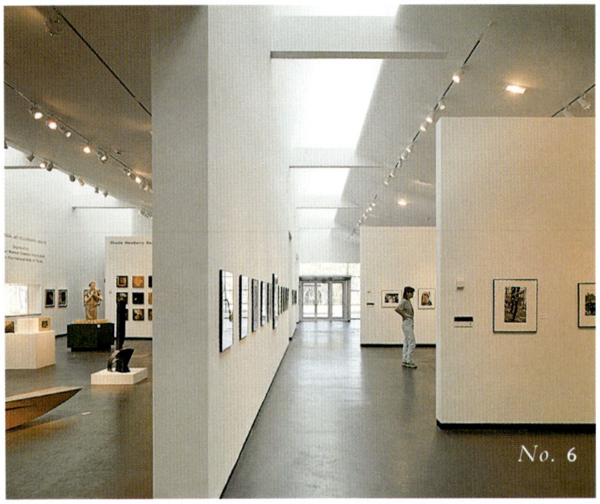
No. 6

CAPTION PHOTO

No. 5, 6 & 7 GALLERY SPACES ARE FLEXIBLE AND ARE BOTH NATURALLY AND ARTIFICIALLY LIT.

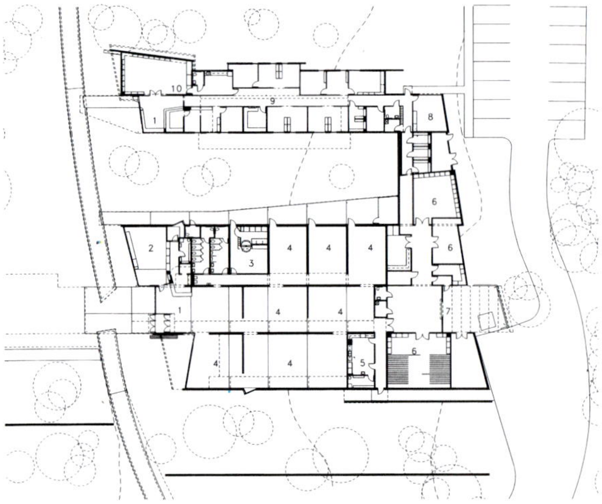

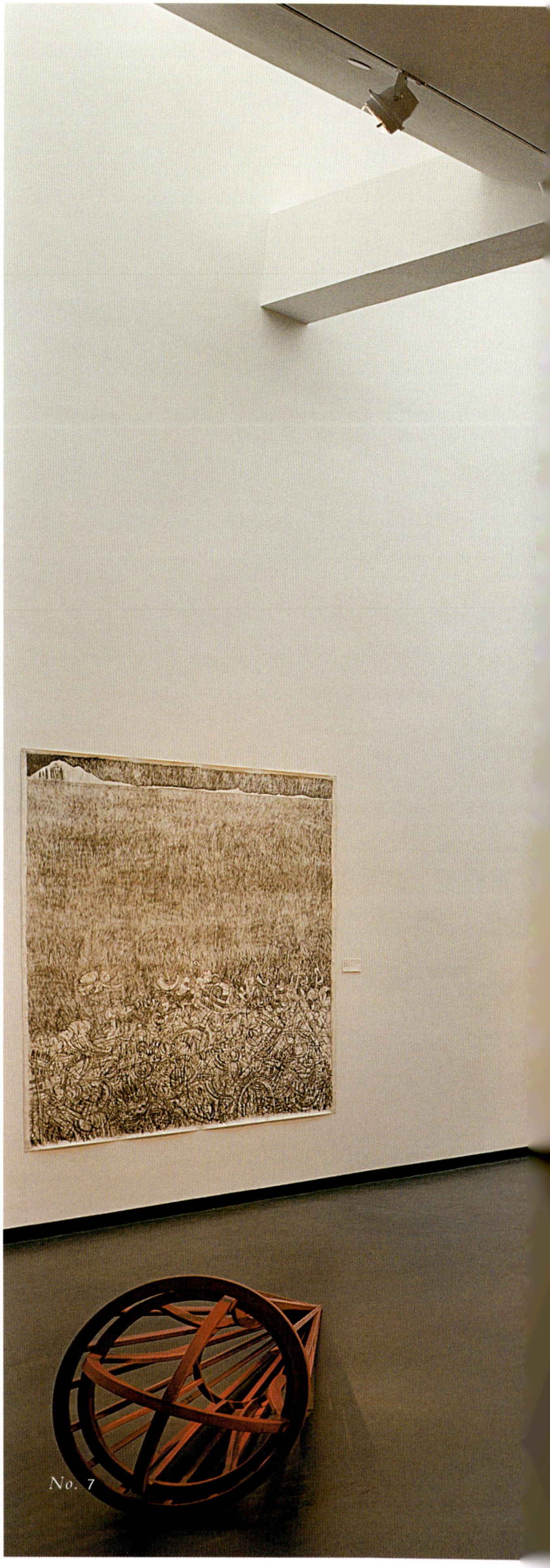
No. 7

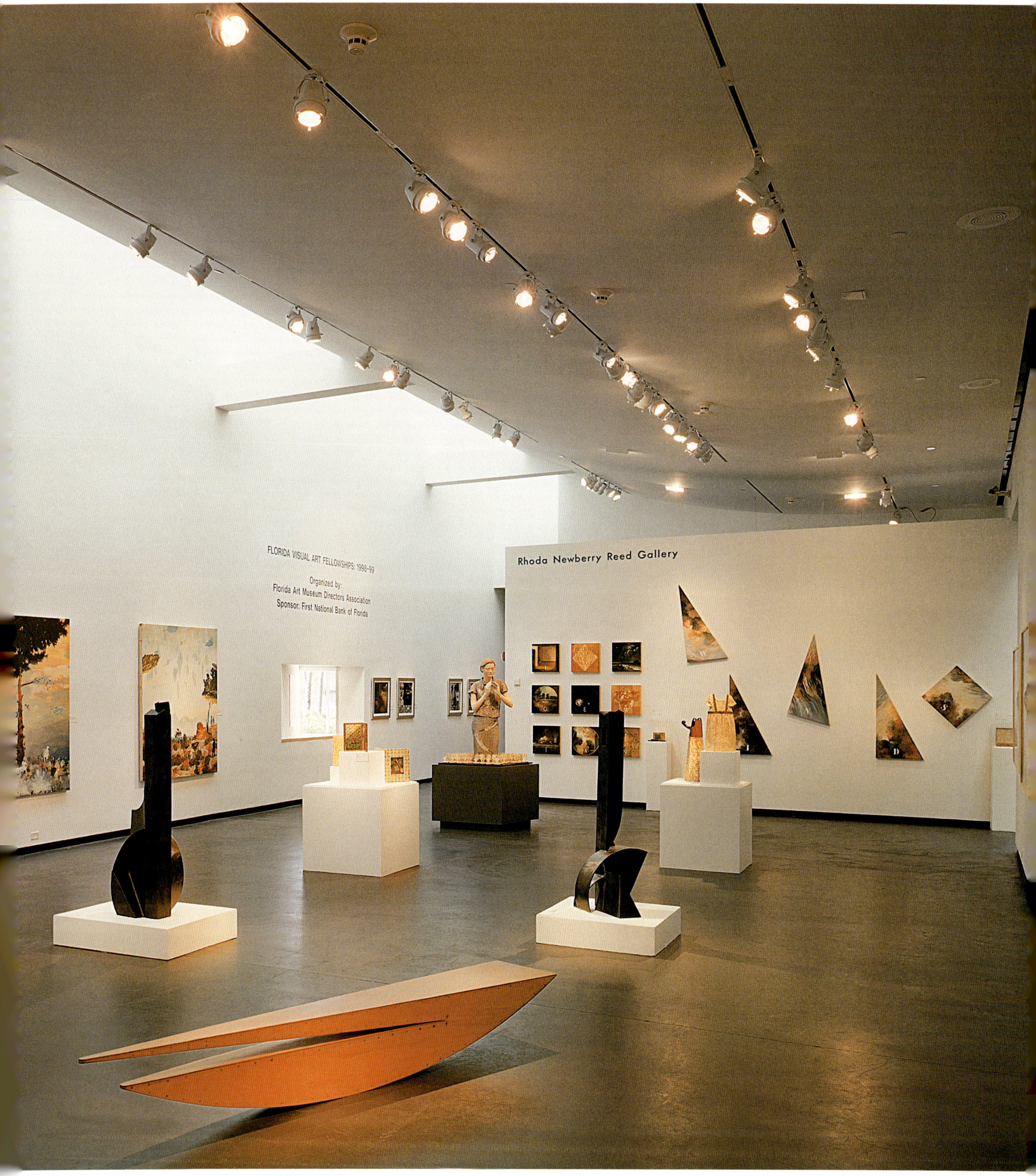
FLORIDA VISUAL ART FELLOWSHIPS: 1998–99
Organized by:
Florida Art Museum Directors Association
Sponsor: First National Bank of Florida
Rhoda Newberry Reed Gallery

Museum Het Valkhof

1 *PROJECT*
Museum Het Valkhof | *Nijmegen, The Netherlands*

2 *ARCHITECT*
UN Studio | *Amsterdam, The Netherlands*

The museum is called the Ice Palace for its glass façade, which shimmers in hues of deep aquamarine and light green and brings the apparition of a structure frozen in time and place. Sited on a hillside overlooking the Will River, where the Roman first settled in ancient Nijmegen, the museum houses the archaeological past, but also modern and pre-twentieth-century art

The architect plays with the visitor's perceptions. The building is basically a two-story, rectangular box, yet from the exterior it appears at points to be four stories. The façade is covered with thin strips of glass that at first glance appear to be parallel but undulate and bow ever so slightly. Attached to a steel substructure with a flexible joint, the glass pieces fan out and up along the length of the façade, making the museum appear thinner and more compressed at the southeast corner, and larger and more transparent at the opposite end.

Inside, a central stair rises to the galleries above, as the ground level houses museum services, offices and education functions. What appears to be a single flight of stairs actually offers eight different routes through the museum. The galleries are organized as parallel streets, through which diagonal pathways cut from one corner of the building to another. By following a zigzag route, the visitor can watch art and crafts unfold in time from the Roman era to the present. Major sections of the roof are cantilevered off the stair's concrete walls. The stair hall, therefore, becomes a major structural element at the museum's core.

No. 1
Description

Caption Photo

No. 1 Thin ribbons of glass are configured so that the museum seems to be four stories when it is actually two.

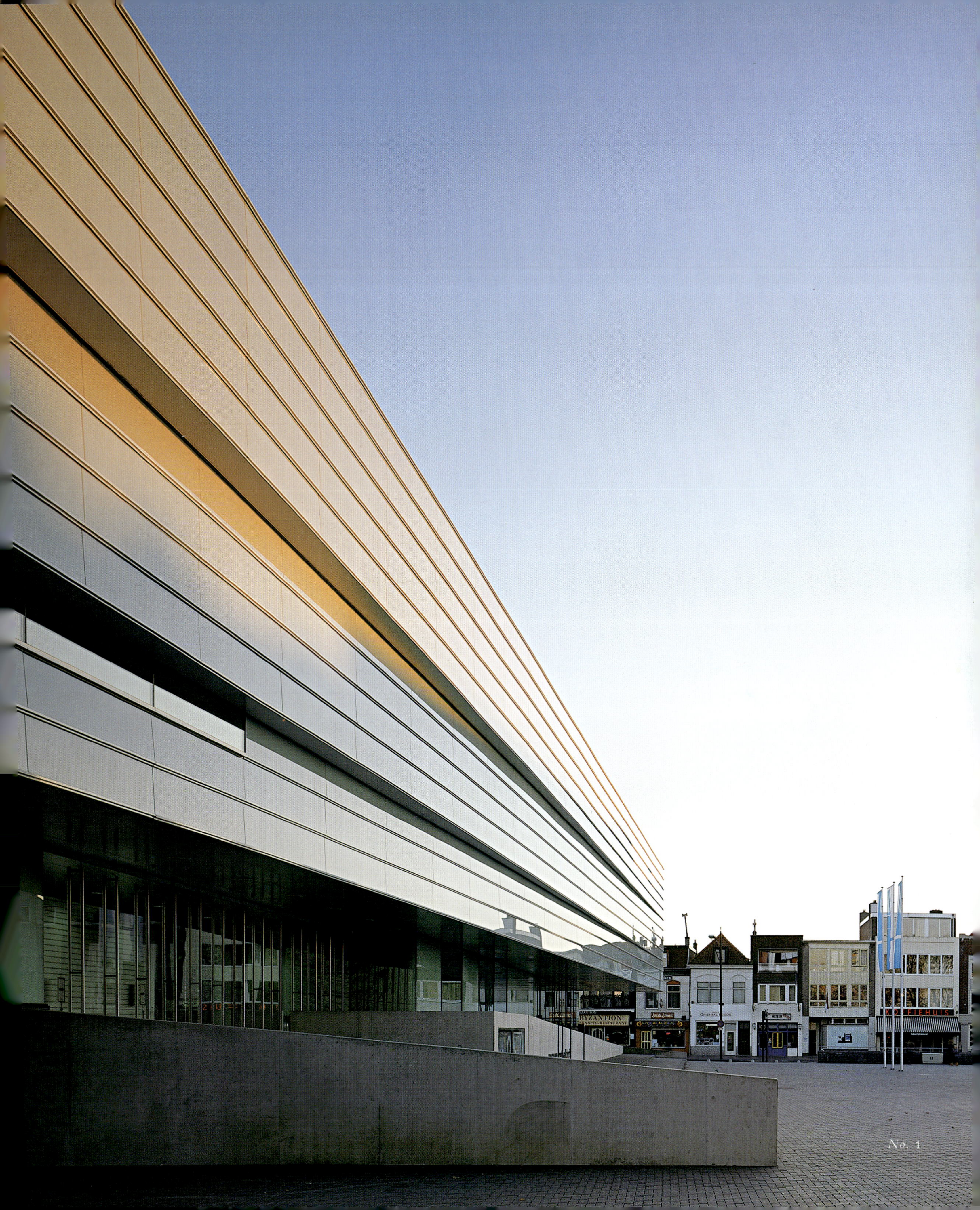

No. 1

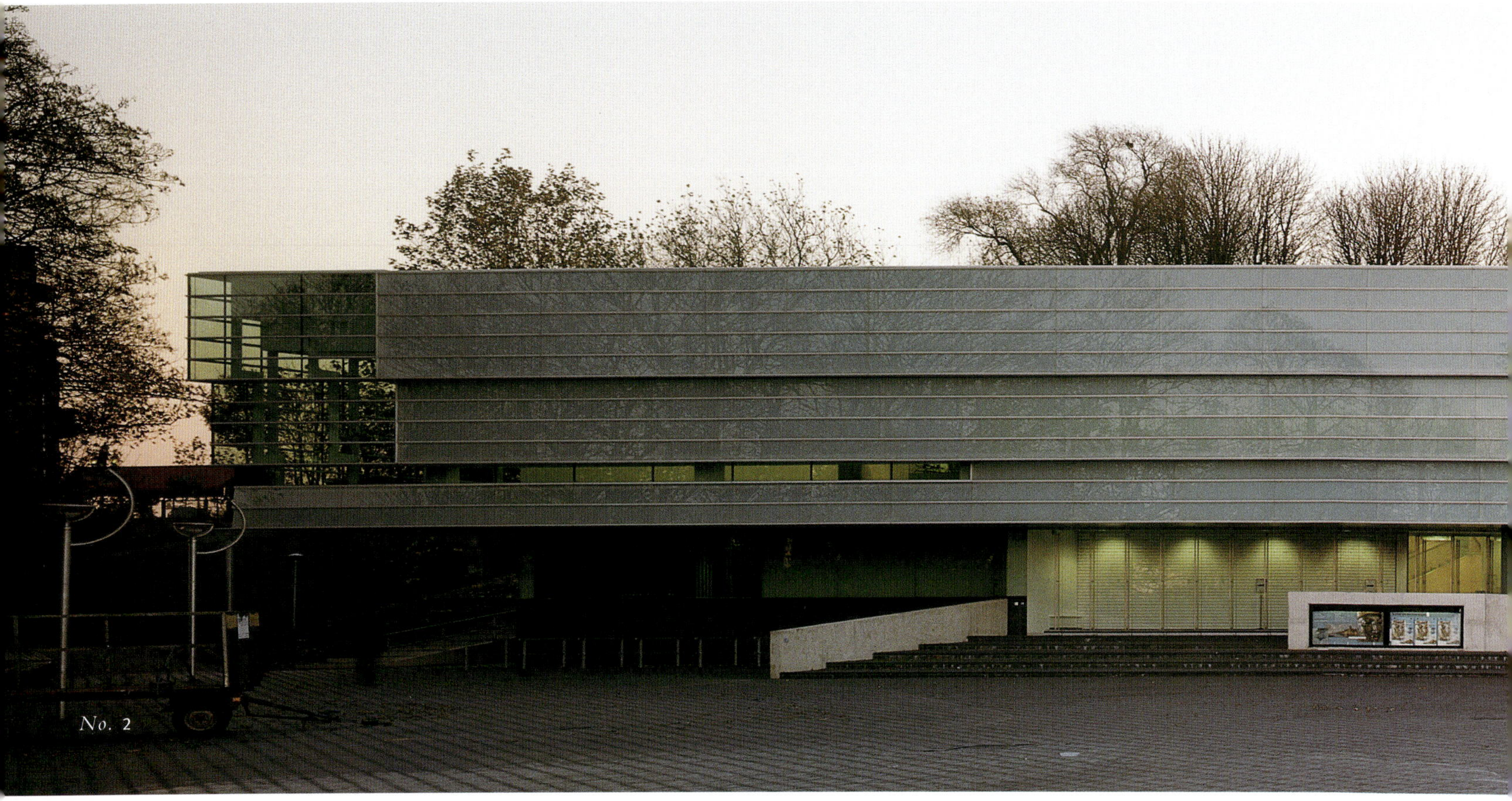
No. 2

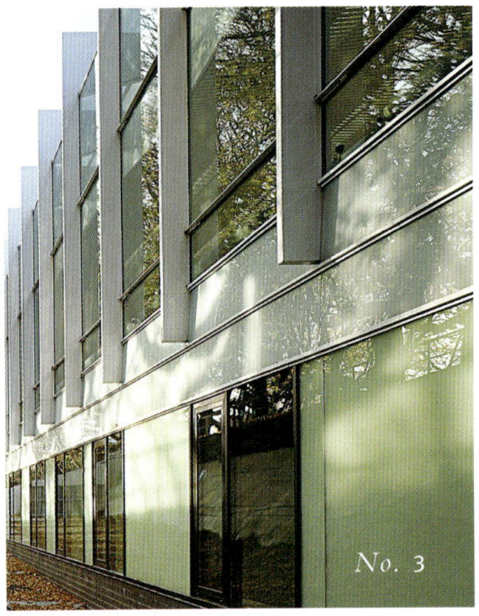
No. 3

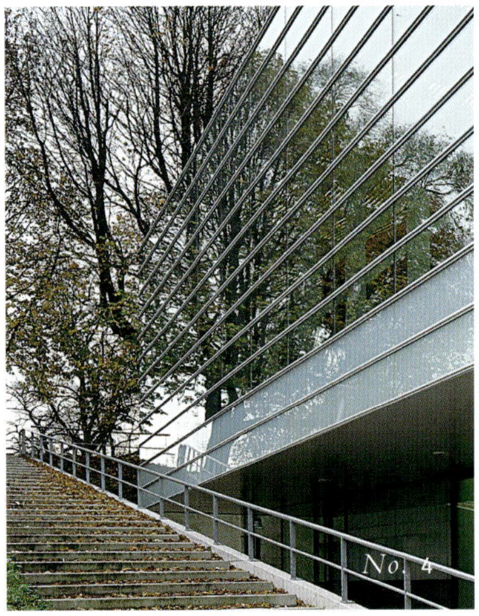
No. 4

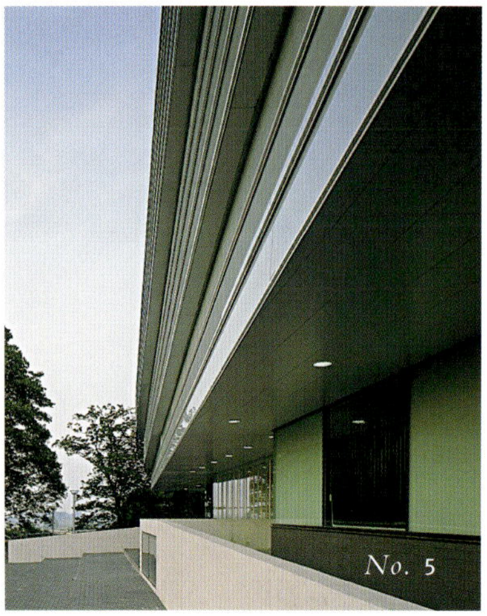
No. 5

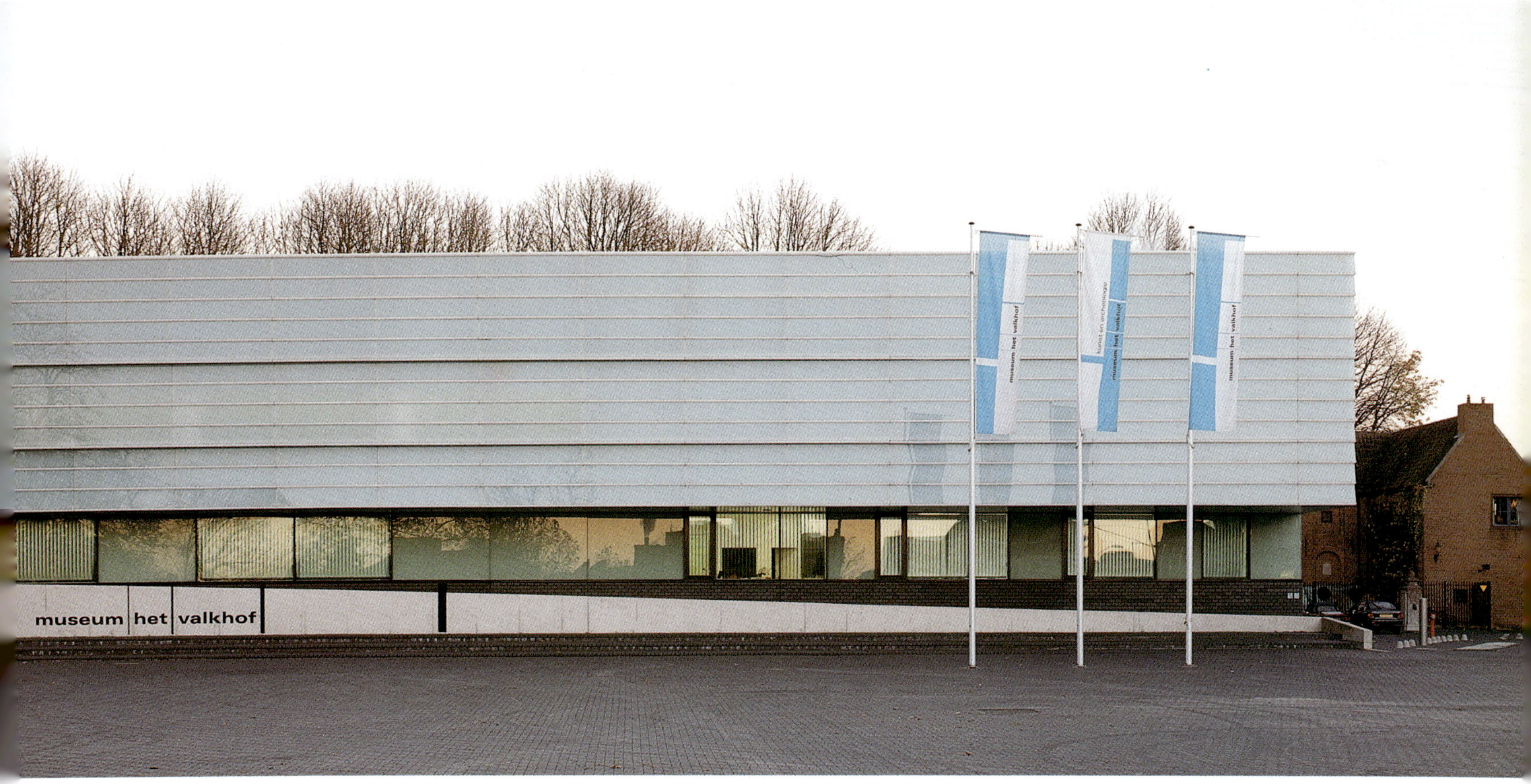

No. 2-5

DESCRIPTION

CAPTION

PHOTO

No. 2-5 The sleek facade contrasts sharply with its Dutch neighbors. The building is called the "Ice Palace" due to its shimmering facade.

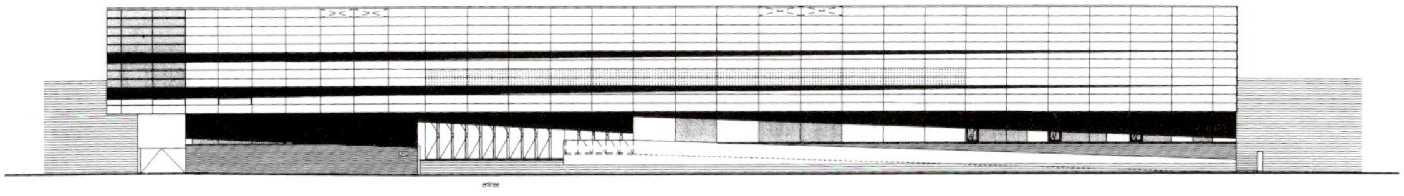

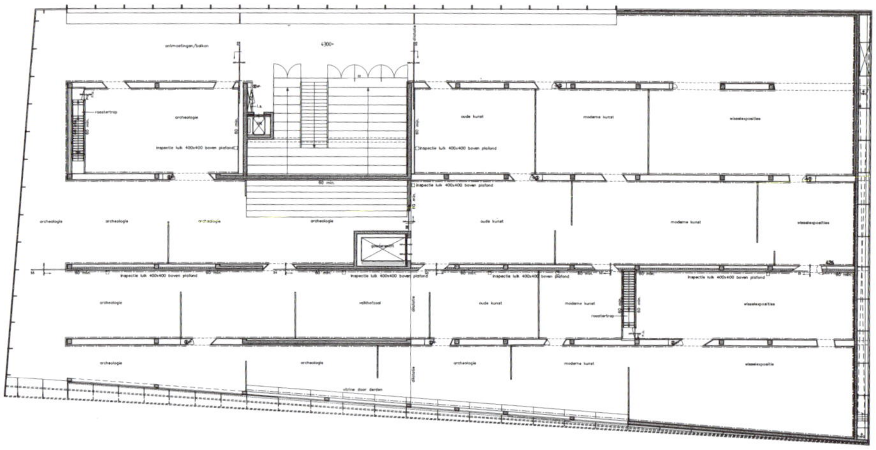

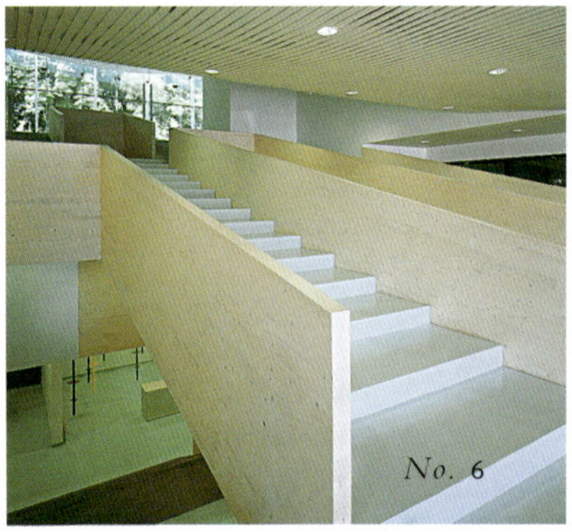

No. 6

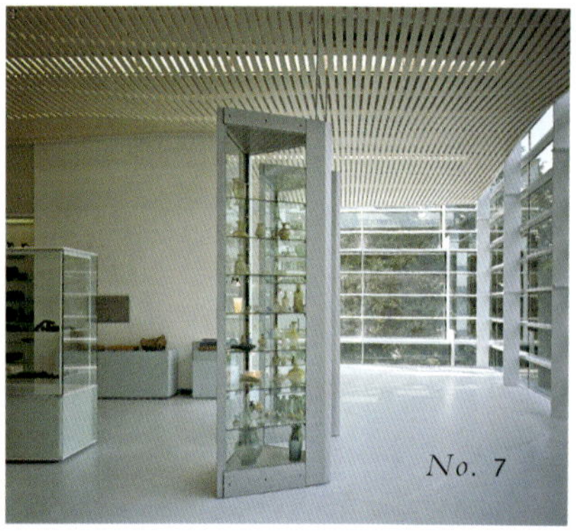

No. 7

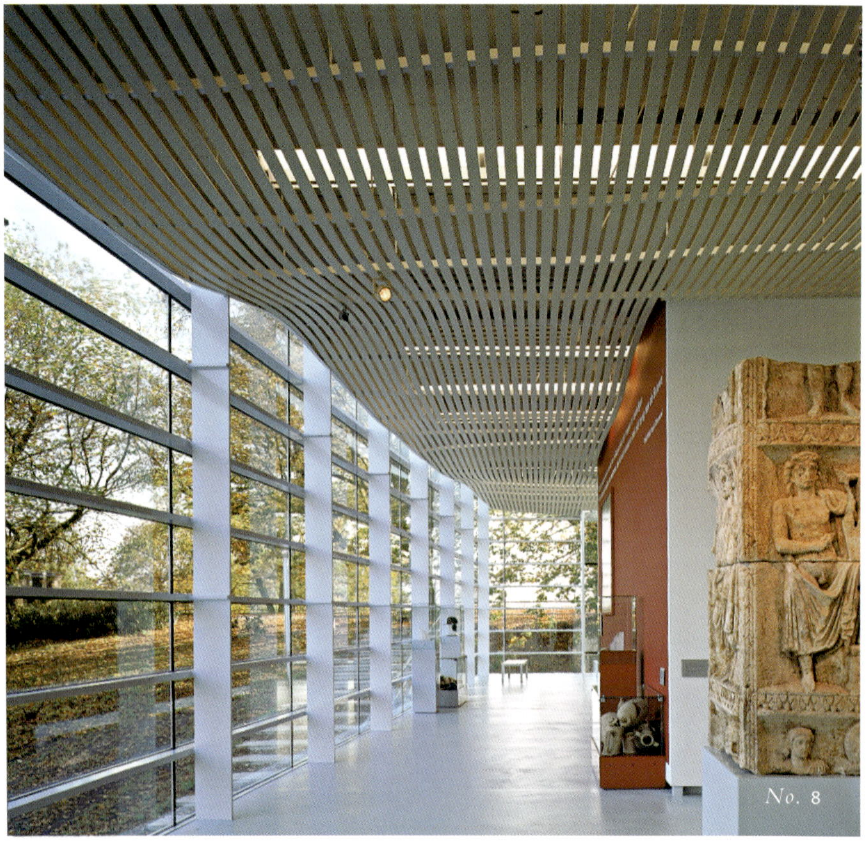

No. 8

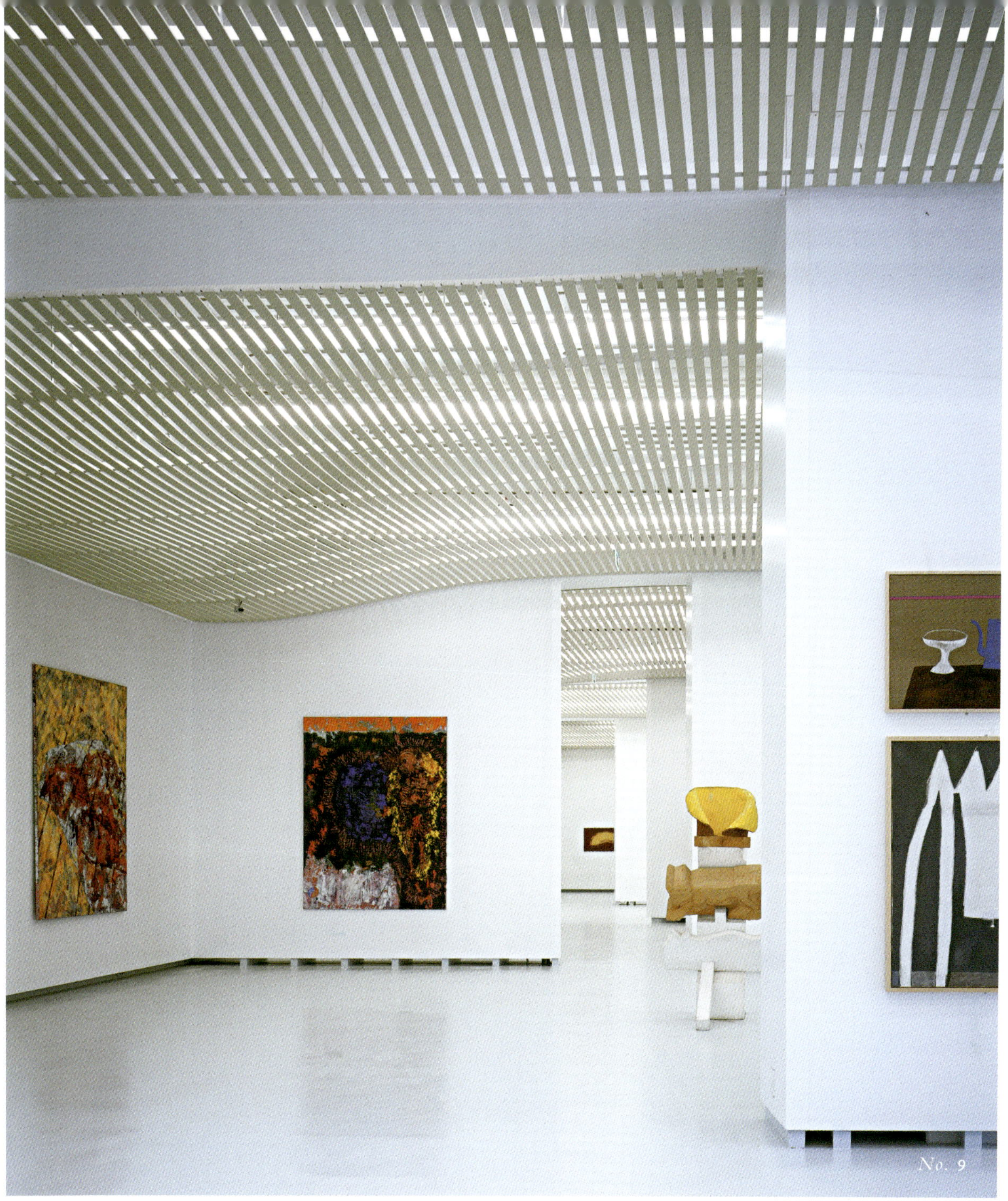
No. 9

No. 6-9
DESCRIPTION

CAPTION PHOTO

No. 6 The staircase forms the structural core of the building.

No. 7, 8 & 9 The ceiling is the second organizing element that lends coherence to the museum. It is like a blanket casually thrown over an object. The ceiling covers but does not conceal or disguise the multitude of installations or lighting, climate control, sprinklers and alarms. The slates of the undulating ceiling are removable for easy access and maintenance.

Rijksmuseum Twenthe

1 *PROJECT*
Rijksmuseum Twenthe | *Enschede, The Netherlands*

2 *ARCHITECT*
UN Studio / Van Berkel & Bos | *Amsterdam, The Netherlands*

Older museums periodically need to upgrade outdated mechanical and electrical systems. The trick is to do so without disrupting the interior fabric of the existing galleries. At the National Museum of Twenthe, UN Studio accomplished such an upgrade by enclosing an exterior courtyard, with minimal alterations to the original 1928 brick building and adding a small pavilion. In the process, the museum introduced new climatic installations and also acquired flexible, light-filled space for temporary exhibitions as well as a new cafeteria.

By simply roofing over one of the two existing courtyards, a new gallery is obtained. Designed for temporary exhibitions, the gallery features a frosted glass ceiling that admits an abundance of natural light. Openings in the otherwise closed facades around the courtyard provide visual and physical links between the old and new sections of the building.

Designed to serve as a restaurant and a small meeting hall, the pavilion is situated in the newly landscaped garden of the second courtyard. Its canted glass and steel walls provide a modern visual contrast with, but do not overshadow, the original brick building.

The only improvements to the original building were to align and enlarge existing room connections. The museumís collection includes fine and applied arts from the thirteenth to the nineteenth centuries and through contemporary times.

No. 1
Description

Caption Photo

No. 1 In the museum's courtyard, new elements juxtapose old.

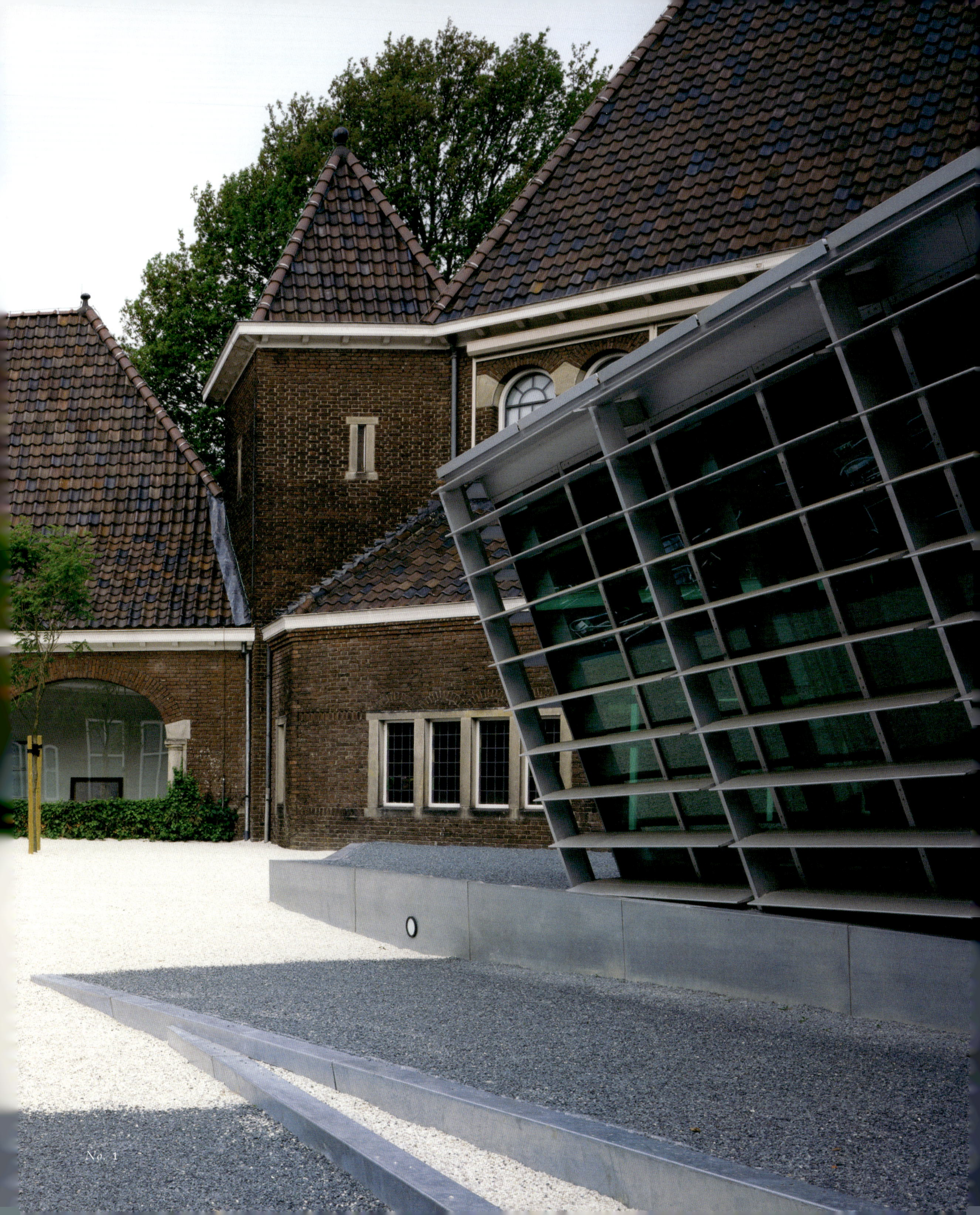

No. 1

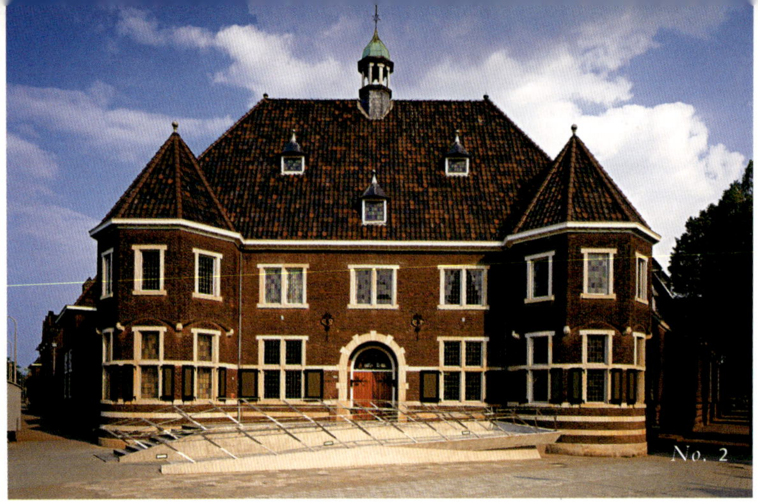

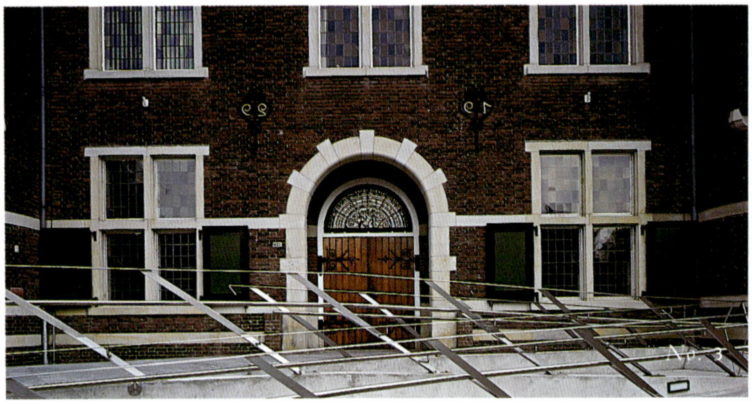

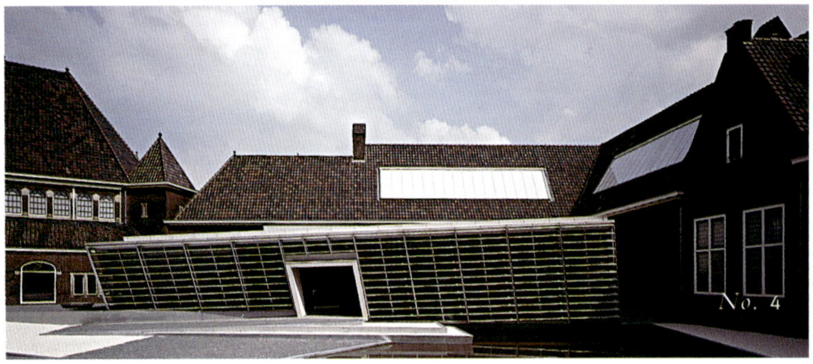

No. 2-7
DESCRIPTION

CAPTION PHOTO

No. 2 & 3 The existing museum, built in 1928, was extensively renovated and its climate control systems upgraded without changing the fabric of the existing building.

No. 4 & 5 A cafè was constructed in the museum's newly landscaped garden. The cafè also serves as a venue for classes, lectures, and other gatherings.

No. 6 & 7 A new gallery was created by roofing over one of the two existing courtyards. Frosted glass in the ceiling draws in natural light. Openings provide visual links with other facades of buildings.

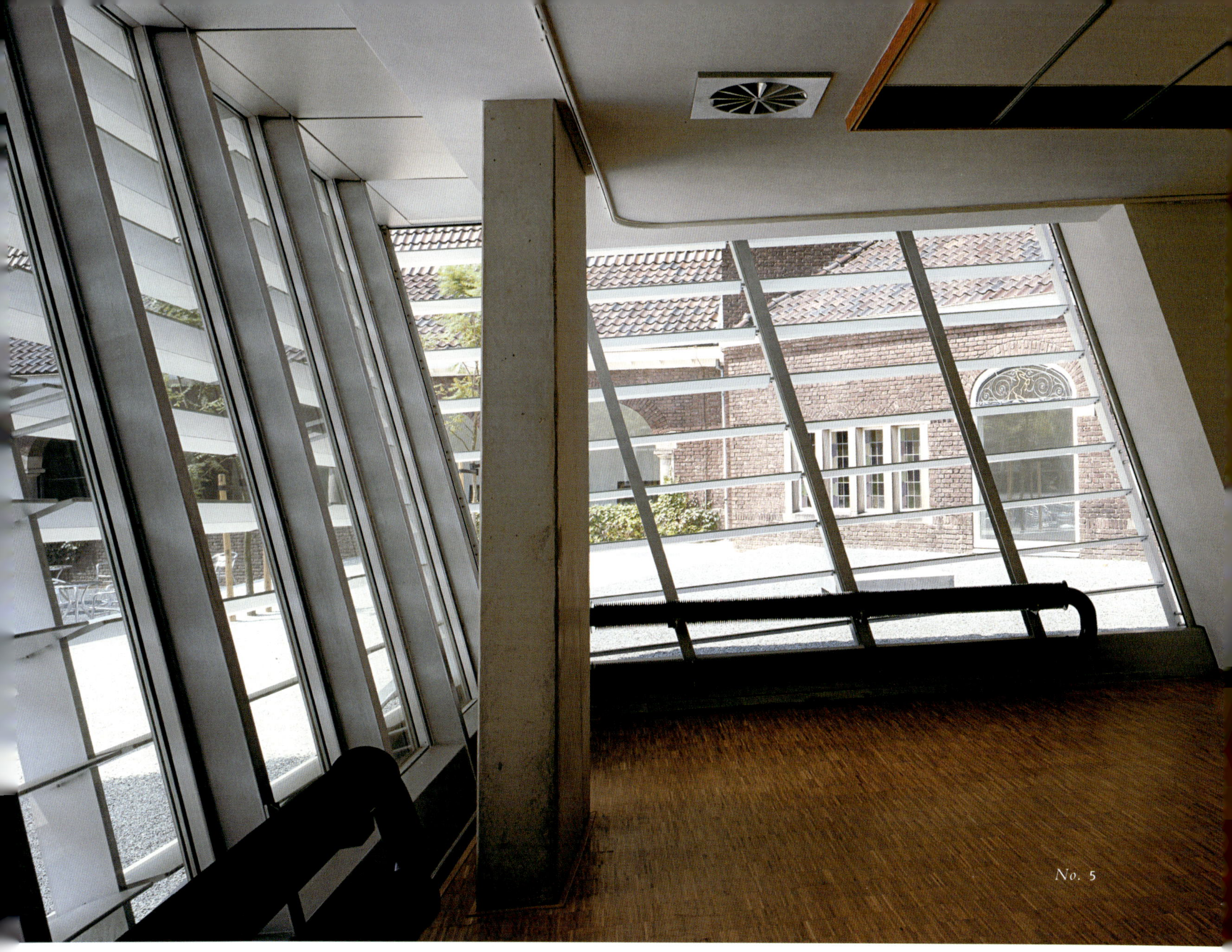

No. 5

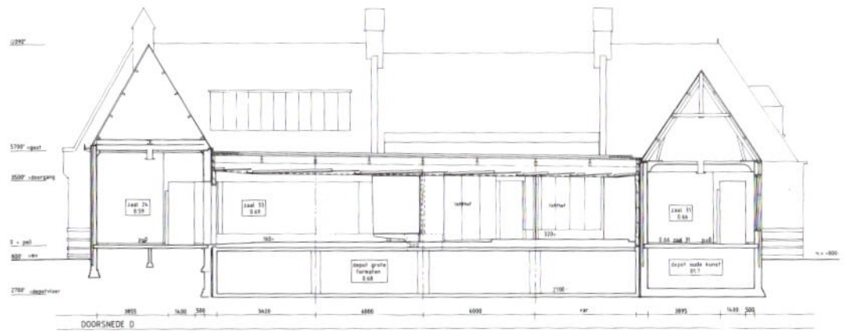

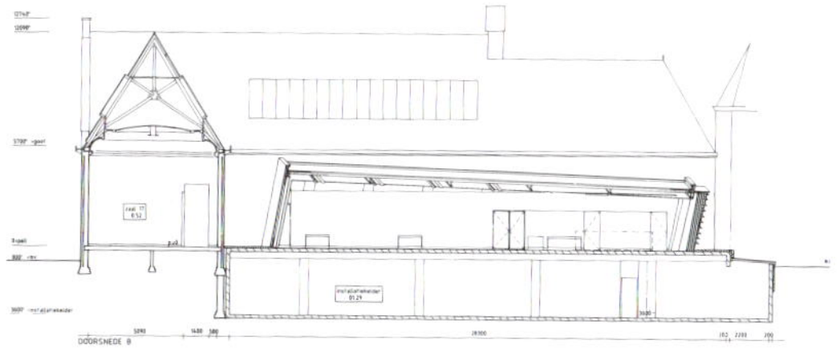

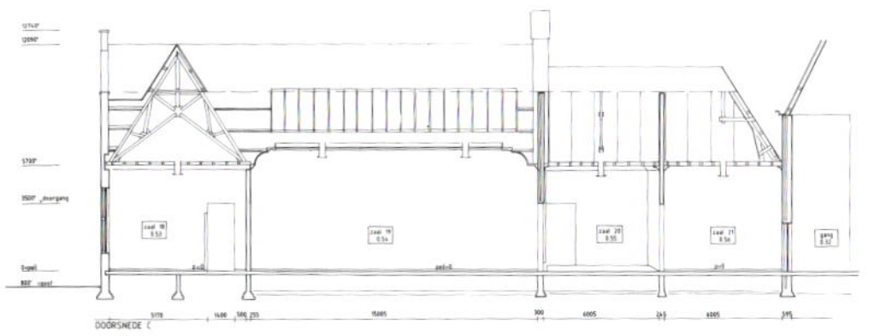

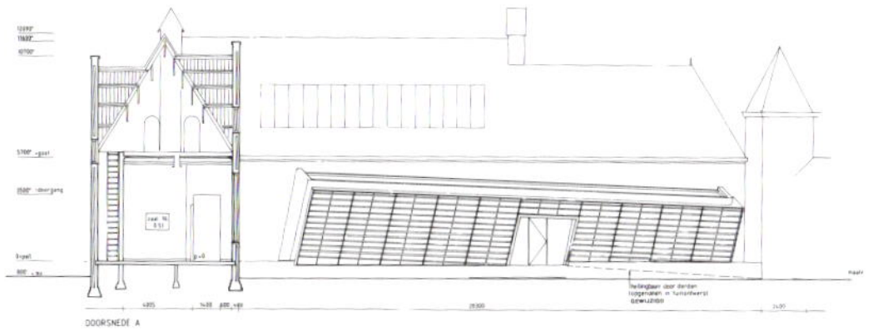

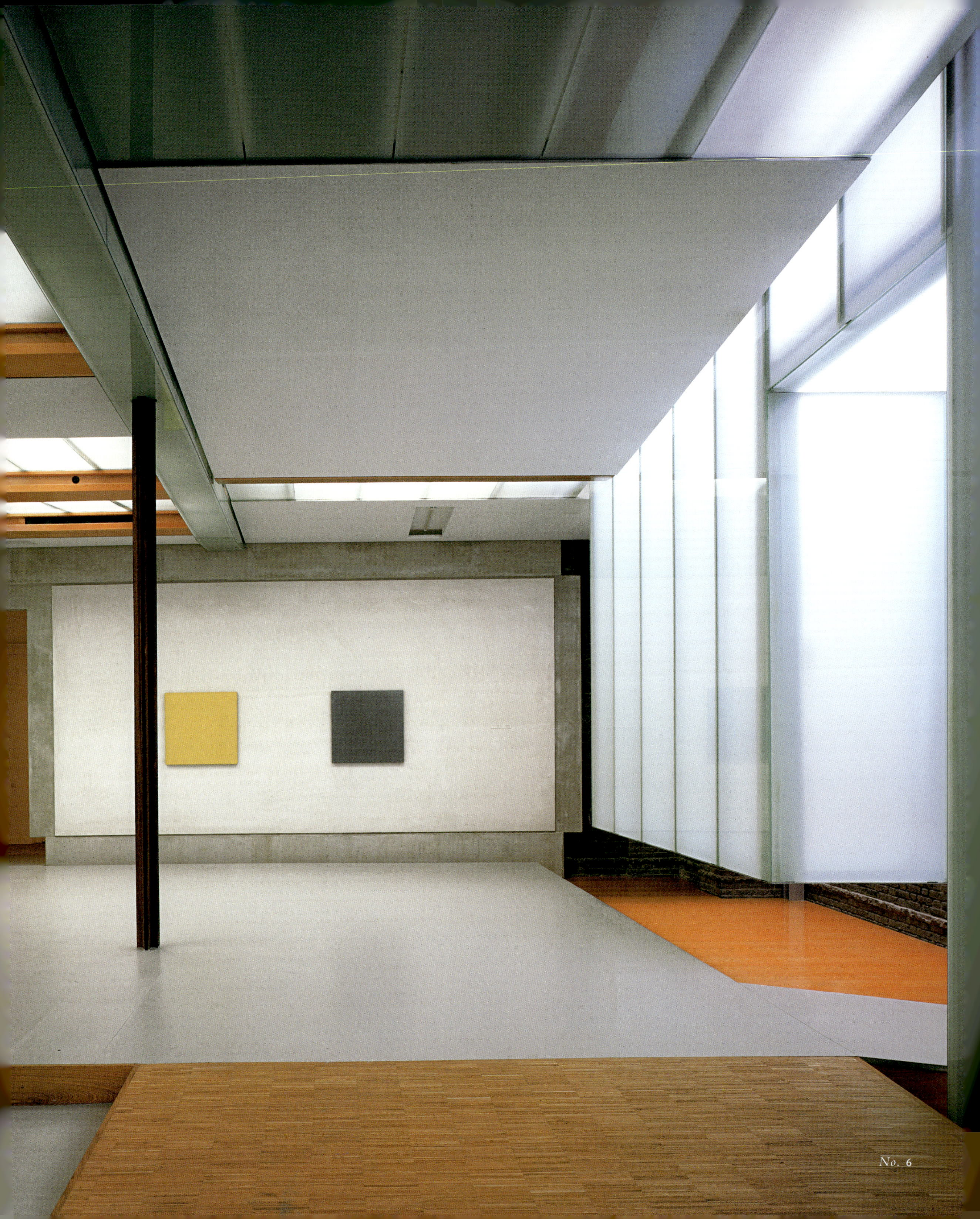

No. 6

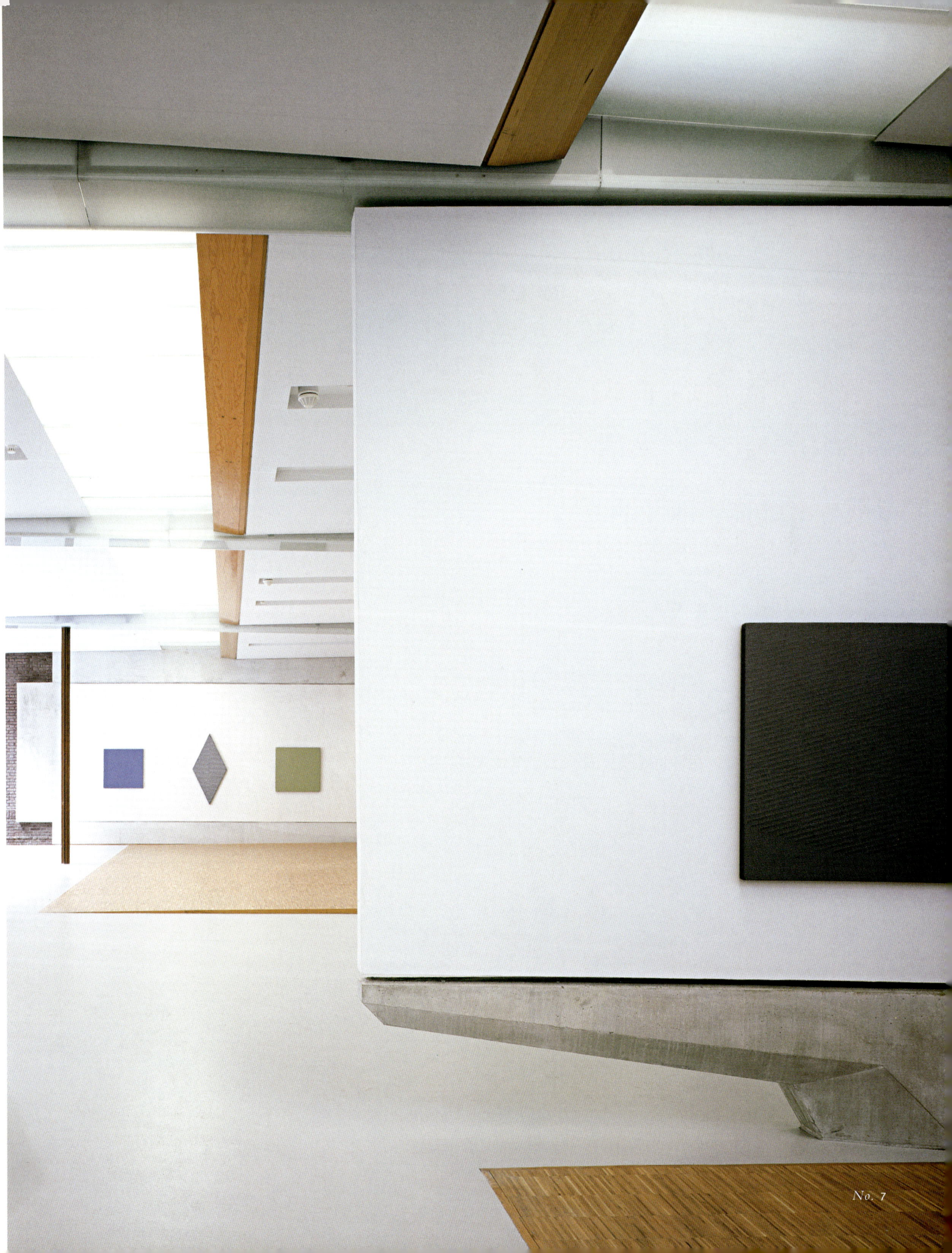

No. 7

SPECIALIZED ART MUSEUMS

North Carolina Pottery Center

1 *PROJECT*
North Carolina Pottery Center | *Seagrove, North Carolina*

2 *ARCHITECT*
Frank Harmon | *Raleigh, North Carolina*

The rich, clay soil of North Carolina is often associated with the tobacco industry. Since Colonial times, however, that soil has yielded clay pots—storage jars, everyday wares, and more aesthetically designed pottery. In fact, more than one hundred potteries have existed over the years in Randolph County alone. Pottery is an art form rooted in tradition and folk lore and to honor this its museum had to be simple yet intricate, solid yet graceful, and most of all, a labor of love. "As the pot always shows the marks of the hands of the potter," architect Frank Harmon says, "I wanted my buildings to show the mark of the builder, with materials and a structure that are both obvious and pleasant to look at."

Set in a grove of oak trees, Harmon designed two buildings as the beginning of a village—a 7,500-square-foot (675-square-meter) museum with a main exhibit area, gift shop, and information desk and a 1,500-square-foot education building with concrete counters for demonstrations and workshops. He choose the vernacular form of a barn and a shed, respectively, with simple massing, metal roofs, southern yellow pine, and coastal white cedar siding—all to give the buildings a look that they had existed on the site for a while.

The main museum—the barn-like building—is entered under a red trellis, which will eventually be covered by vines bearing gourds. This vestibule adjusts our eyes to the lower light levels of the interior. Upon entering, the visitor is surprised by the upward thrust of the museum, which is shaped in the form of a basilica. The space draws natural light from two large clerestories that run the length of the building. Catwalks, visible from below, are used to display archival pottery.

The wood structure is left exposed so that the building could "show its own sense of craft." On the exterior walls, the vertical support members are visible, and roof trusses, lookouts, and outriggers reveal themselves. Inside, columns built-up from pieces of southern yellow pine, seem almost woven together. The education building's wide, shaded porch recollects another common feature of home studios, where artists have long worked the soil into pots.

No. 1
Description

caption photo

No. 1 The interior of the museum is bathed in sunlight, which reflects off the warm knotty pine floor.

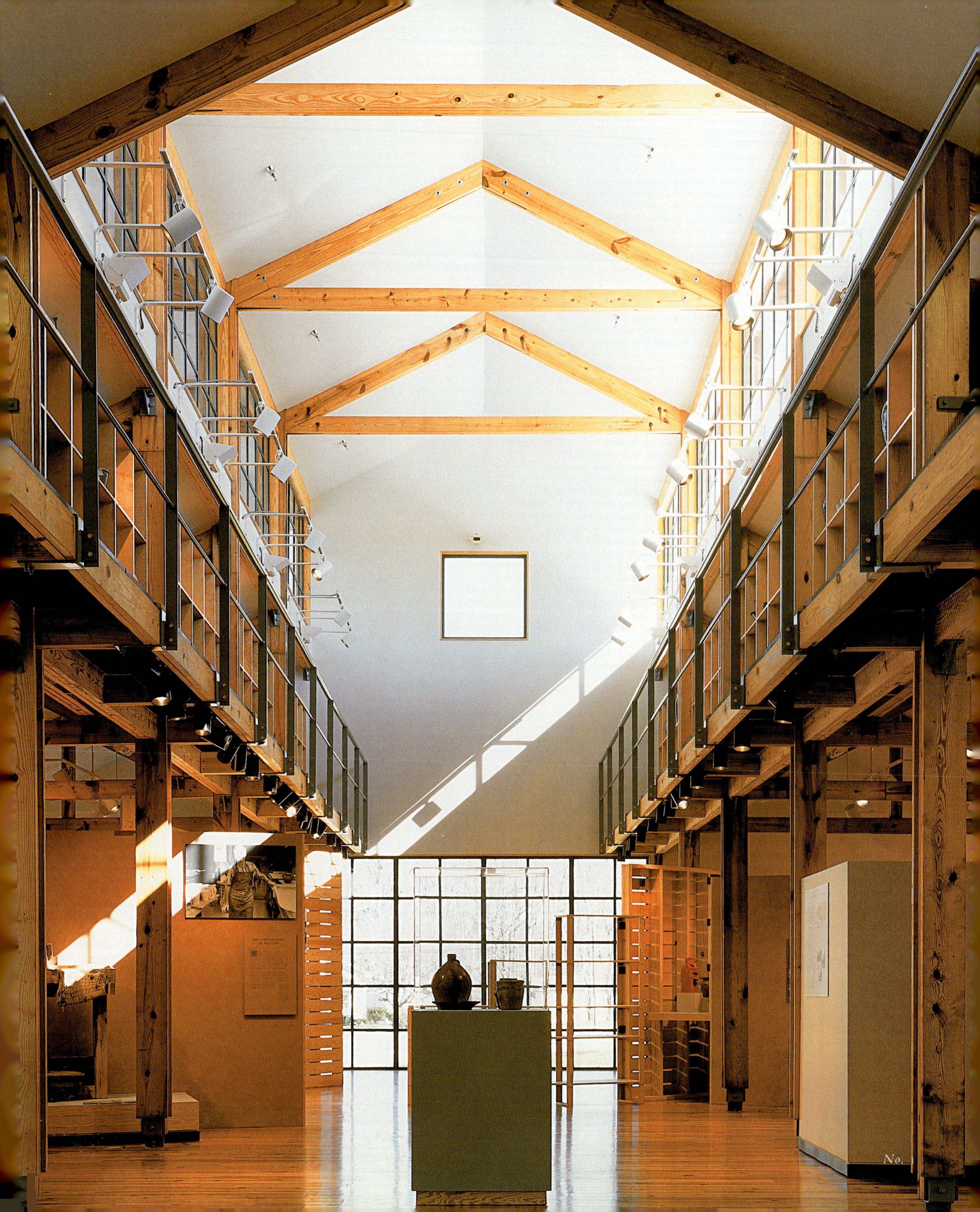

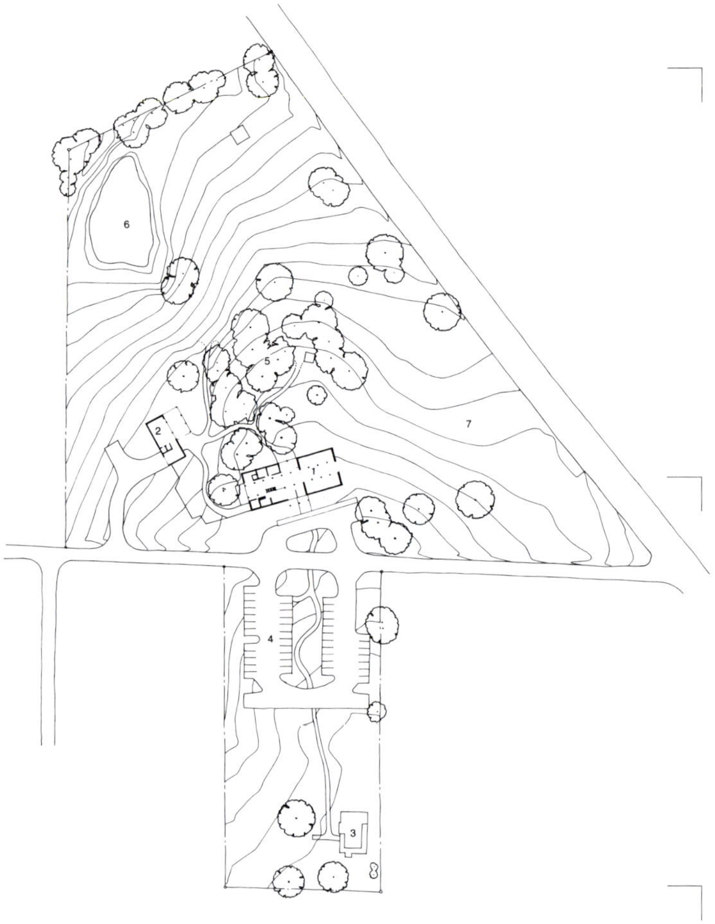

No. 2.5

DESCRIPTION

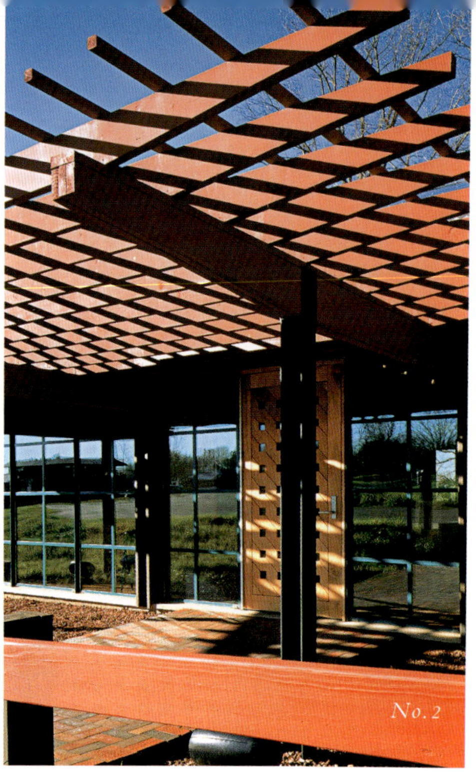

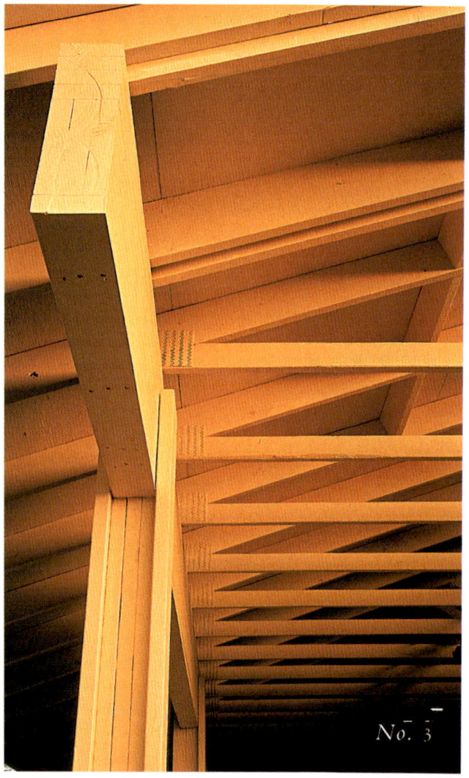

caption photo

No. 2 The trellis that serves as an entrance canopy also acts as a welcoming transition between the bight sunlight and the softer light of the interior spaces.

No. 3 For the building's structure (in detail), southern yellow pine supports a metal roof.

No. 4 The well-crafted exhibition space relates the simplicity of the building's overall design.

No. 5 The 9000-square-foot museum recalls the barn-like structures that dominate the landscape in this rural North Carolina county. The 1,400-square-foot education building with a large porch overlooking a pond is used for demonstrations and workshops.

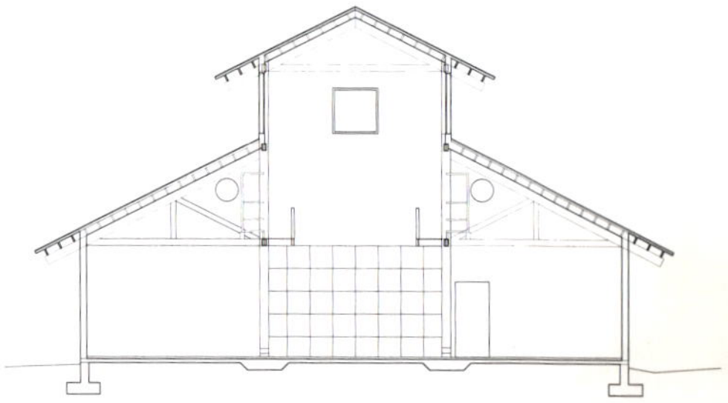

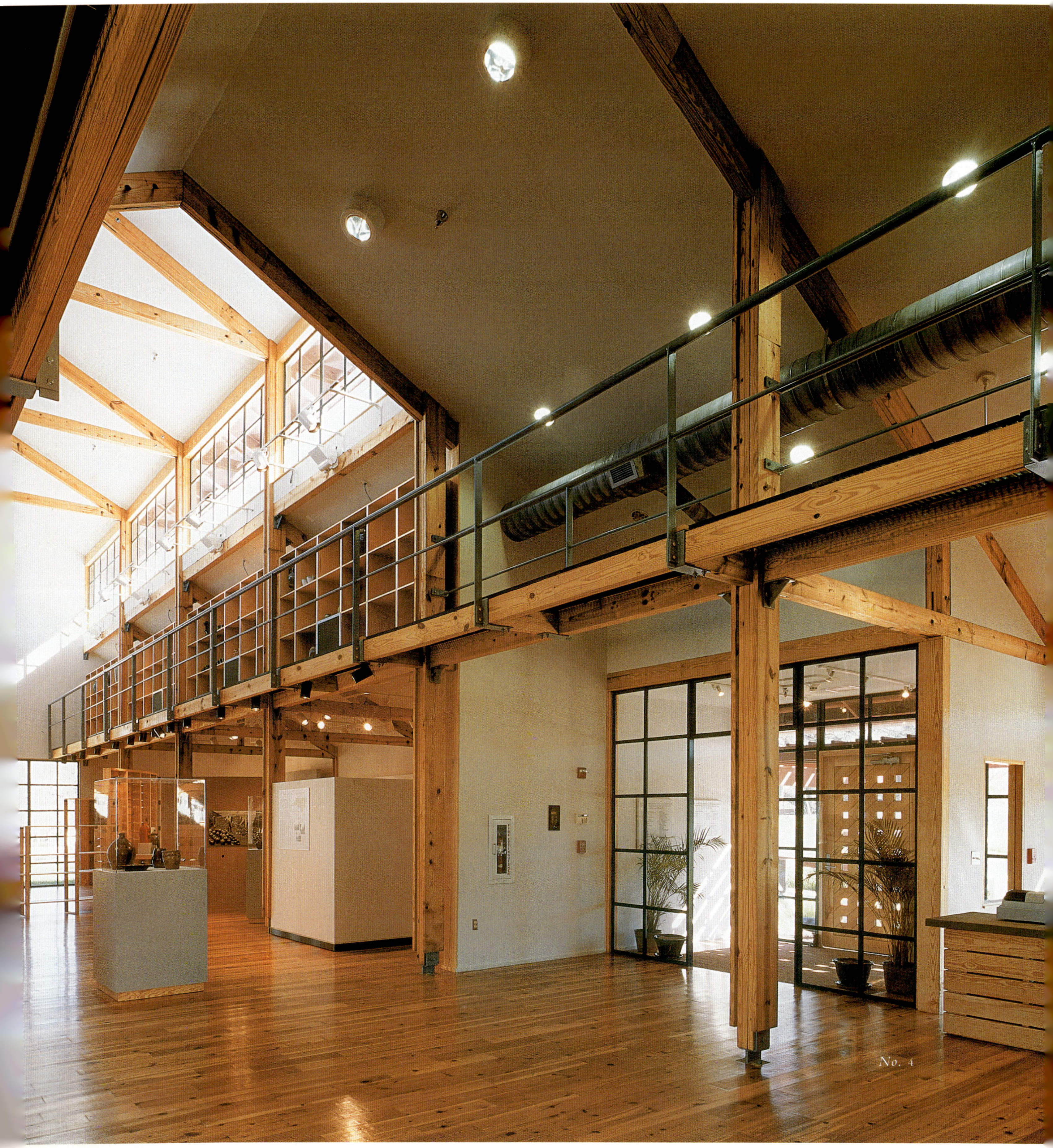
No. 4

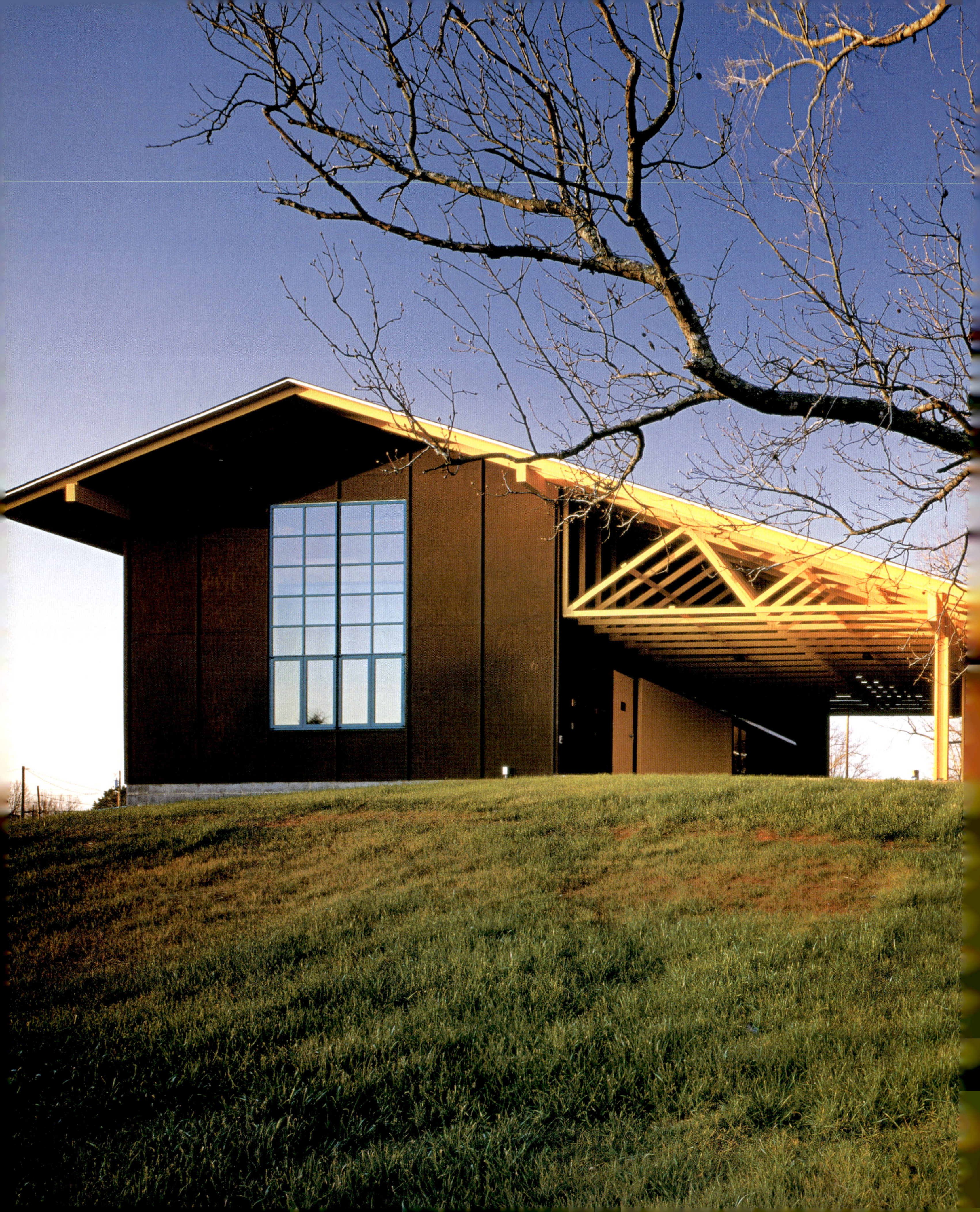

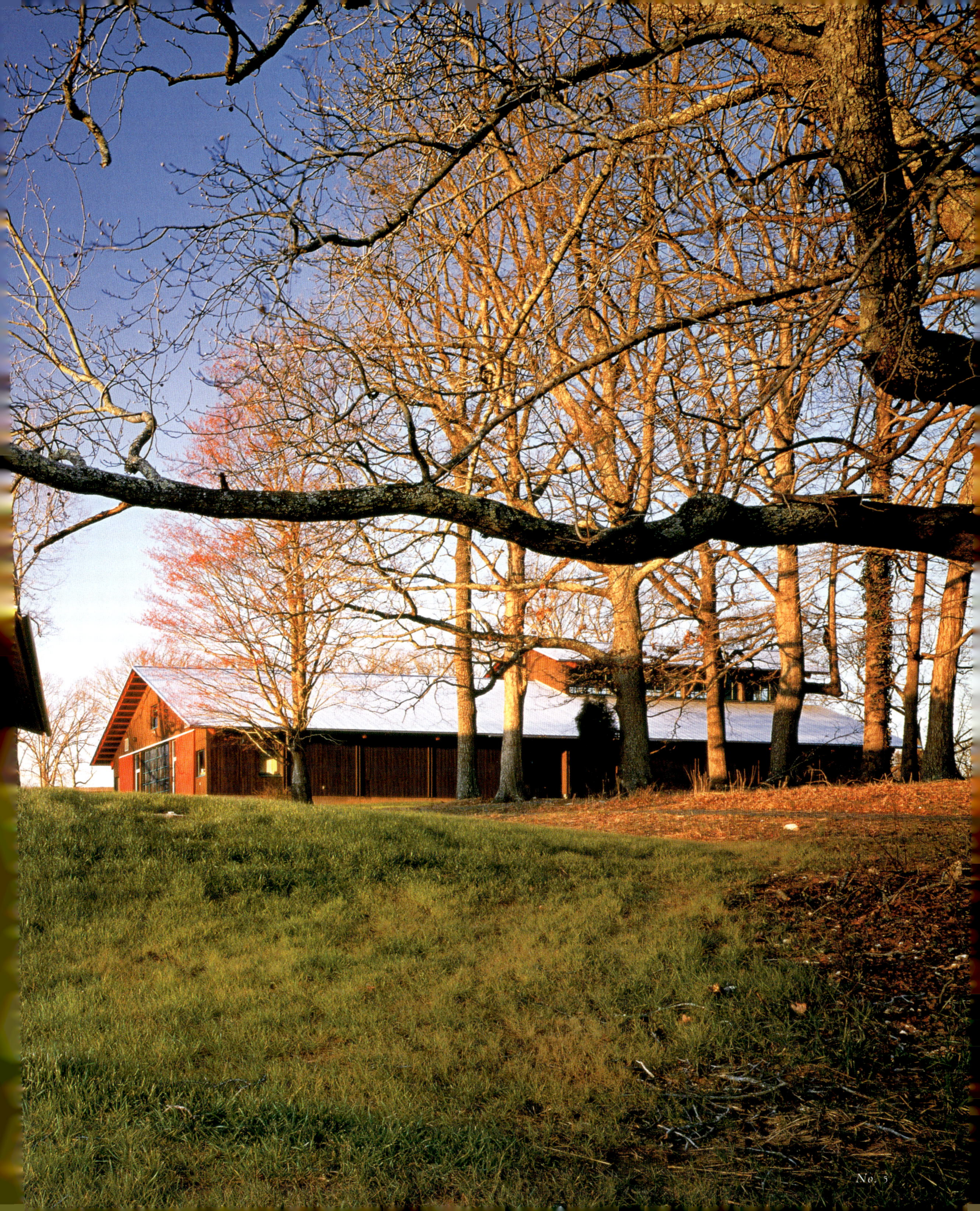
No. 5

Rodin Museum

1 *PROJECT*
Rodin Museum | *Samsung Headquarters, Seoul, Korea*

2 *ARCHITECT*
KPF Associates PC | *New York, New York*

In our fast-paced, twenty-first century cities it's rare to find a shelter for contemplation, where two magnificent works of art are carefully framed for display. Samsung's Rodin Museum, designed by Kevin Kennon of Kohn Pederson Fox, is such a place—a luminous sanctuary set in the heart of Seoul. Within the pavilion, two of Rodin's masterpieces create a unique spatial tension—a "pas-de-deux" between two glass walls.

Originally, Rodin's *Burghers of Calais* and *Gates of Hell* were slated for outdoor display, but Seoul's air quality and environmental conditions necessitated an enclosure. The Samsung Group chose KPF to design a pavilion at the base of its 26-story, headquarters building in downtown Seoul. The architect choose the form of a glass pavilion as a simple gesture that would create tension between the spatial complexity of the *Burghers of Calais* and the frontal nature of the *Gates of Hell*. To recreate the moody light found in Rodin's Paris, three types of glass were chosen—acid-etched, sandblasted and clear-glazed glass. Basically, a flat, glass roof joins two nested glass walls, each canting and curving at different angles and heights. The envelope is made by bolting two layers of glass to an internal steel frame.

Visitors enter through a steel-framed portal in a slot between the curving glass. Directly in front of the entrance is *Burghers*, set against the curving wall so that visitors can view the muscular sculpture from every angle. Across the pavilion is the *Gates of Hell*, cradled by curving walls of glass to permit only a frontal view. The only other object in the pavilion is a chamfered limestone bench. The museum's bookstore and information desk are tucked underneath the Samsung highrise. The result is a space of amazing purity and grace that is filled with softly filtered light during the day and glows luminescently at night.

No. 1
Description

caption photo

No. 1 At the entrance to the gallery, the glass wall system is visible—a translucent exterior glass skin and an interior glass surface attached to blots by structural fins.

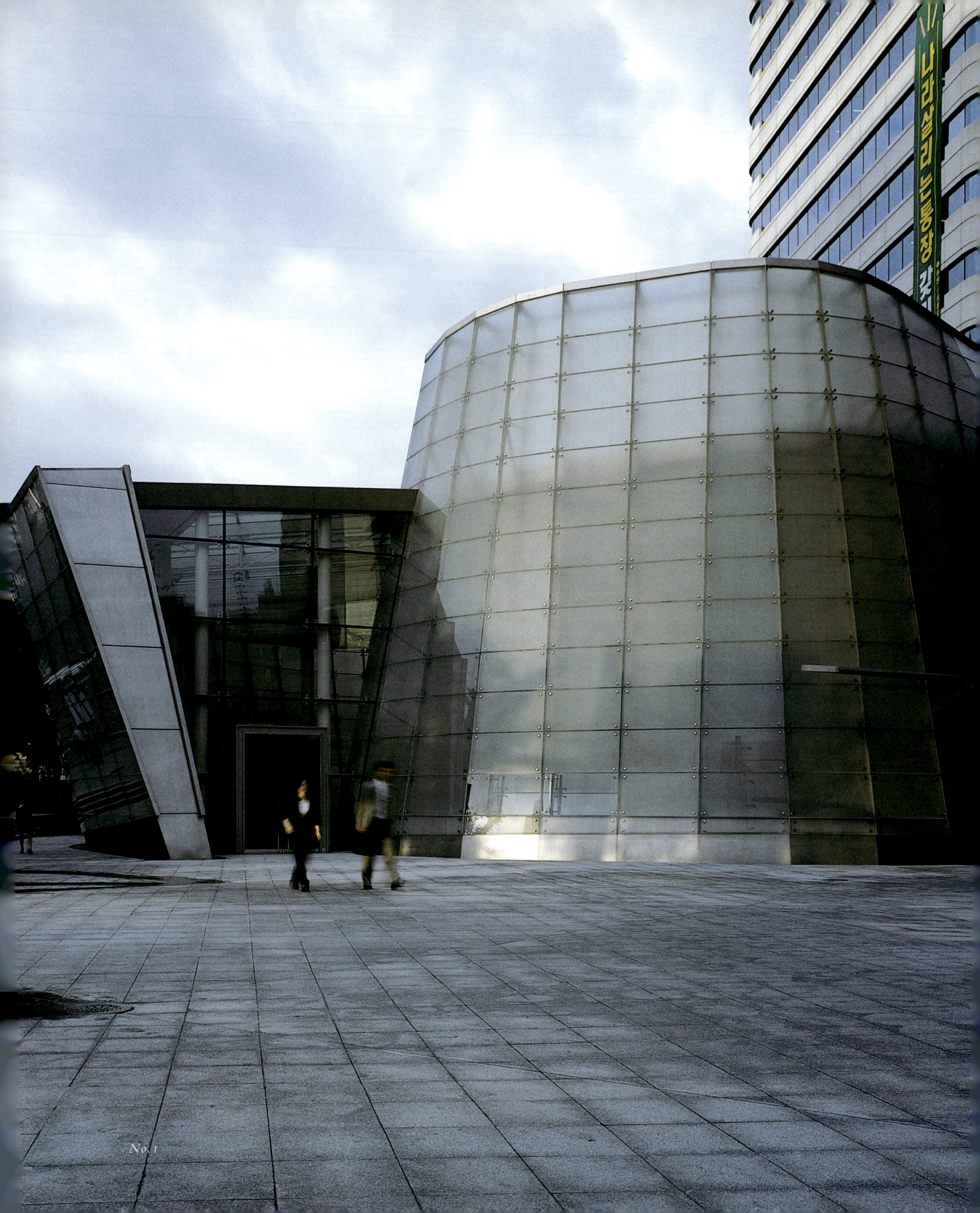
나라살리는통장
No.1

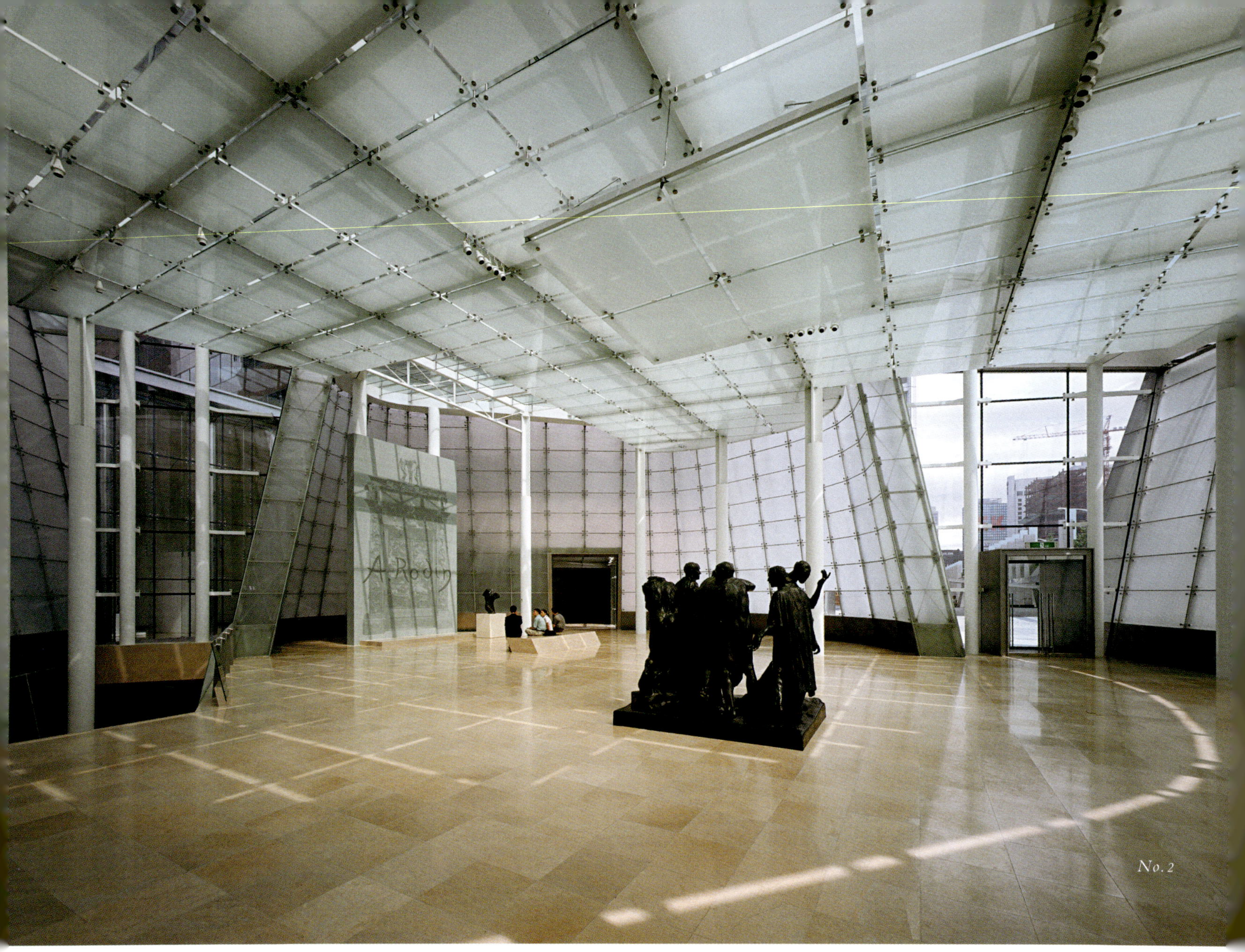
A. Rodin

No. 2

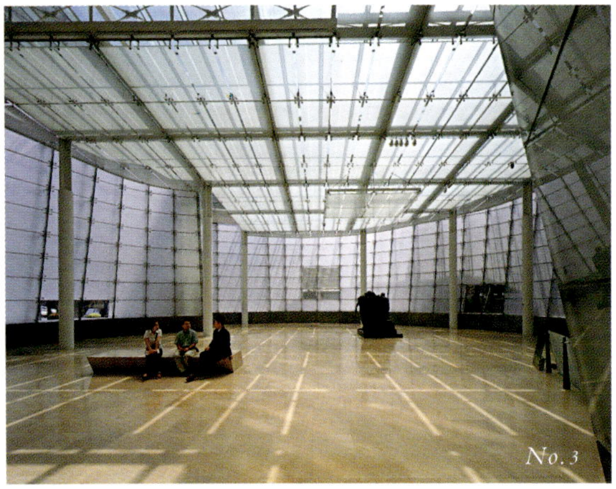

No. 3

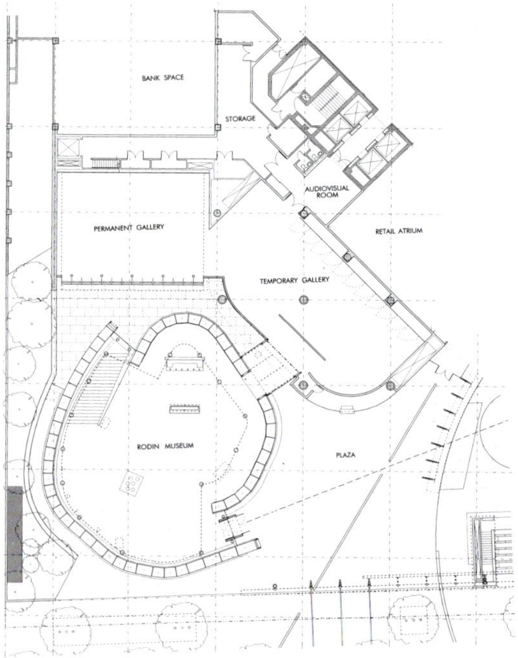
BANK SPACE
STORAGE
AUDIOVISUAL ROOM
PERMANENT GALLERY
RETAIL ATRIUM
TEMPORARY GALLERY
RODIN MUSEUM
PLAZA

No. 2-4

DESCRIPTION

caption photo

No. 2, 3 & 4 The glass roof is supported by steel columns and is conceived of as an independent element, a natural plane sloping below the glass walls. The glass pavilion houses only two Rodin masterpieces—*Burghers of Calais* and the *Gates of Hell*.

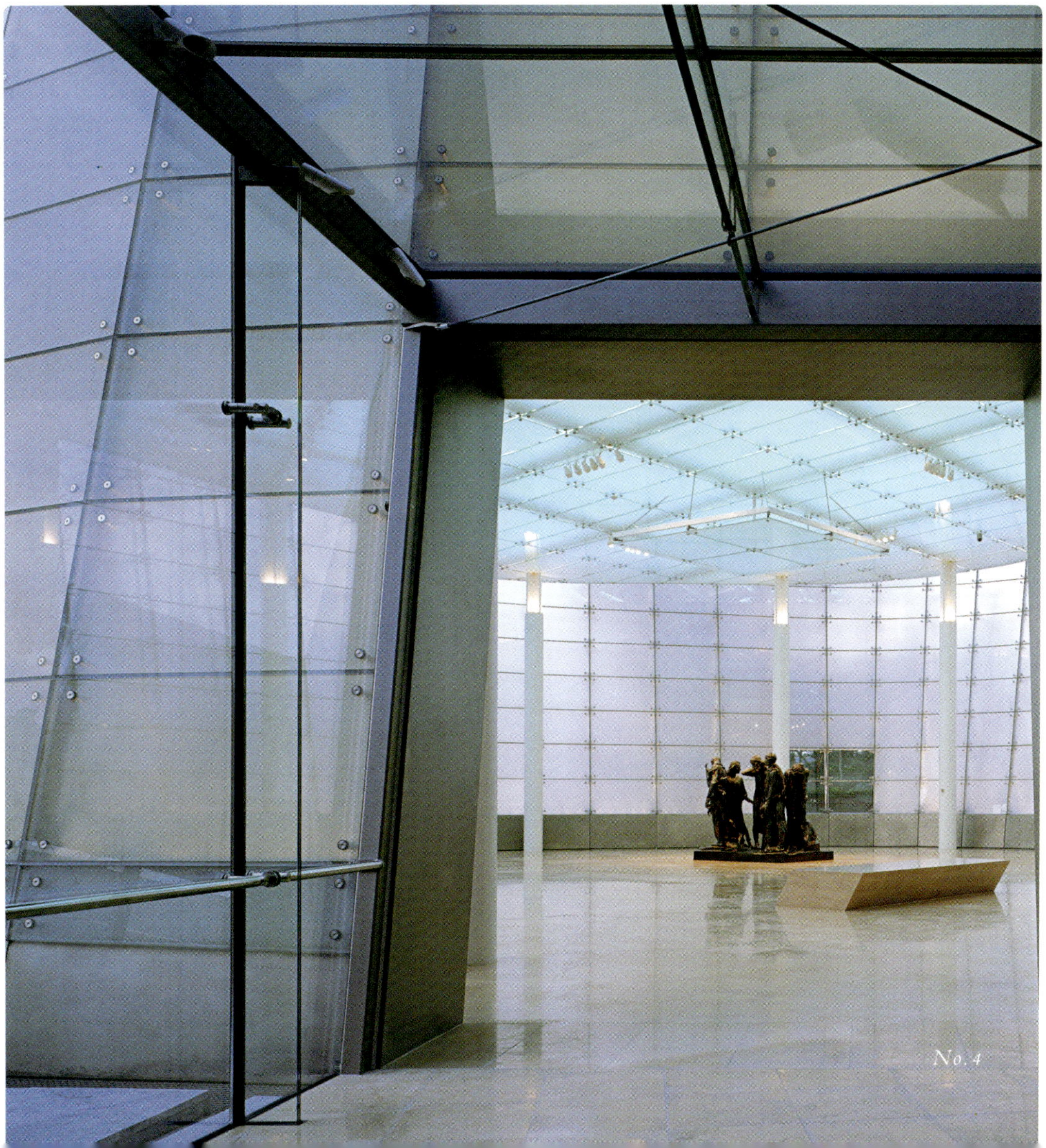

caption photo

No.5 Originally intended to be displayed outdoors, the poor air quality of Seoul's urban environment necessitated the enclosure of Rodin's sculpture. In order to view the sculptures as intended the museum is primarily glass, capturing as much natural light as possible.

No. 6 Located in Tapyungro, one of Seoul's main thoroughfares, the gallery is connected to other main buildings in the area. The entire complex is linked to the Samsung headquarters building by a series of metal columns.

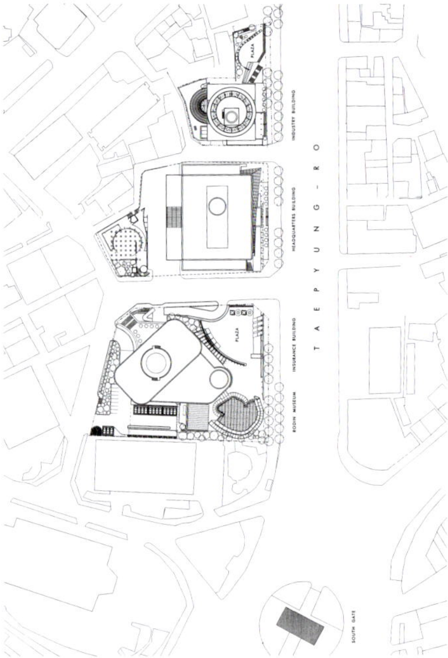

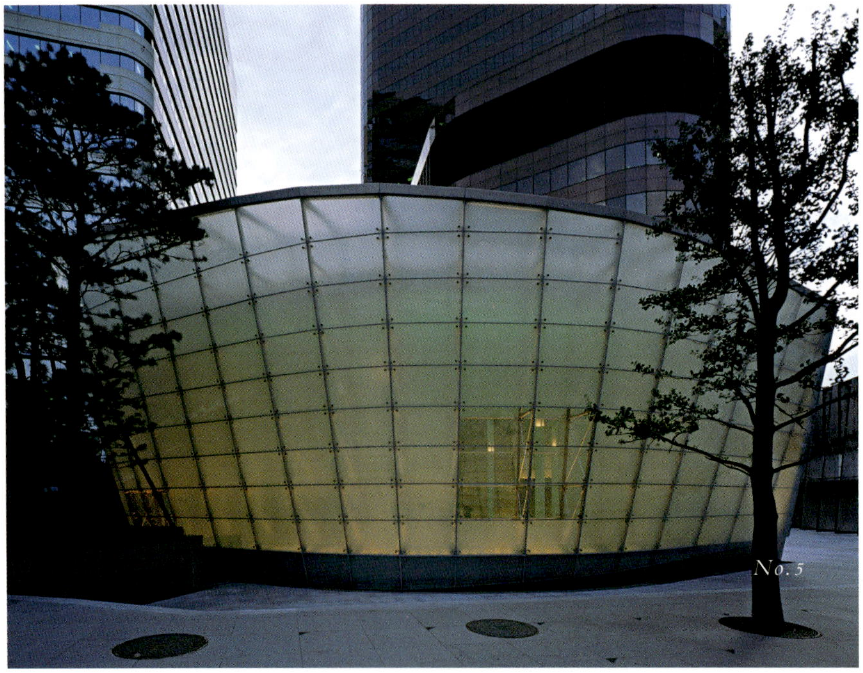
No.5

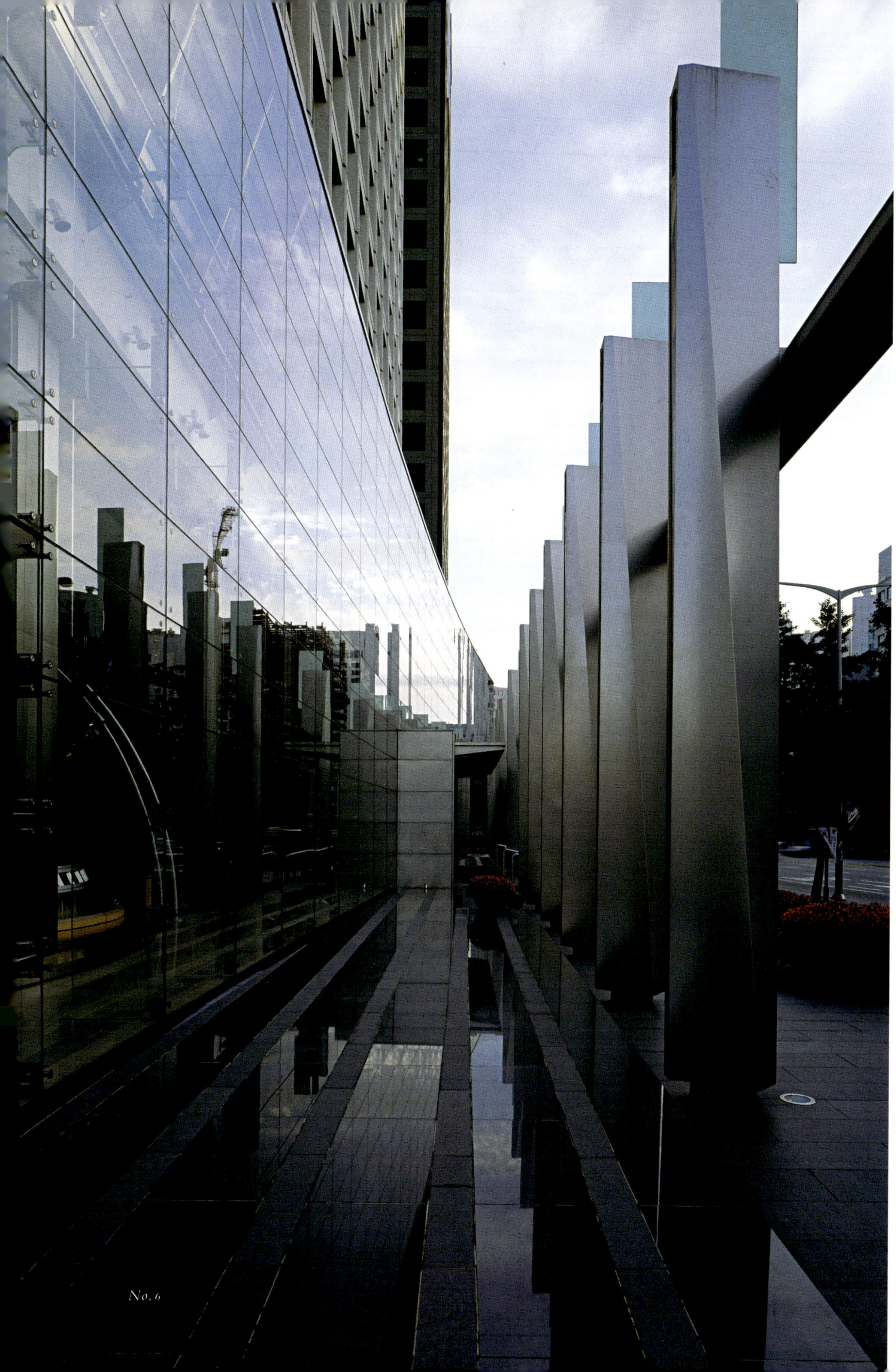

No. 6

New Wing of the Van Gogh Museum

1 *PROJECT*
New Wing of the Van Gogh Museum | *Amsterdam, The Netherlands*

2 *ARCHITECT*
Kisho Kurokawa Architect & Associates | *Tokyo, Japan*

Located in the heart of Amsterdam, the Van Gogh Museum houses the world's largest collection of works by the artist. Since it opened in 1973, it has drawn far more visitors than expected. An addition, however, posed site problems, as it would extend into a significant downtown park. The solution by architect Kisho Kurokawa, was to place 75 percent of the new building underground, thus diminishing its impact on the site.

Dutch architect Gerrit Rietveld designed the original museum, although Rietveld passed away during the planning stage of the work and his disciples finished the project. The original museum does express Rietveld's characteristic use of linear and planar elements. In keeping with this rigorous abstract ideology, Kurokawa uses his own geometry—circular, semicircular, and elliptical shapes—to form the much-needed addition.

The main museum and new wing are connected by a sunken garden. The courtyard functions as a water garden with constantly flowing water, an abstraction of a Japanese garden. The basement exhibition corridor and exhibition rooms are surrounded by the ellipse pond, which creates an intermediate space between the interior and exterior. The wall facing the garden is slightly tilted.

Van Gogh's personal collection of Japanese *ukiyoe* prints are housed in a square shaped mezzanine gallery that has been rotated so one corner juts out of the wall into the sunken garden.

The distorted volumes of the museum aim at creating a spatial composition that echoes the anti-*Bourbaki* world of Japanese art.

No. 1
Description

Caption
Photo

No. 1 The new wing faces the existing museum.

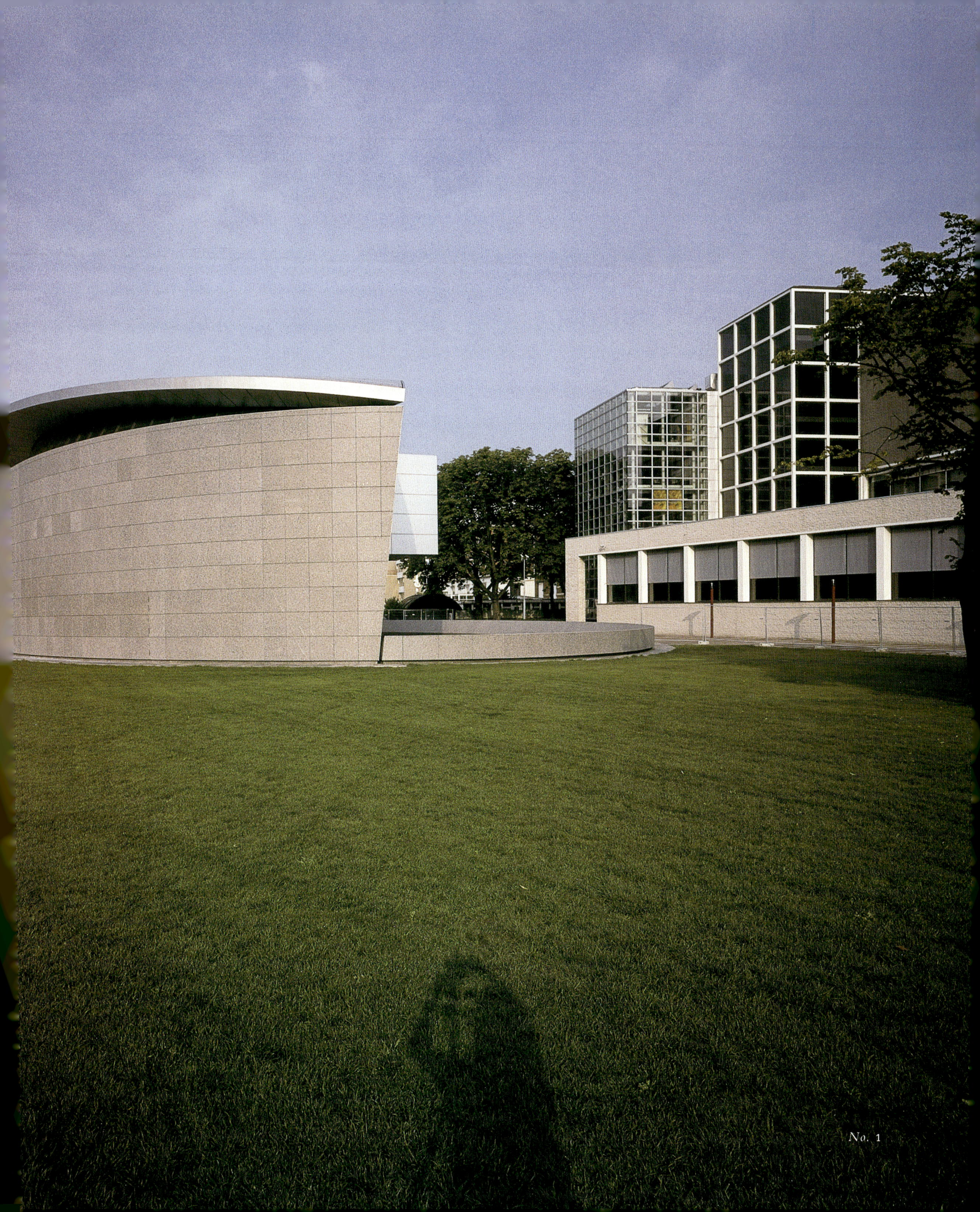

No. 1

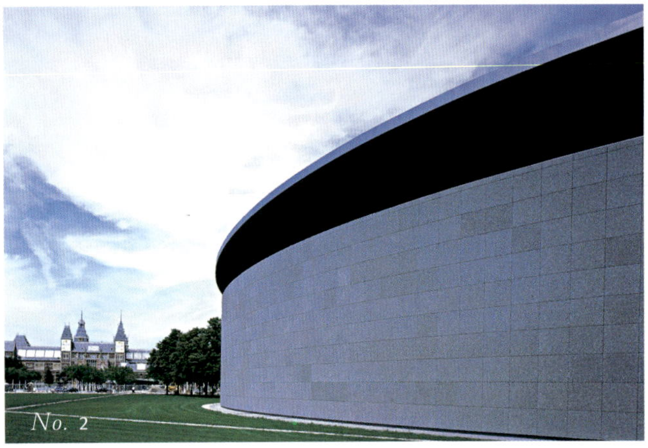
No. 2

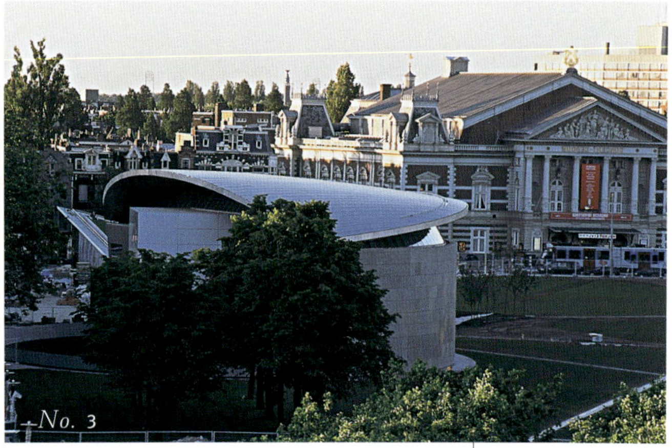
No. 3

No. 2-4

DESCRIPTION

CAPTION PHOTO

No. 2-4 The building's shape reflects the architect's fascination with abstract geometry. Between the new wing and the existing building is a sunken garden onto which the lower level corridor opens.

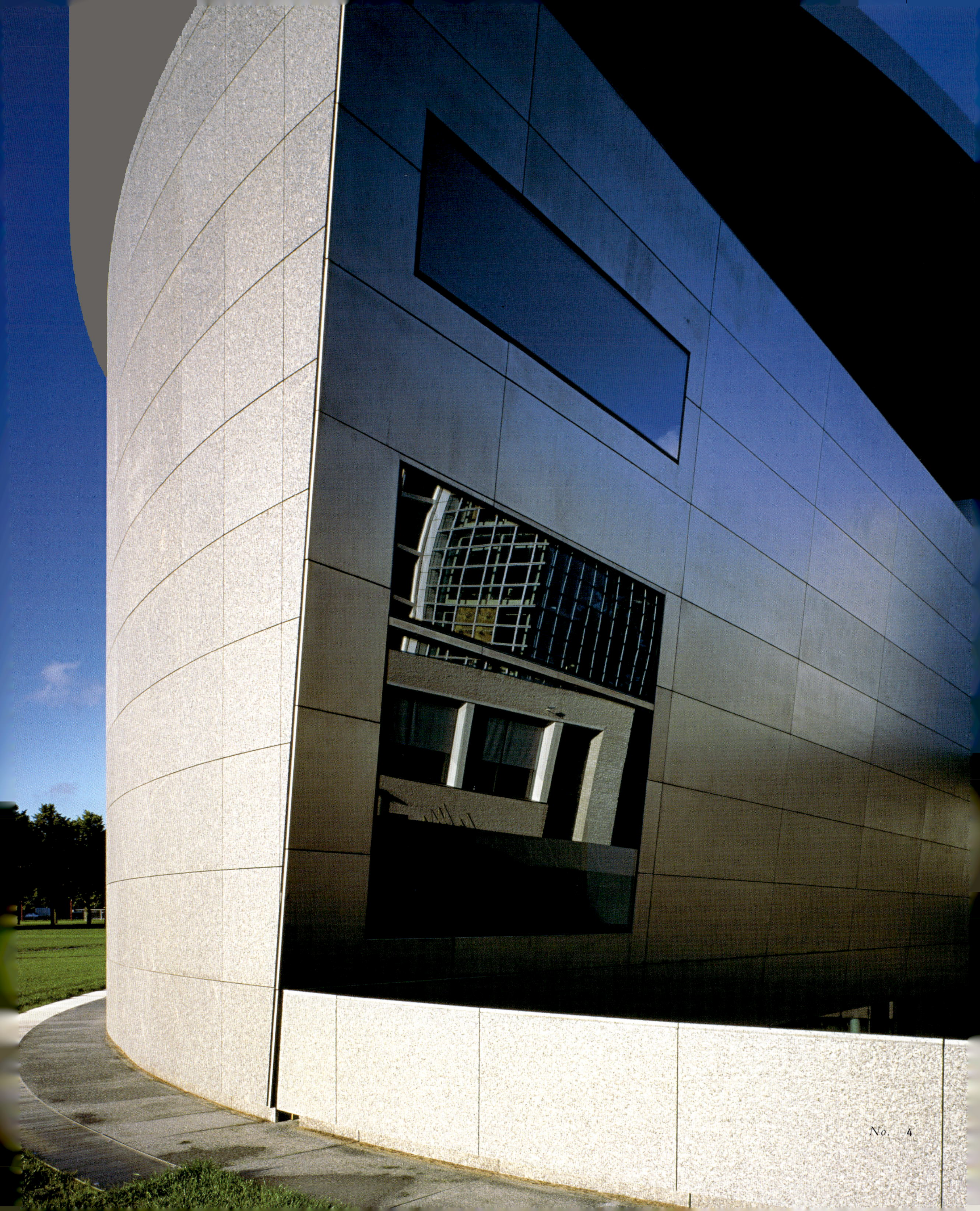

No. 4

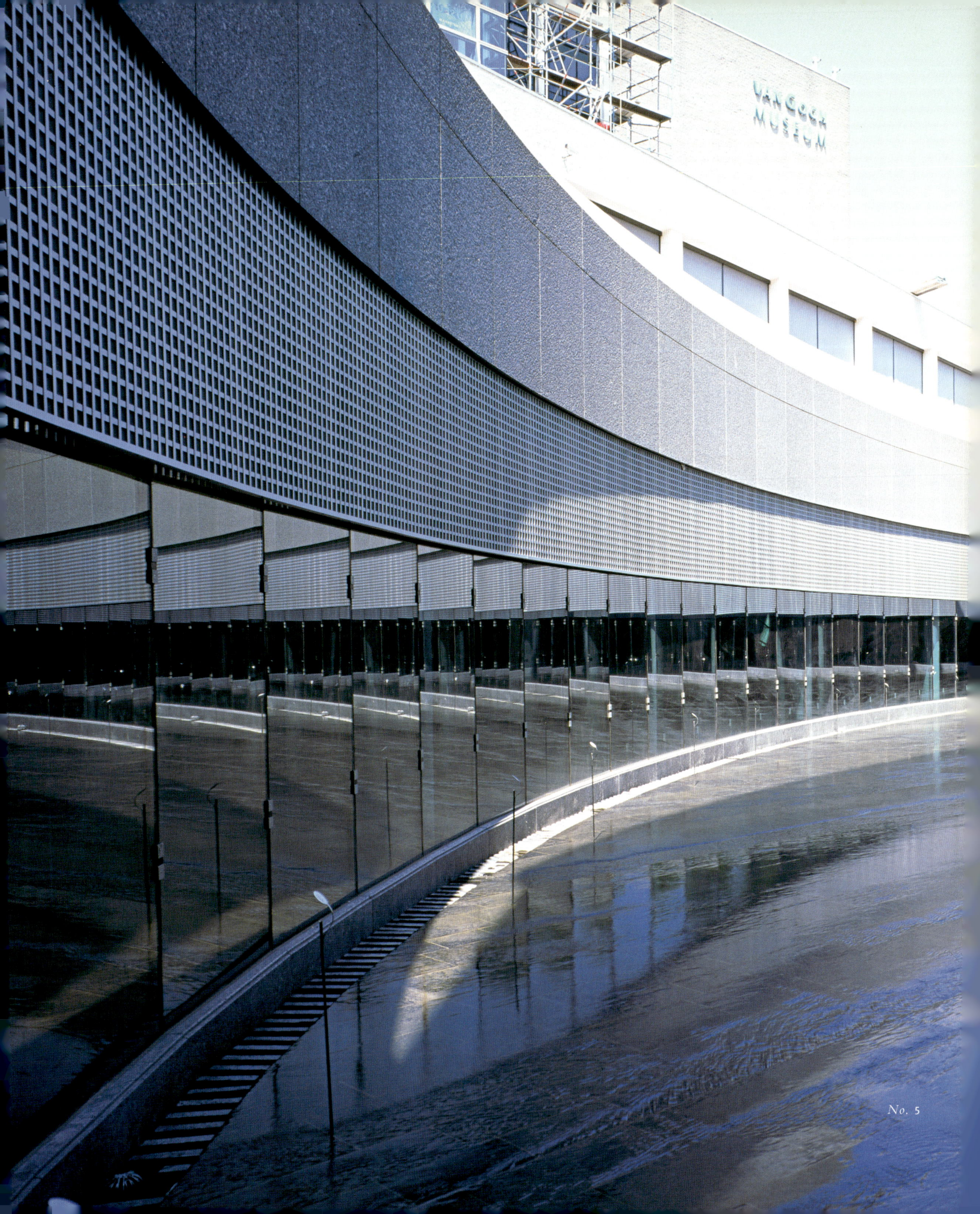

No. 5

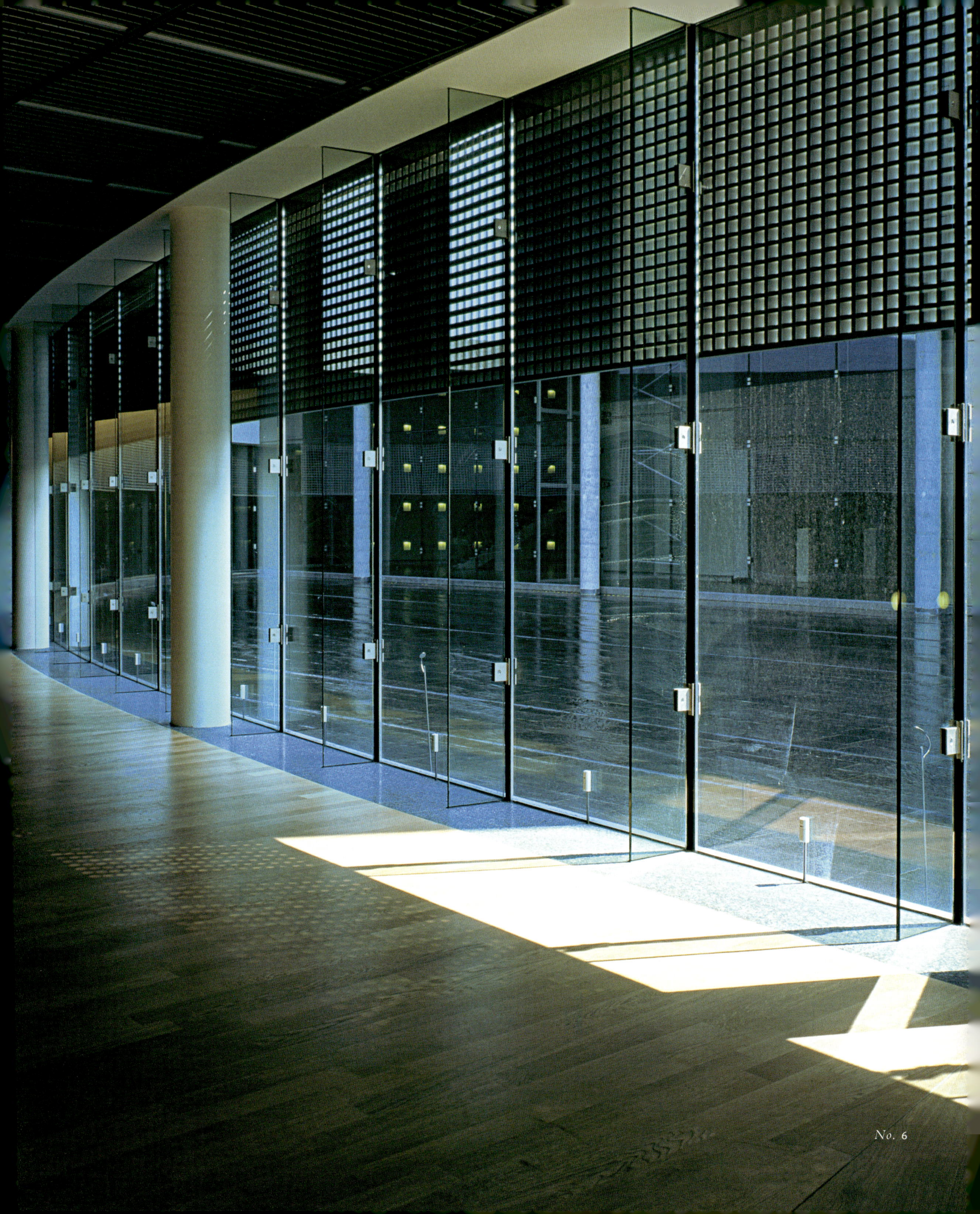

No. 6

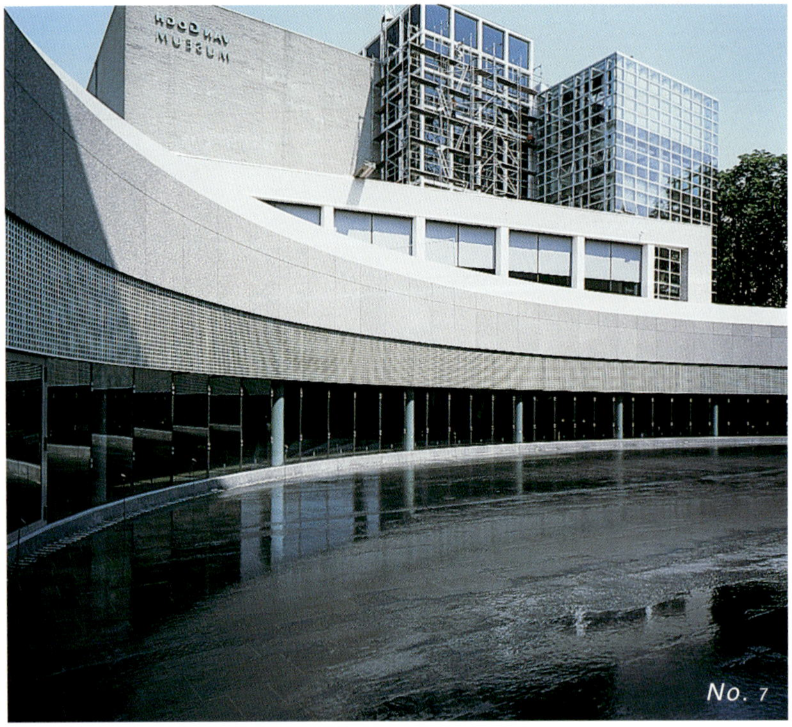

No. 5-8

DESCRIPTION

CAPTION PHOTO

No. 5-8 VIEW OF THE SUNKEN GARDEN BETWEEN THE EXISTING MUSEUM AND THE ADDITION.

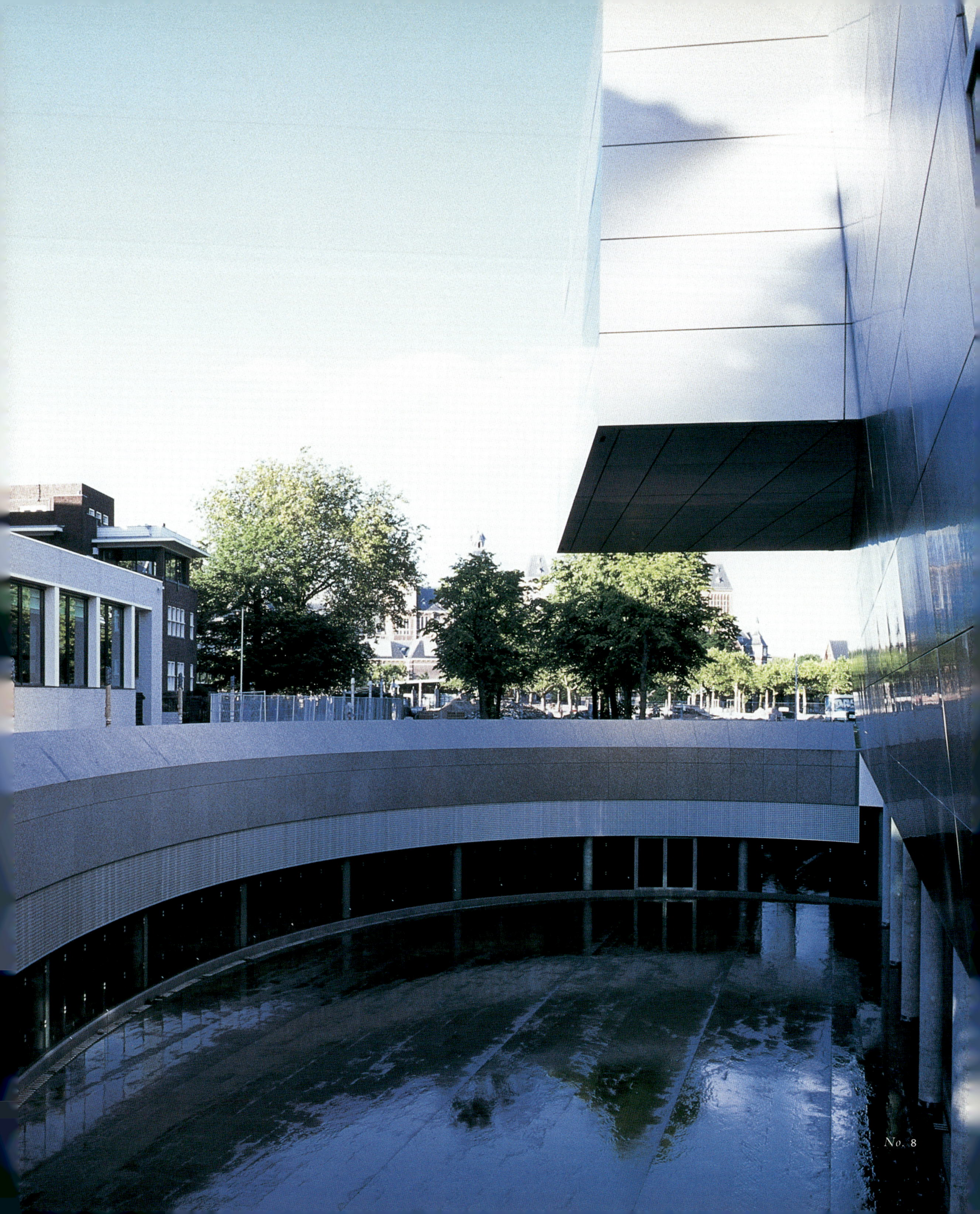

No. 8

Felix Nussbaum Museum

1 *PROJECT*
Felix Nussbaum Museum | *OSNABRUCK, GERMANY*

2 *ARCHITECT*
Daniel Libeskind | *BERLIN, GERMANY*

In plan, particularly, the design of the Nussbaum Museum appears to be a simple intersection of three rectangular volumes. Yet, in reality, the museum is meant to be much more. Architect Daniel Libeskind sought an emotional architectural experience, a "museum without exit," which would symbolize the artist's restlessness, exile, and search for orientation.

Felix Nussbaum was born in Osnabruck in 1904 and studied art in Hamburg and Berlin, where, in 1927 he had his first solo exhibition. In the 1930s, his work was compared to that of Henri Rousseau and Vincent van Gogh. Information about major events in Nussbaum's life's events is scattered throughout the building's spaces—his scholarship period in Rome, his travels via Paris to Berlin, his futile attempts to escape from the Nazis through France and Belgium, his deportation and murder in Auschwitz. Before his imprisonment and tragic end, Nussbaum produced in his paintings one of the most profound expressions of human suffering in this century.

Yet, the museum's design is highly unconventional and reads as a layering of space and meaning. Disorienting effects riddle the interior spaces. For example, a particular space may appear to allude to one thing upon entering and then appear to be something quite different when looking back from another side. Libeskind achieves this with three dimensional spatial manipulations, such as sloped floors and ceilings and nonparallel walls. Spaces even fold back upon themselves. The spaces are familiar, yet different in form and concept, questioning our preconceptions.

The building consists of three main components. Made of exposed concrete, the two-story Nussbaum Corridor is 150 feet long and 10 feet wide (45-meters long and 3 meters wide). The two-level zinc-clad Nussbaum Bridge links the new museum to the old. The oak-clad box contains most of the gallery and work space.

No. 1

DESCRIPTION

CAPTION

PHOTO

No. 1 DEDICATED TO THE LIFE AND WORK OF THE MAJOR TWENTIETH-CENTURY ARTIST FELIX NUSSBAUM, DANIEL LIBESKIND'S DESIGN FOR THE MUSEUM IS BASED ON A SERIES OF INTERRELATED LINES, WHICH SYMBOLIZES NUSSBAUM'S RESTLESSNESS, EXILE, AND SEARCH FOR ORIENTATION.

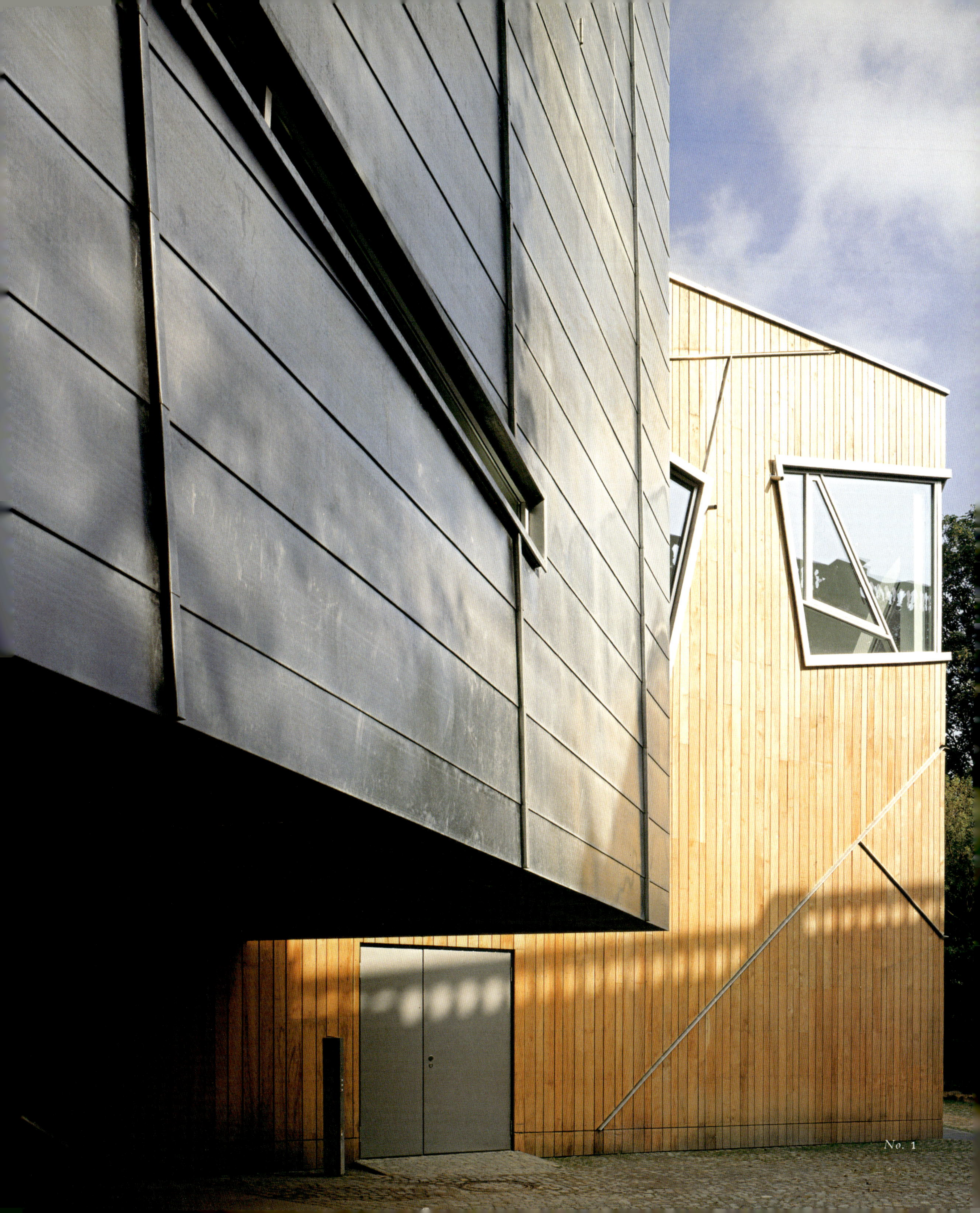
No. 1

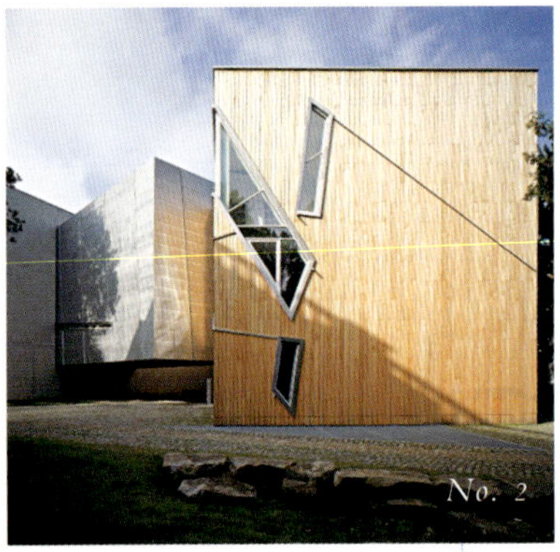
No. 2

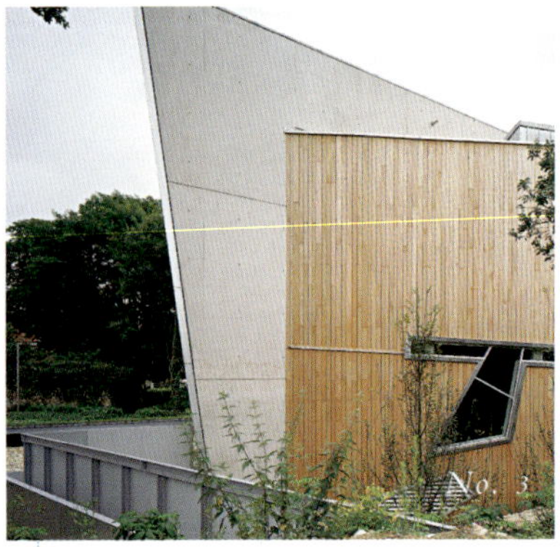
No. 3

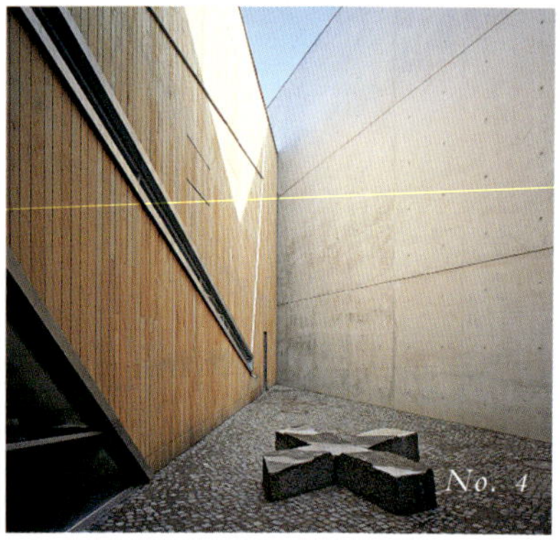
No. 4

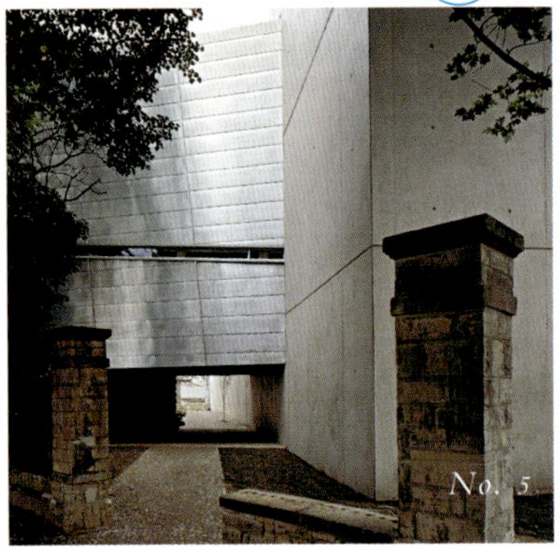
No. 5

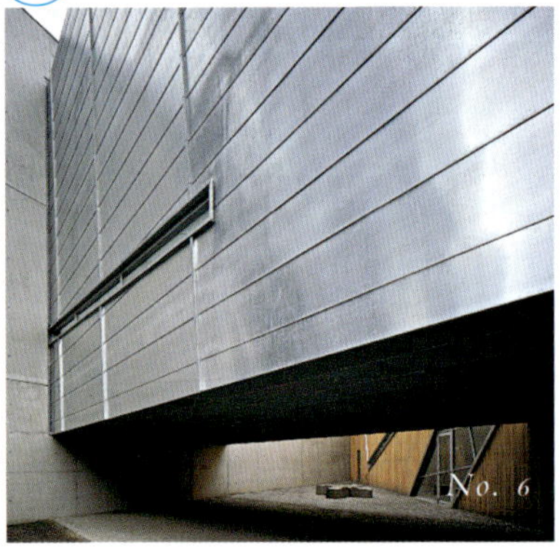
No. 6

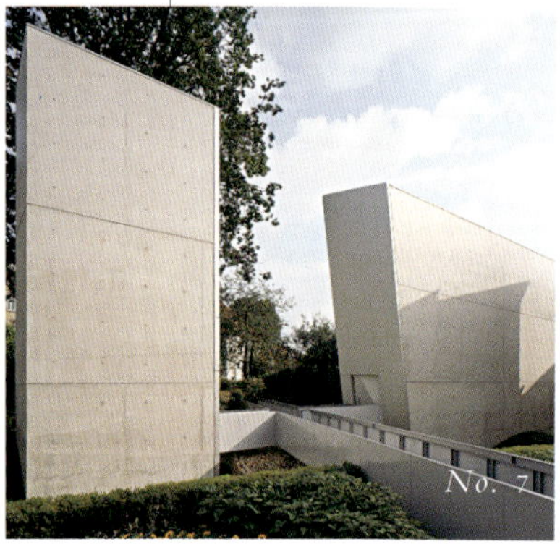
No. 7

No. 2-10 DESCRIPTION

CAPTION PHOTO

No. 2-8 The maze-like building uses wood, concrete, and zinc sheeting and incorporates a seventeenth-century bridge that was uncovered during construction.

No. 9 The Nussbaum Corridor is a long, windowless hallway of exposed concrete.

No. 10 The spatial illusions extend into the gallery spaces.

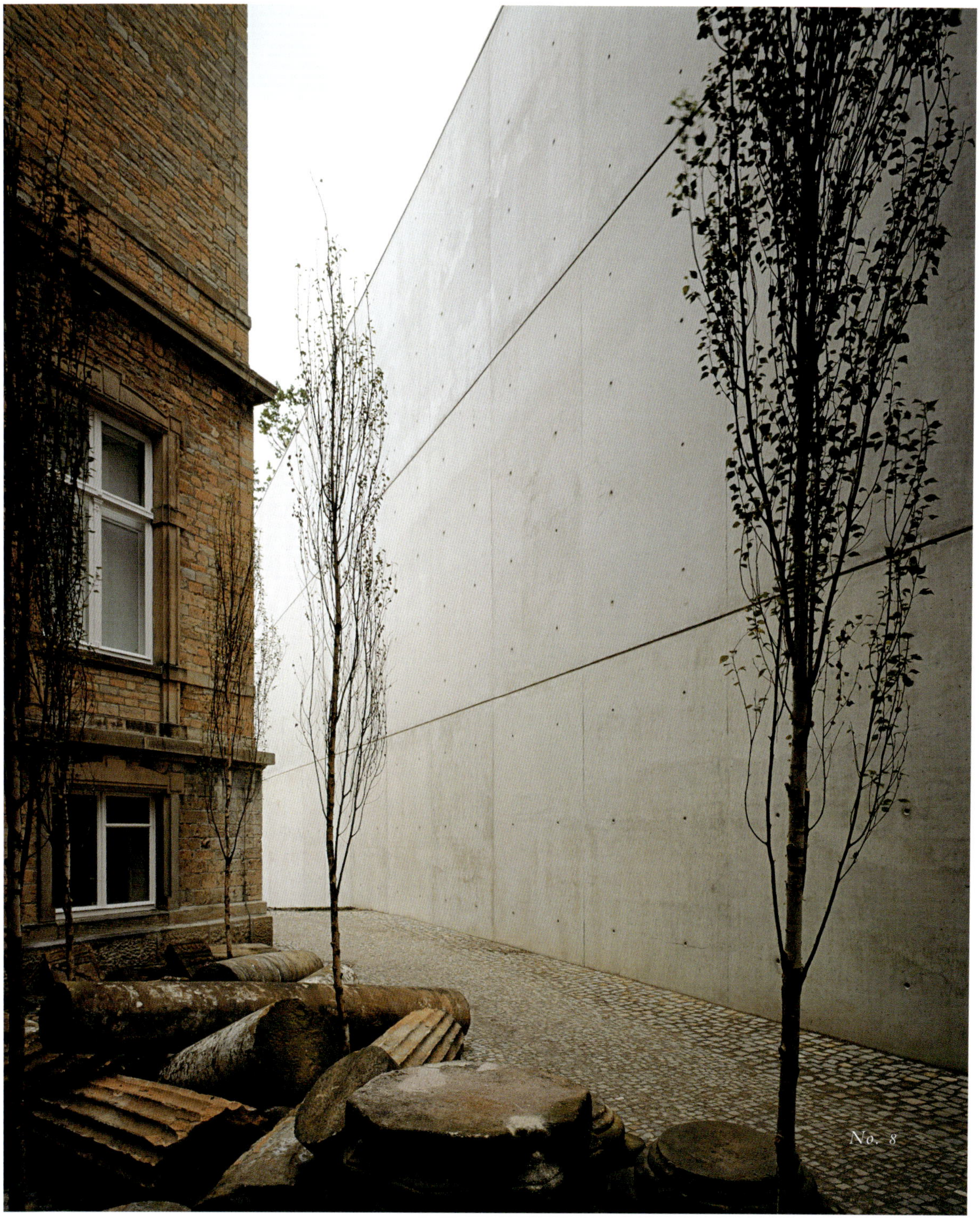
No. 8

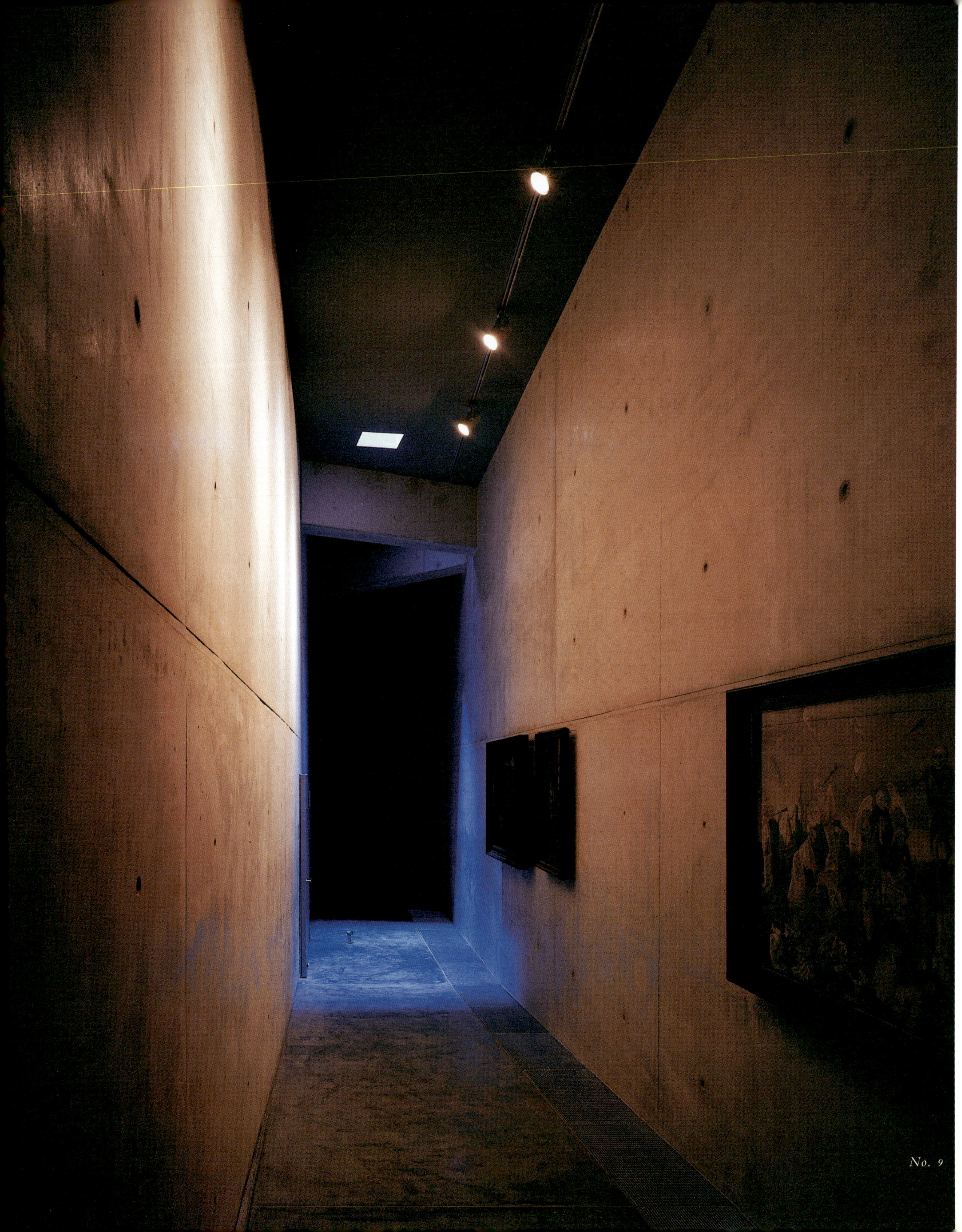

No. 9

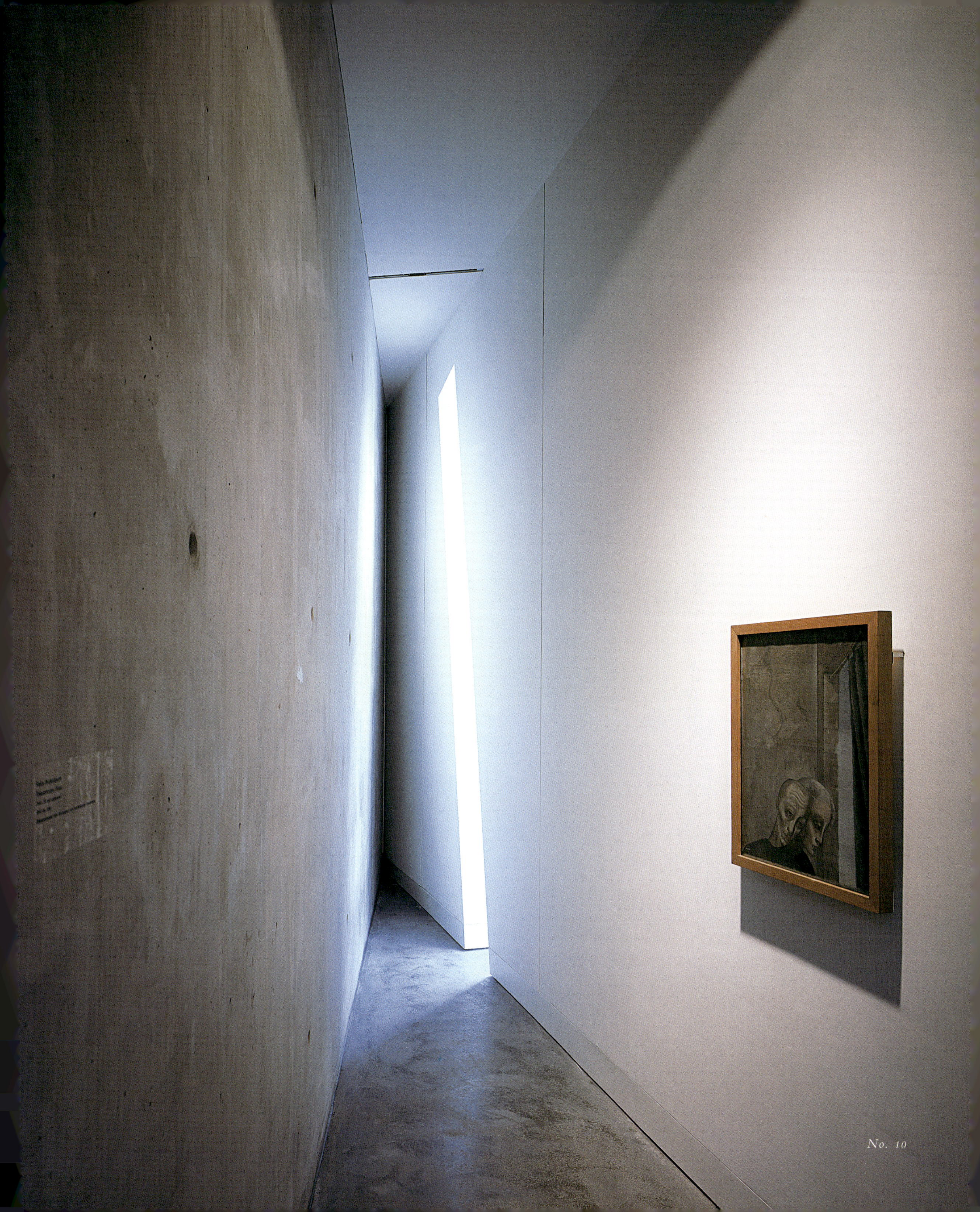

No. 10

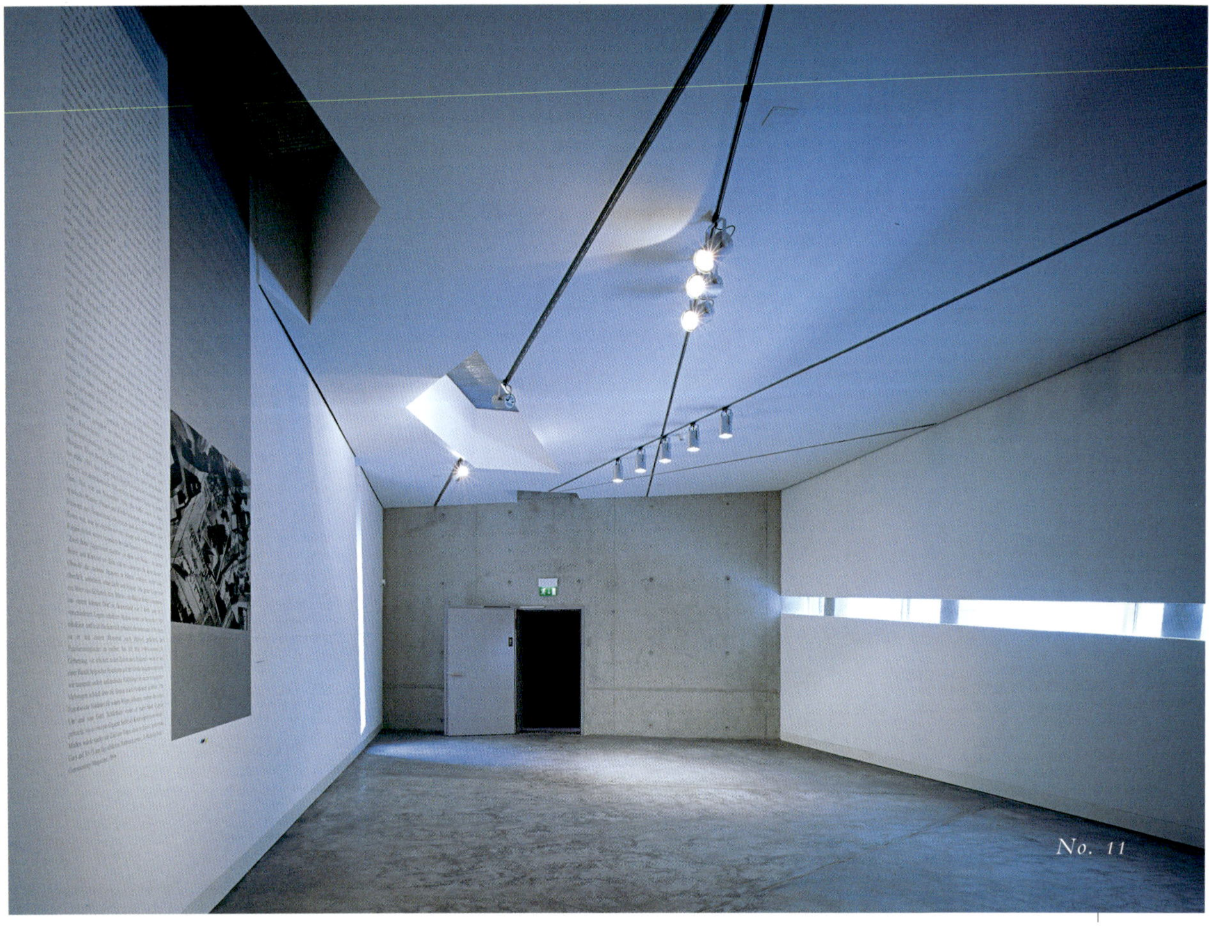

No. 11-13
DESCRIPTION

CAPTION PHOTO

No. 11 & 12 Slightly sloping floors with rising and falling gradients, walls that do not run parallel to each other, windows without right angles, and partially transparent ceilings between the floors are a constant source of tension.

No. 13 The exterior of the building complex is symbolic of Nussbaum's life. The coldness of the materials reflects his violent death in Auschwitz.

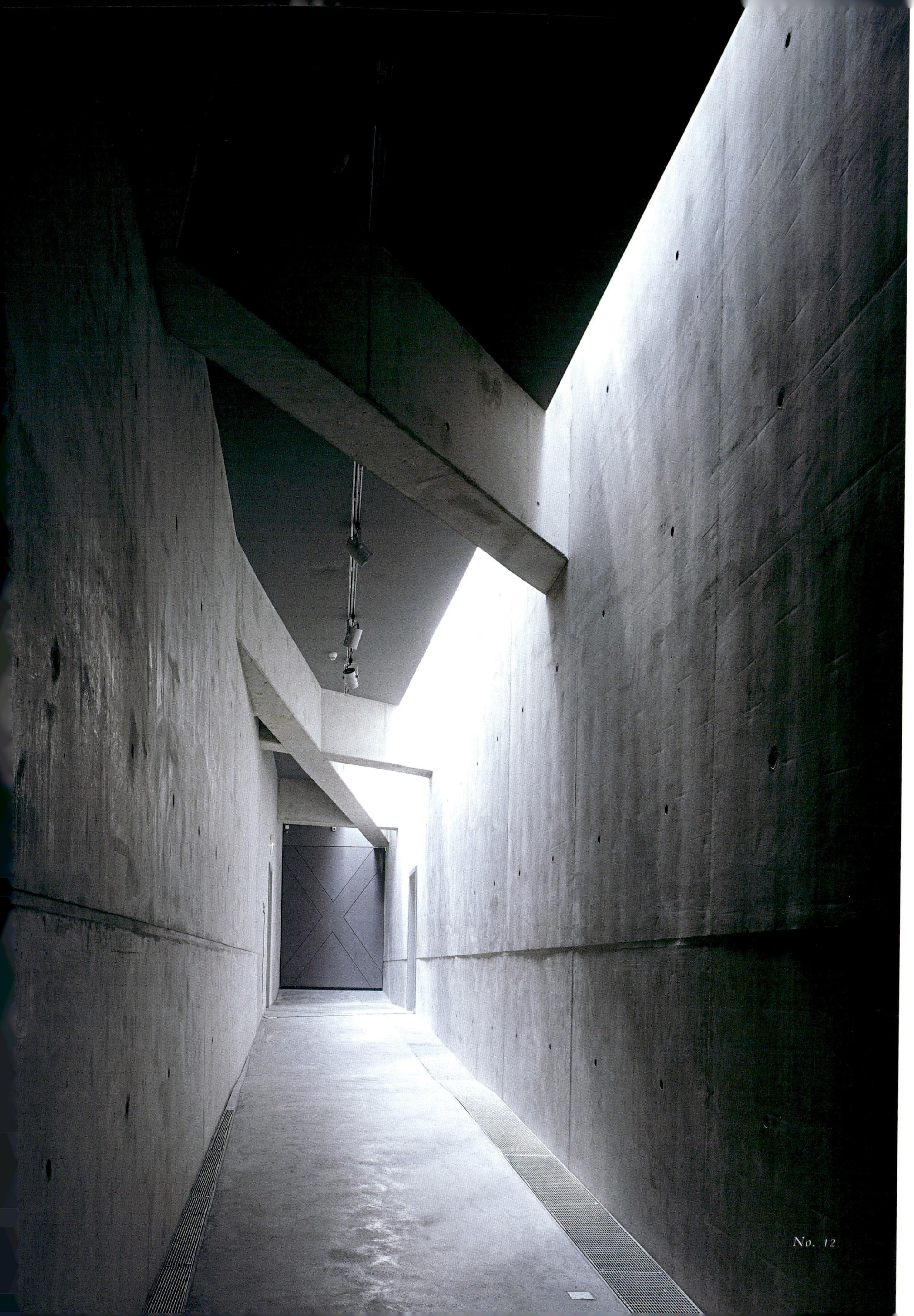
No. 12

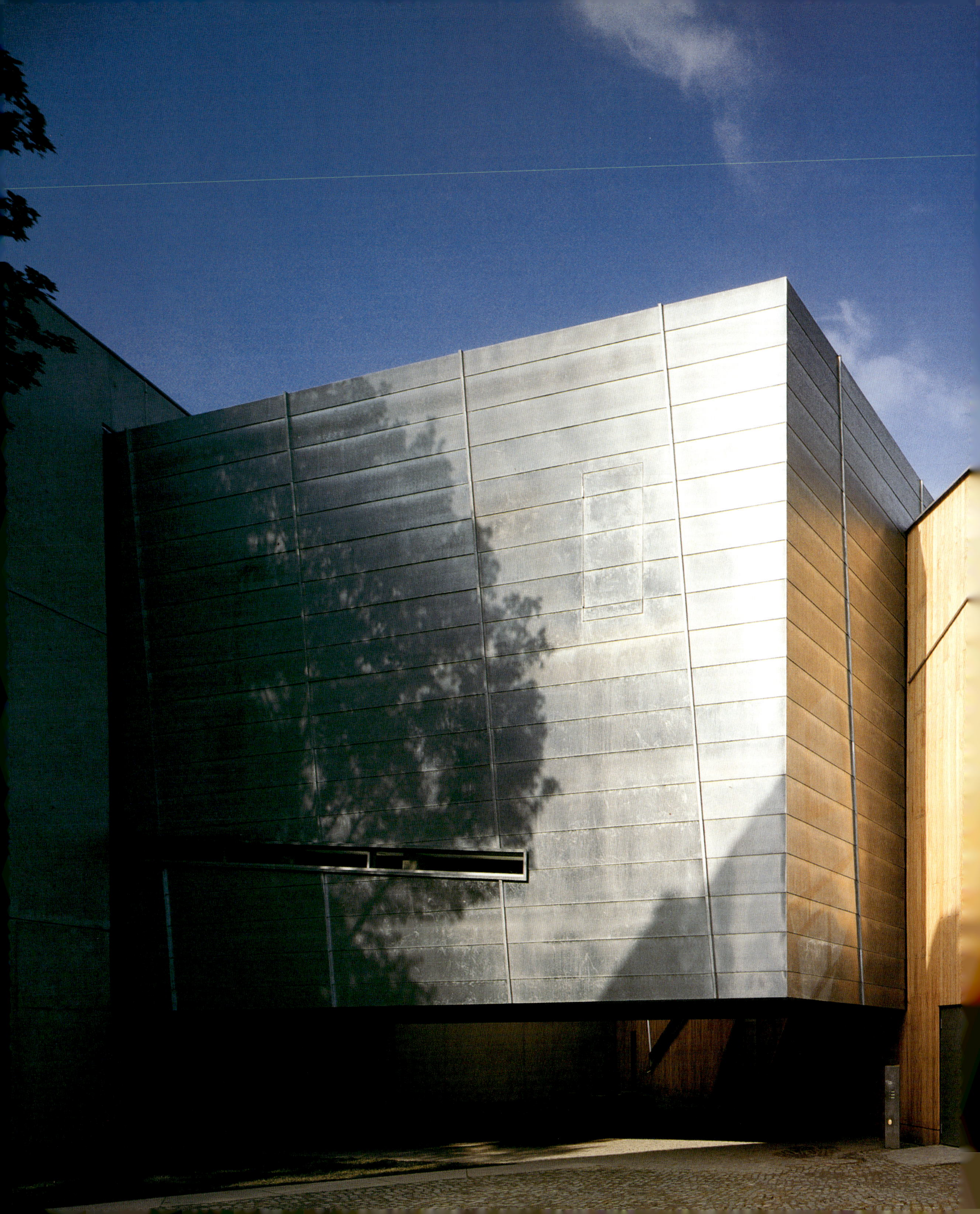

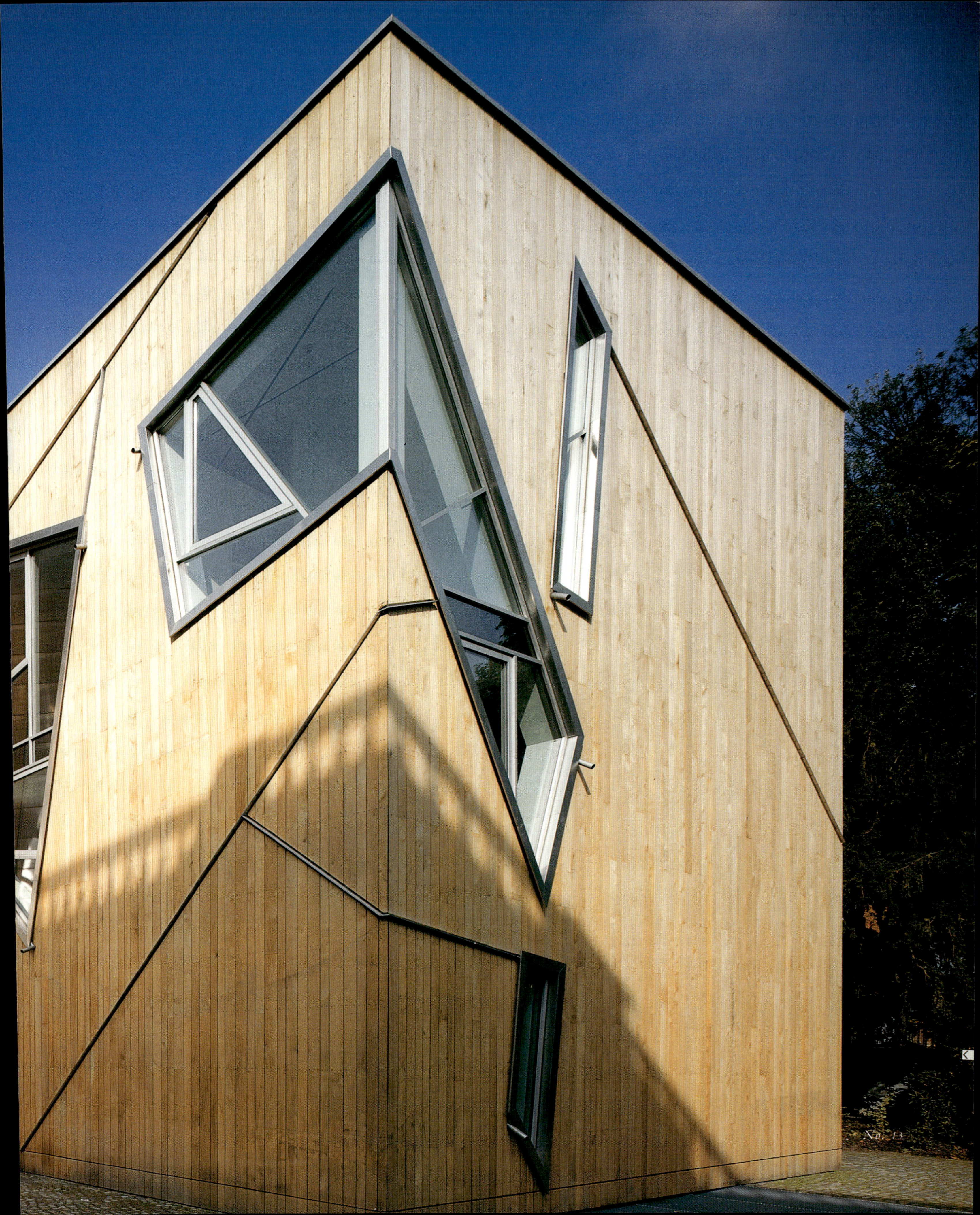
No. 13

Corning Museum of Glass

1 *PROJECT*
Corning Museum of Glass | *Corning, New York*

2 *ARCHITECT*
Smith-Miller + Hawkinson | *New York, New York*

Ever expanding its collection of art glass, the Corning Museum recognized the need to update and expand its physical environment. As with its earlier building, the obvious approach was for the architecture to serve as an exhibition itself—to become a showcase for the material potentials of glass.

The project involved stitching together several existing buildings with a new spine. The institution in 1951 was a pair of buildings designed by Wallace Harrison—an elegant glass box serving as a visitor's center and a modernist shed housing a Steuben glass factory. In 1972, Gunnar Birkerts designed an amoeba-shaped museum attached to one corner of the visitor's center. Over the years, other changes resulted in disorienting circulation routes for visitors. Smith-Miller + Hawkinson were given the task of "filling in the spaces between the new and the old (and improving the circulation routes) and presenting a new skin."

At the same time, Smith-Miller + Hawkinson choose to present a different way to architecturally use glass. In the 1951 buildings, Harrison experimented with various kinds of opaque and transparent glass on the facades Birkerts used glass in an expressionistic way reminiscent of the German architect Bruno Taut. Smith-Miller + Hawkinson are fascinated by the three-dimensional aspects of glass and invite the visitors to look at, rather than merely through, the glass. For example, visitors enter through deliberate "fractures" in the smooth glass skin and pass under and between tilting sheets of glass. The curtain wall uses a mullion-less, point-fitting system with a series of very thin and light stainless steel vertical trusses.

Inside, the architects have created a sculpture gallery, orientation theater, retail shops, café, regional visitor's center, and exhibition gallery, where the major scientific advances in glass from the nineteenth century are told. And the architecture, itself, is part of the learning experience.

No. 1
Description

Caption Photo

No. 1 The architects "embraced the opportunity to bring glass to the forefront of the project—to make glass and its history both the structure and the content of the museum."

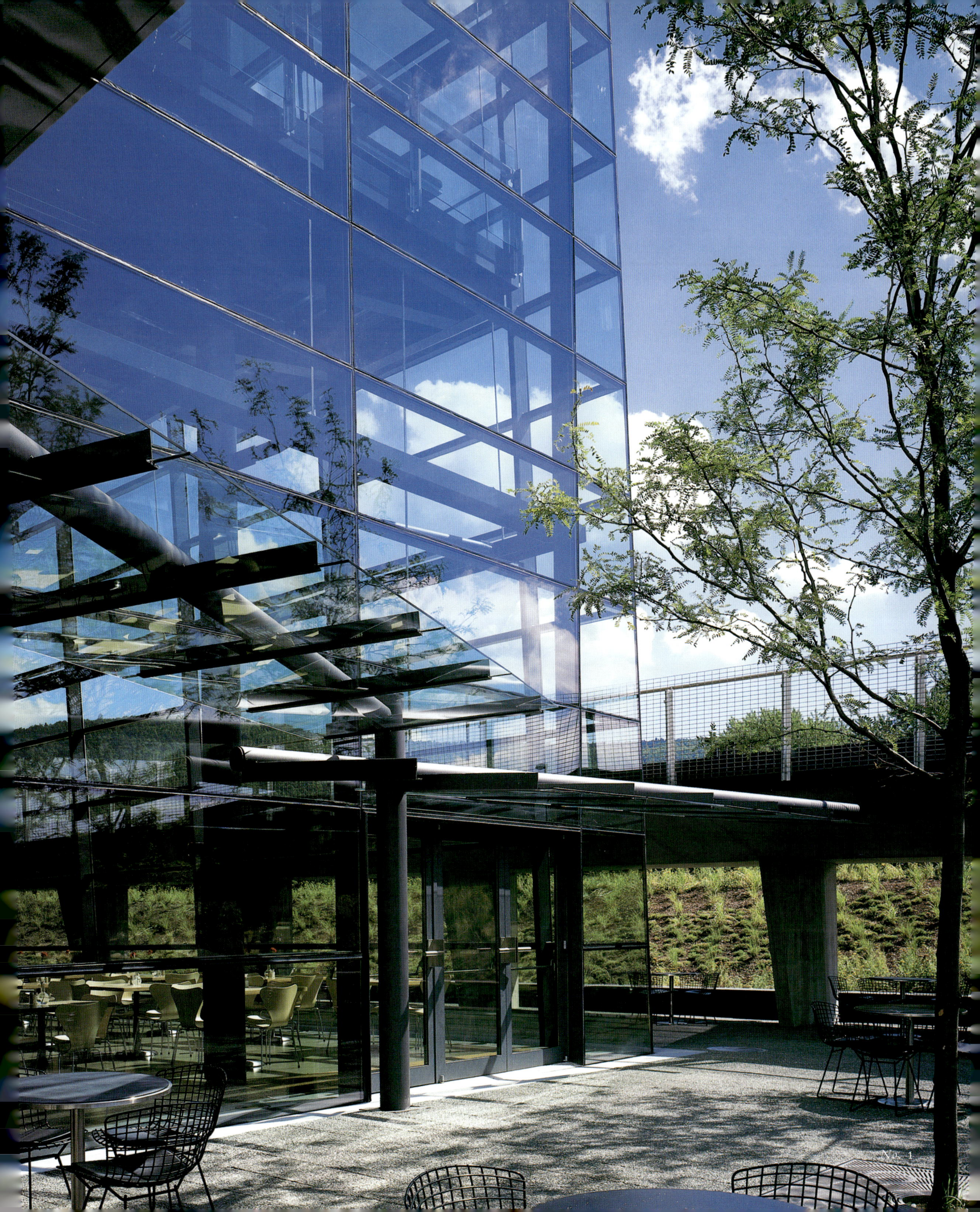
No. 1

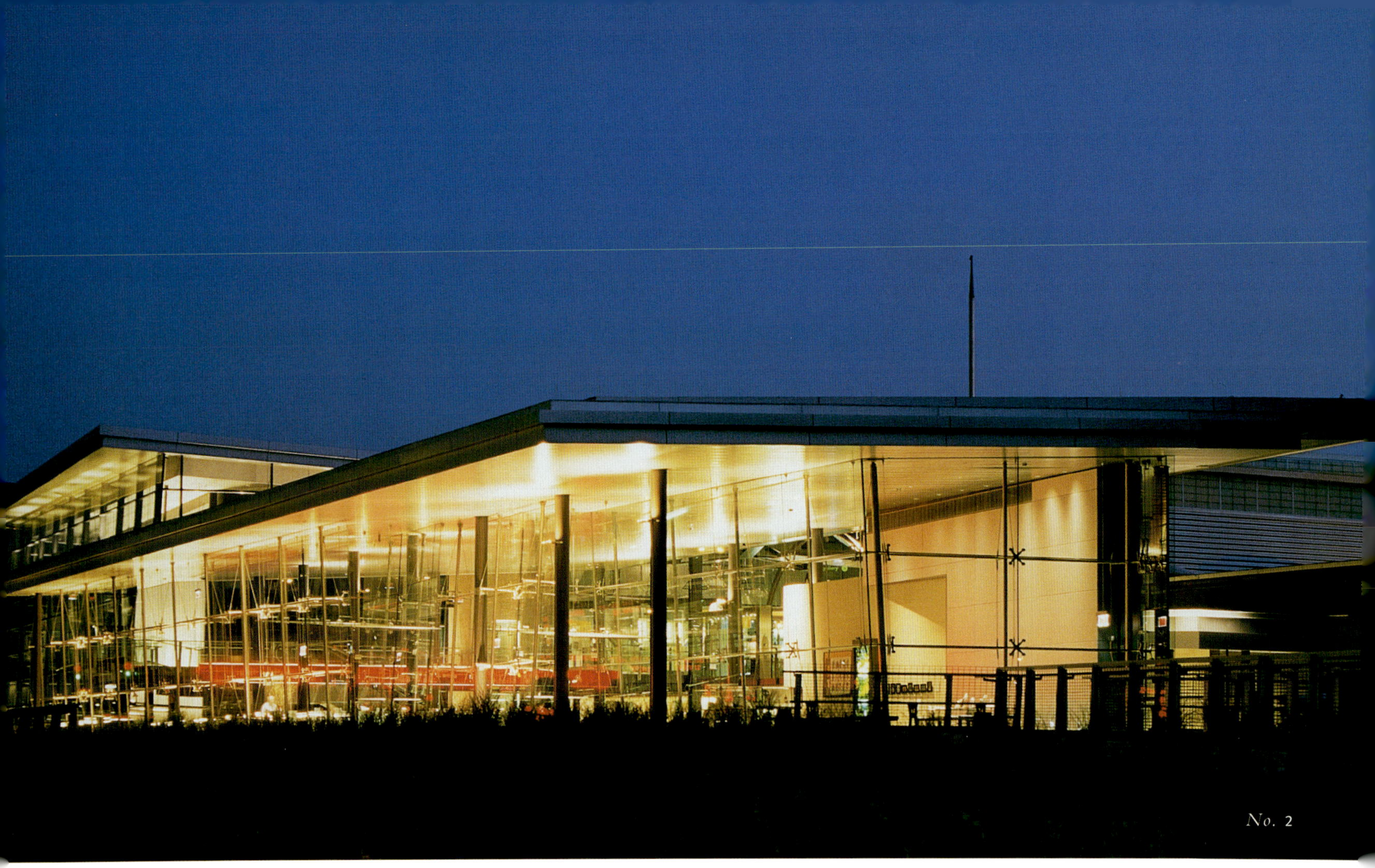

Photo: Frank J. Borkowski

No. 2-8

DESCRIPTION

CAPTION

PHOTO

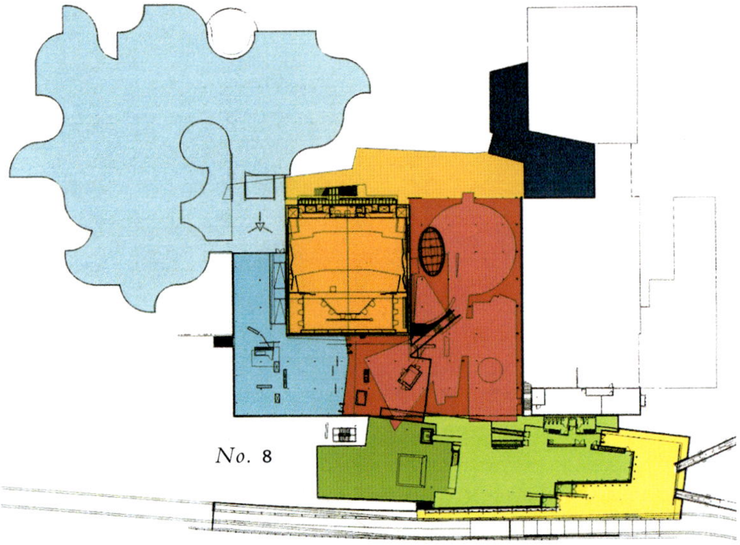

No. 2 The new glass pavilion glows from within.

No. 3 The West Bridge offers ground floor access to retail shops, a cafÈ, and a new 770-seat auditorium.

No. 4 An operating periscope allows visitors to survey the town of Corning and its surrounding environments.

No. 5, 6 & 7 Glass visually unites the spaces and passageways of the complex.

No. 8 The plan shows how the original Smith-Miler-Hawkinson design unites the original Wallace Harrison building, the Gunnar Birkerts building, and the Steuben glass factory into a seamless whole.

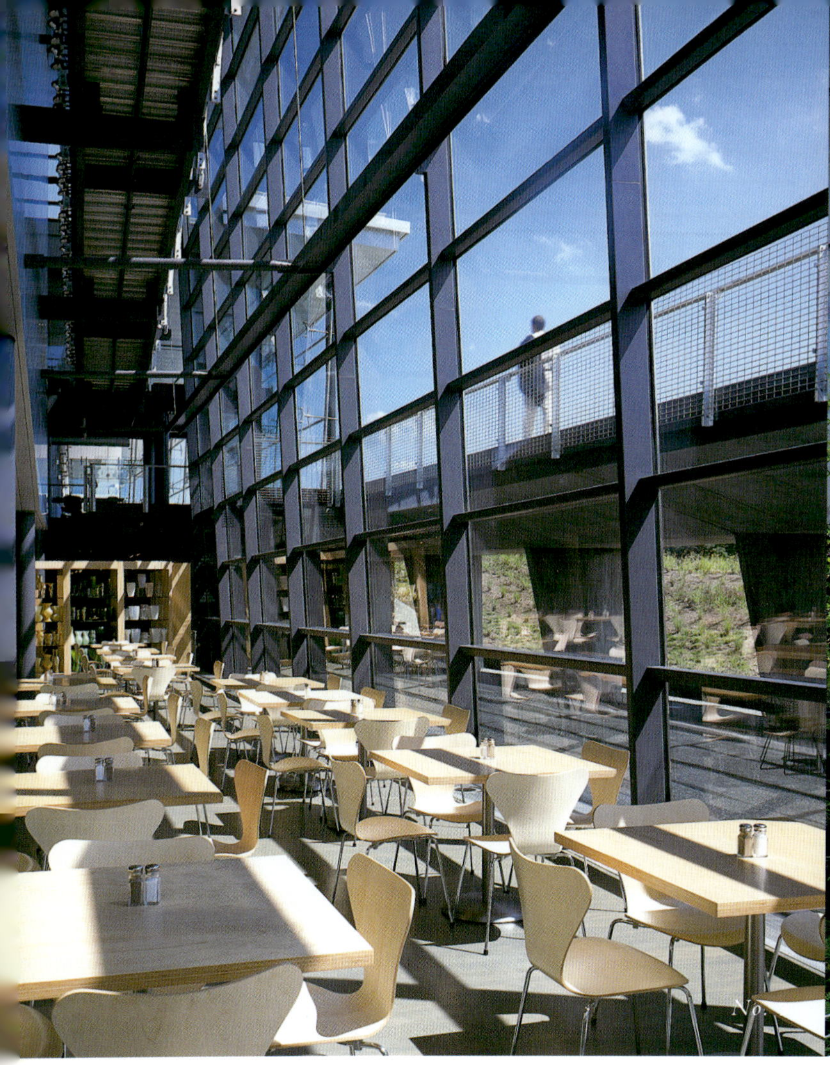

Photo © Paul Warchol

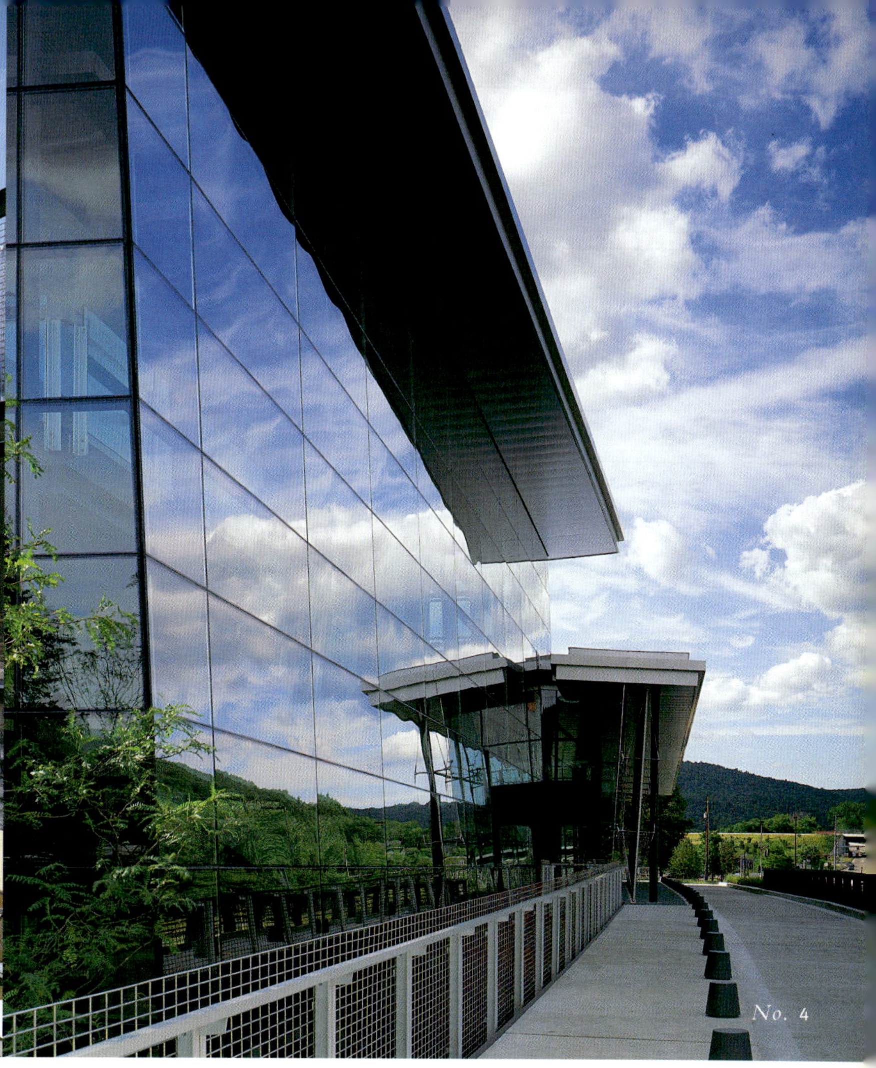

Photo © Paul Warchol

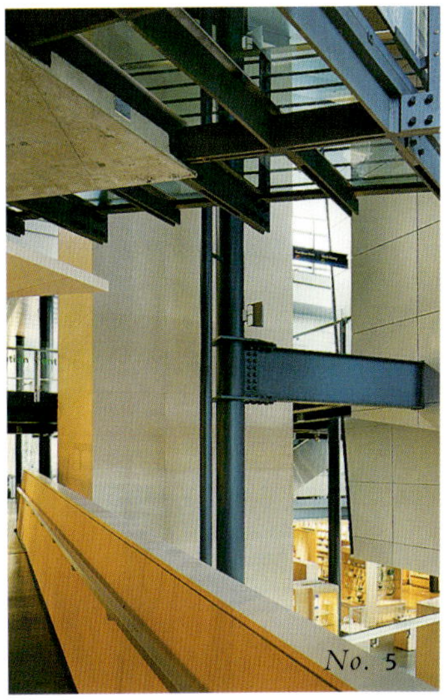

Photo © Paul Warchol

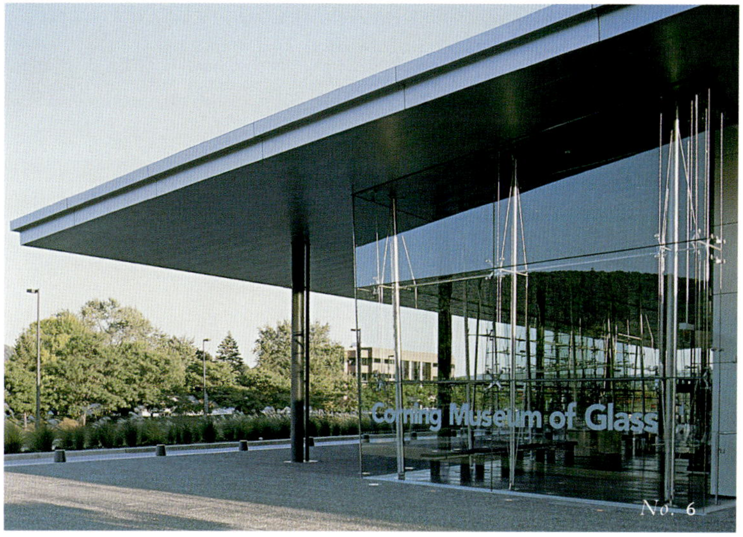

Photo: Frank J. Borkowski

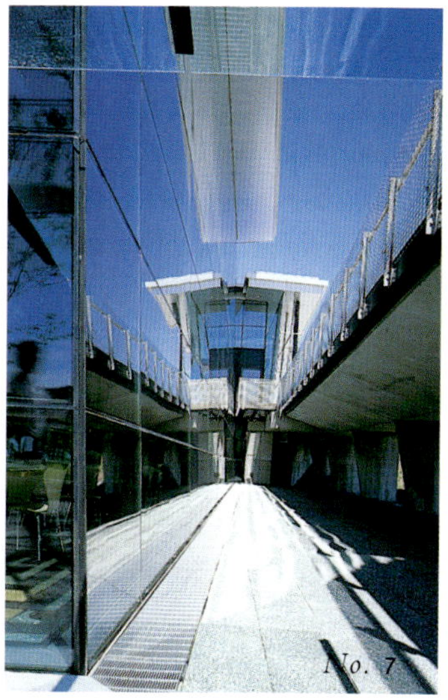

Photo © Paul Warchol

Arts of Korea Gallery

1 *PROJECT*
The Metropolitan Museum of Art | *New York, New York*

2 *ARCHITECT*
Kyu Sung Woo Architects, Inc. | *Cambridge, Massachusetts*

One of the first major museums to commission a gallery solely dedicated to Korean art, the Metropolitan Museum set aside a modest room and chose a Korean-American architect to design a setting that would convey a sense of that culture's architecture and art. Kyu Sung Woo created at the Metropolitan a Korean treasure house, a luminous white box that becomes an emotive space of calmness and beauty.

The austere gallery acts as a neutral backdrop to the treasures on display, especially the prized Korean celadon weares. The ceramics, as well as paintings and sculpture are placed in glass cases that run along the perimeter of the room. The colors and textures of the art contrast against white mylar screens that resemble rice paper and line the cases. The overall composition is further subdued through the use of a nonreflective glass placed on the exterior of the case to reduce glare. The only break in the box is a central partition, which allows for different exhibit configurations, including the display of large scroll paintings. The only other objects of "solid" appearance are the two blackened, steel-plated entrance doors.

The "white box" is made complete with flooring of bleached white oak articulated in an abstract, gray finish. This traditional flooring extends into the display case to purposely blur the separation between object and viewer and, at the same time, enlarge the room.

When daylight enters through a pitched glazed roof skylight, the room luminates. Masked by a white scrim of coarse, stretched cotton, the light is filtered and diffused and bathes the gallery in a gentle radiance.

No. 1
DESCRIPTION

CAPTION PHOTO

No. 1 From the skylight, natural light is filtered through a cotton scrim resulting in a soft diffused glow that touches every corner of the room. Small spotlights supplement the daylight.

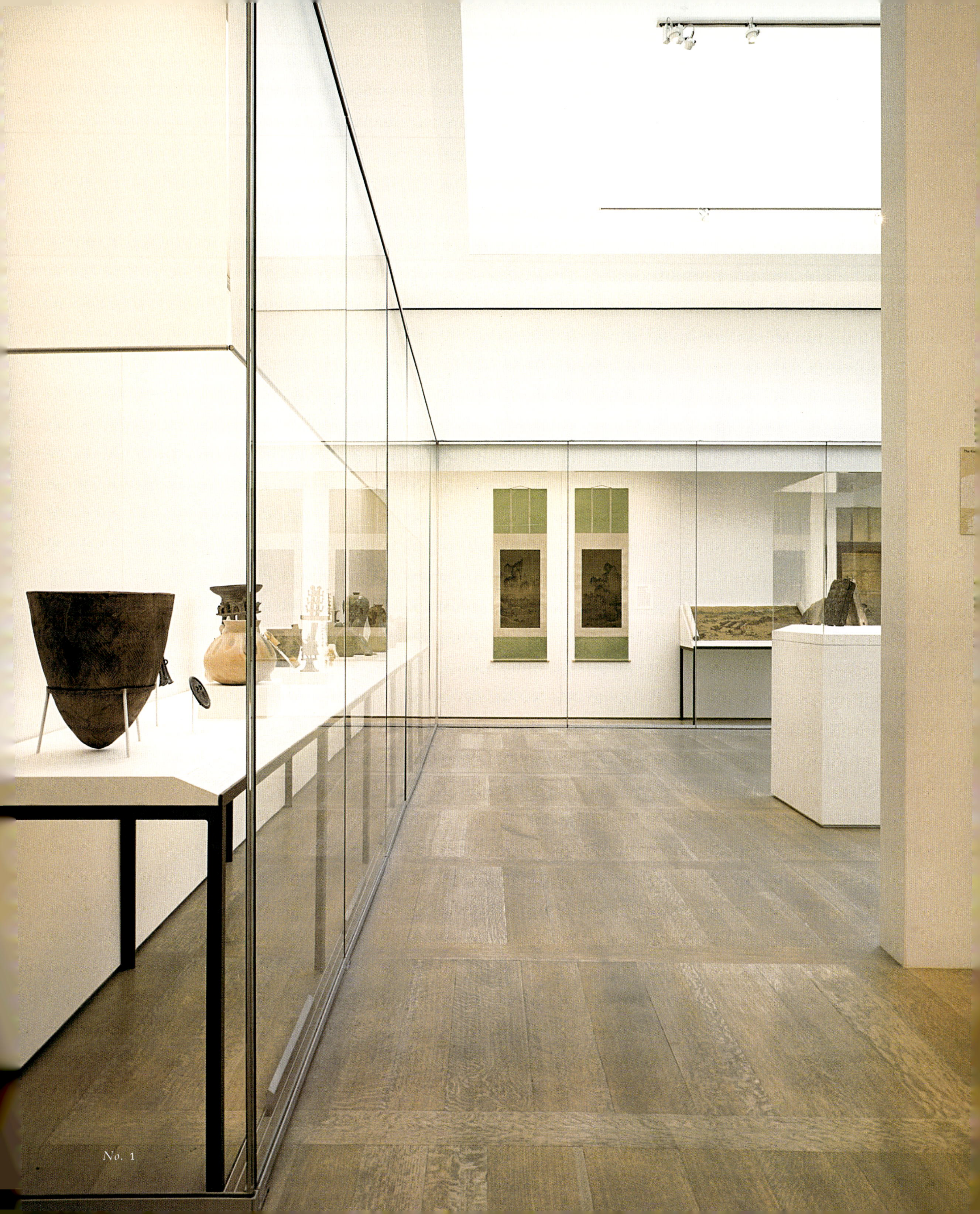

No. 1

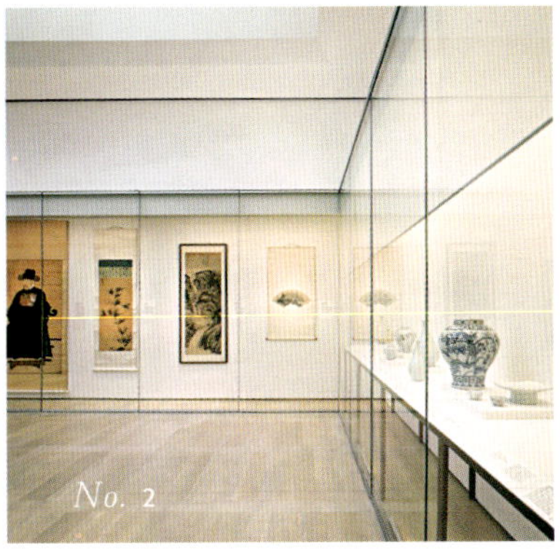

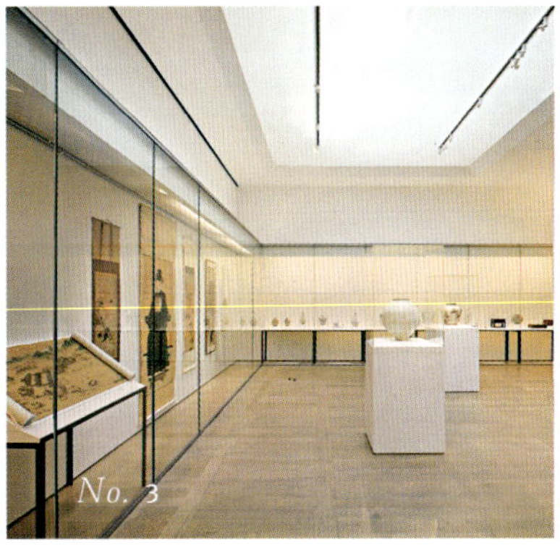

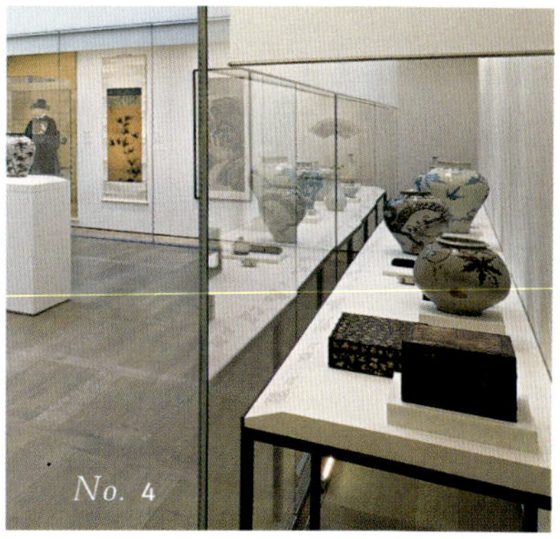

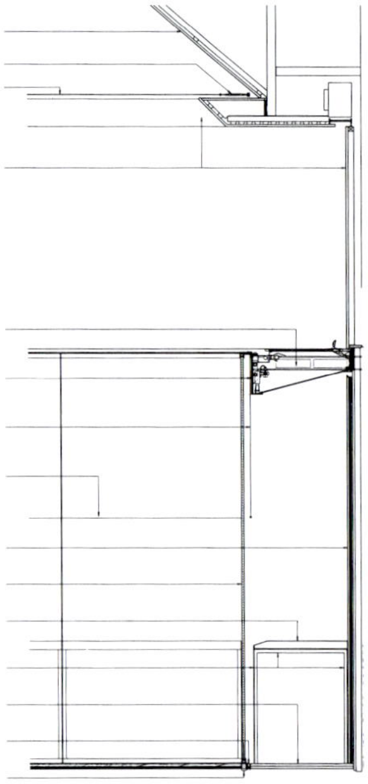

No. 2-5

DESCRIPTION

CAPTION PHOTO

No. 2 It is the art, not the architecture, which dominates the space.

No. 3 A restrained color palette complements the restrained architecture.

No. 4 The freestanding wall is removable to accommodate changing exhibition requirements.

No. 5 The restrained yet deliberate use of architectural elements within the gallery communicates Korean sensibilities without the application of traditional materiality.

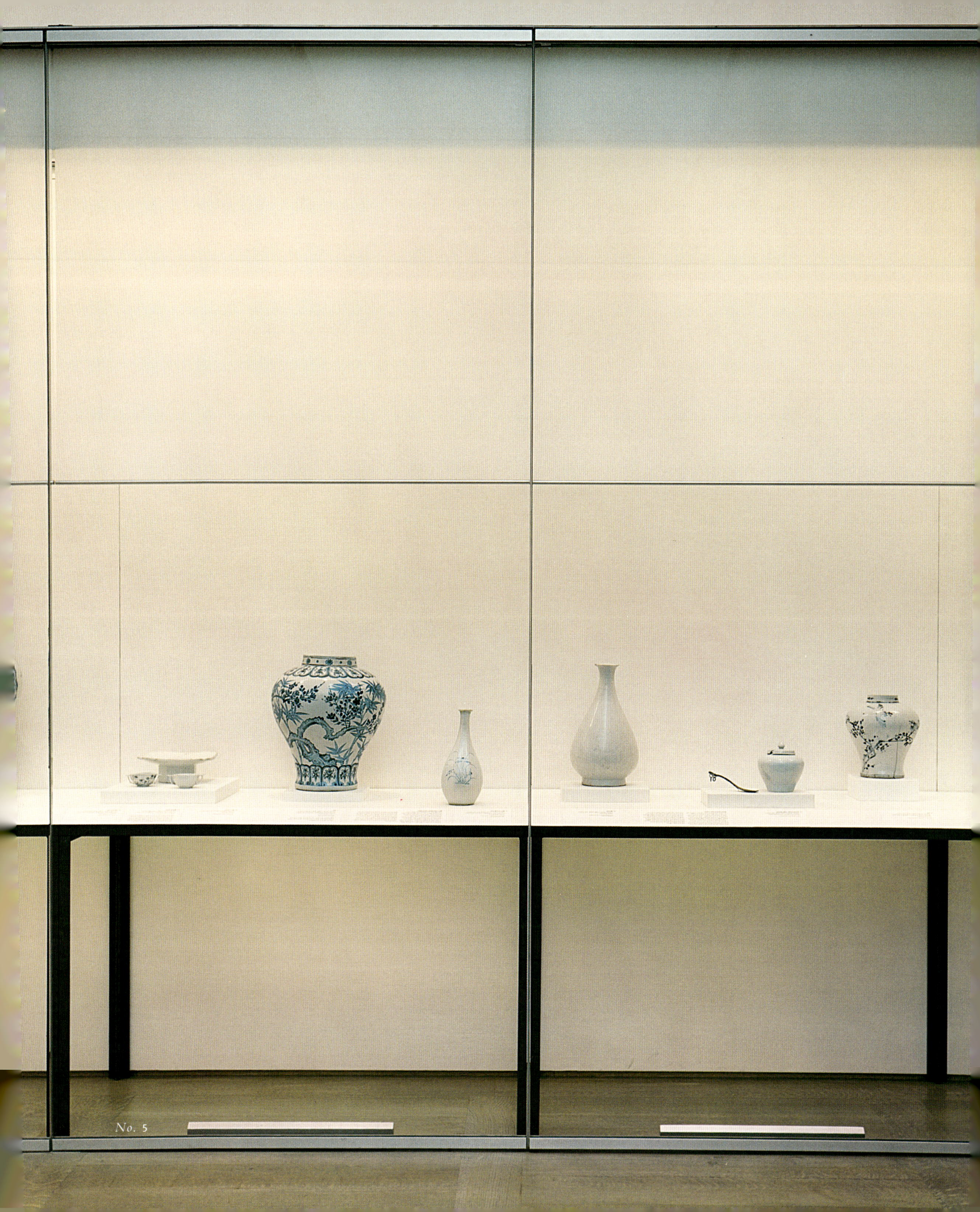

No. 5

OTHER MUSEUMS

Senator John Heinz Pittsburgh Regional History Center

1 *PROJECT*
Senator John Heinz Pittsburgh Regional History Center | *Pittsburgh, Pennsylvania*

2 *ARCHITECT*
Bohlin Cywinski Jackson | *Wilkes-Barre, Pennsylvania*

The nineteenth-century warehouse that the Historical Society of Western Pennsylvania transformed into a museum, library, archive, and education facility had an unlikely beginning, at least in today's terms. This plain, muscular building stored ice harvested from Lake Chautauqua in western New York State. What better setting for an historical museum that commemorates this region's colorful industrial past.

The goal for Bohlin Cywinski Jackson was to upgrade the building's system while maintaining the strong character of the original structure. The first floor had been built high enough to accommodate rail cars that delivered the ice, while the upper floors were structurally re-enforced to accept the weight of the stored ice. This translates into thick, brick bearing walls and heavy wooden beams and columns. The first floor ceiling was of long-span construction with steel transfer girders and a vaulted brick ceiling. The upper levels have relatively few—and small—windows, which matches the current need for a "black box" setting for exhibitions and archival storage areas.

During the renovation, the architect inserted an atrium that runs the height of the seven-story building. This is the primary vertical circulation core in the building. Lit with a combination of clerestory windows and a large westward-facing window, the atrium offers panoramic views of the Pittsburgh skyline to the three upper floors.

Opening the atrium well revealed pieces of the heavy timber frame. Thus, the building itself, is celebrated as an artifact. Some timbers were removed and recycled as the face of the reception desk and end-grain floor in a portion of the lobby. The exterior was cleaned and the brick masonry re-pointed. A new steel and glass canopy and colorful banners mark the entrance.

No. 1-3

Description

Caption Photo

No. 1 The existing building has a plain muscular quality that bespeaks of Pittsburgh's industrial heritage. It was originally used as a storage facility for ice.

No. 2 A newly configured atrium is lit with a combination of clerestory windows and a large westward facing window that offers panoramic views of the Pittsburgh skyline.

No. 3 The primary vertical circulation is organized as an atrium with an elevator shaft.

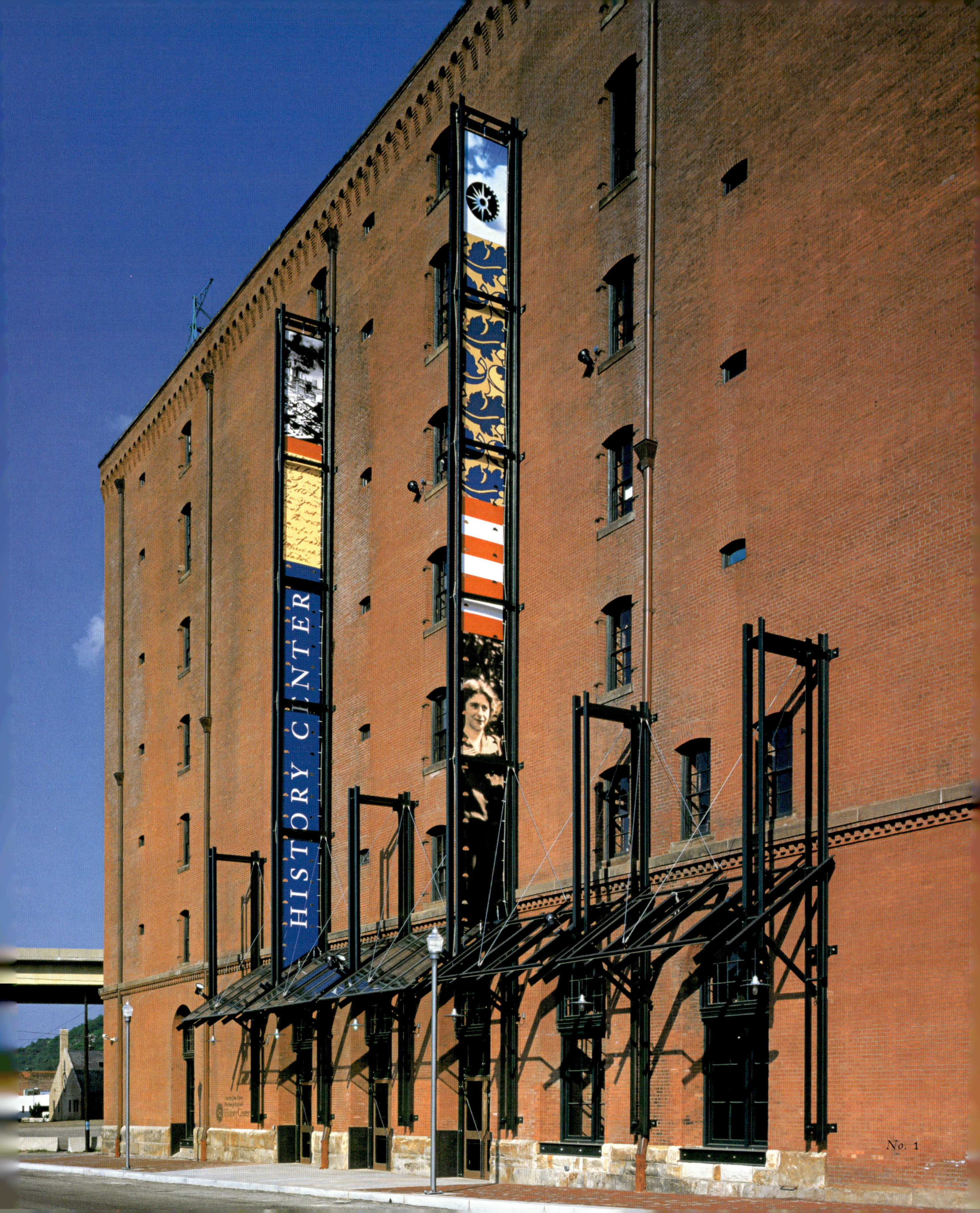

No. 1

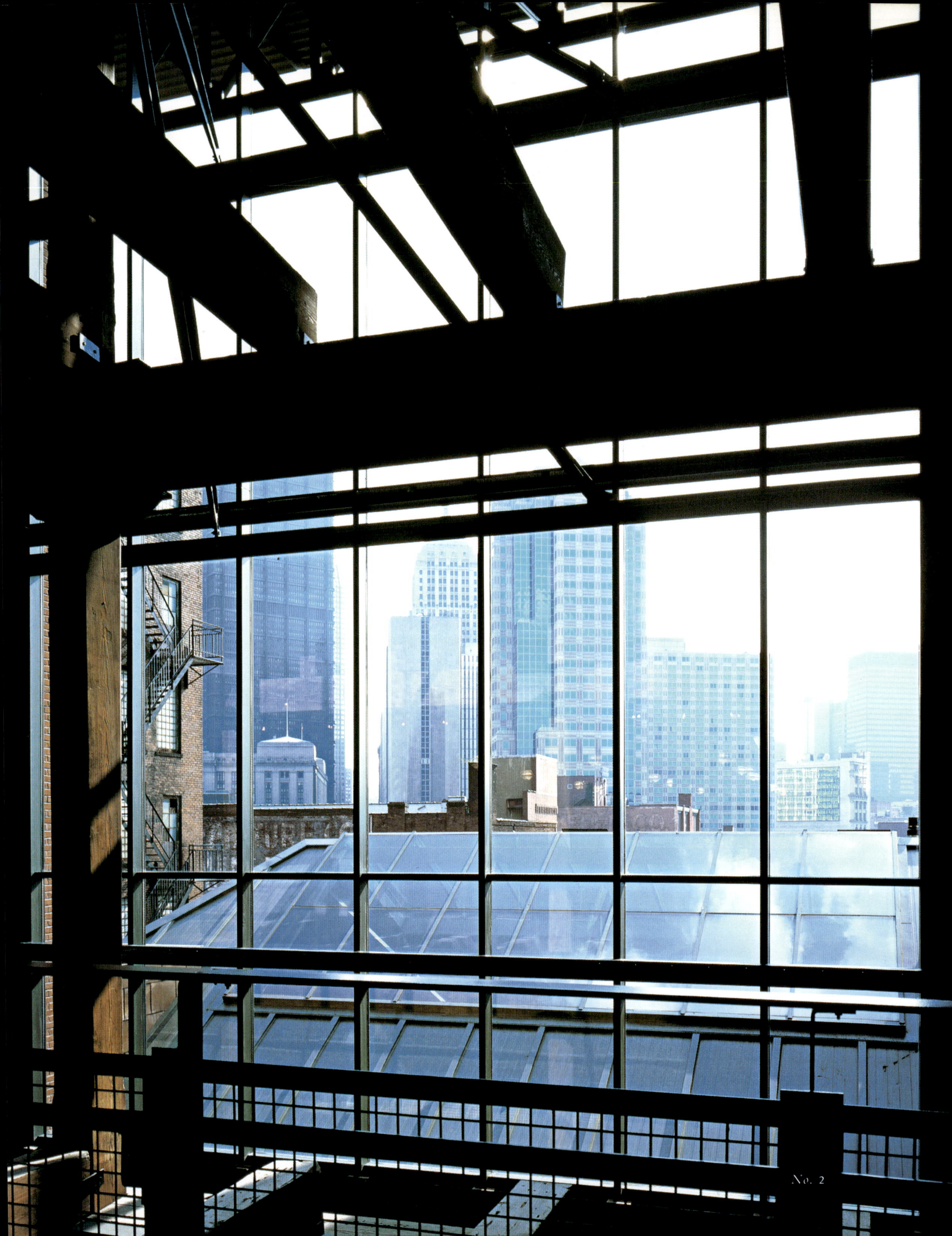

No. 2

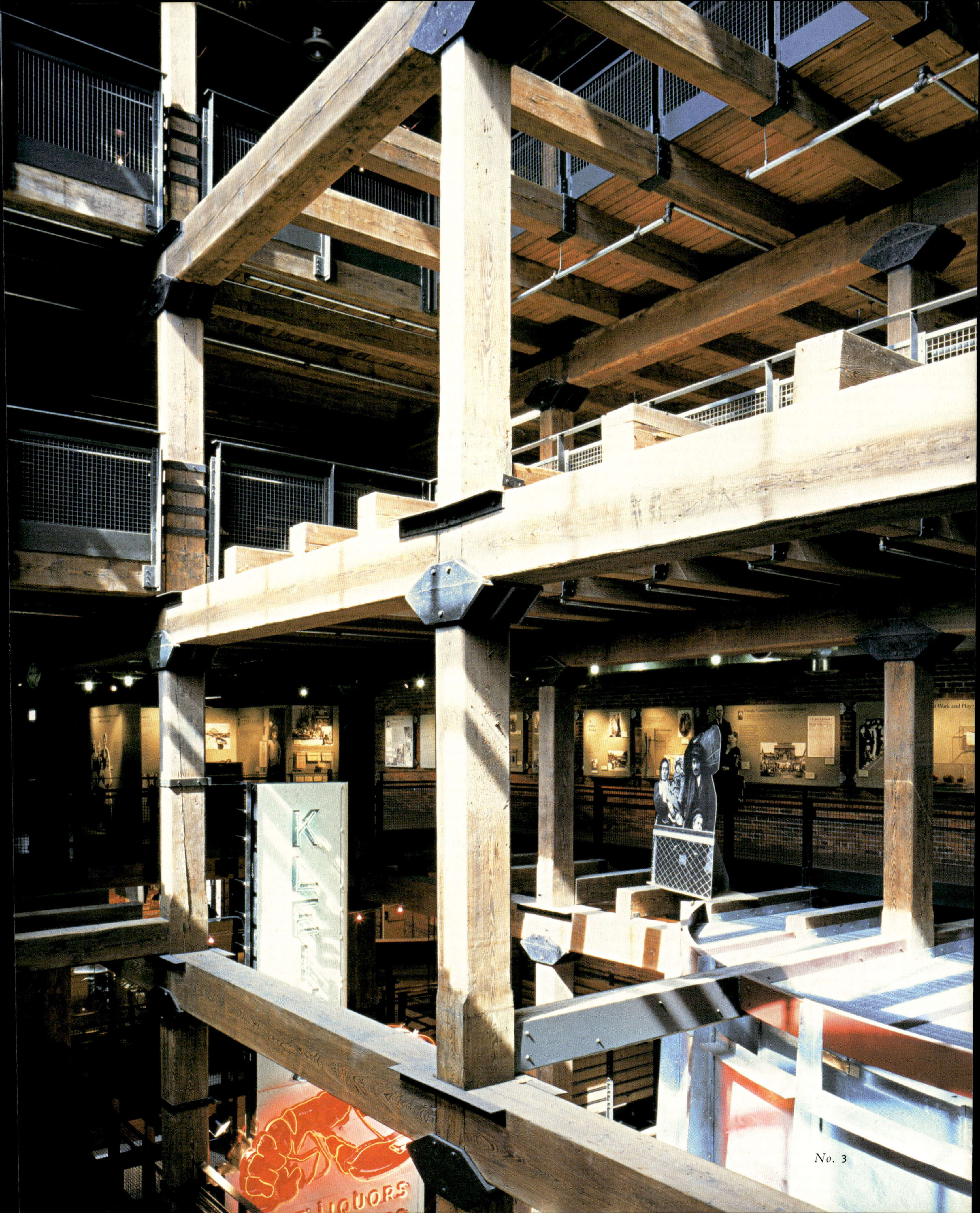

No. 3

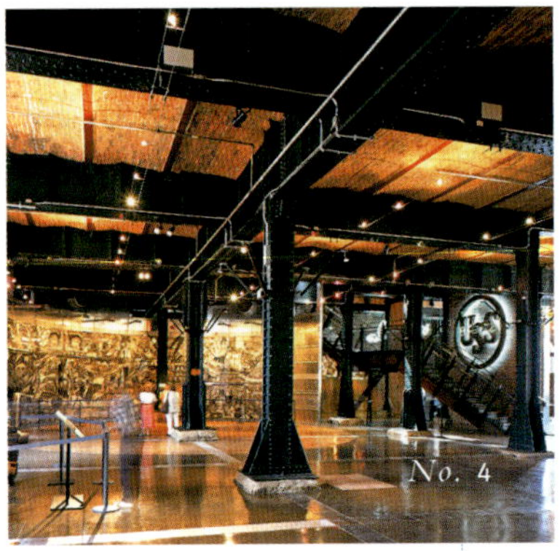

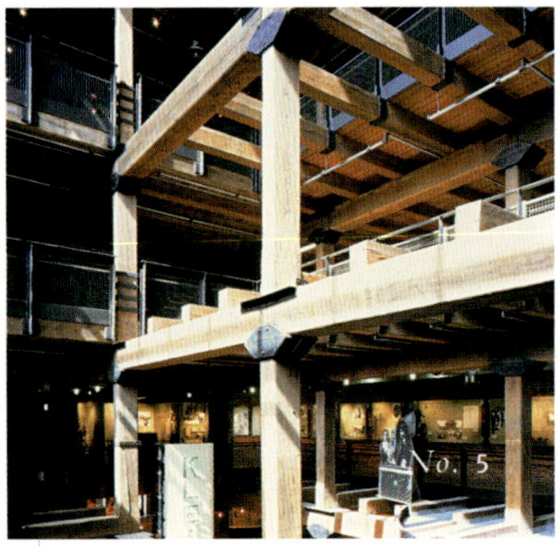

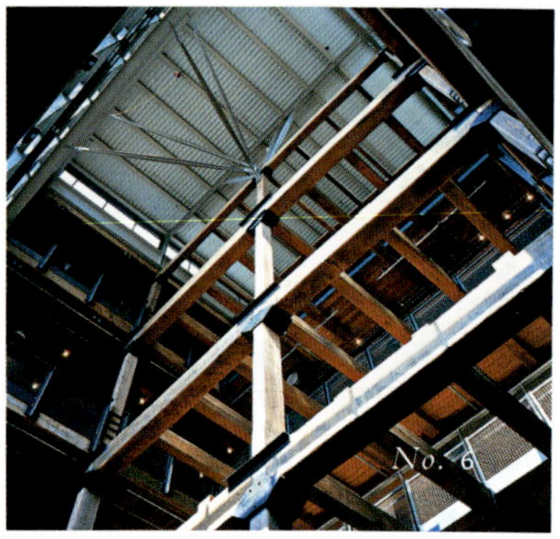

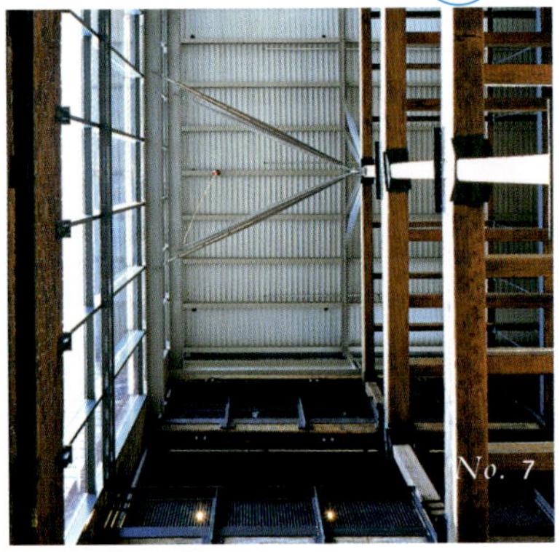

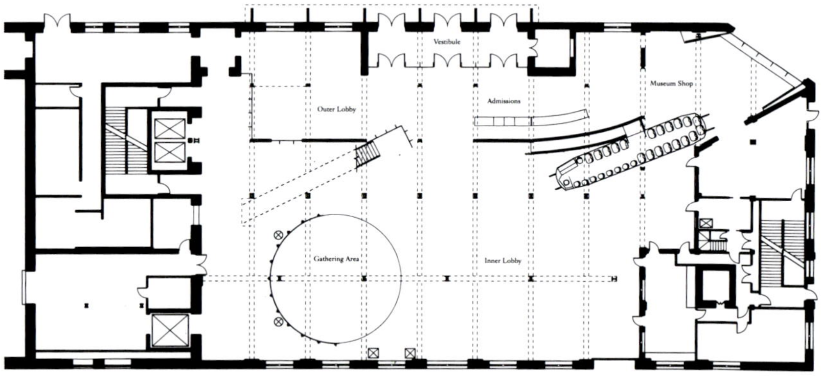

No. 4-8
DESCRIPTION

CAPTION PHOTO

No. 4-8 The overall design strategy emphasizes the strong character of the building's original structure. The heavy wooden beams and columns provide a strong visual aesthetic for the galleries.

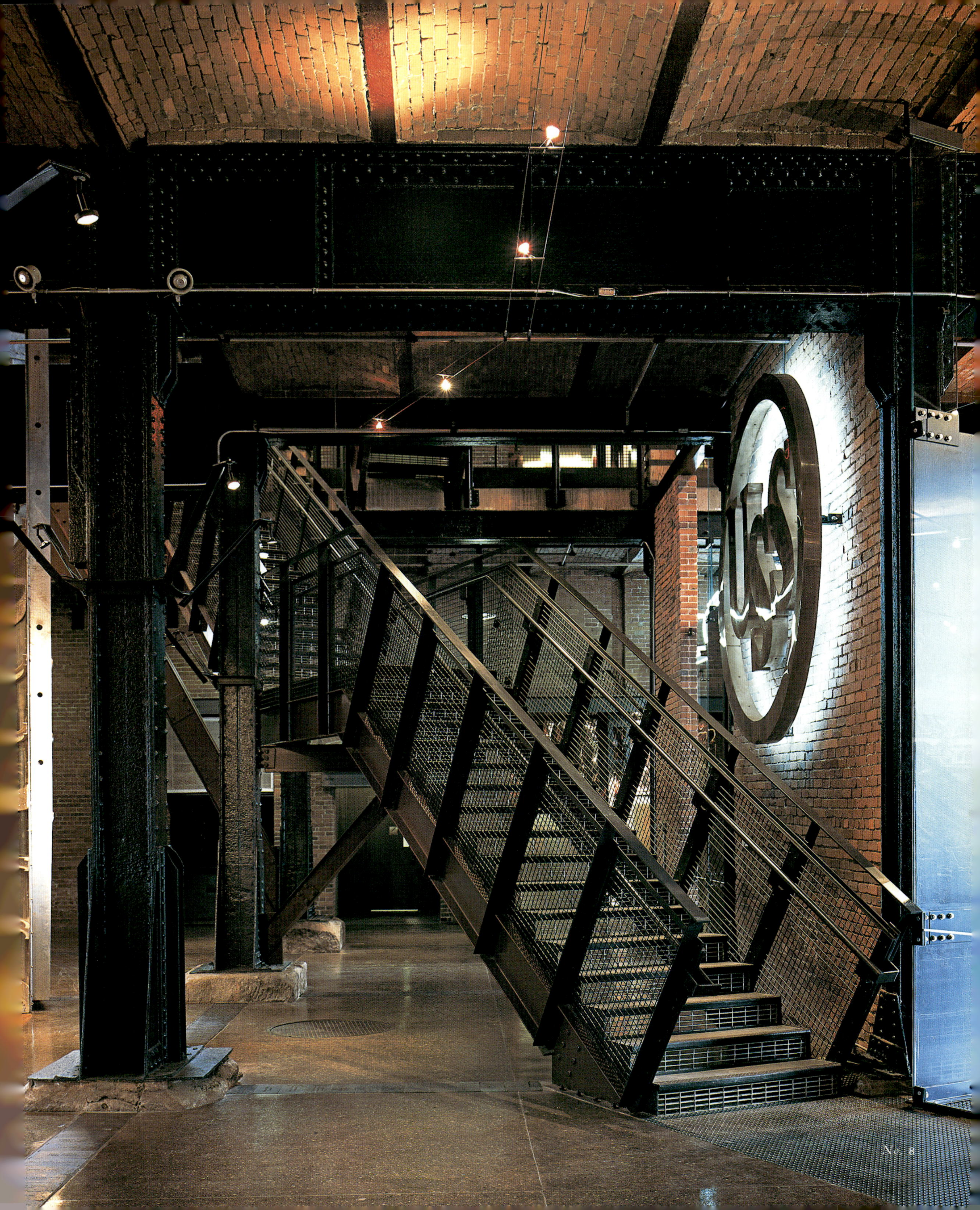

No. 8

Nakatomi Memorial Medicine Museum

1 *PROJECT*
Nakatomi Memorial Medicine Museum | *Tosu, Japan*

2 *ARCHITECTS*
Cecco Bonanotte | Francescomaria Bonanotte | Pier Paolo Maria Bonanotte | *Rome, Italy*

Atop a hill overlooking the small town of Tosu in southern Japan, the Nakatomi Museum celebrates the contribution of pharmaceutical science to society. The building takes the form of a sequence of large boxes assembled together to symbolically suggest that science—and pharmacology—is formed by several elements. Some of the elements are already known (represented as perfect cubes), some are not yet revealed (represented by half cubes), yet the whole is a quest toward complete knowledge.

Developed by the Hisamitsu Pharmaceutical Company to demonstrate the relation of science to nature, the building is integrated into the natural environment. For example, the 5-meter-cubes (16.5-feet-cubes) were cut at 45-degree angles as the building the uneven terrain down the slope.

The goal was to create "an effect of reciprocal response among the various elements composing it" the architect says, "the construction, the water, the garden." The building's form is reflected on the nearby lake as is the garden, both of which are seen from inside the building. So the environment is totally tied together.

The building's skin is a volcanic stone found in the region, which changes color according to different climatic conditions. On sunny days the stone seems to be alive, while on rainy days it looks gloomy, fading into the landscape.

The complex consists of three structures, the largest of which houses the museum exhibit on two floors. The smallest structure is for storage, and connecting the two are research rooms.

No. 1-2
Description

Caption
Photo

No. 1 The building is designed to symbolize pharmaceutical science's contribution to the development of society. The building consists of a series of boxlike forms: some are perfect cubes; others are slashed through at forty-five degree angles.

No. 2 The design is in the form of two pavilions joined together by a passageway.

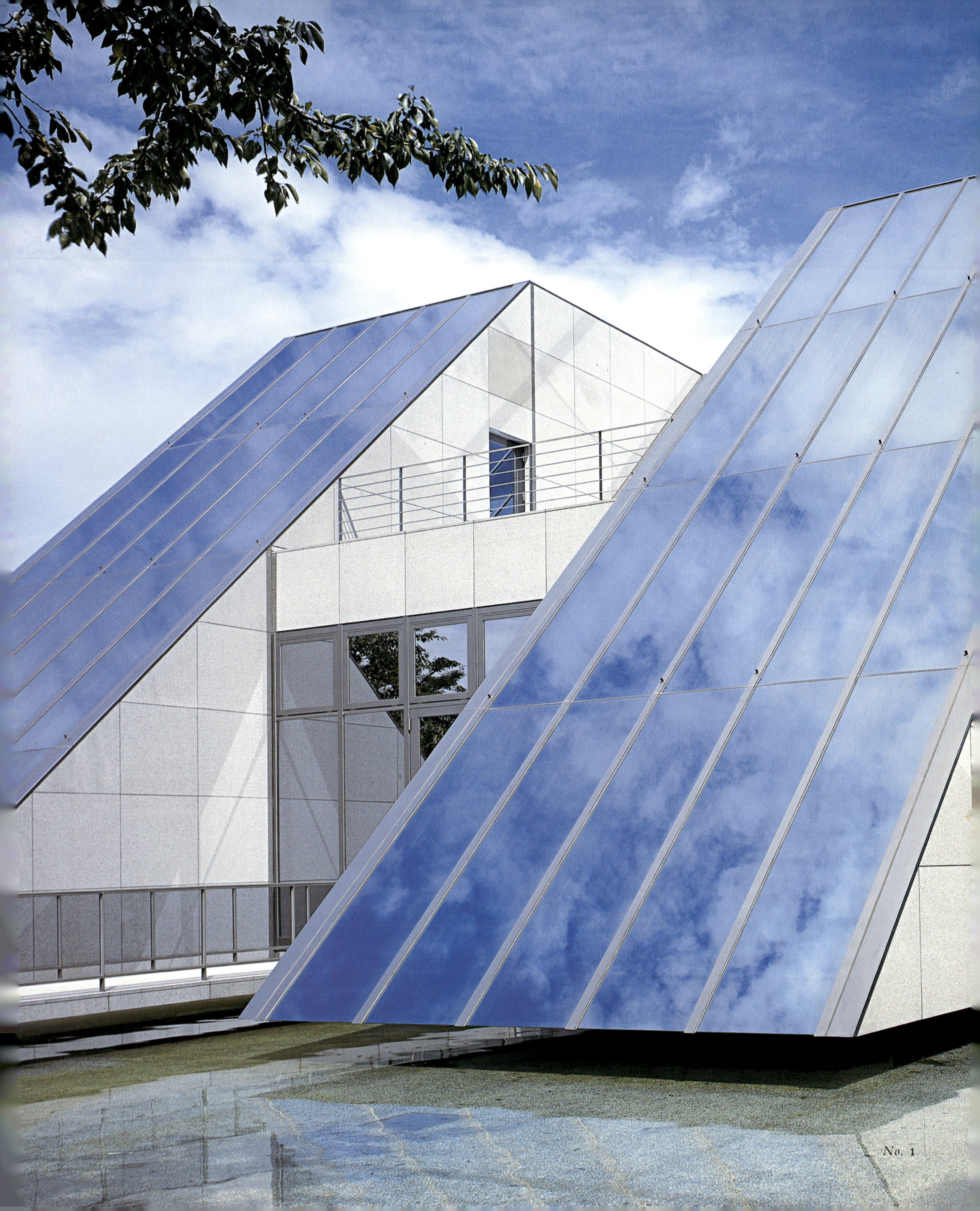

No. 1

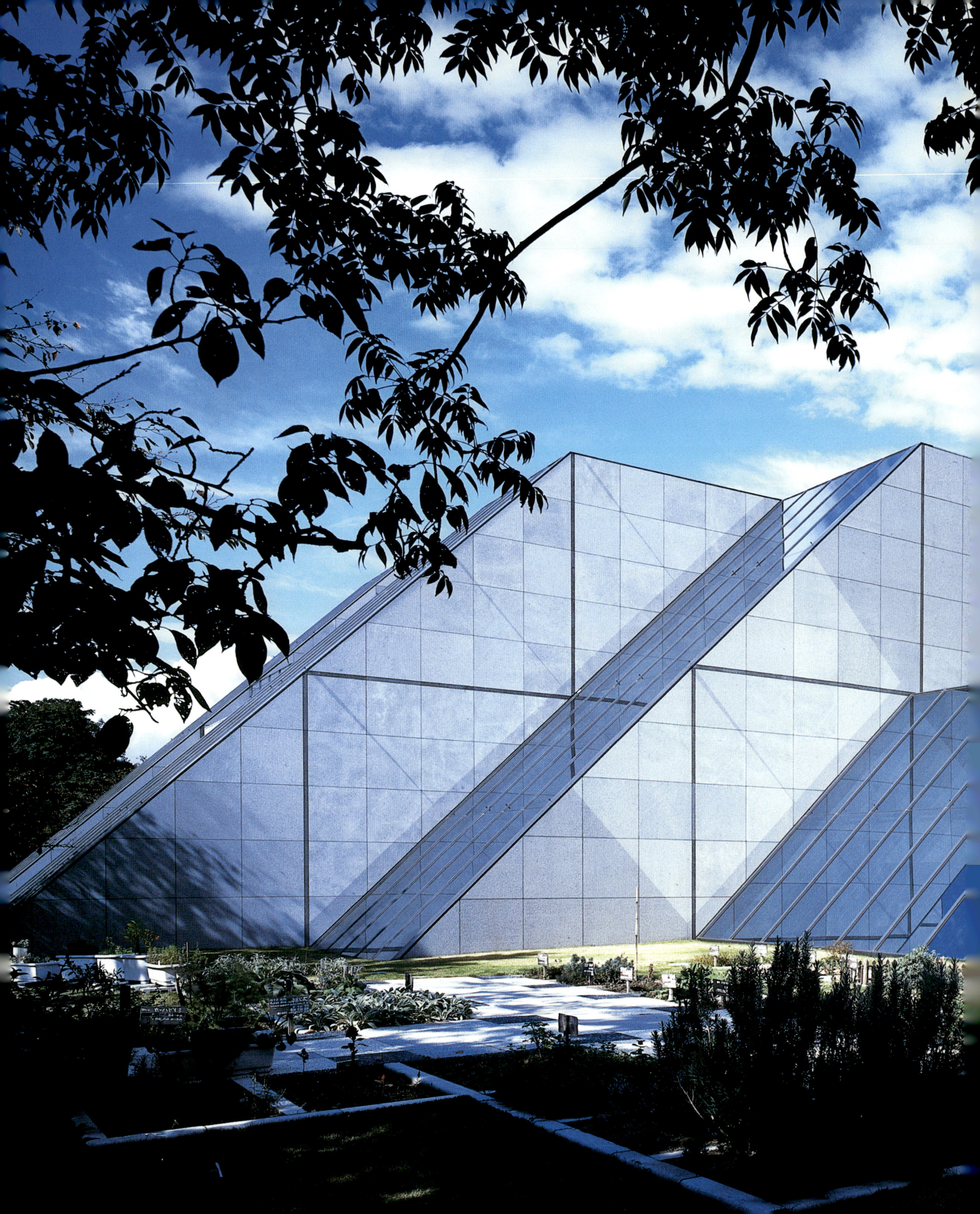

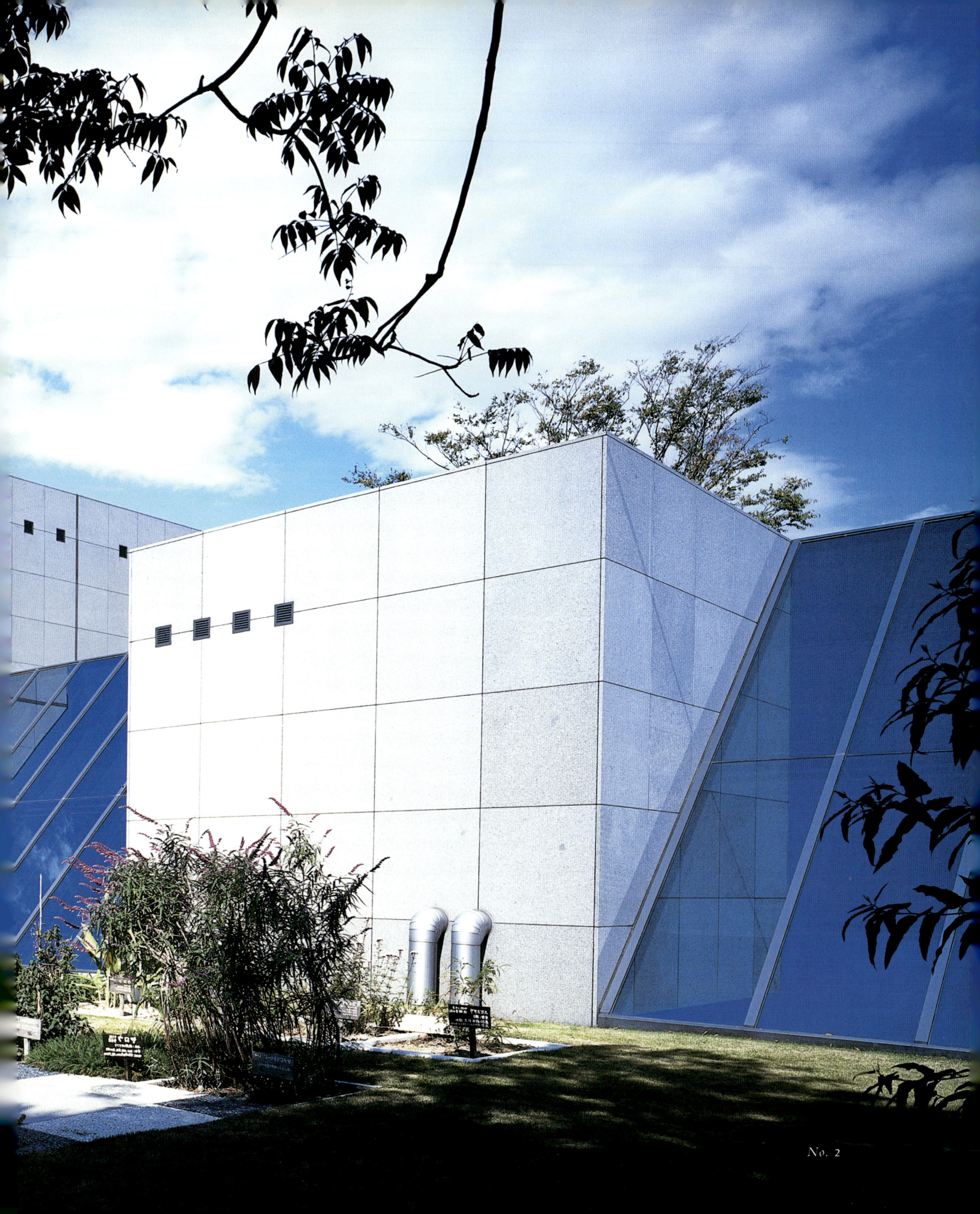

No. 2

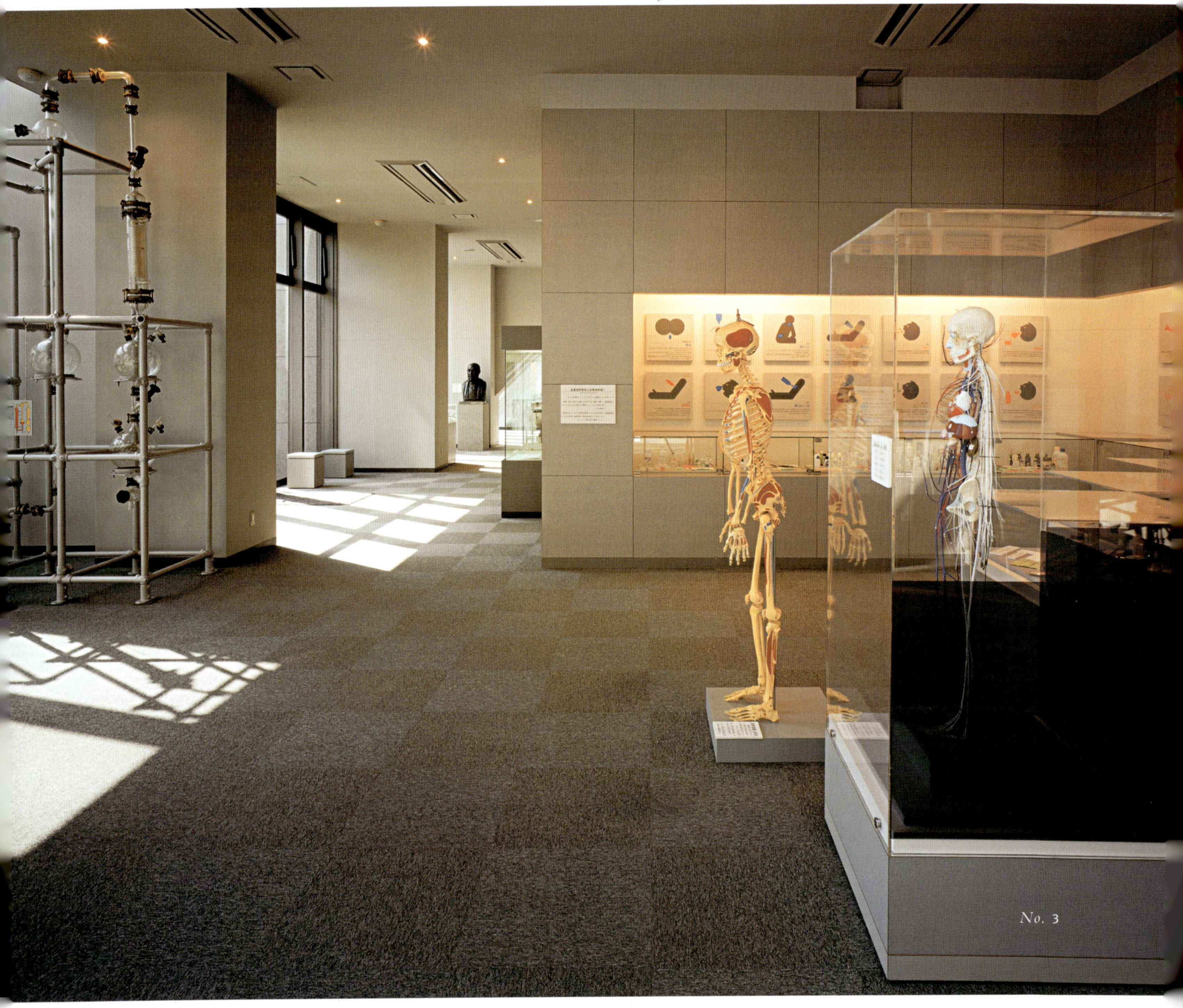
No. 3

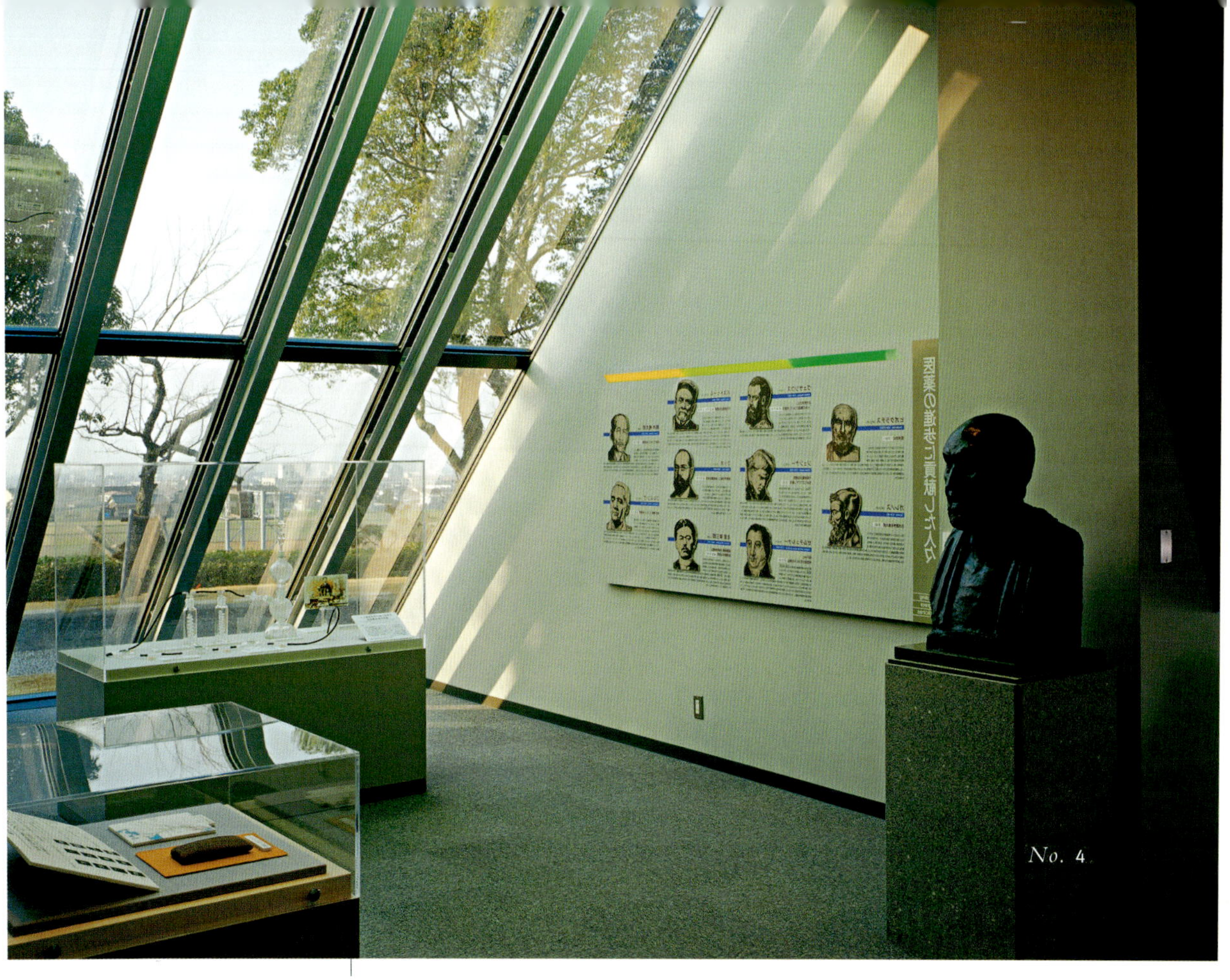

No. 3-4

DESCRIPTION

CAPTION PHOTO

No. 3 EXHIBITIONS INCLUDE RECENT ACHIEVEMENTS IN PHARMACEUTICAL SCIENCE CONTRASTED WITH ANCIENT PRACTICES.

No. 4 THERE IS A STRONG INTERACTION BETWEEN THE EXTERIOR LANDSCAPE AND THE GALLERIES WITHIN.

Musee Archeologique

1 *PROJECT*
Musee Archeologique | *Saint-Romain-EnGal/Vienne, France*

2 *ARCHITECT*
Chaix & Morel | *Paris, France*

The architect approached the site as an archeologist would a ruin, for in fact, the site contains excavated remains of Roman civilization. The solution was to design two different, yet connected buildings that embrace the ruins and allow visitors to experience the archeologist's discovery as their own.

Located along the Rhone River, the museum appears as a rectangular box, except for the monumental staircase notched its entire length. The building sits alongside the road leading from the bridge. The staircase rises from the river and runs up to a projecting point on the roof terrace on the concrete structure. The second level contains the entrance to the concrete and glass building, which houses the reception and museum services (such as bookshop, cafeteria, and amphitheater), and offices.

Set at a skewed right angle, the second building is connected to the first by a glass walkway. Housing the permanent exhibition, this building takes a much different form. Its delicate silhouette evokes the temporary structures used to cover ruins at archeological sites. The building, which shelters the permanent exhibition, is actually suspended over an excavation site by four rows of six columns. Beams carry the weight and support the framing systems for the two internal floor levels.

The interiors are filled with natural light because silk-screen glass slates held by stay cables act as diffusing sunbreakers to allow daylight to enter. Inside a series of mezzanines offers views down over the large mosaics. The displays related to the river are on the riverside. Running down the apex of the museum is a central room housing the masterpiece Lycurgue mosaic.

No. 1
DESCRIPTION

CAPTION PHOTO

No. 1 Mosaic tiles discovered among the ruins, are hung for visitors to review.

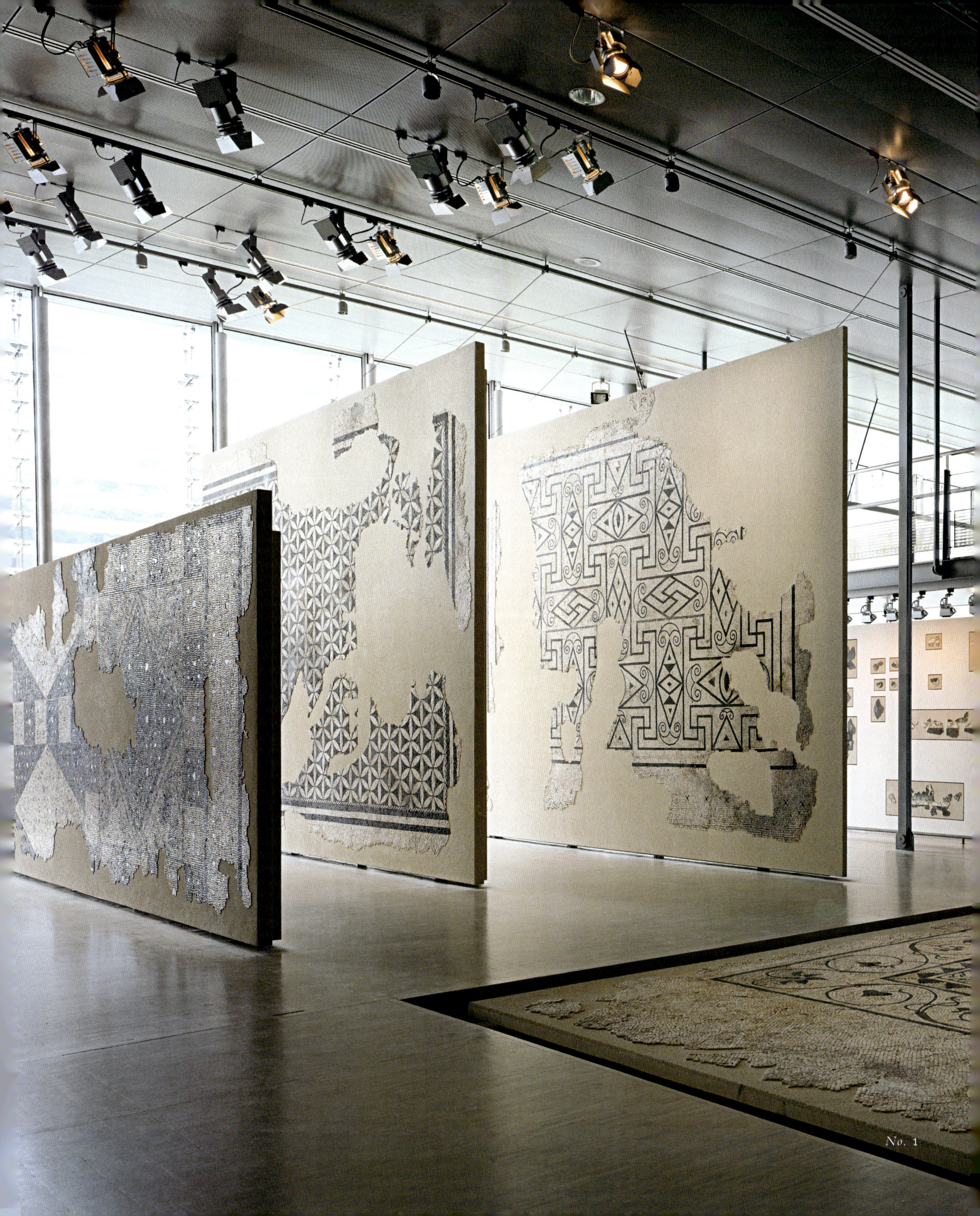

No. 1

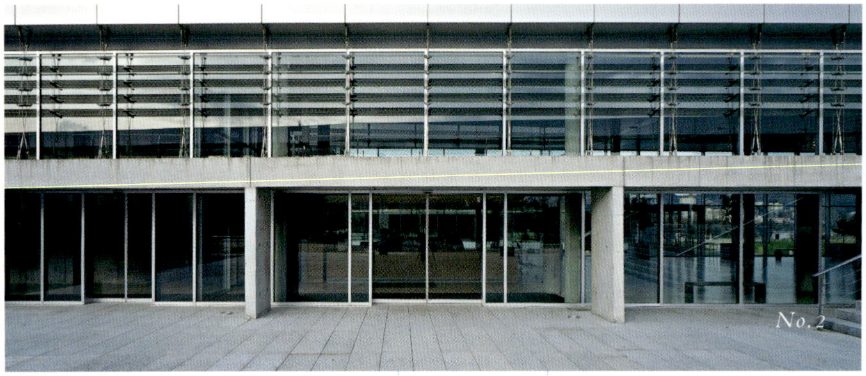

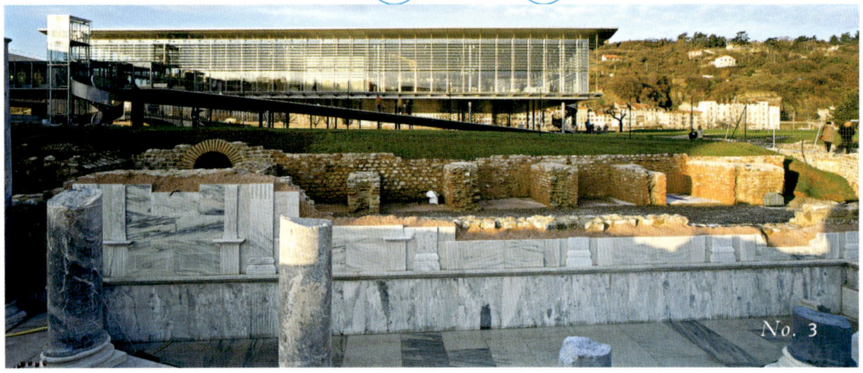

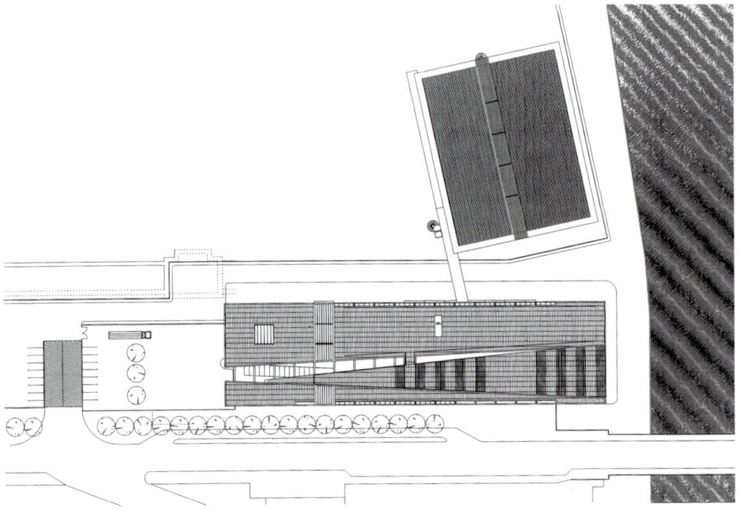

CAPTION PHOTO

No. **2, 3 & 4** The museum complex is composed of two buildings linked by a glass footbridge. The buildings are situated over Roman vintages that have been preserved. The second building contains the permanent exhibition. Glass facades welcome in natural light, which is controlled by silk-screen glass blinds. An inclined footbridge brings the visitor from the nearby archeological site.

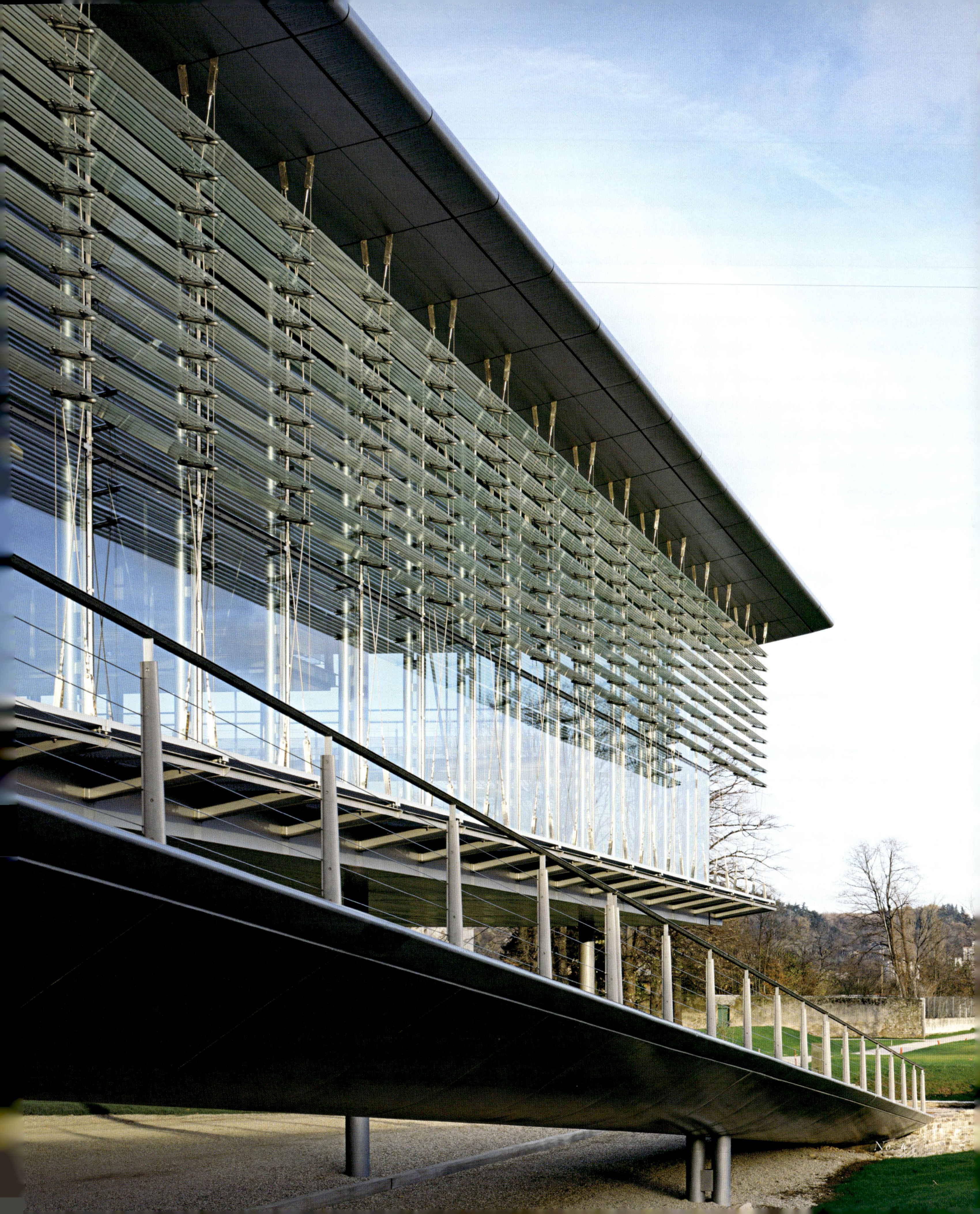

No. 4

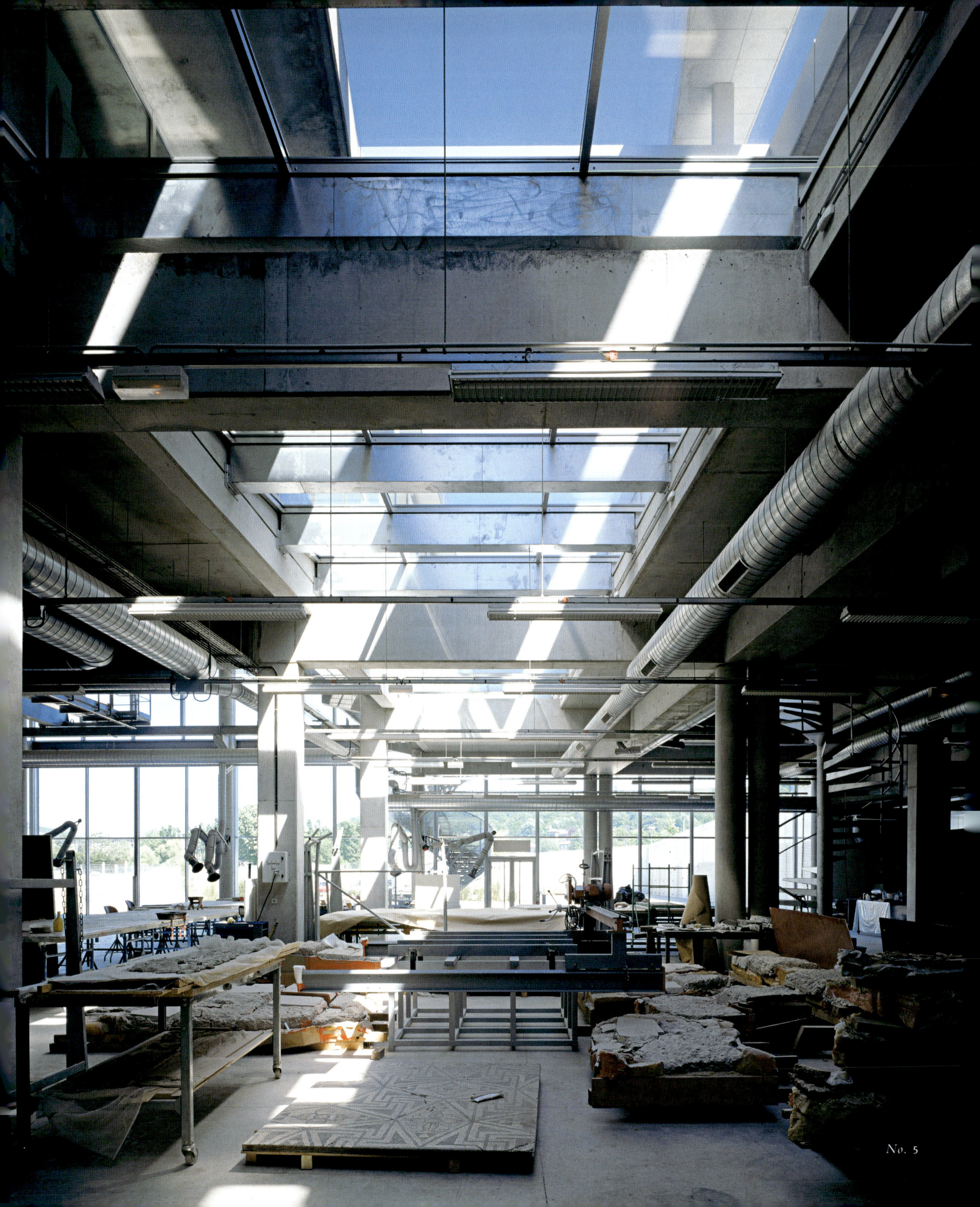

No. 5

No. 5-6

DESCRIPTION

CAPTION

PHOTO

No. **5 & 6** INSIDE THE PERMANENT EXHIBITION IS A SUSPENDED STRUCTURE MUCH LIKE THAT USED TO SUSPEND THE ENTIRE BUILDING OVER THE ARCHEOLOGICAL SITE. THIS SYSTEM ALLOWS THE VISITORS A GOOD OVERVIEW OF THE EXHIBITIONS.

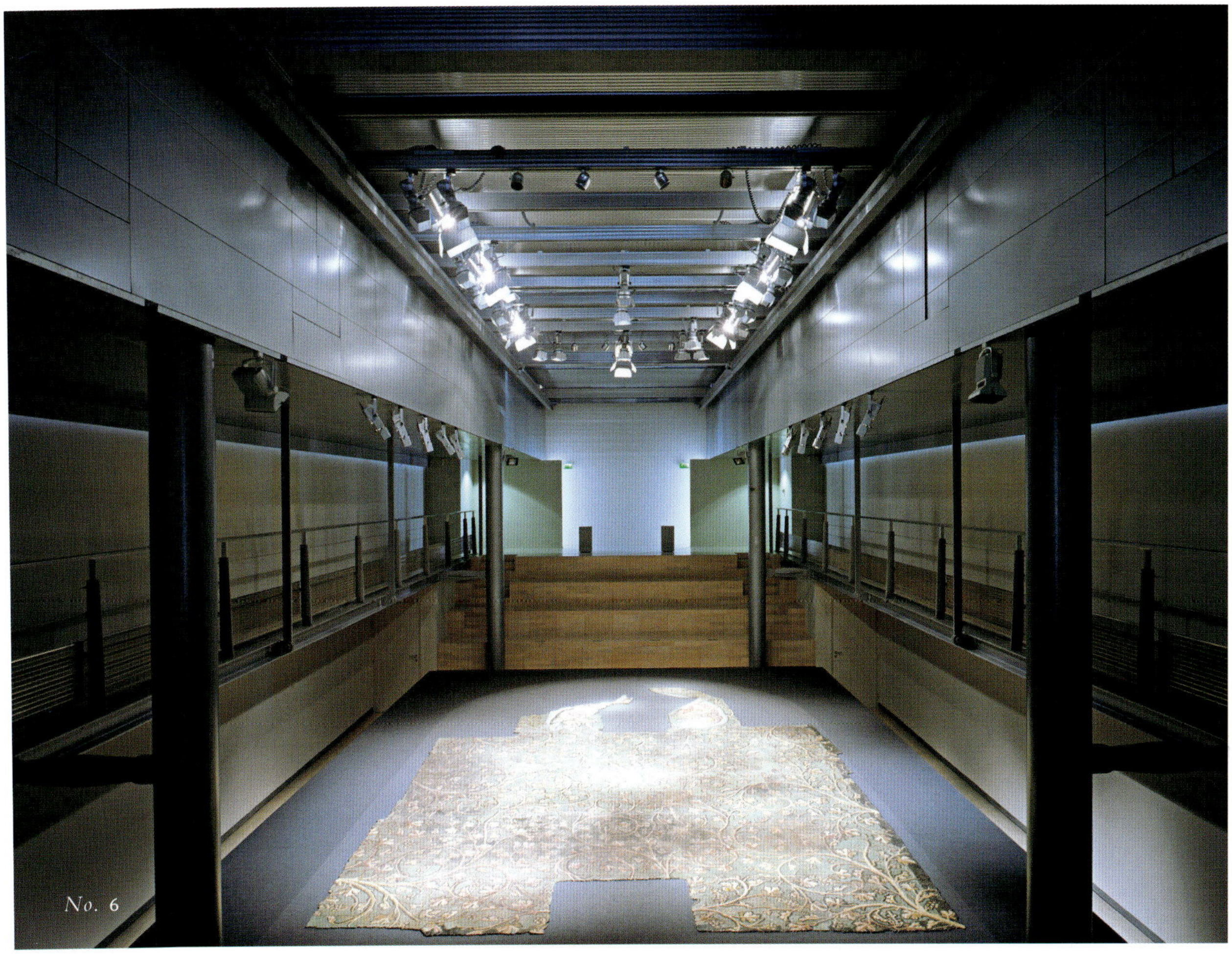

No. 6

Center of Science And Industry

1 *PROJECT*
Center of Science and Industry | COLUMBUS, OHIO

2 *ARCHITECT*
Arata Isozaki | TOKYO, JAPAN

Approach the museum from the east and then from the west and you'll think it's two entirely different buildings: On one side it's a 1920s neoclassical structure, set against a dark screen, overlooking the Scioto River. On the other, you'll discover an abstract, oblong concrete form that acts as a frontispiece for the entire downtown Columbus skyline. Such is Arata Isozaki's design of the Center of and Industry (COSI), which boldly contrasts new against old.

COSI's east side, Isozaki says, "speaks about tradition, memory, the past." The west side "speaks about innovation, hope, the future."

Set along the Scioto River across from downtown Columbus, Isozaki's addition houses 140,000 square feet (12,600-square-meters) of COSI's 230,000 square feet (20,700-square-meter), the rest being a 1920s neoclassical structure that originally served as a high school. Characteristically, Isozaki's work is recognized by abstract, curved forms. At COSI, the western façade of the addition is a 1,000-foot-long (300-meter-long) concrete clothoid curve made of 6-feet by 62-feet (1.8 meter by 18.6 meter) precast concrete panels. Each of the panels curves in two directions. On each side, where the addition plugs into the U-shaped high school, Isozaki carved out the back of the lozenge and plugged in a row of stair towers, which are clad in black-pointed corrugated-metal panels.

A plinth interacts the building's ground floor on the south side and contains the service functions that, because of the museum's position on the Scioto's flood plan, cannot be placed in the basement. Two rectangular boxes protruding from the west wall, along with a cylindrical entrance rotunda in that façade's center complete the interruptions to the pavilion's sweeping envelope.

At the core of the addition, the main public space is designed as a cube. Light enters through skylights; the back façade of the high school forms a stage set at the eastern end, the lozenge's entrance rotunda plays off against the cube's orthogonal frame. Most of COSI's program elements open up to this grand lobby. Deigned by exhibition designers, the museums spaces are a collection of scientifically thematized fantasy environments called "learning worlds," including nineteenth and twentieth century main streets, underwater scenes, and gadget-filled labs.

No. 1
DESCRIPTION

CAPTION PHOTO

No. 1 EACH OF THE 158 PRECAST CONCRETE PANELS IS 6 BY 62 SQUARE FEET (1.8 BY 18.6-SQUARE-METER).

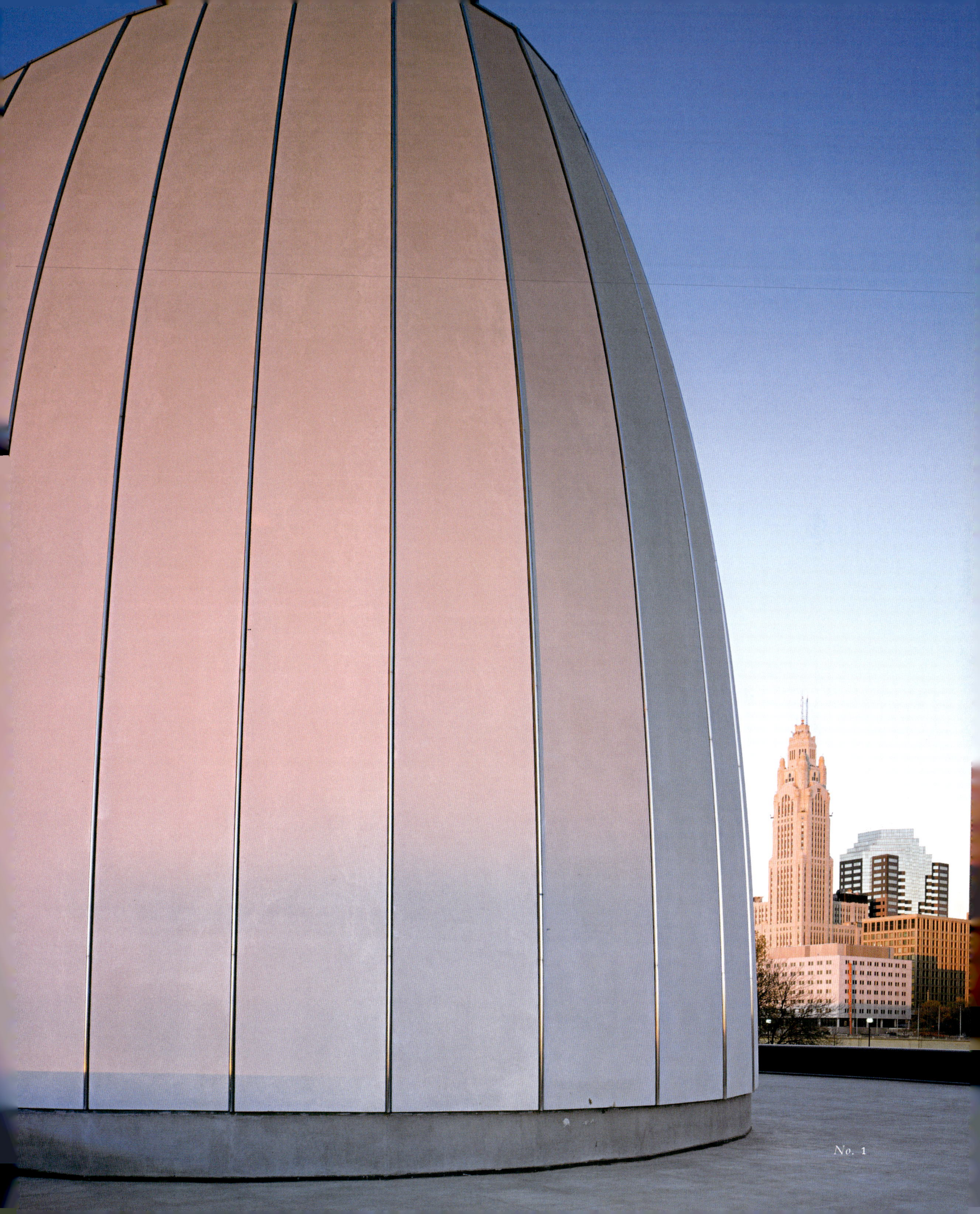

No. 1

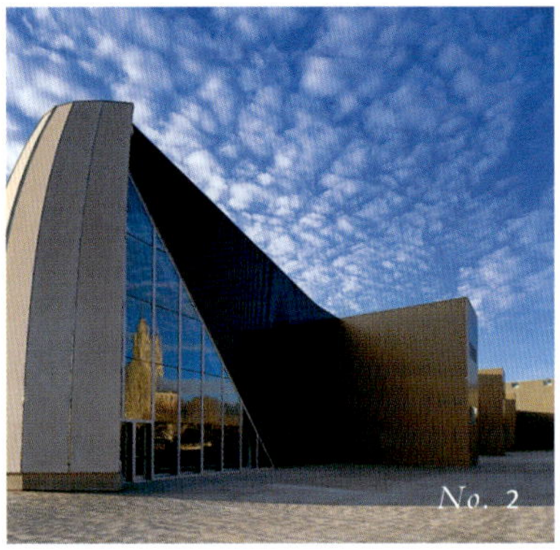

No. 2

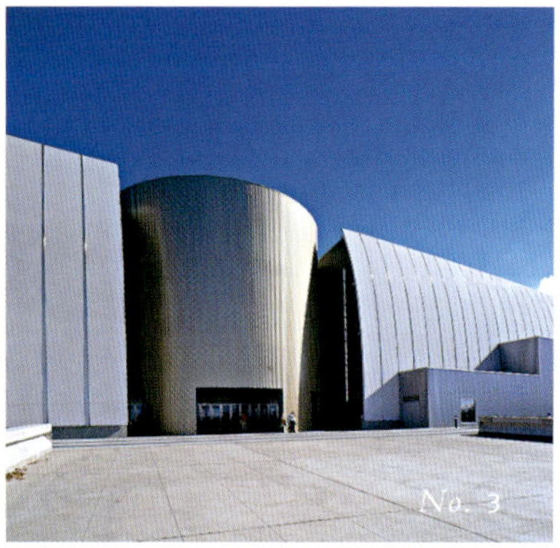

No. 3

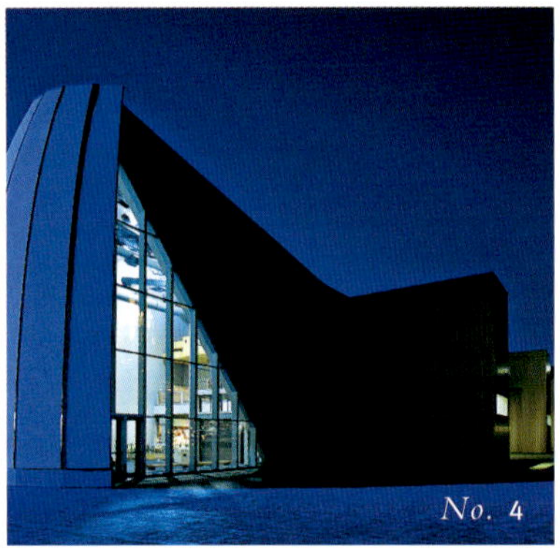

No. 4

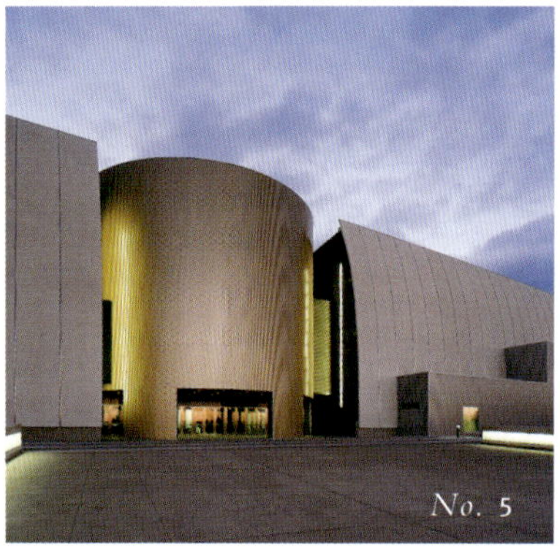

No. 5

No. 2-8

DESCRIPTION

CAPTION

PHOTO

No. 2 & 4 A large triangular window illuminates an exhibition space inside.

No. 3 & 5 A cylindrical form in the center of the west facade encases the domed theater and marks the building's primary entrance, which passes beneath the theater.

No. 6 With downtown Columbus, Ohio, as a backdrop, the museum sits on a 17-acre parcel on the west back of the Scioto River.

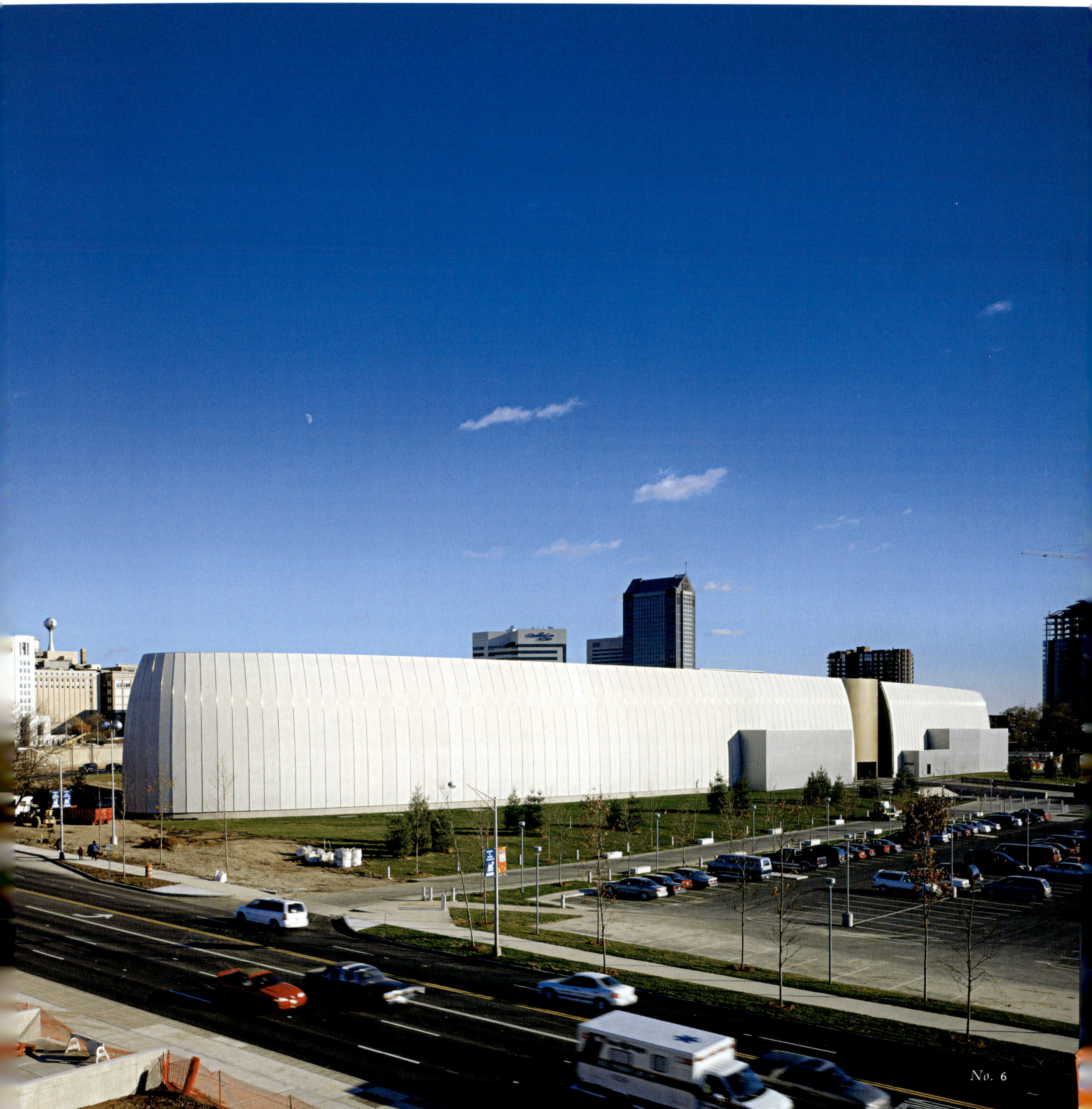
No. 6

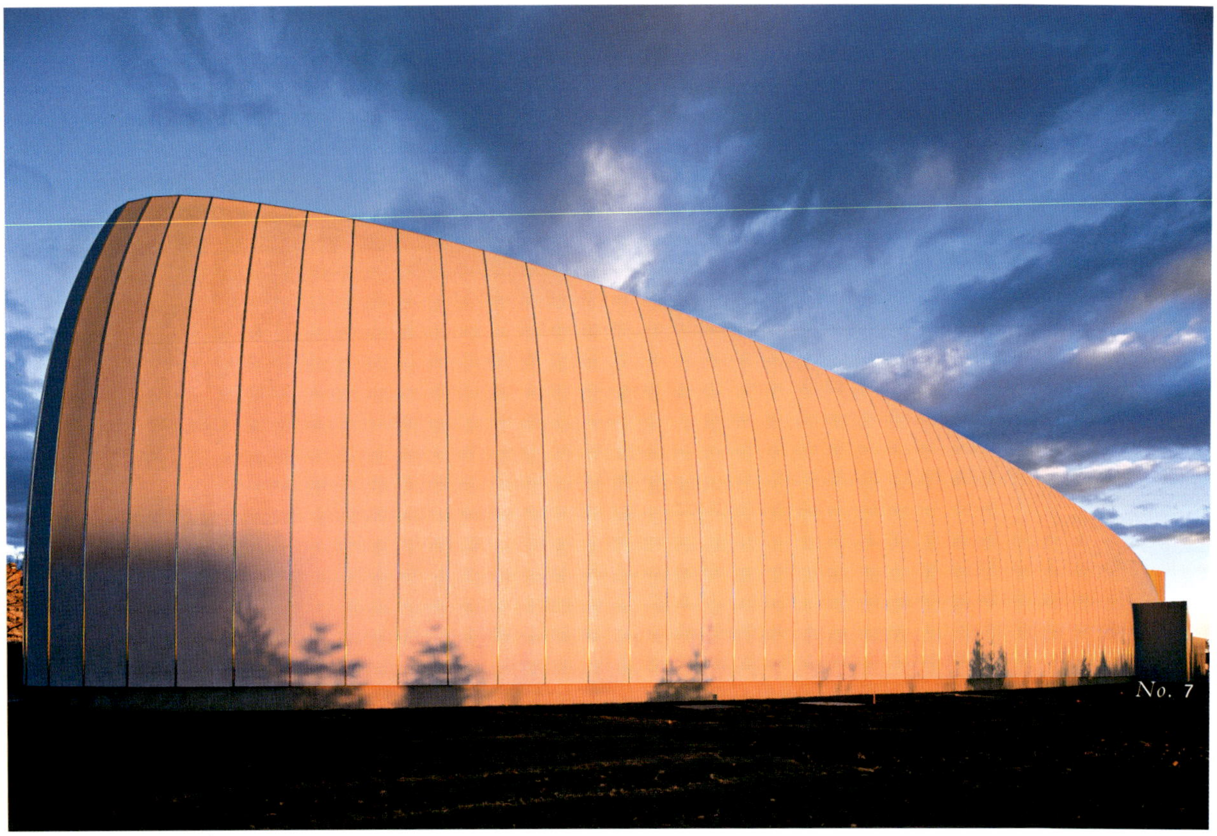

No. 7

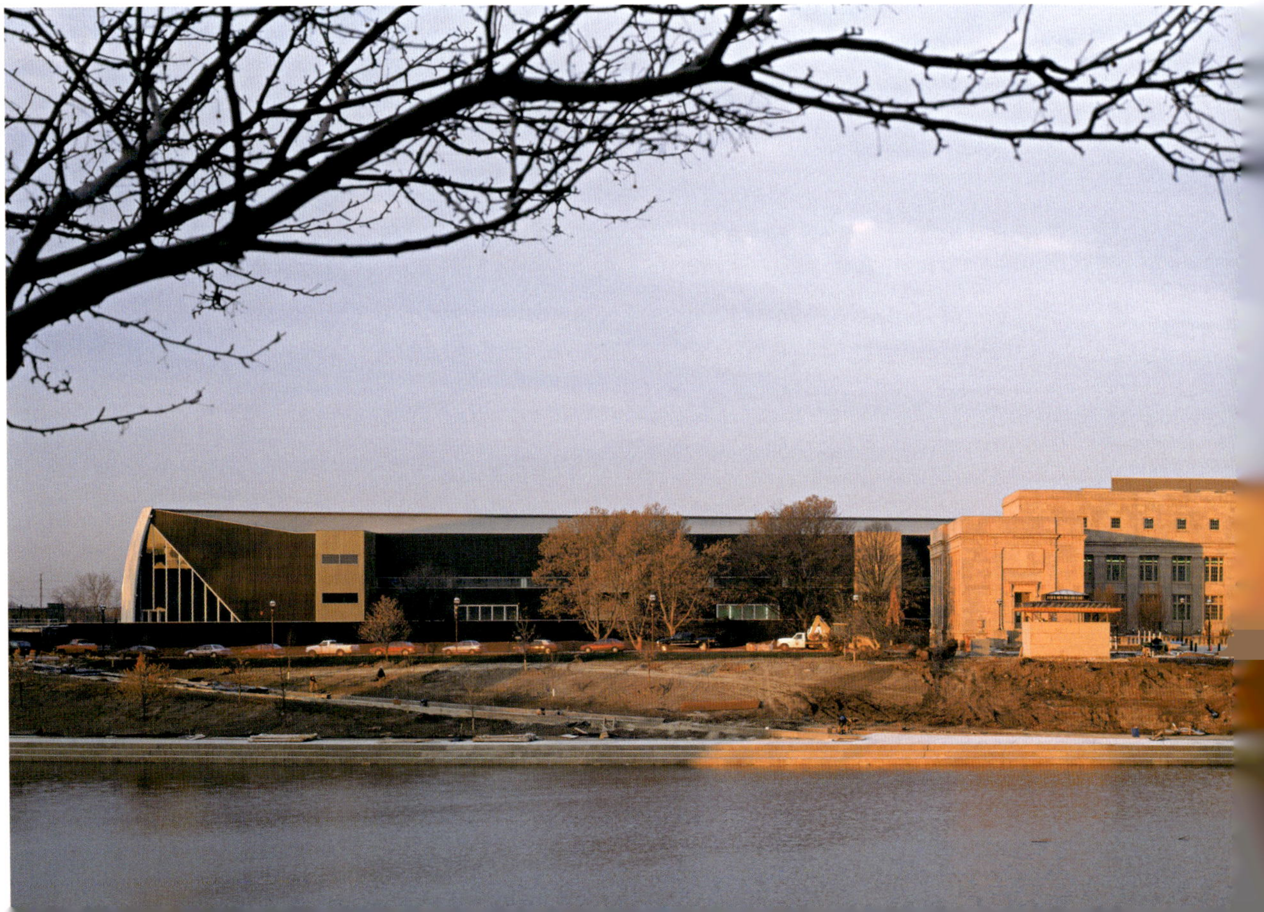

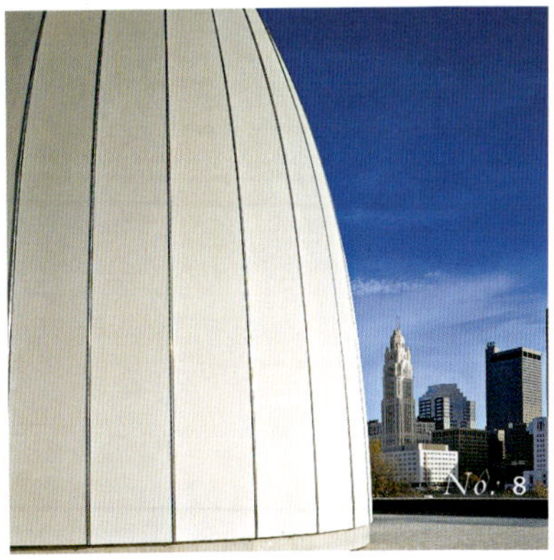
No. 8

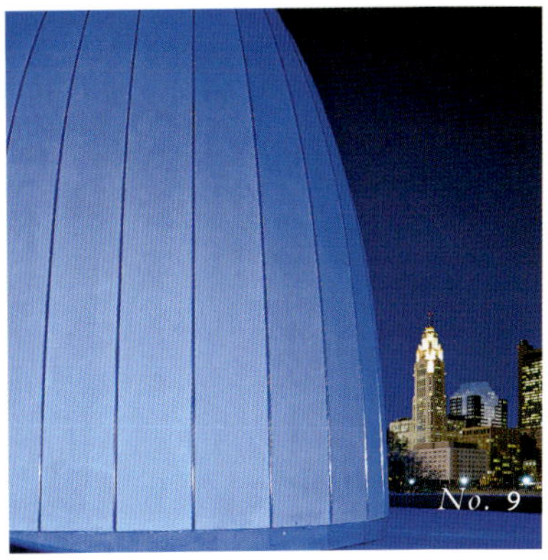
No. 9

CAPTION PHOTO

No. 7 The new museum is enveloped in a long, curved shell, shaped as a partial eclipse stretching 960 feet from end to end and rising to a height of 65 feet.

No. 8 & 9 The city's skyline juxtaposed against the curving concrete shell.

No. 10 The east facade reveals the original 1920s neoclassical structure that the new building wraps around.

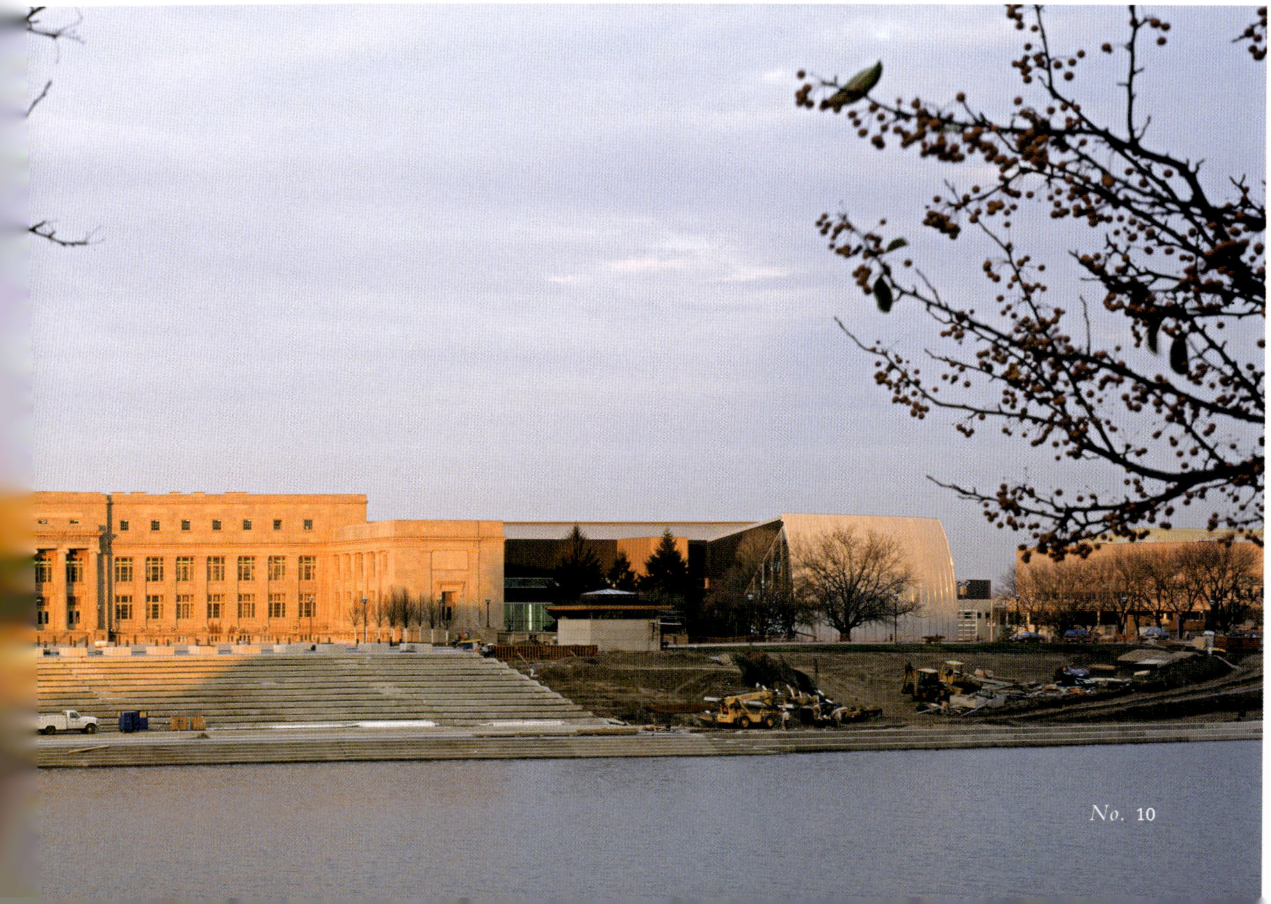
No. 10

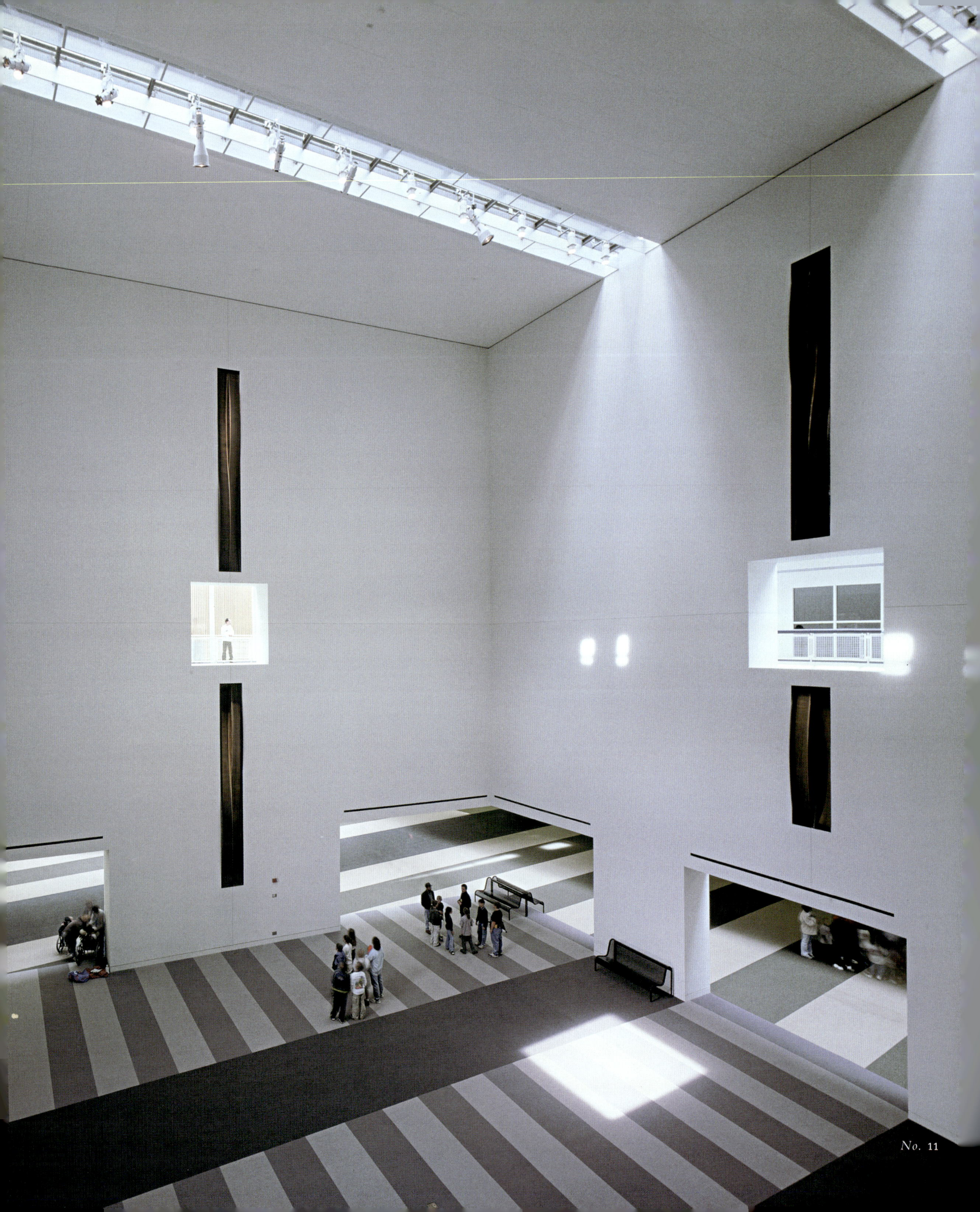

No. 11

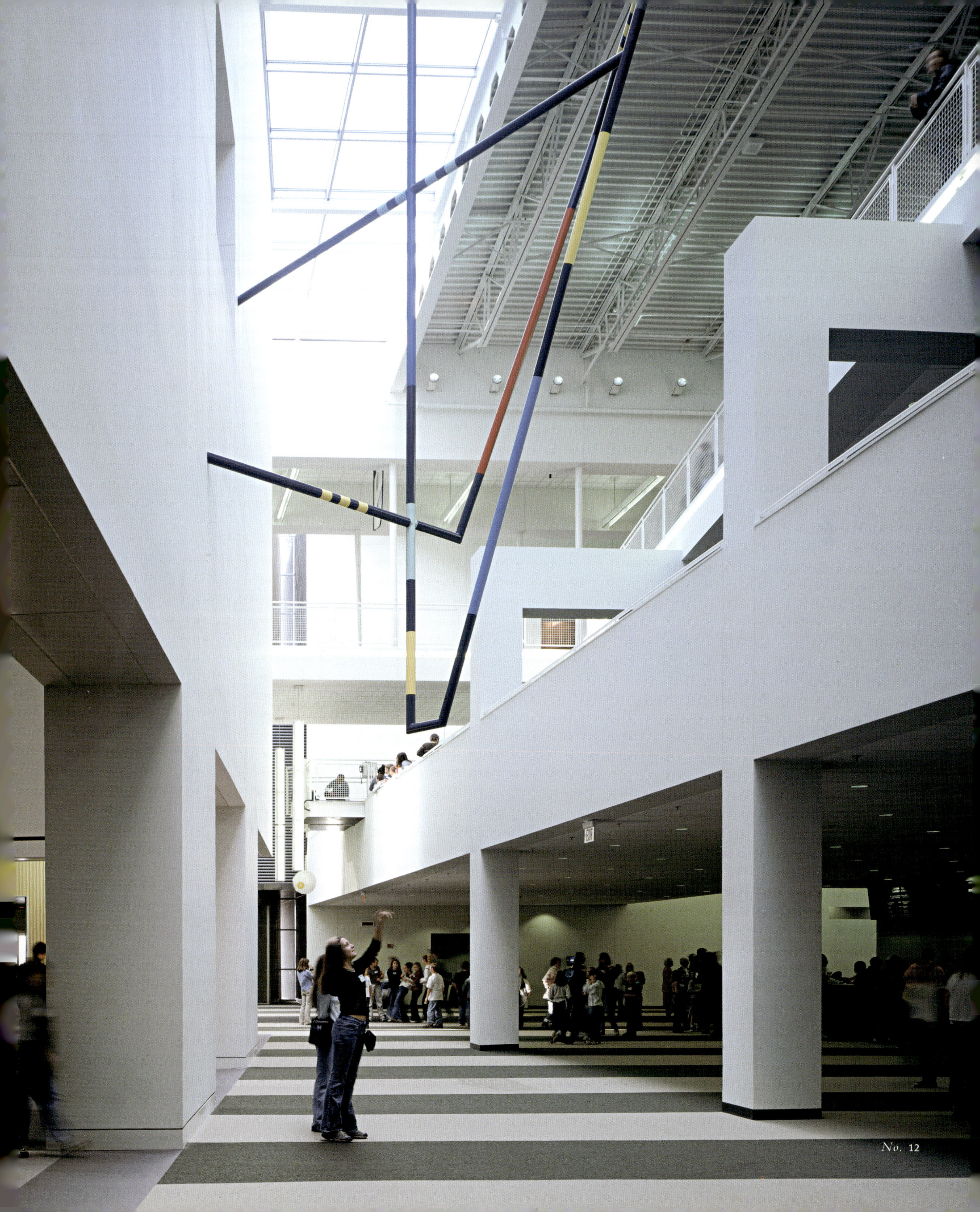

No. 12

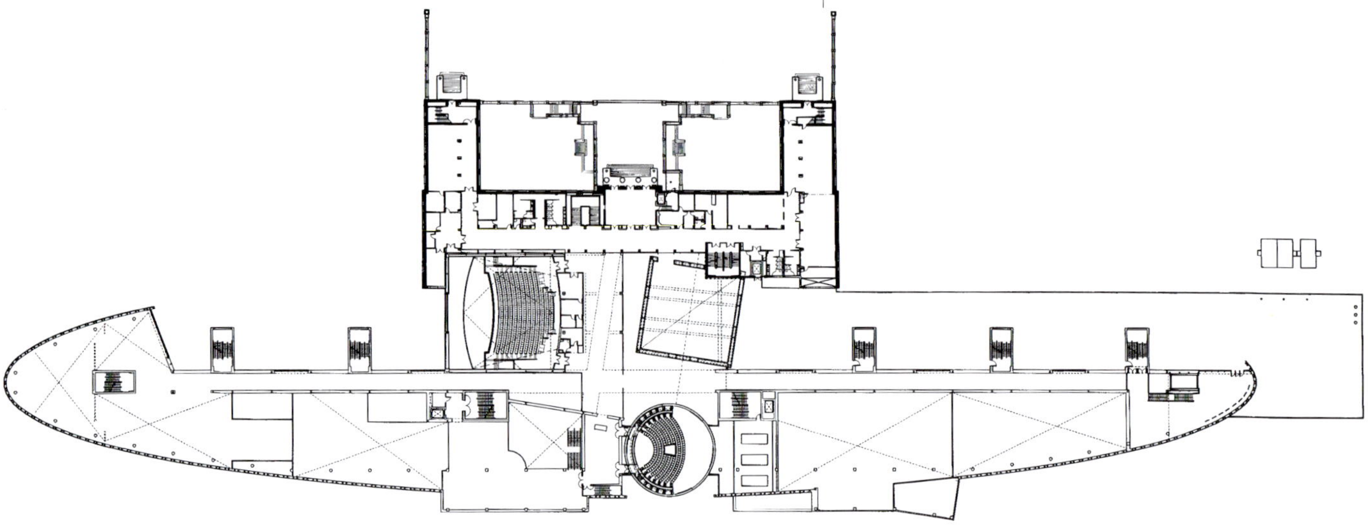

No. 11-13

DESCRIPTION

CAPTION PHOTO

No. 11 The atrium is a perfect cube measuring 75 by 75 by 75 feet, punctuated by skylights.

No. 12 The 960-feet, carpeted circulation spine runs the length of the building.

No. 13 An opening in the atrium's multistory wall.

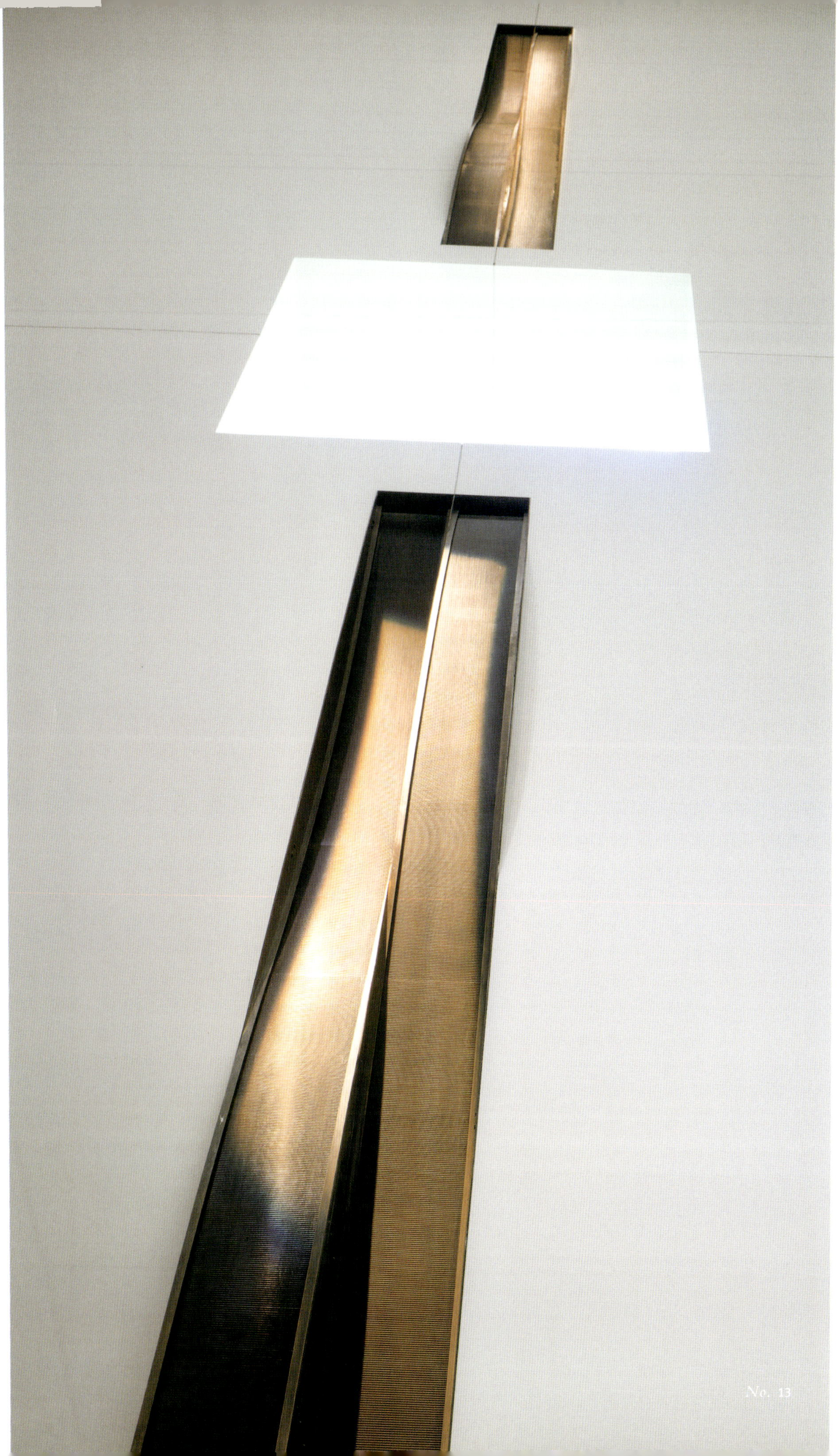
No. 13

Norsk Oljemuseum

1 *PROJECT*
Norsk Oljemuseum | *Stavanger, Norway*

2 *ARCHITECT*
Lunde & Lovseth Architects | *Stavanger, Norway*

Set in Stavanger Harbor, the Norwegian Petroleum Museum needs no signage to announce itself. Architect Lunde and Lovseth call the design a "scenographic interpretation" of Norway's petroleum industry. Its three shining cylindrical platforms mimic a much larger oilrig. The main stone-clad building is meant as a paraphrase of the Norwegian bedrock where the forces of nature have passed sediment to the North Sea and created the basis for the oil. Its exhibition hall resembles a space in the landscape facing the sea where the black slate floors elude sea bottom's the petrified slate and limestone sedimentations.

Norway first discovered oil in the North Sea in 1969, and the museum documents the history of drilling there. It also connects nature, man, and technology. The main building is covered in dark gray Barents Blue gneiss from Varanger. It draws geometric references from the town's wooden houses and long and narrow storehouses, tying the oil industry to the local economy. At the main buildings' entrance and staircases, the gneiss is formed in a wave-like motion to appear as if scrubbed by glaciers, a theme that is repeated in the exhibition hall's glazed façade. Underneath the gneiss is black, spackled concrete, which appears as black granite on the exterior.

The exhibition hall faces the sea and provides a stunning view towards the Stavanger fjord, (a wharf for the oilrigs), as well as the North Sea itself. The interior is designed to feel like a vast cave.

Perhaps the main attraction is the journey to the oilrig, which begins via the "check-in-stairs"—a helicopter cabin that whisks visitors across a bridge to the middle cylinder. The outer cylinder is an exhibit of life on the platform, with drilling tower and drilling rod. The inner platform plunges down to the sea. Set in a well with a cubic cap, audio-visual effects reflect off mirrored sides to create an artificial atmosphere.

No. 1
Description

Caption Photo

No. 1 Celebrating the history of oil, the museum is sited like a giant oilrig in Staranger Harbor.

Photos: Espen Gronli

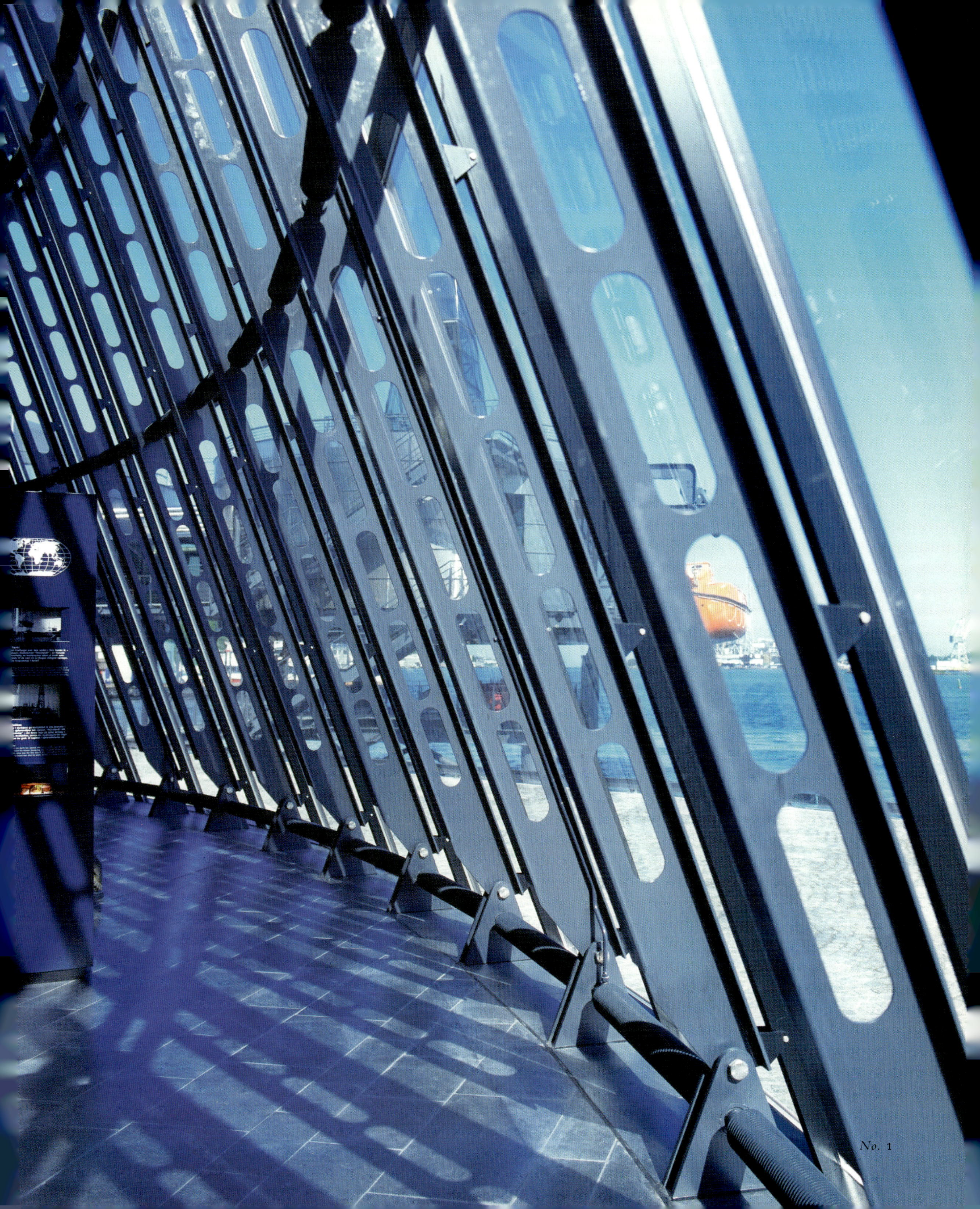

No. 1

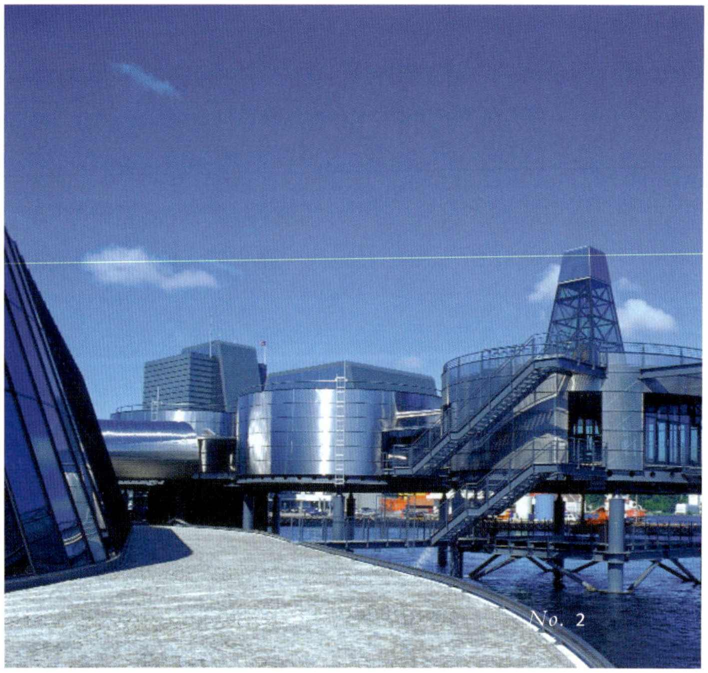

No. 2-3

DESCRIPTION

CAPTION PHOTO

No. 2 A massive granite volume signals the entrance.

No. 3 In the main hall are exhibitions on Norway's maritime history, as well as innovative methods of drilling and the production of oil at increasing ocean depths.

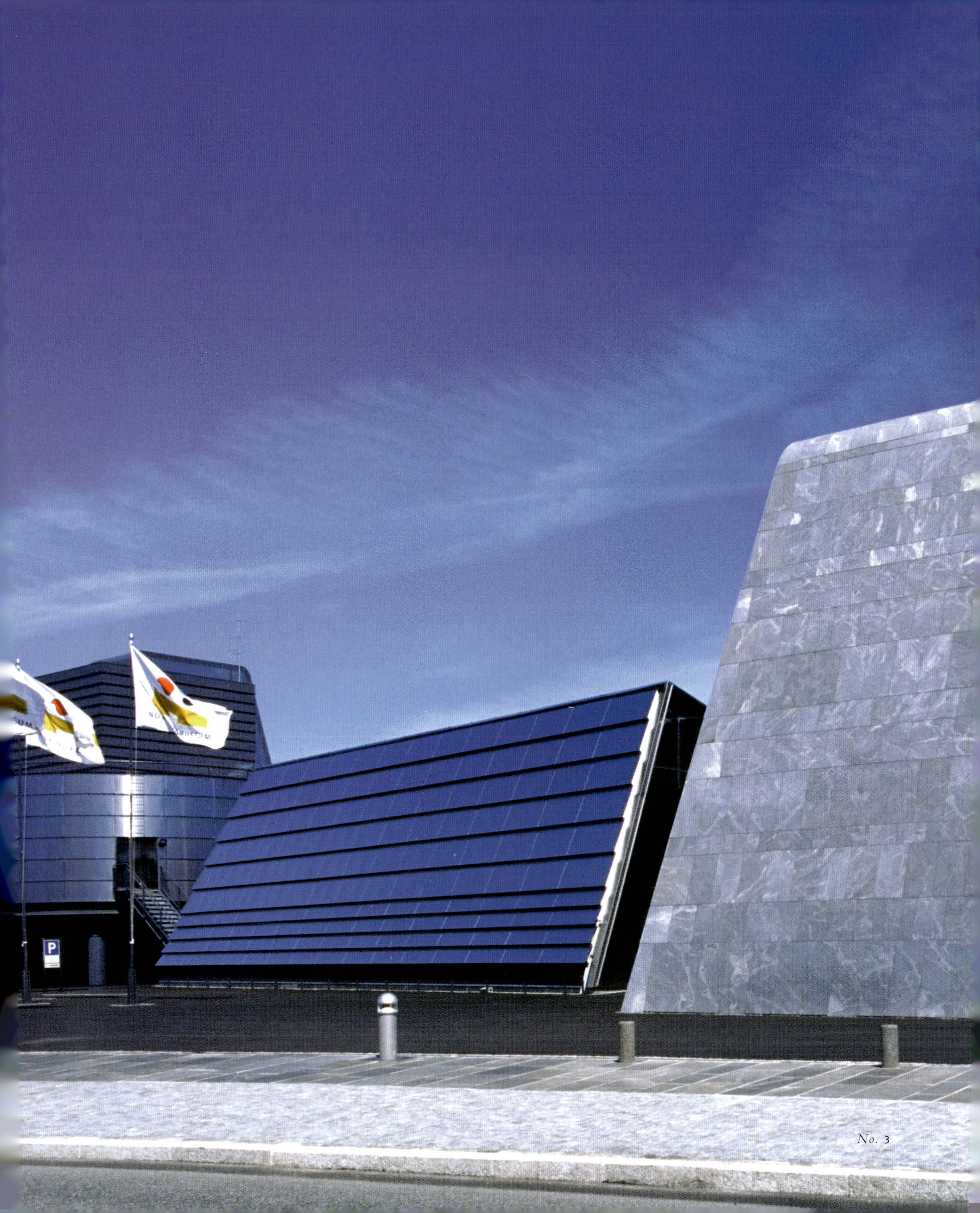

No. 3

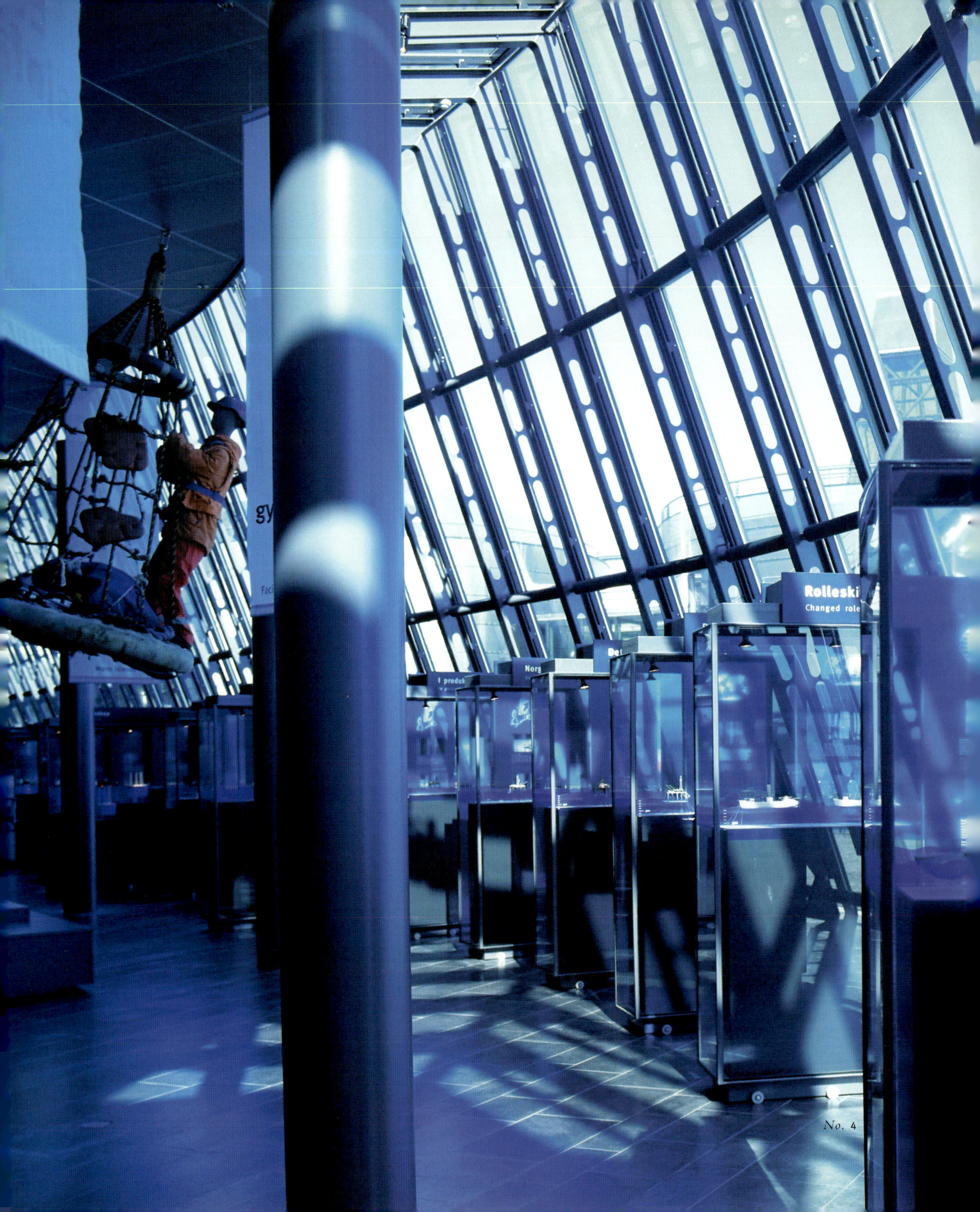

No. 4

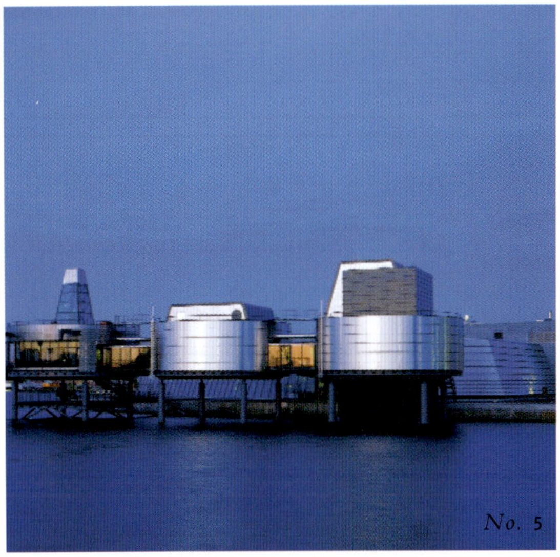

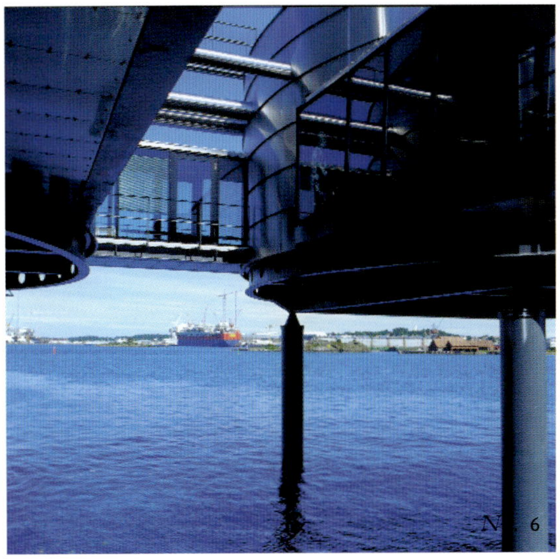

No. 4-6

DESCRIPTION

CAPTION PHOTO

No. 4 THE MUSEUM CONSISTS OF TWO SECTIONS—THE EXHIBITION HALL, WHICH IS ON SHORE, AND THREE OFF-SHORE INSTALLATIONS, WHICH CONTAIN AN EXHIBITION OF NATURAL HISTORY, SCENES FROM WORK AND LEISURE ON AN OFF SHORE OIL RIG.

No. 5 & 6 SITUATED AT THE EDGE OF THE BAY, THIS MUSEUM IS BOTH A ONSHORE AND AN OFFSHORE EXPERIENCE IN KEEPING WITH ITS MISSION.

Mashantucket Pequot Museum and Research Center

1 *PROJECT*
Mashantucket Pequot Museum and Research Center | *Mashantucket Reservation, Connecticut*

2 *ARCHITECT*
Polshek Partnership Architects | *New York, New York*

With new prosperity gained from its lucrative bingo enterprise and casino resort, the Mashantucket Pequot Indians were able to realize a symbolic contribution to their tribal people. The new museum and research center takes the form—albeit a modern interpretation—of the seventeenth century fort lost to British soldiers in 1637. This exhibition and gathering center links past to present while looking toward the future.

The building sits in a wooded, 14-acre site next to the Pequot's Foxwood casino complex located near Mystic, Connecticut. The center's soaring glass atrium recalls the circular form of the seventeenth century fort, yet the architect resists the urge to turn it into a modern-day teepee. The atrium is the heart of the 300,000-square-foot (27,000-square-meter) complex, which houses research and education facilities as well as exhibition space. This is the first tribal complex in the United States to combine such facilities; it is considered a model for other tribes across the country.

Inside the atrium, the canted, curving glass encloses a sweeping ramp that leads down to two subterranean levels, a large auditorium, and two smaller circular cinemas. To minimize the building's bulk, 89,000 square feet (8,010-square-meter) of exhibition space was placed underground. From the exterior, the building edges were bermed and a lawn planted to conceal the edges.

The design incorporates symbolic elements, but at the same time yearns to embrace modern technology. The entire south-facing façade is meant to be a giant wampum, a belt made of purple and white shell beads encased in a girded rectangular sheath. In construction terms, this was translated into a two-story aluminum grid with a rectangular slab of gray limestone, slate, and rosy granite.

Inside, the shimmering indigo-tinted terrazzo floor of the gathering hall, which is constructed of bits of iridescent seashells, recalls the Pequot's coastal history. Throughout the building are reminders of tribal handicraft skills—woven metal screens and balcony railings, leather-wrapped door pulls, acoustical wall panels fashioned from copper and hemp, and horsehair fabrics in the Pequot palette of red, black, and green.

The transition to the modern age is seen in the 200-foot-high (60-meter-high) observation tower's exposed trusses and the complex steel armature of the gathering hall. Technical advances take on a more symbolic importance in the state-of-the-art archaeology and conservation labs in the buried research center.

CAPTION PHOTO

No. 1 Steel and cedar trusses shield skylights that illuminate underground galleries and lead to the main atrium and tower.

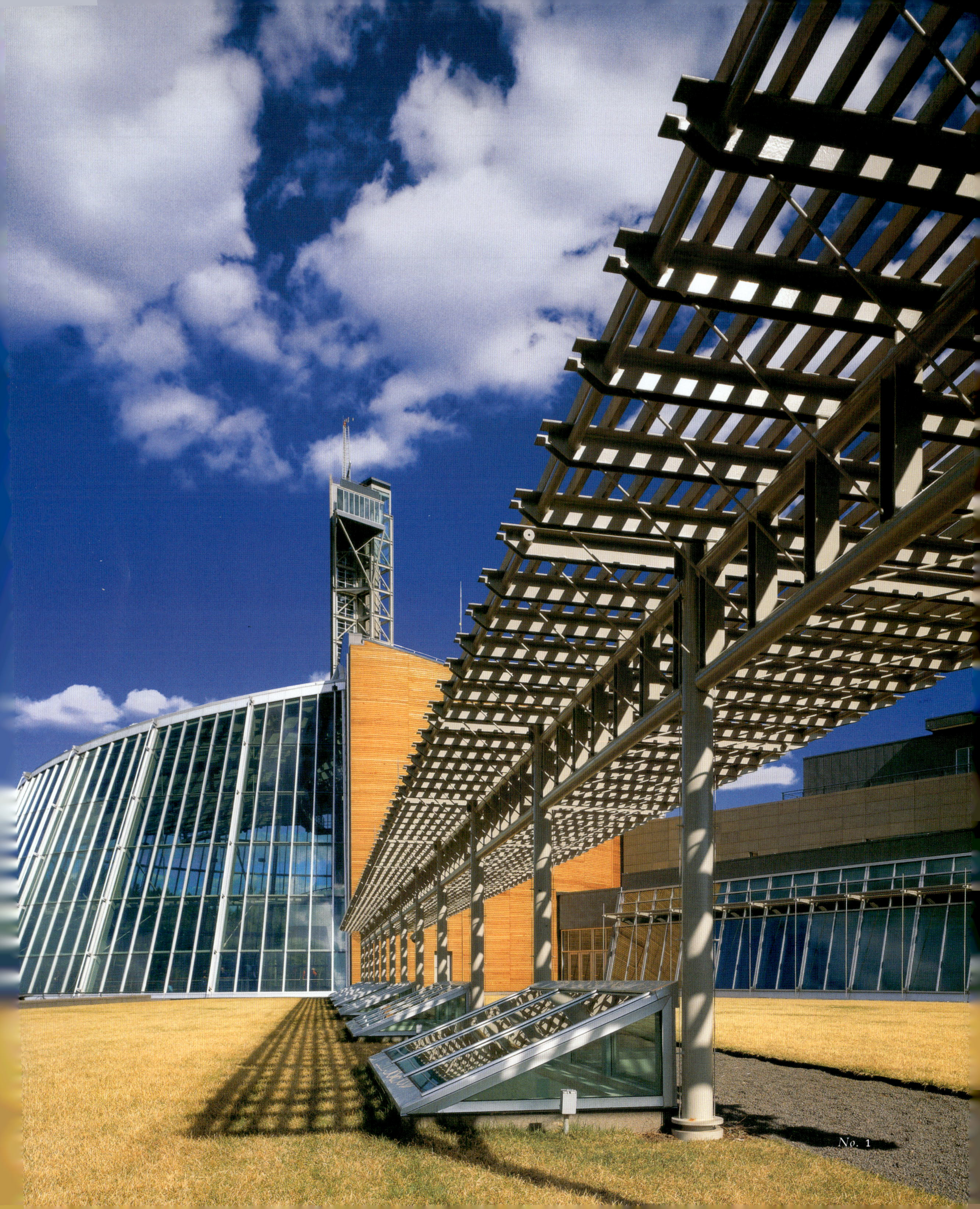

No. 1

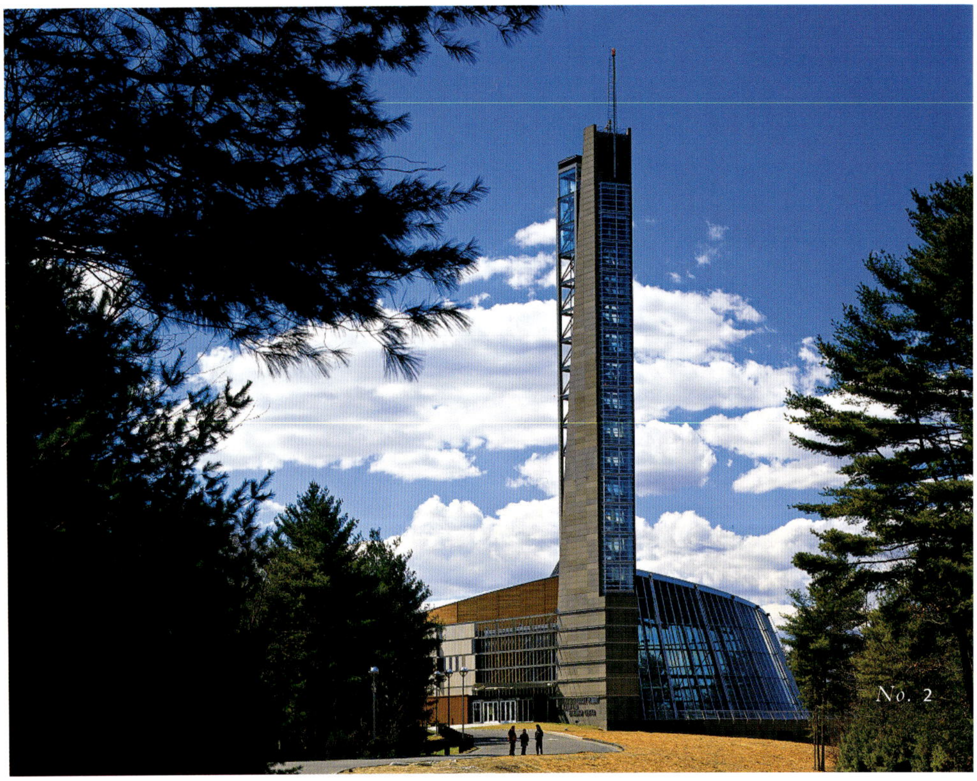

No. 2

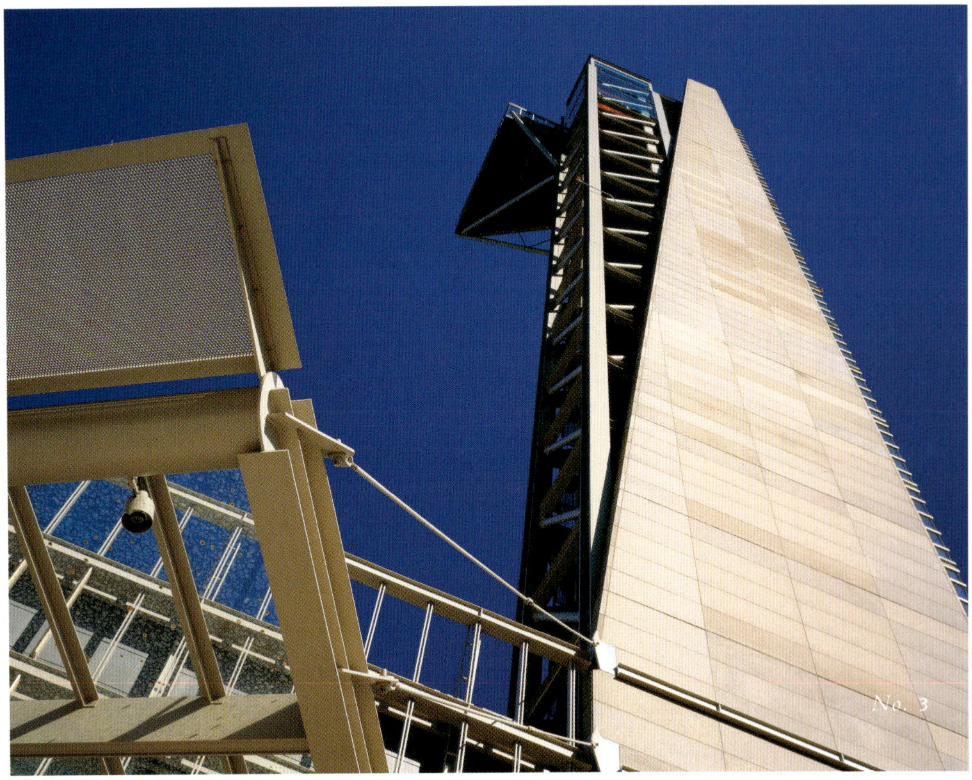

No. 3

No. 2-4
DESCRIPTION

CAPTION PHOTO

No. 2 & 3 On the east, the building terminates at a-200-foot-tall (18-meter-tall), stone clad tower, which marks the entry, identifies the facility from a distance, and provides access to a platform for viewing the entire reservation.

No. 4 The south-facing entry façade symbolizes a giant wampum. It is a two-story aluminum grid inset with gray limestone slate and rose colored granite.

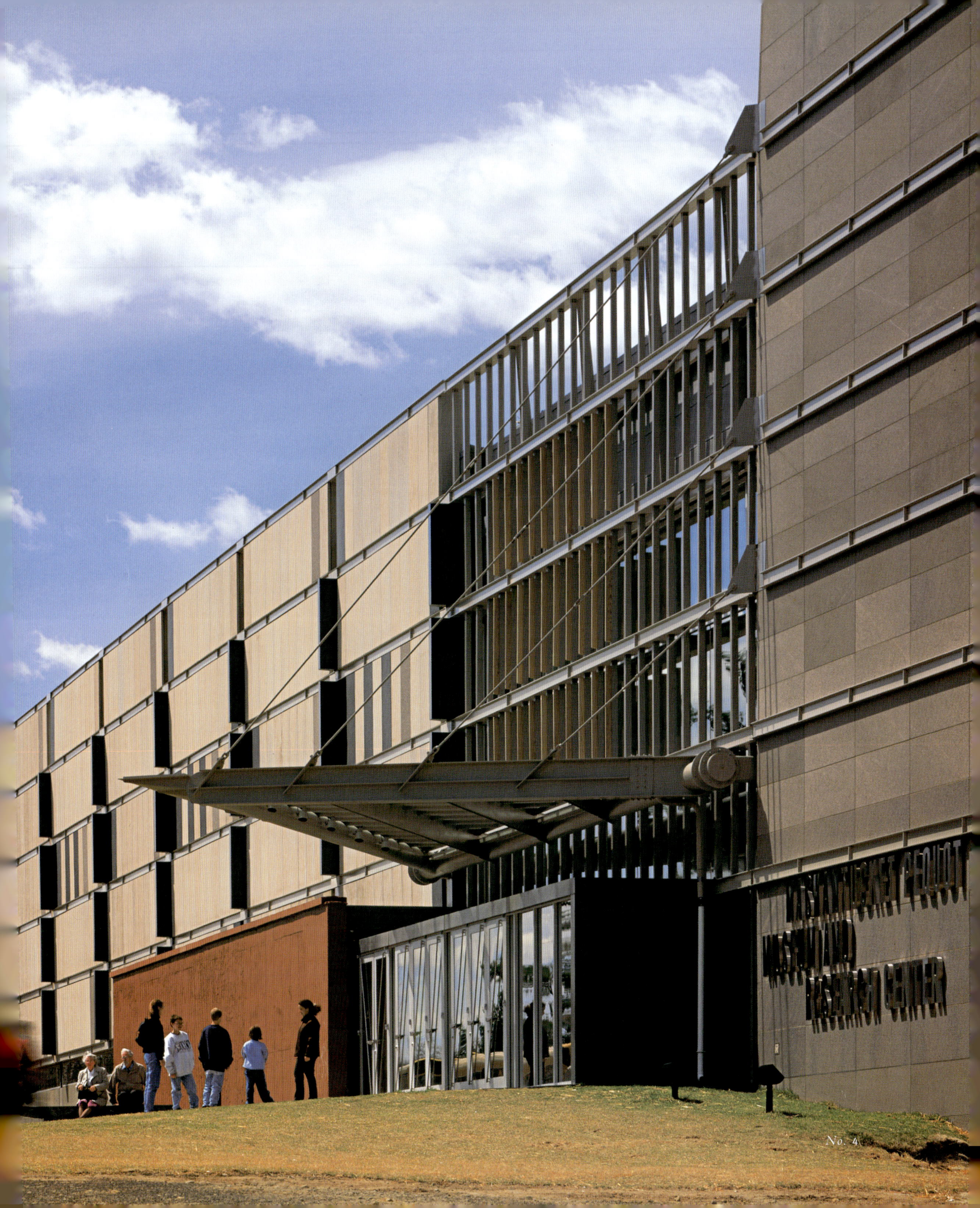

No. 4

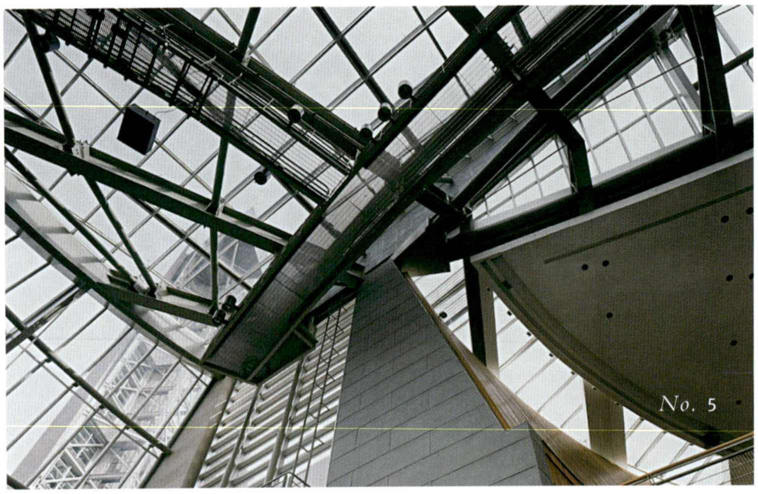

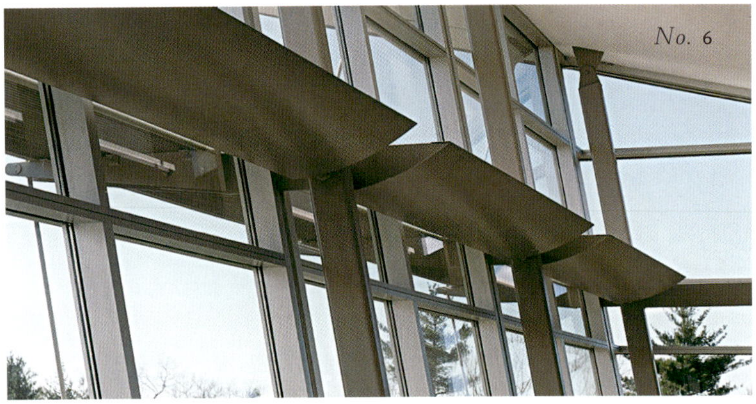

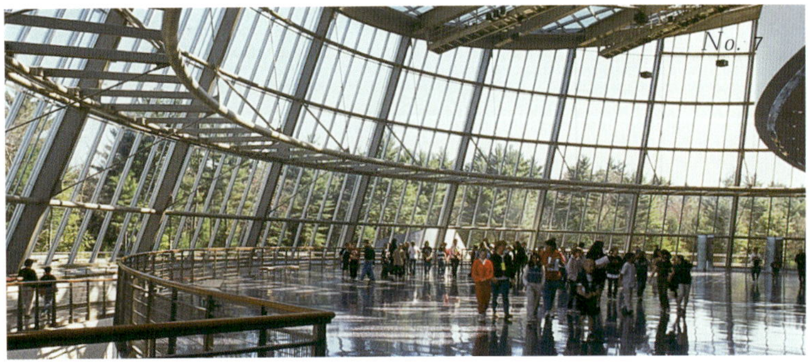

Photo © POLSKEK PARTNERS

No. 5-8
DESCRIPTION

CAPTION PHOTO

No. 5–8 THE MASSIVE GATHERING SPACE CONSISTS OF CANTED GLASS CURVES ENCLOSING THE ATRIUM, ITS SOARING ROOF AT THE HEART OF THE 300,000-SQUARE-FOOT COMPLEX.

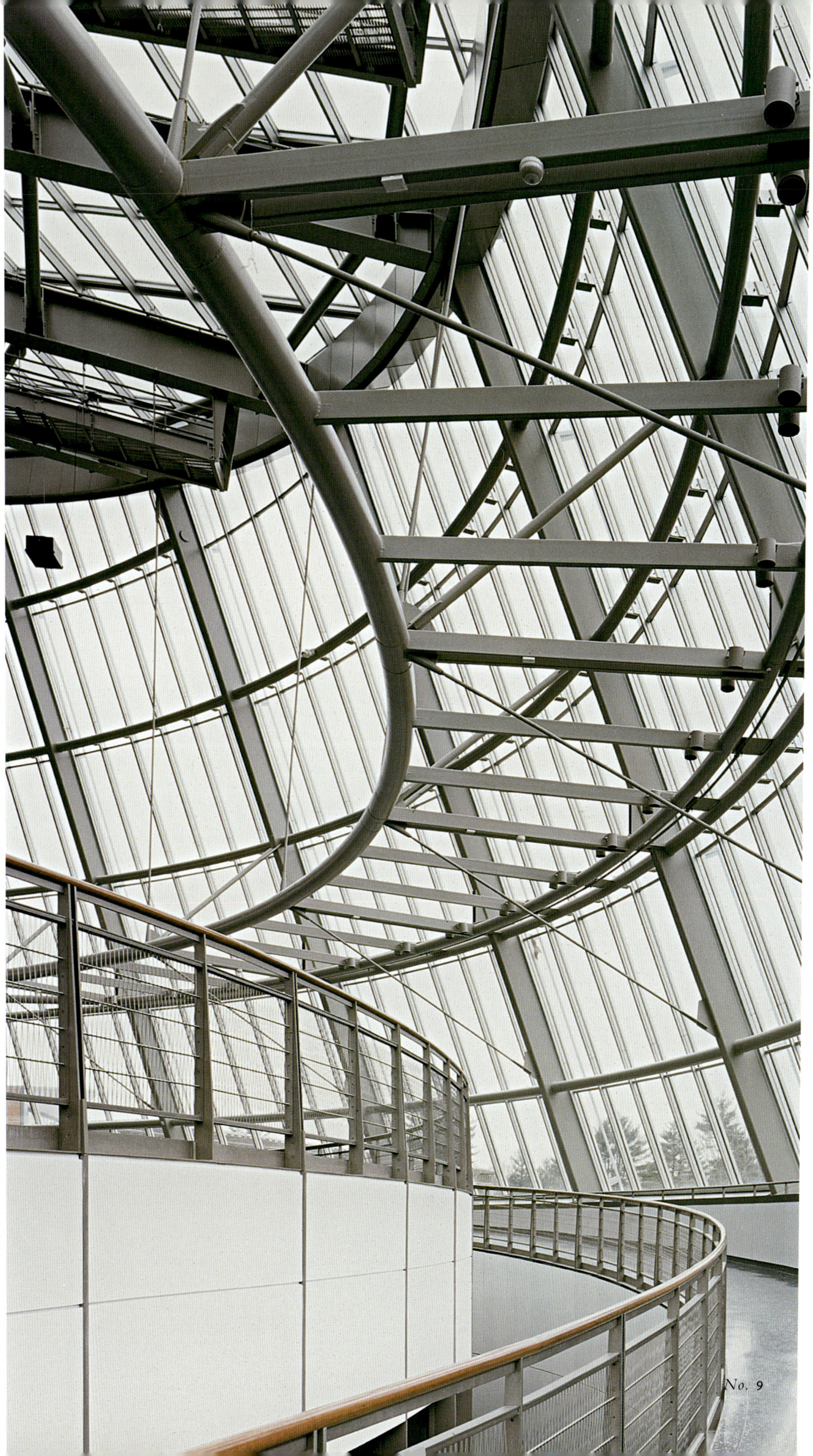

No. 9

Museum of Science and Industry

1 *PROJECT*
Museum of Science and Industry | *Tampa, Florida*

2 *ARCHITECT*
Antoine Predock Architect | *Albuquerque, New Mexico*

Bold geometric forms that rise out of the land itself characterize the architecture of Antoine Predock. Set on the edge of the Florida wetlands, the Museum of Science and Industry in Tampa easily fits this description—its main organizing element is a shimmering blue sphere that seems to clutch the earth and reflect the water and sky around it.

The sphere houses the museum's Omnimax Theater. A journey to the museum, in effect, becomes a journey to the shimmering blue sphere. Visitors enter the museum grounds from heavily trafficked Fowler Avenue along a road that guides them under and through the building. On the way, they get glimpses into the four-story lobby and exhibition spaces. The drive follows the outstretched arm of the wetlands causeway until it penetrates the museum's thick wall, and moves into the woodlands beyond. Visitors park and then return to the museum via the "Florida Biomes" footpath, a journey through several regional environments from the low marshlands to higher and drier, live-oak hummock and a butterfly pavilion near the museum's front door.

A series of truncated legs define an outdoor courtyard. Here the visitors' path penetrates the building and leads to the lobby. The shimmering blue dome is once again visible. Piers lead visitors into the four-story lobby, where they encounter the nested exhibition levels they saw earlier from their cars. From here, the exhibition space flows upward toward the entrance of the Omnimax Theater.

No. 1
Description

Caption
Photo

No. 1 The skin of the sphere is highly reflective stainless steel, recalling the Tampa's blue sky and the waters of its bay. Perched on its massive concrete columns, the piers appear thrust from the earth. The sphere's reflective qualities continue late into the night.

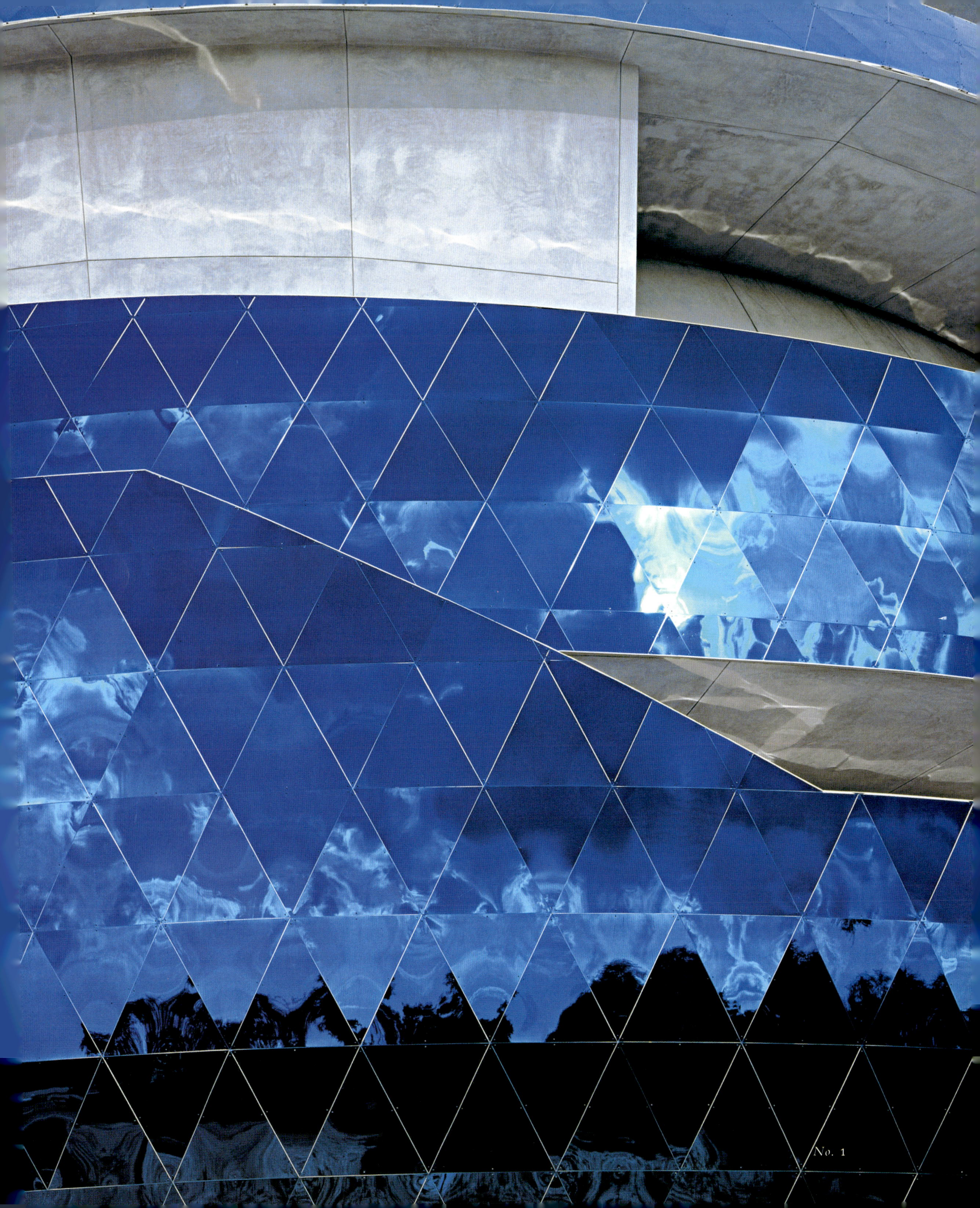

No. 1

CAPTION PHOTO

No. 2 The plan shows bold geometries of Predock's scheme, including the principle organizing elements that culminate at the museum's Omnimax theater.

No. 3 With massive piers supporting the Omnimax theater as a background, visitors have a sweeping view of the Florida wetlands.

No. 4 The museum's powerful geometry sits low and snug in the flat Florida landscape.

No. 5 The auto entrance pierces the entrance the museum and passes by the sphere.

No. 6 The museum's powerful geometries beckon visitors to enter. The Saunders Planetarium and exhibits focusing on the human body, Florida environmental issues, Gulf Coast hurricanes and space and flight are among the more than 450 hands-on activities for visitors of all ages.

No. 7 The space beneath the theater is a ritual observatory and appears like a void against the massive volume of the space.

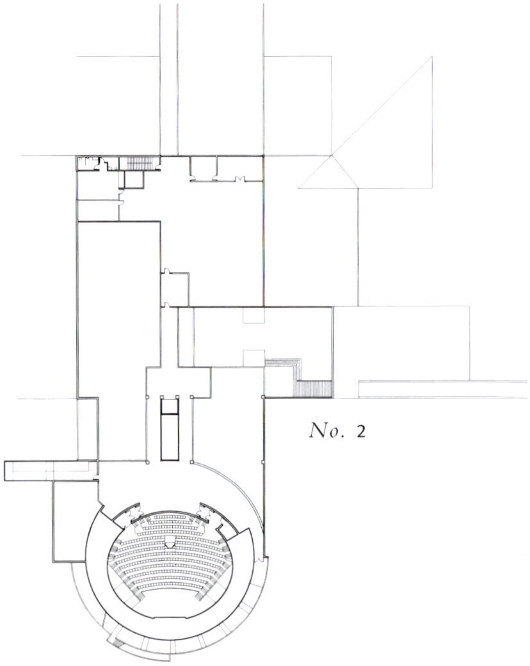
No. 2

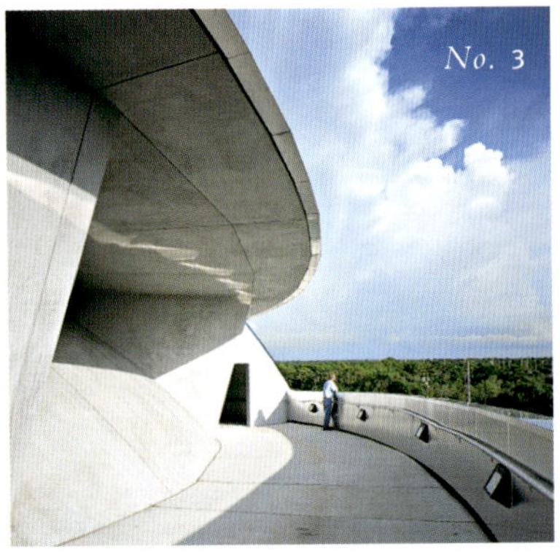
No. 3

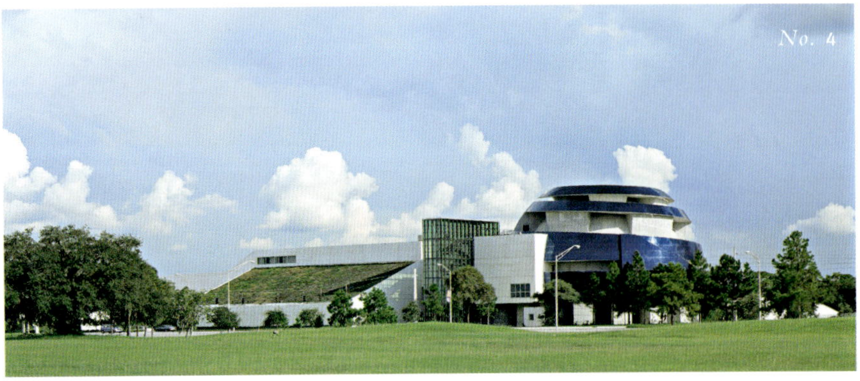
No. 4

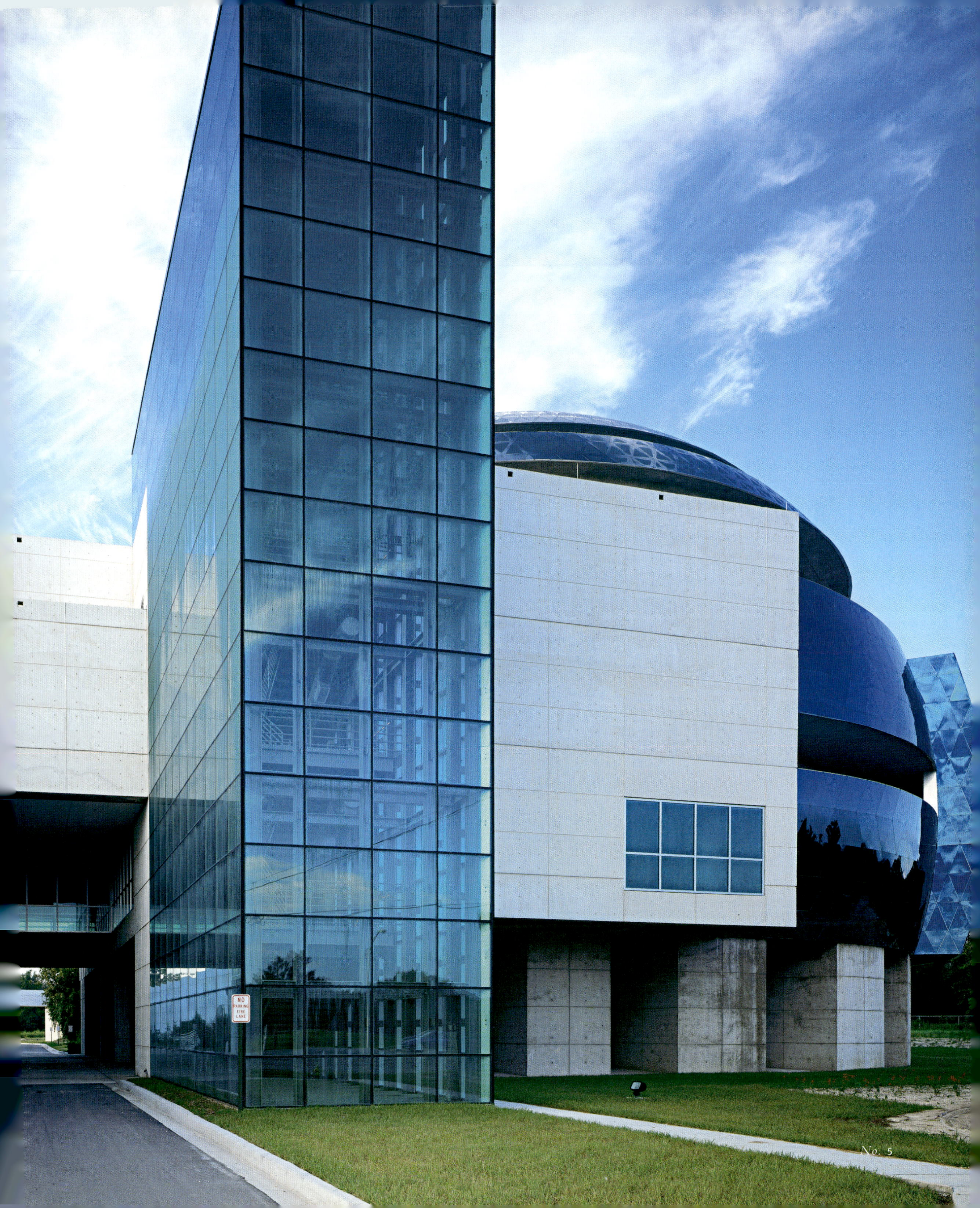

No. 5

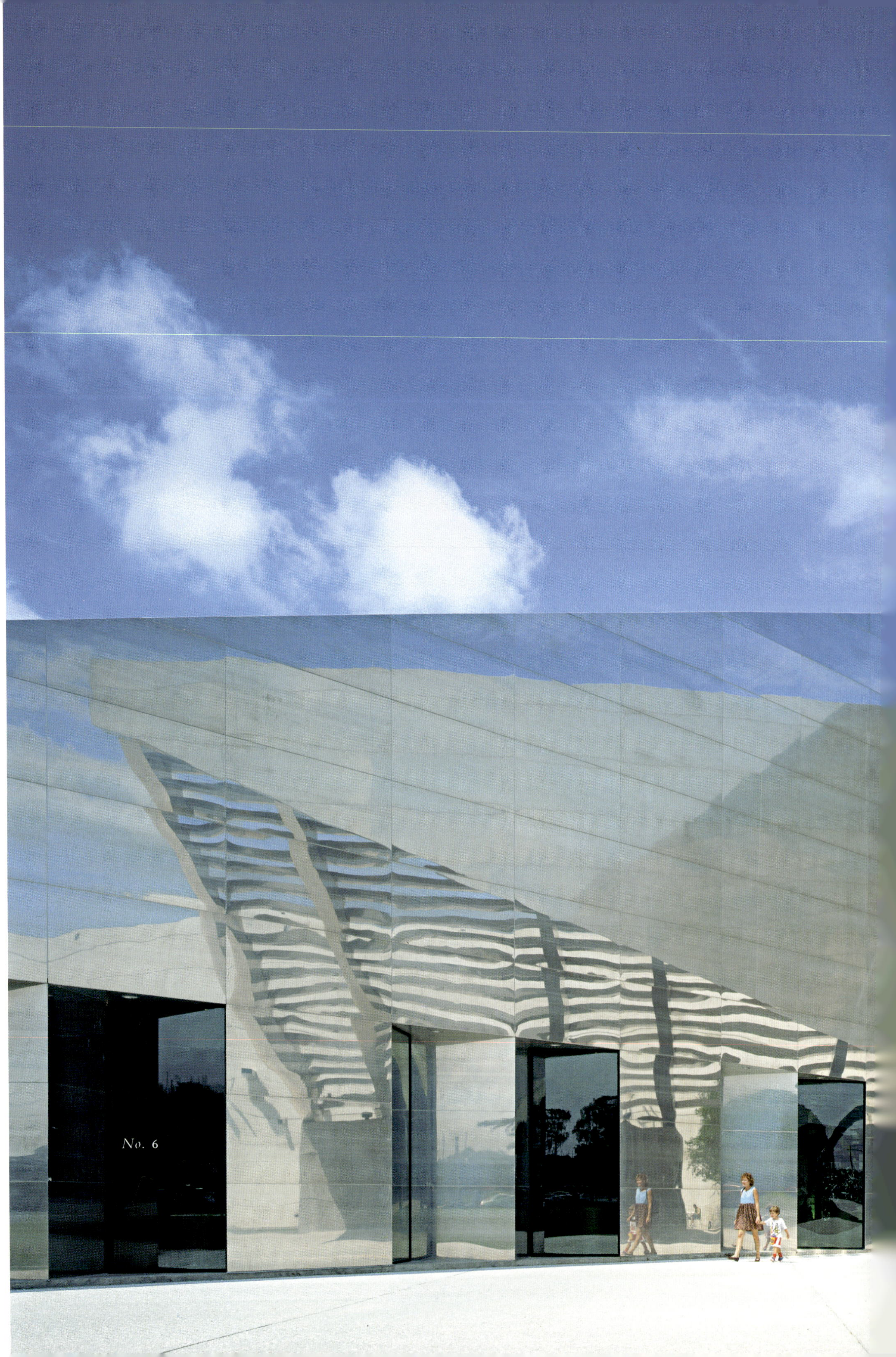
No. 6

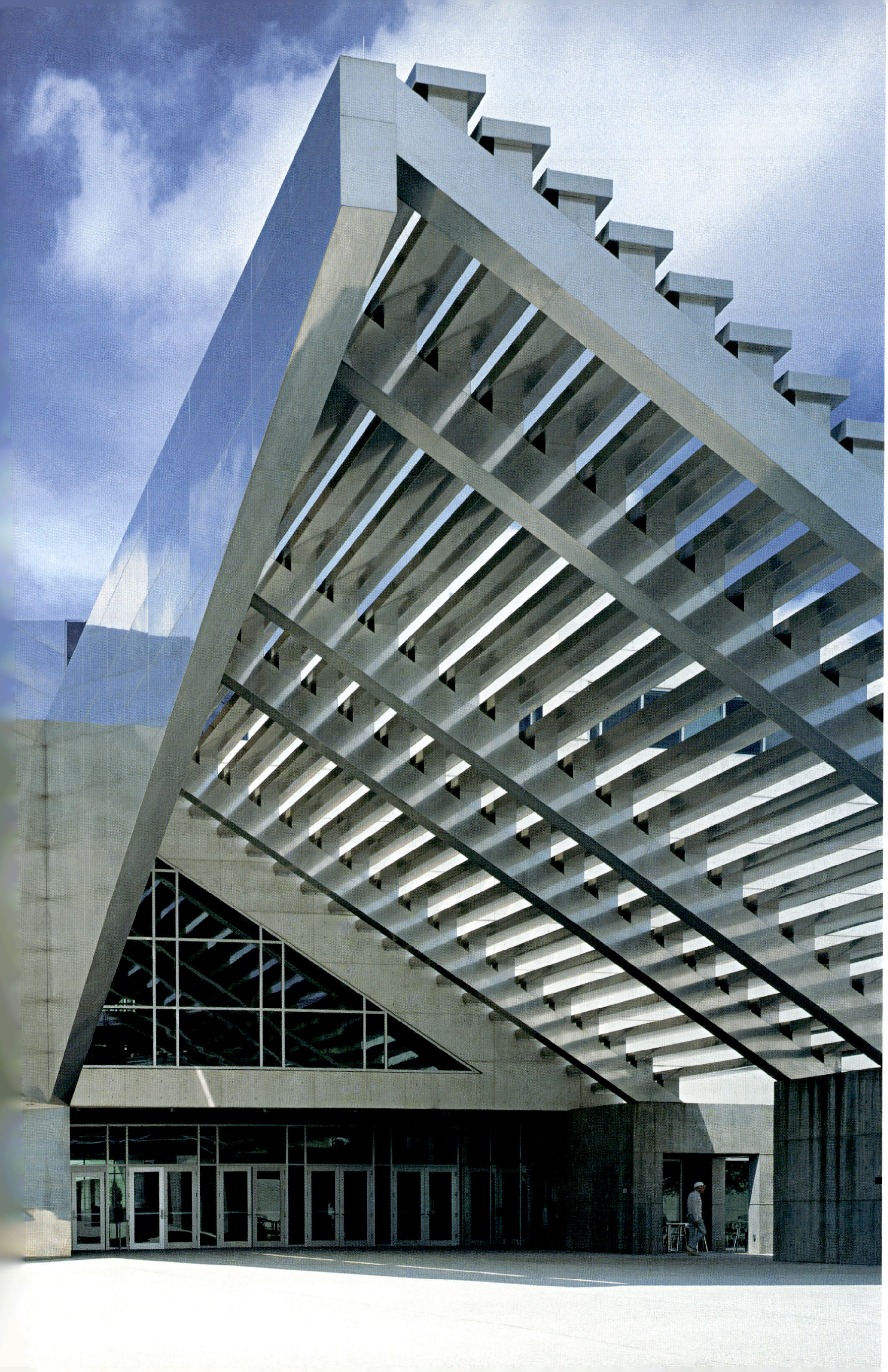

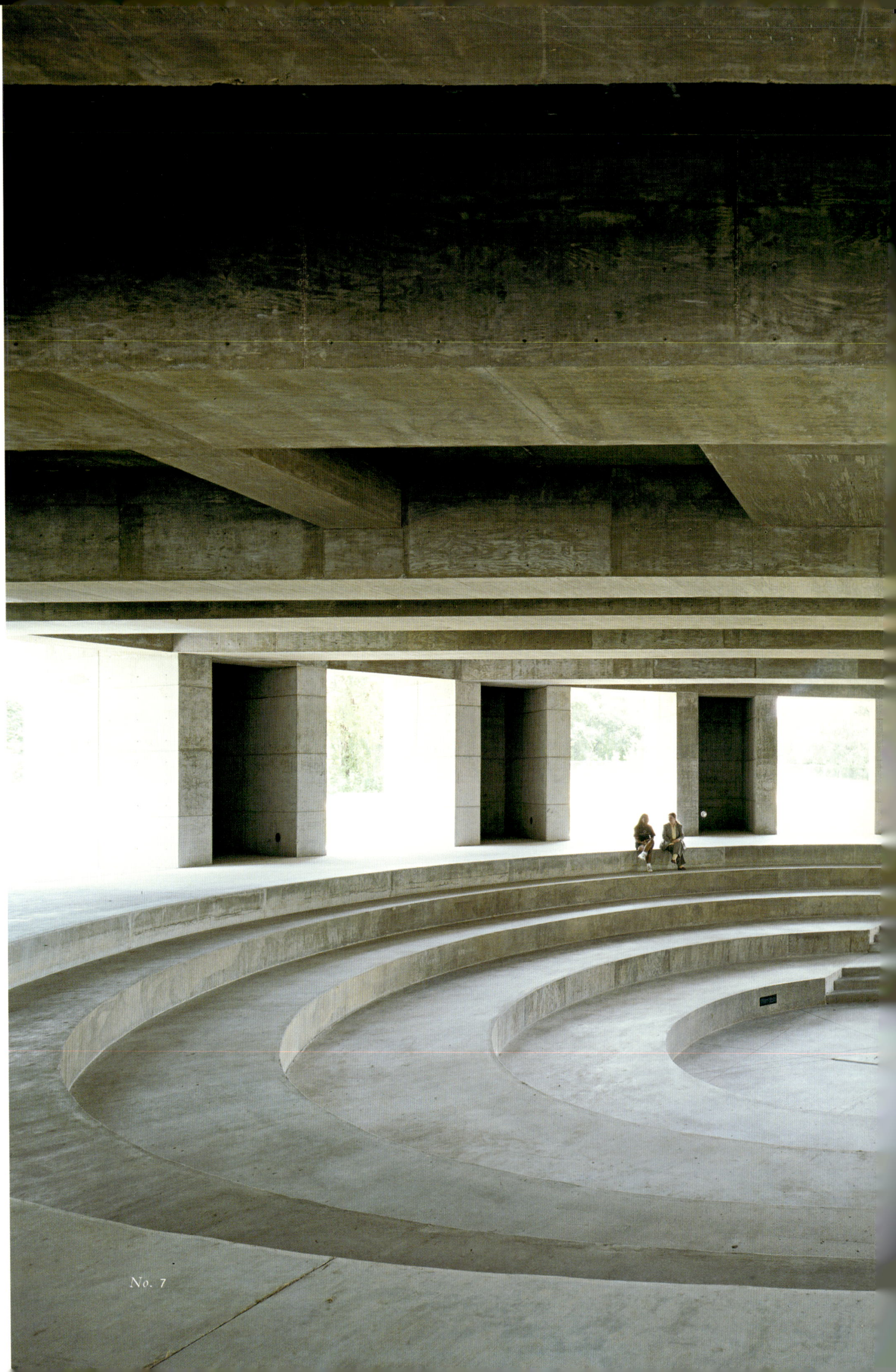
No. 7

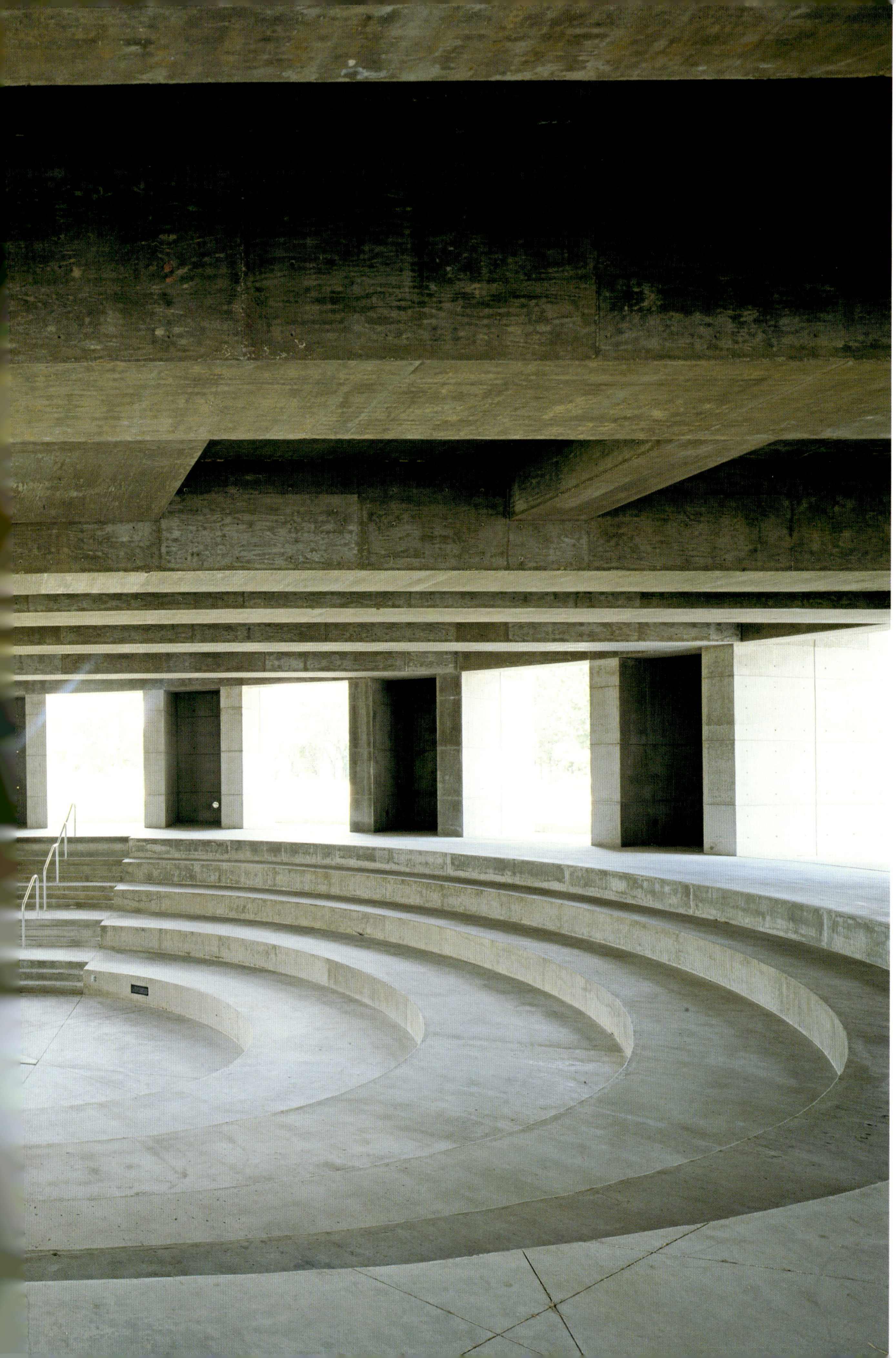

DIRECTORY OF ARCHITECTS

BOHLIN CYWINSKI JACSON
Wilkes-Barre PA, Pittsburgh PA, Philadelphia PA, & Seattle WA
Tel: 412-765-3890; Fax: 412-765-2209; Web: www.bcj.com

Senator John Heinz Pittsburgh Regional History Center
Pittsburgh, Pennsylvania
Owner: Historical Society of Western Pennsylvania
Project team: Peter Q. Bohlin, FAIA (principal for design); Jon C. Jackson, AIA (principal in charge); Robert S. Pfaffmann, AIA (project manager); Gregory R. Mottola, AIA, Charles J. Cwenar, AIA, Rebecca L. Boels, RA, Erik W. Hokanson, Maria K. Wyant, Michael D. Maiese, Keith Cochran, Stephanie Jacobs, AIA, David Senft, Veronica Berchok. Associate Architect: Notter + Associates, P.C. Engineer: RAY Engineering (mechanical/ electrical); Structural Engineering Corporation, (structural). Consulting Engineers: Consentini Assocaites. Exhibit design: Vincent Ciulla Design. Acoustical: Cavanaugh Tocci Associates. Food facility planning: Hammer Design Association. Theater consultant: David Weiss. General contractor: Jendoco Contraction Company.

CECCO BONANOTTE
FRANCESCOMARIA CONANOTTE
PIER PAOLO MARIA BONANOTTE
Via di Quarto Annunziata 120
Rome 00189 Italy
Tel: 39-06-33-111-784; Fax: 39-06-33-111-703

Nakatomi Memorial Medicine Museum
Tosu, Japan

WILLIAM P. BRUDER ARCHITECT, LTD.
1314 West Circle Mountain Road
New River AZ 85207
Tel: 623-465-7399; Fax: 623-465-0109; Web: bruder@netwest.com

Scottsdale Museum of Contemporary Art
Scottsdale, Arizona
Owner: The City of Scottsdale
Project team: Will Bruder, Rob Gaspard, Tim Christ, Ben Nesbeitt, Saskia Harth. Landscape architect: Steve Martino & Associates Design, Todd & Associates, Inc., Bill Peifer. Engineers: Rudow & Berry, Inc. (structural); Baltes/Valentino Associates (mechanical, electrical, hvac); Todd & Associates, Inc. (civil). Consultants: Lighting Dynamics (lighting); Wardin-Cockriel & Associates (acoustical); Construction Consultants (cost). General contractor: Howard S. Wright Construction Co.

BRUNER/COTT
130 Prospect Street
Cambridge MA 02139

MASS MoCA
North Adams, Massachusetts
Tel: 617-492-8400; Fax: 617-876-4002; Web: www.brunercott.com
Project team: Simeon Bruner (principal-in-charge); Henry Moss (principal); Phoebe Crisman (project manager); Maria Raber (project manager, construction); Robert Crosky, (site representative). Landscape architect: Bruner/Cott & Associates. Engineers: Boston Building Consultants, (structural); Abbood Holloran Associates (mechanical). Consultants: Alan Symonds (lighting). General contractor: Peabody Construction.

ATELIER D'ARCHITECTURE CHAIX & MOREL ET ASOCIES
16 rue des Haies
Paris 75020 France
Tel: 33-1-43-70-69-24; Fax: 33-1-43-70-67-65

Musee Archeologique de Saint Romain-en-Gal
Saint Romain en Gal
Project team: Philippe Chaix, Jean-Paul Morel, Remy Van Nieuwenhove Architectes. Project team assistants: David McNulty, Olivier Boiron, Sylvie Merle, Dieter Feichtinger, Nelly Breton, Denis Germond. Engineers: Ingerop, Serge Measso, Jean-Michel Dupuy (coordination); Arcora (structure metallique); Agibat (structure beton); Inex (thermicien, fluides); Peutz & Associes (acoustique); Socotec (bureau de controle); Margaret Grau (graphisme).

GWATHMEY SIEGEL & ASSOCIATES ARCHITECTS
475 Tenth Avenue
New York NY 10018

Museum of Contemporary Art
North Miami, Florida
Tel: 212-947-1240; Fax: 212-967-0890; Web: www.gwathmey-siegel.com.
Project team: T.K. Tam (associate-in-charge); Daniel Sullivan, (project architect). Associated architect: Gelabert-Navia, Architects. Structural engineer: Donnell & Duquesne; Mechanical engineer: MH Engineering. Civil engineer: C.A.P. Engineering Consultants.

FRANK HARMON ARCHITECT
Frank Harmon Architect
706 Montford Street
Raleigh NC 27603
Tel: 919-829-9464; Fax: 919-829-2202; Web: www.frankharmon.com

North Carolina Pottery Center
Seagrove, North Carolina
Client: North Carolina Pottery Center
Project team: Frank Harmon, FAIA (principal in charge); Vincent Petrarca, (project manager); Quan Banh, Charles Holden, Jeff Schroeder, design team. Consultants: Morrison Sullivan Engineers (structural); Stanford White Engineers, (MEP); Dan Gottlieb, (exhibit design); Design Dimensions, (exhibit fabrication); John William Brown Company, (general contractor).

STEVEN HOLL ARCHITECTS
435 Hudson Street
New York NY 10014
Tel: 212-989-0918; Fax: 212-463-9718; Web: stevenholl.com

Kiasma, Museum of Contemporary Art
Helsinki, Finland
Project team: Steven Holl, AIA (principal); Vesa Honkonen (project architect); Molly Blieden, Justin Russli, Tim Bade, Pablo Castro-Estevez, Janet Cross, Justin Korhammer, Anderson Lee, Chris McVoy, Anna Muller, Tapani Talo, Tomoaki Tanaka. Associate Architect: Juhani Pallasmaa Architects; Juhani Pallasmaa (principal); Timo Kiukkola, (project architect); Seppo Mantyla (project manager), Heikki Maattanen, Timo Ruusuvuori, Seppo Sivula, Meita Soini. Consultants: Insinooritoimisto OY Matti Ollila & Co. Consulting Engineers (structural engineer); Insinooritoimisto Olof Granlund OY, HVAC; Tauno Nissinen OY Consulting Engineering (electrical engineer; Ove Arup & Partners Consulting Engineers (structural and mechanical consultant); L-Observatoire International (lighting); Fire Technical Consultant Markku Kauriala Ltd. And Total Walther GmbH (fire technical); Engineering Office Aulis Bertin Ltd, (glass consultant); Teatek, (theater technical); Insinooritoimisto Rakennuslankenta NHL (quantity supervisior); Arkkitehtitoimisto Alpo Halme (acoustical consultant); Seico OY (general contractor).

ARATA ISOZAKI & ASSOCIATES
9-6-17 Akasaka, Minato-ku
Tokyo 107 Japan
Tel: 81-33-405-1526; Fax: 03- 34-75-5265

Center of Science and Industry
Columbus, Ohio
Desgn architect: Arata Isozaki (principal in charge); Yasuyori Yada, (project architect). Project team: Fumio Matsumoto, Atsuhi Aiba, David Gauld, John Bohn, project team; Howan Kong, John O'Reilly, Michie Yahagi, Yusaku Imamura. Architect: NBBJ; Friedrich K.M. Bohm (principal) Bernard J. Costantino (principal in charge); Jerome M. Scott (project architect); Kathy Kelly, Jim Lenhert, Steve Rice, Ed Mendelson, Ray Skonce, A.J. Montero (project team). Associate architect/ civil engineering: Moody/Nolan Ltd.: Curtis J. Moody (principal in charge); Rex W. Hegerling (project archtiect); Jamie Leesburg (civil engineer); Todd Dove, Mark Haker, Lance Timmons, Paul Pryor, Ed Alting, (project team). Consultants: Korda Nemeth Engineering, Inc. (structural engineers); HAWA Inc. (mechanical and electrical engineering); Saski Associate, Inc., and Peter Walker and Partners (site design); Ruscilli Construction Co. (construction manager); Project Control Systems, Inc. (program management); Acoustic Dimensions (acoustics); William Caruso & Associates (food service consultant); Estudio Mariscal and NBBJ, (graphic design); NBBJ (landscape architect), Fisher Marantz Stone (lighting consultant); FRCH Design Worldwide (retail design).

KPF ASSOCIATES PC
111 West 57th Street
New York NY 10019
Tel: 212-977-6500; Fax:. 212-956-2526; Web: www.kpf.com

Rodin Gallery
Seoul, Korea
Client: Samsung Group, Seoul Korea
Project team: Kevin Kennon (design principal); Gregory Clement (managing principal); Andreas Hausler, John Locke (project managers); Luke Fox, Marianne Kwok (design team leaders); Francis Freire (coordination leader); Vladimir Balla, Christopher Ernst, Andrew Kawahara, Michael Marcolini, Chulhong Min, Cordula Roser, Aida Saleh, Trent Tesch (project team). Associate Architect: Samoo Architects & Engineers; Suk Ho Lee (president); Ju Hwan Cho (principal –in-charge); Woo-Chun Rah (project manager), Taean Kang (designer). Consultants Rolland/Towers (landscape architect); Ove Arup & Partners (structural engineers); Cosentini Association (mechanical and electrical engineers); Thomas Thompson Lighting Design (lighting); Cerami & Associates (acoustics); Sussman/Prejza & Company (graphics); Shen Milsom & Wilke (audiovisual); Donald Spector Architect (specifications); Entek (maintenance); Gary Haven Smith Studio (stone); Heitmann & Associates, James Carpenter Design Associates, Tripyramid Structures, (exterior wall); Hanscomb Associates, (cost estimating). General contractors: Samsung Construction; Joseph Bartner & Company; Bruder Eckelt & Company.

KISHO KUROKAWA ARCHITECT & ASSOCIATES
11F, Aoyama Bldg, 1-2-3 Kita-Aoyama,Minato-ku
Tokyo 107-0061 Japan
Tel: 81-3-3404-3481; Fax: 81-3-3479-5088; Web: www.kisho.co.jp

New Wing of the Van Gogh Museum
Amsterdam, The Netherlands
Client: Stichting Nieuwe Vleugel Van Gogh Museum
Local coordinating architect: Bureau Bouwkunde F.B—Rotterdam. Mechanical engineer: Huisman en Van Muijen B.V; Hertogenbosh. Building constructor: J.P. Van Eestern B.V.—Barendrecht.

DANIEL LIBESKIND
Windscheidstrasse 18
Berlin D-10627 Germany
Tel: 49-30-327-782-0; Fax: 49-30-327-782-99

Felix Nussbaum Museum
Osnabruck, Germany
Client: City of Osnabruck, Germany
Design team: Daniel Libeskind (principle): Markus Aerni, Barbara Holzer (architects-in-charge); Anne Marie O'Conner (project architect); Lars Graebner, Ariel Huber, Claire Karsenty (project team); Damon Caldwell, Robert Claiborne, Sonia Dinnebier, Elizabeth Govan, Bernd Lederle, Sang Lee, Dietmar Leyk, Stephanie Riech (competition team). Landscape architects: Lutzow 7; Cornelia Muller, Jan Wehberg + Partner. Engineer: Watermann, structual. Consultants: Reinders + Partner, cost and site control; Jan Dinnebier Lighting, lighting.

LUNDE & LOVSETH ARKITEKTER AS
Oscarsgt 34
Oslo 0258 Norway
Tel: 47-22-12-99-50; Fax: 47-22-12-99-51

Norsk Oljemuseum
Stavanger, Norway

JOSE RAFEL MONEO, ARCHITECT
Cinca 5
Madrid 28002 Spain
Tel: 34-91-564-2257; Fax: 34-91-563-5217; E-mail: cinca5@genio.infor.es

The Audrey Jones Beck Building, The Museum of Fine Arts, Houston
Houston, Texas
Project team: Jose Pafael Moneo (principal in charge); Emilio Tunon, (preliminary design phase); Eduardo Miralles (project architect); Hayden Salter, Jose Luis Gahona. Associate Architect: Kendall/Heaton Associates—Larry Burns (project architect). Engineers: CBM Engineers (structural); Altieri Sebor Wieber (mechanical). Consultant: Fischer Marantz Renfro Stone (lighting design).

PEI COBB FREED & PARTNERS ARCHITECTURE LLP
600 Madison Avenue
New York, New York
Tel: 212-751-3122; Fax: 212-872-5443

Miho Museum
Shiga Prefecture, Japan
Client: Shinji Shumeikai, Shumei Cultural Foundation. Project team: I.M. Pei (principal), Tim Culbert (project architect), Perry Chin (building envelope), Chris Rand (initial design), Carol Averill, Price Harrison, Celia Imrey, Hubert Poole (project team). Associate Architect: Kibowkan Inernational, Tokyo—Osamu Sato, (principal-in-charge), Hiroyasu Toyokawa (prinicpal, administration), Hitoshi Maehara, Fumio Ozaki, Masa Sato, Yasuhiro Sonoki, Miho Toyoda (project team). Landscape architects: Kohseki and Akunuke Zoen; Noda Kensetsu. Engineers: Leslie E. Robertson Associates; Aoki Structural Engineers; Nakata & Associates; Whole Force Studio (structural); P.T. Morimura (mechanical, electrical) Consultant: Fishter Marantz Renfro Stone (lighting). General contractor: Shimizu Corporation—Mikio Noguchi, Mutsuo Takagi (project managers).

POLSHEK PARTNERSHIP ARCHITECTS LLP
320 West 13th Street 8th Floor
New York NY 10014-1278
Tel: 212-807-7171; Fax: 212-807-5917; Web: www.polshek.com

Iris and B. Gerald Cantor Center for the Visual Arts
Stanford University Museum of Art
Stanford, California
Competition team: James Stewart Polshek, FAIA (design principal); Richard M. Olcott, FAIA (design principal); Thomas Wong, Amanda Martocchio, Minsuk Cho, John Fernandez. Design Team, New York Office: James Stewart Polshek, FAIA (design principal); Richard M. Olcott, FAIA (partner-in-charge); Joseph L. Fleischer, FAIA, (partner-in-charge); Amanda Martocchio, Darius Sollohub, Lawrence Zeroth. Design team, San Francisco; C. David Robinson, FAIA (partner-in-charge); Richard Kosheluk, AIA (project manager, project architect, specifications and construction administration, 1996-1998); Stefan Hastrup, AIA (project architect, 1994-1996); Joanne Hermance, Kenneth Ong, Roberto Sheinberg, Thomas Silva, Andrew Tyley. Structural engineers: H.G. Degnkolb Associates. Civil Engineer: Rutherford & Chekene. Mechanical engineer: Flack & Kurtz. Specifications: BCI Specification Systems. Acoustics: Charles M. Salter & Associates, Inc. Code: Rolf Jensen & Associates, Inc. Graphics: Madeleine Corson Design: Historic preservation: Architectural Resources Group. Landscape architect: The SWA Group. Lighting: PHA Lighting design. General Contractor: Rudolph and Sletten, Inc.

Mashantucket Pequot Museum and Research Center
Mashantucket Connecticut
Design team: Susan T. Rodriguez, James Stewart Polshek (design principals); Timothy P. Hartung (principal-in-charge); Don Weinreich, (project architect); James Sinks (job captain, main building); Charles Griffith (job captin, exhibit); Minsuk Cho, Denis Dambreville, Jihyon Kim, Amanda Martocchio, Lois E. Mate, David Shultis, Dan Stube, Crystal Cai Anderson, Gary Anderson, Anya Bokov, Charles C. Brainerd, Francsica Bucci, Victor Colom, Hoang Dang, Carlos Espinoza, Joseoph L. Fleischer, Maria Gray, Price Harrison, Sally Leung, Lisa Mann, E. Tiffany Marr, Craig McInhenny, Lisa Odyniec, Steven Peppas, Victor Rodriguez, James Slade, Kathleen Smith, Mark Thaler, William Truitt, Laurence Turner, Yuri Uceda, Daryl Wugalter. General Contractor: Pavarini, Inc. Consultants: Altieri Sebor Wiebor (mechanical/electrical); Ove Arup & Partners; The Office of Dan Kiley; (landscape architect); Presnell Group, RDA International (library design); FFE; Fisher Marantz Renfro Stone (lighting); Jules Fisher/Joshua Bachs Associates, Inc., (theater); Jaffe Holden Scarbrough (acoustics).

ANTOINE PREDOCK ARCHITECT
300 12 Street NW
Albuquerque NM 87102
Tel: 505-843-7390; Fax: 505-243-6254; Web: www.predock.com

Museum of Science and Industry
Tampa, Florida
Client: The City of Tampa.
Design architect: Antonie Predock Architect. Executive Architect: Robbins, Bbell Kreher Architects.

ALVARO SIZA ARQUITECTO, LDA
Rua da Alegria 399, A-2
Porto 4000 Portugal
Tel: 011-351-22-616-72-70; Fax: 011-351-22-616-72-79; E-mail: siza@mail.telepac.pt

Museu de Serralves
Porto, Portugal
Archtiect: Alvaro Siza. Project director: Clemente Meneres Semide. Project team: Tiago Faria, Christian Gaenshirt, Sofia Thenaisie Coelho, Edison Okumura, Abilio Mourao, Avelino Silve, Joao Sabugueiro, Cristina Ferreirinha, Taichi Tomuro, Daniela Antonucci, Francesca Montalto, Francisco Raina Guedes de Carvalho. Engineers: GOT GET and Commins Acoutics Workshop (Caniel Commins). Structural consultant: Gop-Joao Maria Sobraira. Electricity constultant: Raul Sarafim and Alexandre Martins. Water systesm: GOP-Ines Sobreira. Mechanical engineer: GET-Alfredo Costa Pereira. Landscape architectL Joao Gomes da Silva: General Contractor: Edifer, S.A. Project management: FASE.

SMITH-MILLER+HAWKINSON ARCHITECTS
305 Canal Street
New York NY 10013
Tel: 212-966-3875; Fax: 212-966-3877; Web: smharch.com

Corning Museum
Corning, New York
Project team: Henry Smith-Miller, AIA, Laurie Hawkinson (design principals); Ingalill Wahlroos, (project architect); John Conaty, Ferda Kolatan, Flavio Stigliano, O;iver Lang, Mauricio Salazar, Catherine Bird, Paul Davis, Maria Ibanez de Sendadiano, Christian Lynch, Akira Okaji, Eric Van Der Sluys, Kristina Yu, Karin Taylor, (project team). Engineer: Ove Arup & Partners (structural, mechanical, electrical, plumbing). Consultants: Quennell Rothschild (landscape); Claude Engle, (lighting); R.A. Heintges Architect (curtain wall); Fisher Dachs (theater). General contractor: Welliver McGuire.

THOMPSON AND ROSE ARCHITECTS INC.
1430 Massachusetts Ave
Cambridge MA 02138
Tel: 617-876-9966; Fax: 617-876-9922; Web: www.thompsonandrose.com

Florida Gulf Coast Art Center
Largo, Florida
Project team: David Martin, Christopher Hoxie, Heidi Beebe, Brian Bell, Samantha Pearson, Franco Ghilardi, Erin Cowhey, Lori Sang, David Whitney, Nancy Stabb. Construction manager: Peter Brown Construction Co., Tito Vargas (project manager). Structural engineer: Ocmulgee Associates Inc., Wayne King (principle). MEP Engineer: Bobes Associates, Gus Bobes, Jr. (principal). Geotechnical engineer: BTL Engineering Services, Inc. David Faulkner (engineer); Site engineer: DSA Group, Inc., Jim Bryce (engineer).

UN STUDIO/VAN BERKEN & BOS
Stadhouderskade 113
Amsterdam AX 1073 The Netherlands
Tel: 31-20-570-2040; Fax: 020-570-2041; Web: www.unstudio.com

Museum Het Valkhof
Kelfkensbos Nijmegen
Client: Stichting Museum Het Valkho
Architect: Ben van Berkel (Un Studio/Van Berkel & Bos). Collaboration: Henri Snel, Rob Hootsmans (coorindation); Remo Bruggink (interior); Hugo Beschoor Plug, Walther Kloet, Marc Dijkman, Jacco van Wengerden, Luc Veeger, Florian Fisher, Carsten Kiselowsky. Constructor: Adviesbureau voor Bouwtechniek b.v., VArnhem. Building contractor: Nelissen van Bouwzuid b.v. Venray; Technical installations: Ketel Raadgevenda Ingenieurs, Delft. Landscape: Bureau B&B, Steadbouw en landscapsarchitectuur, Michael van Gessel.

National Museum Twenthe
Lasondersingle 129-131, Enschede
Client: Rijksgebouwendienst, Directie projectmanagement, Den Haag
Architect: Ben van Berkel, UN Studio/Van Berkeeel & Bos. Collaborators: Harrie Poppot (project coordination); Joost Hovenier (project leader); Hugo Beschoor Plug, Pieter Koster, Peter Meier, Martin Visscher, Jan van Erven Doren, Serge Darding, Arjan van Ruyven. Contractor: Bouwbedrifj Punte bv, Enschede. Technical consultants: Rijksgebouwendinst DO&T; Ingenieurs en advisbureau A.H. b.v., Enschede; Adviesbureau Peuta & Associes bv., Molenhoek. Landscape architect: Lodewijk Baljon, Amsterdam

KYU SUNG WOO ARCHITECT, INC.
488 Green Street
Cambridge MA 02139
Tel: 617-547-0128; Fax: 617-547-9675

Art of Korea Gallery, The Metropolitan Museum of Art
New York, New York
Project team: Kyu Sung Woo, Timothy Downing, Steve Lacker, Andrew Wang. Lighting consultant: Fisher Marantz Renfro Stone.

DIRECTORY OF MUSEUMS

(In Order of Appearance)

GENERAL-INTEREST ART MUSEUMS

Page 16
Gerald L. Cafesjian Pavilion
Scottsdale Museum of Contemporary Art
7374 East 2nd Street
Scottsdale, Arizona
Tel: 480-994-2787; Fax: 480-874-4699
Web: www.scottsdalearts.org
Open: Tue, Wed, Fri & Sat: 10 a.m. to 5 p.m., Thu: 10 a.m. to 9 p.m., Sun: Noon to 5 p.m., Closed: Mon.
Admission: Adults: $5, Seniors & Students: $3, Children (15 and under): Free.

Page 24
MASS MoCA
(Massachusetts Museum of Contemporary Art)
87 Marshall Street
North Adams Massachusetts 01247
Tel: 413-664-4481; Fax: 413-663-8548
Web: www.massmoca.org
Open: November through May: Tue though Sun: 10 a.m. to 4 p.m., Closed: Mon. June through October: Sun through Thu: 10 a.m. to 5 p.m., Fri & Sat: 10 a.m. to 7 p.m.
Admission: Adults: $6, Seniors & Students: $4, Children (6 –16): $2, Members: Free.

Page 42
Museum of Contemporary Art
Joan Lehman Building
770 NE 125th Street
North Miami Florida 33161
Tel: 305-891-1472; Fax: 305-891-1472
Web: www.mocanomi.com
Open: Tue through Sat: 11 a.m. to 5 p.m., Sun: Noon to 5 p.m., Closed: Mon.
Admission: Adults: $5, Seniors & Students: $3, Children under 12, North Miami residents, and Members: Free

Page 42
Kiasma, Musuem of Contemporary Art
Mannerheiminaukio 2
Helsinki FIN-00 100
Finland
Tel: 358-9-17-336-500; Fax: 358-9-17-336-503
Web: www.kiasma.fi
Open: Tue: 9 a.m. to 5 p.m., Wed through Sun: 10 a.m. to 10 p.m., Closed: Mon, Check for specific Holiday closings.
Admission: Adults: FIM 25, Pensioners & Students: FIM 20, Children: (under 18): Free. Special exhibitions may be addtional.

Page 52
Audrey Jones Beck Building
Museum of Fine Arts, Houston
1001 Bissonnet
Houston, Texas 77005
Tel: 713-639-7300; Fax: 713-639-7597
Web: www.mfah.org
Open: Tue, Wed & Sat: 10 a.m. to 7 p.m., Thu & Fri: 10: a.m. to 9: p.m., Sun: 12:15 p.m. to 7:00 p.m., Closed: Mon (except Mon holidays).
Admission: Adults: $5, Seniors (65+), Students & Youth (6-18): $2.50, Children (5 and under), Members & All on Thu: Free.

Page 60
Miho Museum
300 Momodani, Shigaraki-cho, Koga-gun
(20 miles from Kyoto)
Shiga Prefecture 529-1814 Japan
Tel: 81-748-82-3411; Fax: 81-748-82-3414
Web: www.miho.or.jp
Open: Spring: March 15 to June 10, Fall: September 1 to December 15, Check for Special Opening periods. Tue, Wed, Thu, Fri & Sun: 10 a.m. to 5 p.m., Sat: 10 a.m. to 8 p.m. Closed: Mon (When Mon is a holiday, open that day but closed the following day).
Admission: Adults: 1000 yen, Students: 800 yen, Children under 16: 300 yen.

Page 66
Iris and B. Gerald Cantor Center for Visual Arts
Stanford University
328 Lomita Drive at Museum Way
Stanford, California 94305-5060
Tel: 650-723-4177; Fax: 650-725-0464
Web: www.stanford.edu/dept/SUMA
Open: Wed, Fri, Sat & Sun: 11 a.m. to 5 p.m., Thu: 11 a.m. to 8 p.m., Closed: Mon & Tue, holidays.
Admission: Free.

Page 72
Museu de Serralves
(Museu de Arte Contemporanea de Serralves)
Rua D. Joao de Castro, 210 Porto Portugal
Rua de Serralves 977
Oporto 4150-708 Portugal
Tel: 351-2-615-6500; Fax: 351-22-61-56-533
Web: www.serralves.com
Open: Tue, Wed, Fri, Sat, Sun, & Holidays: 10 a.m. to 7 p.m., Thu: 10 a.m. to 10 p.m., Closed: Mon, Christmas Day & New Year's Day.
Admission: Museum & Park: 800, Students, Youth, and Seniors (over 65): 50% discount, Children under 12 and All on Sun from 10 a.m to 2: p.m: Free.

Page 82
Gulf Coast Museum of Art
12211 Walsingham Road
Largo, Florida 33778
Tel: 727-518-6833; Fax: 727-518-1852
Web: www.gulfcoastmuseum.org
Open: Tue, Wed, Fri & Sat: 10 a.m to 4 p.m., Thu: 10 a.m. to 7 p.m., Sun: Noon to 4 p.m., Closed: Mon.
Admission: Free.

Page 86
Museum Het Valkhof
Kelfkensbos 59
Postbus 1474
Nijmegen BL 6501 The Netherlands
Tel: 024-360-8805; Fax: 024-360-8656
Web: wwwmuseumhetvalkhof.nl
Open: Check museum, Closed: Mon.
Admission: Check museum.

Page 92
Rijksmuseum Twenthe
Lasondersingel 129-131
Enschede BP 7514 The Netherlands
Tel: 31-53-435-8675; Fax: 31-53-435-90-02
Open: Tue through Sun 11 a.m. to 5p.m., Closed: Mon.
Admission: Check museum

SPECIALIZED ART MUSEUMS

Page 100
North Carolina Pottery Center
250 East Avenue
Seagrove North Carolina
Tel: 336-873-8430; Fax: 336-873-8530
Web: www.ncpotterycenter.com
Open: Tue through Sat: 10 a.m. to 4 p.m., Closed: Sun & Mon.
Admission: Adults: $3, Students (Kindegarden through high school): $1.

Page 106
Rodin Gallery
Samsung LIfe Insurance Building 150,
2-ga Taepyung-no Chung-ku
Seoul 100-716 Korea
Tel: 82-2-2259-7789; Fax: 011-82-22-259-7795
Web: www.rodin.co.kr
Open: Tue, Wed, Fri, Sat & Sun: 10 a.m. to 6 p.m., Thu: 10 a.m. to 9 p.m., Closed: Mon.
Admission: Varies by exhibition.

Page 112
New Wing of the Van Gogh Museum
Paulus Potterstraat 7 (Between the Rijksmuseum and the Stedelijk Museum)
PO Box 75366
Amsterdam 1070 AJ The Netherlands
Tel: 020-570-52-52; Fax: 31-20-673-50-53
Web: www.vangoghgallery.com
Open Daily: 10 a.m. to 6 p.m.
Admission: Check museum.

Page 120
Felix Nussbaum Museum
Lotter Strasse 2, D-49078 Osnabruck, Germany
Postfach 4460
Osnabruck 49034 Germany
Tel:49 –41-3-23-2207; Fax: 49-5-41-323-4353
Web: www.osnabrueck.de/fnh
Open: Tue through Fri: 11 a.m. – 6 p.m., Sat & Sun: 10 a.m. - 6 p.m., Closed: Mon.
Admission: Adults: 8 DM, Concessionary Tickets: 4 DM.

Page 130
Corning Museum of Glass
One Corning Glass Center
Corning, New York 14830
Tel: 800-732-6845/607-937-5371; Fax: 607-974-2077
Web: www.cmog.org
Open: Daily 9 a.m. to 5 p.m., July and August: 9 a.m. to 8 p.m.
Admission: Adults: $10, Seniors: $9, Youth (6-17): $5, Children: Free, Family: $30.

Page 134
Arts of Korea Gallery
The Metropolitan Museum of Art
1000 Fifth Avenue at 82nd Street
New York, New York 10028-0198
Tel: 212-535-7710; Fax: 212-570-3825
Web: www.metmuseum.org
Open: Tue, Wed, Thu & Sun: 9:30 a.m. to 5:30 p.m., Fri & Sat: 9:30 a.m. to 9 p.m., Closed: Mon, New Year's Day, Thanksgiving Day, and Christmas Day.
Admission: Adults: $10, Seniors & Students: $5, Children under 12: Free.

OTHER MUSEUMS

Page 140
Senator John Heinz Pittsburgh Regional History Center
1212 Smallman Street
Pittsburgh Pennsylvania 15222
Tel: 412-454-6000; Fax: 412-454-6031
Web: www.pghhistory.org
Open: Daily 10 a.m. to 5 p.m. Closed: New Year's Day, Easter, Thanksgiving, and Christmas.
Admission: Adults: $6, Seniors (62+): $4.50, Children (4-18): $3, Children (3 and under) and Members: Free.

Page 146
Nakatomi Memorial Medical Museum
288-1 Kounde-machi Toso
Saga Prefecture 841 Japan

Page 152
Musee Archeologique de Saint-Romain-en-Gal
2, chemin de la Plaine a St. Romain en Gal
Vienne BP 3 69560 France
Tel: 04-74-53-7400; Fax: 33-4-74-53-74-54
Web: www.cg69.fr
Open: Tue through Sun: 9:30 a.m. to 6 p.m., Closed: Mon.
Admission: check museum.

Page 158
Center Of Science and Industry (COSI)
333 West Broad Street
Columbus, Ohio 43215-2738
Tel:614-228-cosi; Fax: 614-629-3150
Web: www.cosi.org
Open: Daily: 10 a.m. to 5 p.m.
Admission: variable, based upon exhibits visited, check museum.

Page 168
Norsk Oljemuseum
Postboks 748
Havneringen
Stavanger N-4004 Norway
Tel: 47-51-93-93-00; Fax: 47-51-93-93-01
Web: www.norskolje.museum.no
Open: May through August: Daily 10 a.m. to 7 p.m., September through April: Daily 10 a.m. to 5 p.m. (Thu & Sun to 7 p.m.)
Admission: Check museum

Page 174
Mashantucket Pequot Museum and Research Center
110 Pequot Trail Road
P.O. Box 3180
Mashantucket, Connecticut 06339-3180
Tel: 800-411-9671; Fax: 860-396-7013
Web: www.mashantucket.com
Open: Wed through Mon:10 a.m. to 6 p.m., Closed: Tue, Thanksgiving Day, Christmas Day, & New Year's Day.
Admission: Adults (16-54): $12, Seniors (55 & older): $10, Youth (6-15): $8, Children (under 6): Free.

Page 180
Museum of Science and Industry, Tampa, Florida
4801 E. Fowler Avenue
Tampa FL 33617
Tel: 813-987-6300; Fax: 813-987-6310
Web: www.mosi.org
Open: Open 365 days per year at 9: a.m. Closing hours vary by season.
Admission: Adult (14-49): $13, Seniors (50+): $11, Child (2-13): $9, Children under 2: Free.
4801 E. Fowler Avenue
Tampa FL 33617
Tel: 813-987-6300; Fax: 813-987-6310
Web: www.mosi.org
Open: Open 365 days per year at 9: a.m. Closing hours vary by season.
Admission: Adult (14-49): $13, Seniors (50+): $11, Child (2-13): $9, Children under 2: Free.

Authors' Notes

James Grayson Trulove has written, edited, or published nearly thirty books on architecture, landscape architecture, art and graphic design. He is the co-editor with Il Kim of *Big Ideas for Small Studio Apartments* (Watson-Guptill, 1999) and *Studio Apartments* (William Morrow/HBI, 2000), and author of *The New American Garden* (Watson-Guptill, 1998), *Pocket Gardens* (William Morrow/HBI, 2000), *Ten Landscapes: Raymond Jungles* and *Ten Landscapes: Shunmyo Masunno* (Rockport Publishers, 1999). As co-founder of Spacemaker Press, Trulove published over twenty titles on landscape architecture and monographs on landscape architects. He resides in Washington, D.C., and New York, N.Y.

David C. Levy is President and Director of the Corcoran Gallery of Art in Washington, D.C., the oldest art museum and school of art in the nation's capital and its largest non-federal cultural institution. An administrator, art historian and sociologist, Dr. Levy's career has been strongly identified with the revitalization of important American art institutions. The Corcoran Gallery of Art is currently involved in a major expansion project to include the renovation of its landmark beaux art building and an addition designed by Frank O. Gehry that will create an additional 140,000 square feet (?-square-meter) for the museum and college of art. Dr. Levy resides in Washington, D.C.

Il Kim has collaborated with James Trulove on several books on modern architecture including *The New American Cottage* (1999) and *Big Ideas for Small Spaces: Studio Apartments* (2000). Kim is an architect who is completing his doctoral studies in architectural history at Columbia University. His publications include studies of Italian Renaissance architecture and translations into Japanese of architectural books and articles. He resides in New York and Rome.

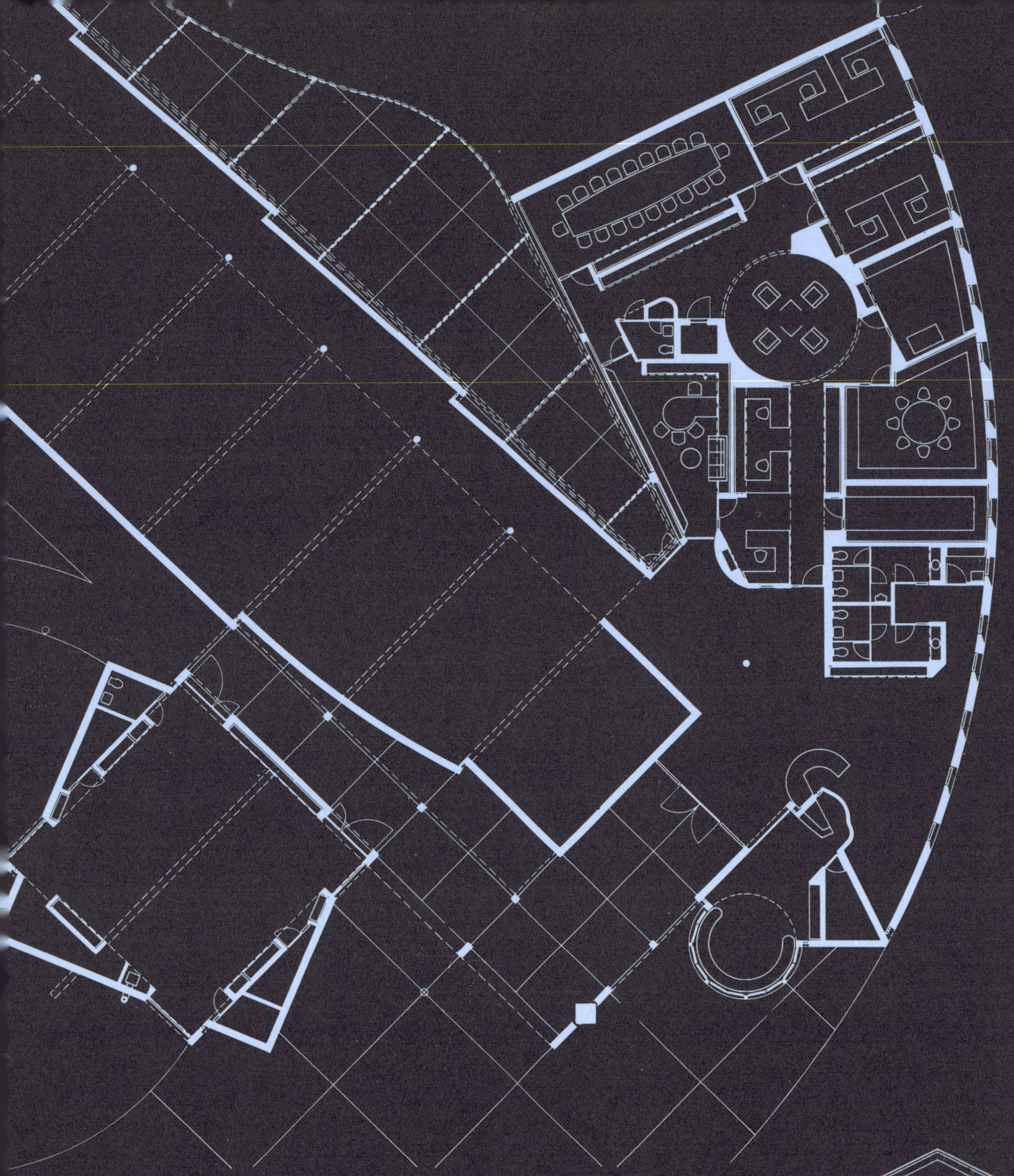

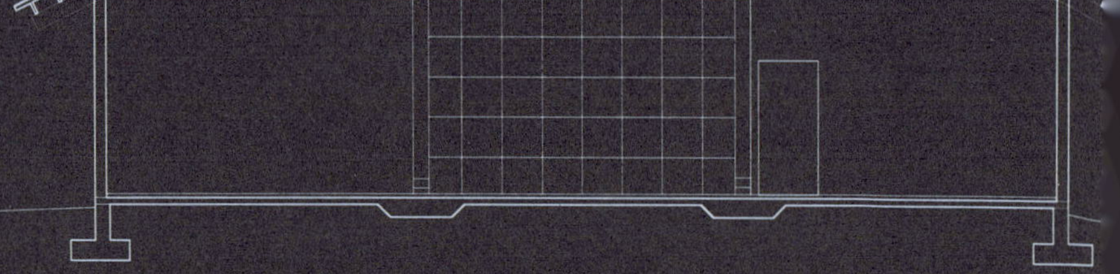